Women Workers in Urban India

In recent years, Indian cities have emerged as spaces of anonymous identities and seamless opportunities, sites that are balancing both modernity and traditional forms of living. This book engages with the role of women workers who are joining the workforce in the cityscape and bringing to surface contradictions that this duality offers. While employment opportunities have opened up and are constantly expanding for women, this edited volume interrogates whether their working status is breaking gender stereotypes or reaffirming them.

It surmises that whether women are working in offices or from home, contributing to the IT sector or labouring as petty producers, they are unable to break out of the gendered codes that place them at the lower rungs of the occupational ladder. More importantly, the hierarchical social order, comprising of caste, class and ethnic identities seems to echo in the gendered structure of the labour market as well. This volume studies the intertwining of work with embedded patriarchal notions of women's place in designated spheres, and the overt and covert processes of resistances that women offer in defining new roles and old ones anew.

Saraswati Raju is Professor at the Centre for the Study of Regional Development at Jawaharlal Nehru University, New Delhi. In 2010 she won the Janet Monk Service Award by the American Association of Geographers, USA in recognition of outstanding service contribution to women in geography and feminist geography which is first ever outside the Anglo-Saxon World. Professor Raju's areas of research interest include gender and social development with focus on literacy skills, labour market, juvenile sex ratios, and social space and place.

Santosh Jatrana is Associate Professor and Principal Research Fellow at the Centre for Social Impact Swinburne, Swinburne University of Technology, Australia. Currently she holds an honorary senior research fellow position at the University of Otago, New Zealand and conjoint appointment at Deakin University, Australia. She is a demographer and social epidemiologist with particular research interest in the fields of gender, migrant health, ageing, health and primary healthcare. Dr Jatrana is Editor-in-Chief of the *Journal of Population Research*.

Women Workers in Urban India

Edited by

Saraswati Raju

Santosh Jatrana

CAMBRIDGE
UNIVERSITY PRESS

CAMBRIDGE
UNIVERSITY PRESS

314 to 321, 3rd Floor, Plot No.3, Splendor Forum, Jasola District Centre, New Delhi 110025, India

Cambridge University Press is part of the University of Cambridge.

It furthers the University's mission by disseminating knowledge in the pursuit of education, learning and research at the highest international levels of excellence.

www.cambridge.org
Information on this title: www.cambridge.org/9781107133280

First published 2016
Reprint 2019

Printed in India by Thomson Press India Ltd.

A catalogue record for this publication is available from the British Library

ISBN 978-1-107-13328-0 Hardback

Contents

List of Figures

List of Tables

Preface

Very often, cities are seen as spaces of anonymous identities and seamless opportunities. They have also been conceived as spaces of transition from traditions to modernity although its supposedly linear trajectory has long been questioned and contested. Indian cities, for example, continue to display an ambiguous mix of both – the so-called modern trends existing in close proximity with traditional values and anchoring. Women's work in labour market provides an interesting site to interrogate these contradictions.

The 'shining India' paradigm talks about the expanding new generation employment avenues of work for women and the recent official discourses eulogizes about rising incidences of employment amongst urban women. Much of the available literature, however, suggests that global capitalism, while providing new opportunities to women, not only exploits the prevailing gendered stereotypes, but it also rearticulates them.

The most recent accounts from India suggest that the growth in paid employment has taken place largely in the informal sector. Whether or not such informalization works in the interest of women is a debatable issue. While some maintain that emerging occupational avenues, such as those available in export processing zones or in case of Business Process Outsourcing (BPO), have helped women significantly to access labour market, there are others who contend that progressively increasing use of technology in urban context offers opportunities only to those who have education and appropriate skills. Moreover, it has been argued that even the export-oriented production is largely driven by informal work. Notwithstanding these propositions, the urban labour market has a range of women – in high-tech IT sectors working from posh offices or from home; they are in home-based work as petty producers; they are, at times, in the so-called masculine professions even as the absolute levels may vary and be miniscule. Intriguingly, their location in varied professions – high-end technically advanced work and/or petty work; home-based or outside homes – does not seem to necessarily alter the socially constructed gendered codes that are instrumental in assigning them places at the lower rungs of occupational ladder. More importantly, the hierarchical social order, encompassing overlapping caste, class and ethnic intersectionalities that typifies India in general seems to echo in the gendered structure of labour market, whether they are salaried, self-employed or at home as paid as well as unpaid family labour. In other words, there are common threads running through the heterogeneity within the working women, both in terms of the types of work and the context in which such work is performed.

That said, it would rather be imprudent to argue that structures are super-efficient in erasing or overcoming sparks of the resistances and negotiations that women may manage to enter into by virtue of their access to paid work, however limited or indirect the struggle may be, through individual agency or collectively. Rather than positing structure and agency as binary opposites or privileging postmodernist take on individualized subjects over foundational metanarratives (such as overarching patriarchy, for example), the book proposes to juxtapose these appositional constructs and analyse the interplay of both. The complexities involved therein make it possible to theoretically study the intertwining of work with embedded patriarchal notions of women's place in designated spheres. In other words, pulling together the different strands of occupational diversity in which women are engaged, the main purpose of this book is to understand whether or not the new economic spaces, contingent upon neoliberal market changes, have been able to redeem women from the traditional gender relations in the sphere of work. What, if not so overtly, are the splashes which are marked by struggles and intercession by women questioning the status quo.

Overall, the working premise that binds through the volume is that the metro cities – presumable panacea of social change – continue to harbour socio-culturally engraved gendered norms irrespective of where women work. However, it would be of interest to trace the specifics of the various occupational avenues that engage women workers; to what extent they create differences and where they forge a collective identity amongst workers by virtue of being women. The underlining concern would also be to look into the disruptions that intersect the traditionally operative gendered specificities in the labour market. That is, what are the ways in which the resilience of traditional gender ideologies and structural constraints limiting women's options are maintained over time and importantly, the sets of circumstances under which such ideologies and constraints can be challenged, weakened, defused and renegotiated? Such a framing allows one to juxtapose the socially encoded gendered locations of women workers with the continuing and emerging material realities at the ground.

It is almost an impossible task to acknowledge who all contributed to this endeavour – directly or indirectly our lived experiences have been the culprit. And yet, transcending them to a visible and concrete outcome could not have been possible without our contributors who readily shared with us their understanding with much support and cooperation. We are grateful to them. The anonymous reviewers with their diligent and thought-provoking remarks helped us rethink and fine-tune many of our propositions. We would like to express our gratitude to them.

The idea of the book took shape when the first editor was on a Thinker-In-Residence program at the Alfred Deakin Research Institute (ADRI), Deakin University, Geelong Campus in Australia. We greatly appreciate the encouragement and bonhomie we received from colleagues there.

We both remain blissfully obliged to Jawaharlal Nehru University which has always been an academically active space: challenging, inspiring and cajoling at the same time! While Saraswati teaches at the Centre for the Study of Regional Development, it is the Alma Mater for Santosh.

The publication process has been joyful. We would like to acknowledge and thank the editorial team at Cambridge University Press for their collaborative and meticulous supervision at every stage of putting together the book.

Saraswati Raju
Santosh Jatrana

1

Setting the Backdrop

Saraswati Raju and Santosh Jatrana

Introduction

One of the turning points in India's recent trajectory has been the liberalization of the Indian economy in response to neoliberal compulsions, which thrives on free-market regime and involves the encounter of the local with the global capital (Ramaswamy 1999; Stiglitz 2004). Briefly, the change has been from an earlier state-controlled and relatively more job-secure environment to a gradual withdrawal of the state-controlled regulationist market, which also 'absolved the employers the responsibility of providing benefits, which usually came with tenured jobs' (Sen and Dasgupta 2009 xiii; Corbridge and Harriss 2000). The ensuing change in the process of production – from assembly-line Fordist model to a more flexible post-Fordist regime – has also brought in with it contractual and flexible labour, particularly in the manufacturing sector in the post-1980 globalizing phase. Although it would be rather erroneous to suggest that the pre-reform period was characterized by secure jobs, the recent decades have witnessed a more insecure employment scenario. As per the National Sample Survey estimates, the share of workers in the total organized manufacturing sector was 26.47 per cent in 2010–11 compared with 15.7 per cent in 2000–01. However, this increase has largely been attributed to the substitution of directly employed workers with contractual workers (Kapoor 2014).

Earlier, it was the public sector including government, quasi-government and local bodies that was the main employer of labour in the organized sector. However, over the years, its share has been declining because of disinvesting policies that accompany the changing role of the state. A concomitant shift to the privatization of industrial production (with its emphasis on cost cutting and profit maximization) has also been responsible for the enhanced employment for women. According to one estimate, although the increase in the absolute number of women workers was almost the same in the public and private sectors in the recent past, the increase of women in the private sector has been nearly double (Khandelwal 2004). This is despite the fact that the overall employment of women workers in India has always been comparably lower than that of other countries in the region, such as Bangladesh and Sri Lanka (Maringanti 2008; Banerjee-Guha 2009).[1]

In general, the increase in urban women's workforce participation has invoked contested and often contradictory debates on 'feminization of labour'[2] as well as on informalization of labour.[3] These discourses can perhaps be anchored to the trade liberalization in general and the emergence of spatially designated export processing zones (EPZs) in particular (Pearson 2010). It would, however, be helpful at this juncture to address very briefly the question as to whether trade liberalization is something new, if not a continuation of patterns previously observed. In this regard, we borrow from Standing's observations. Accordingly, earlier – until about the 1970s – trade was largely confined to countries with similar labour rights and therefore, roughly equivalent labour costs. Since then, international trade and investments have progressively been directed at economies with relatively lower labour costs. In contrast, the labour rights in industrialized countries were increasingly perceived as costs of production, to be avoided in the interest of enhancing or maintaining national competitiveness. Trade openness ensures export-oriented growth, which often sustains cheap labour the world over, as regions are forced to compete on cost. In addition, the technological advances in the recent past have created a wider range of technological–managerial options in working arrangements of labour across the globe. Cost cutting in labour inputs by accessing cheap labour across developing countries has thus emerged as a more significant determinant of allocations and divisions of labour. Although the exploitation of cheap labour, informality, home-based production have always been the case, these changes coupled with structural adjustment and other supply-side economic policies have accelerated these tendencies, bringing about, in recent times, radical changes in labour market relations sans protective labour legislations, regulations, wage parity, employment security and statutory regulation, etc. (Standing 1999). It is now clear that India took the first important, albeit small, steps towards liberalization around 1985 to loosen various regulations having a bearing upon trade liberalization; the reforms announced in 1991 went much further in this direction.

Such growth opens up heightened opportunities for women who can be lured to enter the labour market as paid labour instead of remaining engaged in unpaid household work (Standing 1999; Deshpande 1992).[4] The last decade has also seen an impressive expansion in the outsourcing of services related to business from countries of the North to labour-intensive countries of the global South, facilitated by the use of Information and Communication Technologies (ICTs) and Business Process Outsourcing (BPO) – of which call centres are a significant component. Apart from supportive 'political–economic' changes, locational advantage in terms of appropriate time zone and lower wages has made India a significant player in the ICT-enabled services, leading to a prominent share in offshoring of call centres. India's advantage also stems from her location in the knowledge economy and English language competency (Taylor and Bain 2010). Since these services thrive on an educated and skilled workforce, which is largely urban-based in India, urban labour markets become particularly important in such endeavours both for men and women, more so for the latter, as about 92 per cent of all women in ICT are in urban areas as compared to 84 per cent of all men (Sen and Raju 2012). On the other hand, a production system linked with global market in manufacturing is subject to the vagaries of product demand and market uncertainties leading to emergence of temporary and contingent workers with generalized erosion of job security (Mazumdar 2007, 8). Scholars point out how a huge proportion of contingent workers are usually women in export-oriented garment and electronics industries because of their production regimes, which thrive on cheap, easily manipulable and flexible labour. There is thus a contradictory relationship that exists between women and labour market that is simultaneously oppressive, exploitative and liberating even if partially (Ong 2000). Sen (1999 cited in Razavi *et al.*) sees the glass as half empty. On one hand, rural women escape their patriarchal homes through these types of work while on the other the 'choice' may not indicate positive changes in their lives working in the factories (also, Kabeer 1995, 2000).

This chapter explores how such complex and highly debated processes apply in different contexts and how they bear upon women in the urban labour market in general.[5] In doing so, we also look at the newly emerging sectors of work such as ICTs and BPO, which are presumably global in their orientations, but continue to be framed by socio-spatially articulated constructs of gendered stereotypes pushing women, despite being at the relatively more privileged positions, to disadvantages. We maintain that the labour market processes have to be multiply placed, layered and textured to decode the dialectics between socio-structural barriers that impinge upon the gendered responses vis-à-vis agential resistances and contestations, if any in the labour market. Even if at the risk of stating the obvious, a caveat is in order. Women also have multiple age-specific, caste/class/ethnic and rural/urban locations. Intersectionalities of these provide a complex framework to understand how the capitalist production system reproduces discriminatory practices in the Indian labour market through wage differentials, job security/insecurity, enclaving of job placements for certain social groups, etc. More importantly, two paradoxical processes seem to be happening in India. One, the labour market had undoubtedly drawn on the pool of cheap labour of women almost in all spheres of work and yet socially encrypted and regionally embedded gendered codes that characterize India, result in spatially differentiated labour market outcomes (Raju 2013).[6] As Razavi *et al.* point out (2012 vii), 'both the formal rules and the informal practices that structure the operation of labour markets often reflect the gender norms of the societies in which they are embedded'. Hence, women's increased participation in the labour force is not a straightforward story of progress in gender equality. Moreover, many of the factors that structure labour markets and women's position within them are in turn shaped by broader policies and processes of social change.

Urban labour market: How global is the global

Any discussion on work in contemporary urban India needs to discuss transnational labour force. This invariably brings us to practices of globalizing forces and the contested nature of their implications. Scholars tend to divide in their opinion on the exact enactment of globalizing processes – some calling them inevitable and irreversibly universalizing while others look at them as a project – both dominated by capital.[7] Increasingly, however, the hegemonic metanarratives (of globalization) that basically have masculine undertones are being challenged, particularly when seen through gender lenses and evidence-based analyses in local contexts (Freeman 2001). As Mirchandani (2004a) points out, treating globalization as a 'meta-myth' (Bradley 2000, quoted in Mirchandani 2004a) does not sufficiently allow for an exploration of the incomplete and contested nature of the movements of capital and labour. She further observes that workforces are neither homogeneous nor passive in a globalizing context.[8]

It may perhaps be argued, as Krishna does, that present-day labour geographies need to be situated beyond the nation–state boundaries instead of being bounded by self-spatialization of a kind that 'names itself as a destiny, a genius, a culture, a civilization, or homeland – a contiguous and identifiably discrete and separate entity'(2001, 412). The proposition that spatial contextualization be avoided while looking at labour markets in a global environ can be questioned by bringing in the discussion of localized influences on globalizing processes. Rather than privileging one over the other, the labour market as it exists today allows one to argue for intersected effects of both global and local forces whichever way they are framed. In such situations, the local is not peripheral or incidental; there are enough sustaining as well as 'ironies and resistances' of local makings (Appadurai 1996, 29). So, while educated and skilled women workers can take advantage of emerging employment opportunities in the IT and BPO sectors, they may still be governed by contextual specificities of gendered constructs that do not differentiate their world of work from those illiterate or lowly literate and unskilled workers who are home-based in petty businesses. We will discuss this point later.

Urban labour market: Encountering the gendered constructs

However contradictory it may seem, it has to be acknowledged that the earlier invisibility and the dichotomous spilt in 'productive' and 'reproductive' spheres and the gendered division of labour within that, which had trivialized women's contribution to the labour market in the past is now gradually disappearing (Chhachhi 1999). Although young women with good education appear to be more privileged in ITC-enabled services, the 'unmarried young women as symptomatic of export-oriented growth' syndrome no longer carries as much weight as it used to do.[9] Likewise, one can observe women's move away from stereotypical occupations such as teaching and caring/nursing – extension of familial responsibilities in the market – to semi-industrial and new generation ITC and BPO jobs. And yet, the essential nature of markets as gendered institutions, because of the ways they operate at the intersection of the 'productive and reproductive' economies and under-privileging those who are in reproductive economy, continue to haunt labour market dynamics (Deshpande 2007; also see Chapter 10 in this volume).

An earlier study on migrant women in urban India, which looked at the intersection of marriage, marital responsibilities and career paths, observes that working women do not necessary escape from their traditional roles. Thus, the study revealed a higher proportion of married women were self-employed in home-based work presumably managing both productive and reproductive responsibilities, while the proportion of never married women engaged in regular salaried jobs was almost twice as that of married women. Moreover, nearly all the unmarried women were full-time workers as compared to married women (Banerjee and Raju 2009).[10] Interlinked with immediate familial responsibilities are larger kin relations that impose their own restrictive limits and codes on working women (Ong 1991).

Although diligence, patience and concentration are often cited as women workers' virtues, women are confined to soft-skilled jobs that are usually concentrated at the lower rungs of occupational hierarchy. Such a segmented division of labour may not always be overtly visible. Unni, Bali and Vyas (1999, quoted in De 2012) studying subcontracting in the garment industry in Ahmedabad, point out the variability of segmentation depending upon the size of the manufacturing structures: large factory sector, small units, shops and home-based garment workers. Although all the three segments are marked by subcontracting, it is of interest to note how even such work is embedded in gender stereotypes that requires rethinking about how the sexual division of work perpetuates different and distinct types of work. The authors observe a clear division of the type of garments stitched by women and men. By and large, women were engaged in stitching dresses and hosiery items and very few stitched men's pants and shirts, vice versa in the case of male tailors. Most women in this study felt that even the sub-contractors preferred trousers sown by men compared to women. Men were employed as supervisors, cutters and also marketed products whereas women were mostly stitchers and were also involved in the finishing and ornamentation of the product. Not surprisingly, women's work fetched lower remunerations than men. Also, comparatively large numbers of women were in the household segment of the production units.[11]

The new generation jobs

With women's entrance in rapidly expanding IT workforce, one would have expected that there would be a loosening up of the grip on traditional gender roles, but as Patel and Parmentier (2005)'s study suggests 'not only does women's participation fail to occur at the same speed as IT expansion, but that their participation is based on a continuation of traditional gender roles' whereby 'technology and its development ... adapt[s] to the existing social structure'. Further, '[t]he persistence of ... gender divides perpetuate the notion of gender segregation and do not enhance women's socio-economic and political status, nor provide equal participation in the information economy' (2005, 29; Kelkar, Shrestha and Veena 2002; Raju 2013).

The gendered segregation at workplaces is yet again visible in the engineering field, which as a profession has traditionally been characterized by male dominance. Of late, women's enrolment in the field of engineering has been increasing, but their employment rate has not only been low but they are found to be in teaching departments of Technical Educational Institutes (Parikh and Sukhatme 2004). There is a curious ambivalence at display here. On the one hand women have been able to break away from the stereotype, but on the other they are stuck with the traditional typecast of practices. Banking is another such arena where societal factors impact both the individual and organization levels in perpetuating the existing stereotypes, which ultimately harm the advancement of women in their careers, especially in management (Mirza and Jabeen 2011; see Chapter 11 in this volume).[12]

It is of interest to see how financial independence amongst young educated metropolitan girls in the IT sector eventually gets tied up with marriage prospects despite their exposure to western work-culture. The IT industry is attractive to many young people because of the salaries offered – often much lower than international standards – they are handsome enough. The monotony of the work itself is compensated for by the benefits of indoor facilities, recreational centres, gyms, etc. Jobs have attractive titles such as Customer Care Executive, Customer Support Executive, and so on. And yet economic resources do not necessarily seem to provide women opportunities to exercise their agency in personal lives. Women have to negotiate their socio-cultural rural/urban backgrounds (rural versus urban); despite unprecedented exposure, the women' bargaining agency is contingent upon which regional background they come from (Tara and Ilavarasan 2011).

There are interesting, if not peculiar, contradictions. Despite increasing women workforce in ITCs and IT-enabled services, their upward mobility in the workplace continues to remain constrained, essentially because of household ties. However, their lower mobility prompts human resource managers to prefer hiring them rather than men, as in women's case frequent poaching is minimal (Kelkar, Shrestha and Veena 2002; D'Mello 2006). One's position in the occupational hierarchy makes a difference, but very few women occupy higher echelons of the IT industry.

The spatial and temporal elasticity and the contextual disconnect have made several scholars argue for the emergence of a 'flat' world and to treat call centres as 'disembodied entities' (Taylor and Bain 2010, 439). However, we dispute such claims to point out how social context beyond the workplace has consequences, particularly for women, in terms of conflicting demands between domestic responsibilities and the pressure of social mores that continue to dominate workplace sensitivities. That is, socially constructed spaces create a mix of high-tech operations and indigenous values instead of homogeneous spread of work culture (Ong 1991).

In furthering as well as explaining our arguments, we borrow from Kagitcibasi's concept of the 'autonomous–relational' self (2005). Seeing autonomy and agency being used extensively and often interchangeably, Kagitcibasi questions the often-posed separation of autonomy/agency and their intersections with relatedness. According to him, the separation between agency and relatedness has a root in the Euro-American cultural context with its ideological background of individualism. For him, autonomy and heteronomy are two ends of the same spectrum. An individual can have an interdependent as well as an independent self in a 'dialectic mutuality' or 'coexistence of opposites'. These selves are embedded within societally encoded gendered constructs, which are internalized during socializing processes (D'Mello 2006, 139). What we see in the Indian context is very little scope for mutually dialectic exchanges in the built-up of women's identities. Instead, the 'independent self' (which could have been drawn upon the bases of education and work status) annihilates itself under self-efficacy and self-definition vis-à-vis other means of overwhelming presence of relational self in the making of the 'self'.

What D'Mello contends on the basis of her empirical study of professionals in the field of information technology in Mumbai is apt in this context and we quote:

> The autonomous-relational self ... is operationalized among IT workers, in ways that are more dichotomous than dialectically mutual. The breadwinner ideology predominated as a central aspect of masculine identity constructs, while the relational self occupied center stage in feminine identity constructs. Individual responses as well as the coping means used by women, reinforce the view that the relational self was the predominant pathways [for women]... Negotiating for power and equality in the family system [was found to be] a challenging task, threatening disintegration of family relationships'... many women in this study ... compromised their own career aspirations (D'Mello 2006, 152)

Urban labour market: Gender and class sensibilities

Very often, the notion of urban India is coincident with the emergence of the 'new' middle class – the middle class where working women, particularly professional IT women, signal the arrival of 'global nation, rather than a parochial or traditional one' (Radhakrishnan 2009, 197). Historically, the idealized construct of (Hindu) women into middle class domesticity had become the site

> ... for the production of modern nationalist culture ... [which] was based on a powerful dichotomy between the "inner" and the "outer" ... translated into a set of binaries that were inevitably gendered: spiritual/material, home/world, inner/outer... the outside world [was] to accommodate the changes occurring in society, a burden to be borne primarily by men. The (essential) inner world, the real of the 'spiritual', however, ... must remain free contamination ... maintaining the purity of bourgeois woman ... (Radhakrishnan 2009, 200).

It may be argued that the application of the category of middle class is so broad that it serves to obscure significant socio-economic differences within the middle-class morality. And yet, collective essentializing of women's primary location within homes seems to have overwhelmed the discursive realm of its cultural discourse. As opposed to the earlier emphasis on the spiritual, the more contemporary construction of middle-class domestic, according to Radhakrishnan, hinges upon the notion of family (and the location of women within it). Using Bourdieu's notion of symbolic capital along with his conception of gender and the family, she puts forward the concept of 'respectable femininity', the primary framing of women within the familial realm – family assuming perceived 'normalcy' 'legitimated through middle-class status'. According to her, the symbolically authoritative dominance of middle class values allows the conception of 'family-first' to bear upon the national consciousness, opening 'up space for grappling with the embeddedness of gender', which continues to shape labour market outcomes of even those in new generation employment such as IT, limiting individual negotiations and inter-linkages with the global economy. Her IT women themselves enact highly competent 'professional' femininity, but one which remains 'markedly Indian' (Radhakrishnan 2009, 200–201, 209).[13]

Bourdieu's 'symbolic capital' can be invoked somewhat differently to assert the inevitability of gendered encoding of the sort theorized so far. The multiple location of women across caste, class, ethnicity and rural–urban divide does mean that women occupy differentiated layers of larger structures of social relations – Bourdieu's concept of fields, a site of struggle between the competing claims of different forms of capital. However, individuals, on their own or collectively, may still attempt to decipher what comprises enduring and legitimate capital within available spaces. Thus, symbolic capital may be the signifier of a legitimacy of a particular type of cultural capital.

Undoubtedly, the new middle class in contemporary India occupies the nation's imagination in no small measure (Deshpande 2003; Rajagopal 2003 quoted in Radhakrishnan 2009) and yet one can argue that the ambivalent nature of urban India – a curious mix of urban characteristics with rural – would not only mean that the urban middle class is not the only iconic symbol of re-imagined modern India, but also that middle class is not an undifferentiated monolith.[14] Notwithstanding such a critique, interestingly enough, certain gendered values that the middle class's symbolic capital appropriates, despite being capricious and particularistic, is the idealized location of women within the domestic sphere. We take a cue here from what Chatterjee has to say. Without engaging with her elaborate and nuanced critique of the co-opted feminism by neoliberal capital, we want to reiterate her idea about women as 'embedded in an assemblage of social relations ... of class, gender, caste, and religious position' for many of whom 'household work [remains] women's work as it was destined to be' (2012, 12).[15] Chatterjee's women are Hindus and Muslims from the lower strata of the society in Ahmedabad city.

To the multiple locations of women has to be added the spatial contextualization, which has its own enactment upon how women's lives in India are constructed and socially articulated (Raju 2011). It seems in a way then that some of the middle-class gendered sensibilities eventually get institutionalized to reflect the broader Indian culture.

Labour market: Gender, structure and agency

Let us contend that any discussion on structure and agency particularly with reference to urban labour markets in India is severely constrained by inadequate information on one hand and by repetitive assertions of the continuation of traditional gender roles even in rapidly expanding new sectors on the other. Admittedly, any discourse on structure and agency has to be multiply placed, layered and textured. Although the available space here does not allow us an elaborate expansion of each and every aspect of it, we will touch upon a few of the concerns.

In decoding the dialectic between labour and agency, Coe and Jordhus-Lier identify four distinct thematic strands of labour geography each of which is underpinned by its own bodies of theory. The first deals with the unionized labour and the reassertion of the potential agency thereof; second is about the formation of geographically specific local labour markets/regimes and their ongoing regulation and segmentation; the third talks about the intersections of employment relations with other facets of personal and workplace identity and the last one explores historically placed material landscape in shaping labour struggles and their outcomes. We confine our exposition to the third thematic strand, which prioritizes workers to create their own economic geographies through pursuing their own spatial fixes.' (2010, 212). We do not talk about organized strategies as in trade union activities (at the expense of worker's agency) or isolated success stories from the developed countries in this book. Our 'labour geographies' centre upon the 'spatial hold', not so much on the 'spatial fix' of the capital.[16] Our spatial hold on workers is that of socio-culturally ambivalent spaces where labour navigates, sometimes individually and more often collectively, where the labour market sensitivities cannot be straightjacketed in oppositional traditional and modern categories or in individual and collective strategies.[17] Coe and Jordhus-Lier use Katz's (2004) distinction between resilience, which in fact is 'getting by' with everyday realities without challenging the existing status quo – the coping strategies, so to speak (Mullings 1999). Reworking refers to attempts at materially improving one's conditions of existence albeit 'enfolded' into hegemonic social relations. The participants may not always participate in the hegemonic system, but they do not question it either.

Resistance is about direct challenges to capitalist social relations. Such 'game-changing' resistance is much harder to find in the contemporary era. Let us look at some of the examples.

According to Kelkar, Shrestha and Veena (2002, 65), '... information technology increase[s] women's capability to take decisions on their own and construct greater space to enhance their agency, though within the limited terms of the socially sanctioned structural inequalities of women' (also, Groves and Chang 1999). Mirchandani (2004b, 179–180) seems to concur with such an observation when she suggests that 'understandings of individuals' micropolitics of resistance need to be situated within analyses of the structures, institutions and power relations which, in themselves form other micropolitics of resistance'. Drawing upon her research on the Indian call centres in Delhi and its surroundings involving three sets of people – workers, managers and customers – she illustrates the ways in which the everyday resistance is performed at the workplace. Accordingly, workplace processes are continuously constituted and reconstituted in response to global and local impulses. The industry has a number of groups occupying different social location resisting in their own ways the forces that structure their locally embedded lives – together these form a web of resistances. She is, however, conscious not to claim that such acts slow down the proliferation of the global economy nor fundamentally shift the unequal power relations between rich and poor countries that form its bedrock.

Patel's (2010) work on call centres in Mumbai is an ethnographic study. While challenging the often-held interlinking of women's financial independence with their empowerment, she brings in the concept of 'mobility-morality', which puts constraints on women's physical mobility. Call centre employment seems to release women from such a trap and yet family members and even neighbours circumscribe their movement in the garb of security and respectability given their unsocial working hours; these women have to continuously struggle with the broader patriarchal structures.[18]

The debate of the primacy of either structure or agency in human behaviour is a central debate in the social sciences. Risking simplification, agency here can be defined as the capacity of individuals to act independent of the context and to make their own free choices. Structure, in contrast, refers to the recurrent patterned arrangements that influence or limit the choices and opportunities available. As would be seen, the chapters in the book are largely concerned with the structures, which are occasionally intercepted by agency; both seem to co-exist in a delicate balance often mediated through some overarching paradigms, in our case the gendered regime.

Our proposition may resonate with Giddens's ideas which see social life as being continually produced and reproduced through a process of structuration although our conception of agency is neither confined to only knowledgeable social actors nor do we see agency and structure as two almost automated analytical isolates – criticisms against Giddens's approach (Jessop 2001). It was seen in the earlier discussion that even in the contemporary context of India, the knowledgeable 'middle class' does not always function as the 'agents' of actual social change. What we see is largely a situational change rather than processive one. In fact, women's framing within 'respectable femininity' and 'household domain' reinforces more stringently the structural encoding on gendered behaviour withholding several occasional sparks or resilience and resistance in covert ways.

We may seem to underestimate the 'messiness of real-world struggles over worker politics' (Hayter and Harvey 1993 quoted in Coe and Jordhus-Lier 2010). And yet we would like to suggest that but for a few sporadic examples, the available avenues for organized political struggles are now shrinking. The kind of profiles the urban market is attaining, works as a deterrent for collective agency with very little or no scope for unionization. In the 'new' economic regime, the trade unions have become defunct (Razavi *et al.* 2012);[19] even otherwise, they have been functioning within patriarchal paradigms ignoring women as (equal) partners nor paying attention to their gender-specific issues of concern. In the world of work, 'there is a pronounced absence of conflict-based struggle [defining] protagonists and antagonists' (Roy-Chowdhury 2005, 2250).

While the neoliberal labour regimes privilege the educated urban masses, the poor and the subalterns get busy in day-to-day survival. Quoting Friedmann, Mahadevia (2002b) argues that economic space overrides the life space in the global environment. Elaborating the changing economic landscape of Ahmedabad, she charts the new systems of resource mobilization, forms of governance, privatization and commercialization of infrastructure and ideological mooring that sees economic prosperity taking 'care of everything' – processes which ironically enough legitimately exclude the welfare of the poor who 'have been very much left to fend for themselves' (2002, 4854, 4858).

That said, we are not suggesting a complete negation of women's agency.[20] We do maintain that placed within the overall encryption of 'this far and no further' gendered framework, as far as their lives are concerned, women workers are essentially socio-structurally contained. At the same time, however, there are small and perhaps persuasive strategies that women adopt to negotiate such well-entrenched regimes in order to bring about changes in their own working lives. These examples may be few and far between, and may not offer huge challenges to hegemonic discourses, but as recent literature argues, it is in the small negotiations that we can see the 'pathways of empowerment' (Cornwall and Edwards 2010). Admittedly, the concept of patriarchy as a universal construct has lost its analytical significance; it has been variously reintroduced as a loose descriptor or spelt under the rubric of patriarchal structures, i.e., 'the multiple forms and loci of masculinist domination which prevail' (Qayum and Ray 2010, 112).

At this juncture, it will not be inappropriate to invoke, very briefly, the works of the classical scholars on social change and the enactment of 'urban' therein. That is, whether or not urban locations are distinct in some ways as the pivots of social change or they 'must be subsumed under a broader analysis of factors operating in the society as a whole' as a microcosm. While Marx, Weber and Durkheim acknowledge the cities as primate locales where fundamental social changes are reflected, they all maintain that 'they could in no way explain them'. Their viewpoint was largely based upon the then hugely rising urban population and rural–urban blurriness in the advanced capitalistic society. For these scholars, distinguishing the cities 'was significant only at a specific period in history … [and not in] contemporary capitalism … The city, in other words, is [to be] analysed not as a cause, but as a significant condition, at certain developments'. In contrast, other scholars such as Simmel and Wirth see the urban as a mark of modern society – a unique entity for sociological processes, particularly in modern period (Saunders 1986, 2).

Without indulging in the critical assessment of some of these theoretical constructs, one can still see that they are located primarily in the western urban context. For one, the process of urbanization has been of a slower order in India much of which bears the historically evolved social, cultural and economic footprints, whereby the rural relations did not change radically enough to create an alienated uprooted peasantry that could occupy the cities as industrial labour – unlike western cities where urbanization is often coterminous with industrialization. Instead, the close and dependent relation between cities and villages led to the formation of an internal organic affiliation between the two entities (Tacoli 1998; Mohan and Dasgupta 2005). An implication of such a relationship is that cities are not independent of the context to act as individuate isolates; they do not function as prime catalyst for social change, but continue to be part of an overarching socio-cultural ethos transcending the rural–urban divide, particularly so with regard to gendered behavioural norms. Thus, contrary to expectation that the overarching gendered codes would be questioned and challenged more forcefully in cities because of their heightened sense of cosmopolitan culture and dynamism, we subscribe to the position that there is a pressing need to challenge such assumptions.

The review of scholarly literature here shows the overarching umbrella of socio-cultural ideology that seems to contribute substantially to the concrete reality of work settings, labour relations and gender statuses. Overall, the productive/reproductive divide continues to echo through the conception of women labour and influences labour relations; women's autonomy and power are not synonymous with entry into the workforce in greater numbers; changes seem to be mostly superficial, often in response to specific circumstances rather than triggered by genuine interests. Drawing upon a framework that questions the presumably liberating city spaces for working women, the authors in the book showcase the common threads that connect the women workers as women trapped in constraining gendered ideologies despite their varying work statuses – ranging from domestic workers at one end to body screeners on the other. The focus is on metro cities, i.e., cities that could as well be anticipated as spaces of emancipation from long-standing social hierarchies instead of continuing to foster marginalization along gendered axes.

* * *

This introductory chapter by the editors has tried to systematically bring out the nuances and contradictions in the urban labour market created by the multiple locations of women. Women do provide easily exploitable, cheaper and flexible labour and yet their work visibility is socially architected and governed by spatially embedded gender codes. These codes frame and restrict even those who are in the so-called 'new generation' jobs within the 'so far and no further' paradigm.

The chapter that follows by Saraswati Raju and Debangana Bose is an empirical overview of the labour market as it functions in urban India. It points out how despite employment patterns being different in the million plus cities as compared with other urban centres, overall women are not free from prevailing gendered norms. Although women are part of the ever-increasing 'self-employment' group as are male workers, a relatively higher proportion of them work from home. Home-based work emerges from the market logic of maximization of cost-cutting through unorganized, unprotected and inexpensive labour pool, its persistence and overall presence through the country also fits in well and is sustained under the discursive domain of men as 'bread-winners' and women as primarily 'housewives' (Soni-Sinha 2011; Raju 2013).

The conceptual separation of domains between private/public, inside/outside and the ideological undervaluation and tendency to underestimate activities carried out in the private domestic spheres, seems to transcend even the paid domestic work, outside in the public domain. This is also because those who perform as domestic workers have multiple vulnerabilities in terms of their social positioning, skills and educational attainments. Ironically, however, these vulnerabilities do make them ideal contenders for entering the sphere of domestic workers. The fact that the workplaces are inside the homes and the work is essentially undertaken by women, makes it outside the purview of 'productive' labour market scrutiny by government/academics. Ironically, similar services, when formally regulated outside the home carry somewhat different connotations (ILO 2010).[21] Yet, whether carried out at home or in a more professional setup, domestic work continues to have several socio-cultural underpinnings that do not seem to alter with change in the location of such work.

The next set of chapters explores some of these issues in the lives of domestics in different settings along with several strategies the women adopt for survival.

Chapter 3 by Kaari Mattila is about everyday negotiations of domestic workers in Jaipur in Rajasthan. Based on an ethnographically oriented study, the chapter interrogates the premises under which urban girls and women participate in paid employment. Given that several socio-cultural gendered norms shape their employment trajectories, the chapter argues that in order to understand the meaning of paid employment in women and girls' lives, one must explore their broader life situations. The author talks about the intra-generational transmission of work from working mothers to daughters and the intra-familial survival strategies of the poor working class families. Despite this work bringing a significant contribution to the household economy, the restrictions on mobility in the urban space limit women's participation in paid employment. While class differences between employers and workers are evident, the ways in which the market is stratified through other social attributes are multi-layered and are being constantly renegotiated. Mattila juxtaposes gender with less explored dimensions of age and life course to point out how adult women working as part-time maids were in a much better position to negotiate with the employers in resisting their demands for overtime or extra work. Even young workers do try to resist their employers in subtle ways. However, workers' diverse positioning vis-à-vis employers hinder the formation of collective identity; such separation/individuations mean these resistances do not become formidable.

In Chapter 4, Karen Coelho looks at women' domestic work, housekeeping and factory work in a resettlement colony in Chennai. She explicitly examines yet another less explored role of urban spatial restructurings within the strategies of capital. That is, how spatial politics in globalizing cities facilitate the creation of cheap 'reserve' labour through the mobilization of gender, caste and/or race ideologies within segmented labour markets. Drawing from a study of work and livelihoods in Kannagi Nagar, Chennai's largest resettlement site (settled since 2000, housing about 15,000 families), this chapter reveals the profoundly gendered impacts of peripheral resettlement on the urban poor. Despite abundantly available local jobs, albeit under fluctuating, insecure and poor conditions combined with the living environs in the settlement, women in Kannagi Nagar were at the same time underemployed and overworked. At times challenges of balancing household and paid work, juxtaposed with issues of distance, travel, timing and transport and the lack of social networks, posed serious constraints for women, forcing them out of the labour market. For these women, non-economic parameters such as health, relationships at workplace, hardships, access and most importantly balancing of work and household responsibilities were the deciding factors in accepting/ rejecting or continuing in a particular job. Bringing out the similarities in working conditions between the formal and informal sectors, the author raises questions regarding the 'formal sector' as the preferred option for women.

What is important to note here is that some women transcended the gendered ideologies to actively shape and negotiate the spatial limits along with their participation in the labour market. Women in Kannagi Nagar, almost universally, saw themselves as workers even when they were not active in paid work. Even for those with significant household and care responsibilities, the world of paid work beckoned strongly and they believed it was only a matter of time before they returned to paid work, often against the wishes of their husbands. For these women, the ideology of the household responsibilities and that of the workers overlapped and acted as a source of skill; this was work they knew how to do. In this schema, flexibility of timing was a pivotal enabling mechanism, built on the shared ideologies of domesticity and work between middle and lower class women. This was despite the fact that such negotiations were costly, as these 'flexible' jobs occupied the bottom end of the wage spectrum.

In dealing with paid domestic work, Chapters 3 and 4 explore the caste/ class overlap, the extension of home-based responsibilities to the market and the exploitative nature of such work. In both cases, the subtle intergenerational differences and aspirations along with the younger workers 'subtle resistances and the older generations' efforts to wriggle out of oppressive manual work are common.

Kiran Mirchandani, Sanjukta Mukherjee and Shruti Tambe in Chapter 5 continue to engage with housekeeping, although the setting now shifts to professional services, catering to IT/ITES firms in the city of Pune in Maharashtra. These firms and call centres profess to hold completely different and explicitly 'westernized' approaches to hygiene and cleanliness, having norms where cleaning is technologically defined with heavily scripted and monitored work and workplace behaviour. Cleaning contracts to recruit and train workers are obtained either directly or through smaller subcontractors who may hire local workers. A complex and nested web of operators thus emerges. This together with the connections between discourses of professionalism still located in a historically defined (pure/impure) caste system lead to contradictory experiences of privileges and vulnerabilities. On one hand, gendered stereotypes of women's assumed 'natural' skills in domestic work are challenged through the introduction of modern technology and training, and on the other, notions of appropriate cleaning jobs for women and men are inscribed. Few women have a sense of pride in the use of modern gadgets and uniforms while for others subcontracting chains result in significant work intensification as well as job uncertainty. The authors argue that these factors are key to understanding the changing nature of work in the transnational and IT/ITES service sectors and its with their attendant gender, class and caste based implications in neoliberal India.

Overall, the housekeeping sector provides both promise and an entrenchment of gendered norms for women workers. Apart from regular salaries at the legislated minimum wage, the employees presumably have a rightful access to pensions and subsidized medical services. However, there is little standardization of wages in the sector and women are routinely paid less than men. In order to reduce attrition rates and monitor demands for pay increases, employers provide pension benefits to loyal and hardworking workers only. Thus, there is a disjuncture between the proliferation of transnational business norms in terms of disciplining the workers and maintaining flexible labour regimes for the companies, but reluctance at ensuring social security benefits.

The professionalization of housekeeping services therefore brings several tangible advantages for workers. Cleaning has been discursively resituated as a key organizational function, which demands efficient and standardized management styles. The employment is formalized through written contracts. Practices discriminating against the cleaning/office staff are absent, for example, eating in the same canteens, generally an uncommon phenomenon, is empowering. At the same time, a degree of work informality pervades the sector, which is further masked behind the veneer of professionalization. Workers feel as though they are the benefactors of and dependent on subcontractors' goodwill, often reminiscent of older feudal relations, rather than treated as formal wage earners. Informal hierarchies of work structured by caste and gender stereotypes continue to operate. Although women are paid less than men, some housekeeping women earn approximately the same amount as their husbands and as a result they can exert some influence over household decisions and children's' futures. There is, thus an ambivalent mix of new opportunities as well challenges.

The presence of formal sector establishments, even within the globalized economies of the IT corridor, does not necessarily epitomize a liberal world of work; the vast majority of jobs for women remain semi-casual, highly insecure, and poorly paid with physically taxing working conditions and scant opportunities for economic mobility (see, Chapter 4).

The importance of domestic workers cannot be undermined in the wake of emerging trends in the proliferation of nuclear and dual-income families, emerging 'new' middle classes, working women and an aging population. However, the fact that the workplaces are inside the homes, with work essentially undertaken by women, makes it outside the purview of 'productive' labour market activity, what Adam Smith initially referred to as 'non-productive' personal care services. Similar services, when formally regulated outside the home are treated differently (ILO 2010). Overall, the three chapters demonstrate how domestic work is one of the most marginalized constituencies of workforce because of the workers' conflation with the care economy. However, when the domestic work is drawn out of homes to a professional company/or operation in public domain – ILO's latest endeavour to bring some sense of formality to the informal sector (ILO 2014) – certain things change. The professional obligations are observed; there is professionalism and yet, the nuanced caste and gender subscriptions in the allocation of duties do not disappear fully. They continue to function sub-territorially and subtly.

The underlying concern of the editors in bringing out this book has been to examine whether the changing contours of labour market has made lasting difference to the lives of women workers. Neetha takes up this issue in Chapter 6 by interrogating a crucial hypothesis that poses modern workspaces as more egalitarian and gender sensitive because of the profile of women workers, which constitute the young and better educated workforce. The loci is the city of Delhi and the discussions are based on fieldwork covering factory workers, live-out domestic workers, teachers in informal employment, sales workers, clerical and public relations and customer care workers; the last three categories collectively termed as 'modern service sector workers' as they largely share similar work profiles and working conditions. Individual and group choices and agencies do operate, albeit within the limits imposed by the structural distribution of rules, norms, assets and identities.

The chapter provides distinct and yet overlapping evidences of women workers' subordination in the city. While the low workforce participation of women in Delhi remains the central issue, constraints such as skill-shortage, workload and timings, inadequate wage/earnings and more importantly, pregnancy and childbirth dominate. Though newer sectors of employment bring in diverse opportunities, women workers continue to be bunched in select sectors and occupations. Moreover, the presumption that newer and modern workspaces are more egalitarian and gender friendly fails when subjected to critical scrutiny. More than the prevalence of poor wages, the fact that many workers were not aware of their right to minimum wages or eligibility for a higher wage was particularily striking in the context of new service sector workers, given their educational and other social profiles. It is puzzling that these workers, supposedly capable of questioning social norms and values, constitute an exploited yet voiceless workforce. Even in sectors where their presence is striking, no discernible difference was noticed. Under these circumstances, the author argues that the possibility of renegotiating existing gender norms, be it at workplaces or at homes, seems to be a distant goal.

Amit Basole's Chapter is on Banaras (Varanasi) where he uses field observations, interviews, and time-use surveys to explore the world of home-based women workers in lower-caste Muslim (Ansari) and Hindu weaving communities, the makers of the world-renowned, Banarasi silk sari. He shows that women form a crucial part of this industry doing unpaid as well as paid work and are conscious of their role as such. The contribution of women to the industry is also recognized by male weavers. But lying at the intersection of caste, class, and gender hierarchies, their skills and their time are undervalued. The work is publicly invisible (carried out in purdah by Muslim women) and no statistics are available on the number of women involved, piece-wages, or hours worked. Using examples of a type of unpaid work (such as yarn winding) and a type of paid work (embroidering of sequins, beads, zari, etc. on woven fabric), he explores the labour process involved as well as quantifies the hours spent in paid and unpaid work. He shows that despite performing paid work for up to eight hours a day, women are still seen as working in 'spare time' because paid work fills the 'interstices' of care-work. The low wages that accompany the work are 'justified' on basis of the 'spare-time' discourse. For women, the paid work in the public domain is usually an extension of their household tasks. However, here even the paid work, undertaken by women within the household, is considered as a 'natural' extension of their unpaid work.

The author comments on how the continued prevalence of home-based work in artisanal industries has contradictory effects on gender relations in the society. The time-use data show that women have no leisure time, yet the work performed in groups with intermittent sharing of personal stories, jokes, and gossip provides some bonding. Work-time is also care-time that mothers spend with their children and elder siblings with younger ones; as feminist economists have pointed out, such emotional labour is simultaneously tiring and fulfilling. Ansari women are strikingly embedded in the family and community. The importance of the family as a support-structure is illustrated clearly by the challenges faced by women who have walked out of bad marriages, have been widowed, or have been forsaken by their natal families. It is tempting for the author to conclude that within the dualism of the individual versus the family, it is the family which takes precedence in an Ansari woman's life choices. However, the author is of the opinion that such 'other-regarding behaviour' can be due to the internalization of caring labour from a young age, which is not surprising for women's subjectivities have been perceived as being constituted within family and social relationships in other South Asian contexts.

Chapter 8 by Swati Sachdev on home-based workers in textile and garment industries in the city of Kolkata echoes what Basole has to say about women workers' self-efficacy regarding their contribution to home economy and perception about the (paid) work as being carried out during the 'spare time' that women have. Her respondents also belong to the Muslim community. Sachdev, however, touches upon a rather underexplored feature of the informal sector, i.e., the heterogeneity therein about workspaces and workers and the implications for their relative vulnerabilities. For example, she points out how women workers in the informal sector suffer on multiple counts as women and as home-based who not only receives less wages per hour than men, but also less compared to other non-home-based women workers.

The study includes some extremely relevant sections on the different outcomes for men and women working with agents and subcontractors as well as differentiation among women themselves depending upon age, marital status and class. Women tend to concentrate in home-based work with increasing age as their responsibilities towards care-work expand. The importance of a life cycle approach, i.e., the interplay of age and inside/outside confinement of women's work has also been commented upon by Neetha (Chapter 6) when she observes the absence of older women in customer oriented modern services and factories carried out in public domain. That the working conditions of women cannot be seen in circumstantial vacuum, that their economic roles are intrinsically woven with their familial responsibilities on one hand and contingent environs on the other, resonates through these chapters. Ironically, however, the household commitments and engagements, which are often conceived as socially restrictive for realising women workers' full potentials, can come in as a handy alibi to escape over/extra time work that some workers are routinely assigned in export-oriented factories (Chapter 9).

While pointing out the peculiarities, Sachdev argues for decoding the larger economic and cultural milieu, within which these women workers are placed, in order to understand not only the exact type of work they do, but also how they cannot really escape the nuances of traditional patriarchal structures that segregate women into specific occupations and compel them into particular sections and work places of employment, leaving them little choices. The intersectionalities of gender, poverty and location in specific communities seem to aggravate the marginalized conditions of home-based working women further in consonance with what the author calls 'glocal' inter-linkages.

Neethi discusses women workers in an Apparel Park in a major urban centre in southern Kerala in Chapter 9. The setting is somewhat different, as women workers are now located in an export processing zone, governed and regulated by stricter codes of conduct and surveillance. At the personal level, their status as workers does not seem to lead to any empowering process per se, as the very decision to participate in the labour market is not within the ambit of the women workers' own choices, but a choice that is taken for them by community, family, and even religious bodies – these bodies almost always consisting entirely of male members. Hence, despite being 'urban' or 'semi-urban' women, the very idea of working away from home is framed within patriarchal institutions.

Contending the proposition that the expansionary nature of capital, accompanied by the new economic and political reality, univocally controls the economic responses by labour, irrespective of the constraints of locations and localities, the author argues for multiple ways in which globalizing processes may unravel over space. The study reveals how local labour markets develop their own strategies to control labour, and reinforce gendered norms to exploit women workers. These tactics are achieved by means of involving agents in the local communities and local religious bodies in the region. As an overall argument, the indigenous patriarchy along with global capitalism work hand in hand to control women's bodies and labour.

However, the ambivalence is striking for, contrary to the tendency to portray workers, particularly women workers, as structurally defenceless in the face of globally organized hypermobile capital, Neethi argues for a much more active conceptualization of women workers as agents/actors in the uneven development of capitalism. At times not clearly visible, these workers organize around locally specific concerns to challenge the hegemonic limbs of local capital, although the aim is not to suggest that labour is in any way 'successful' in conquering the overarching power of capital. While being actively involved in the global economy and the expansion of local capital, the women workers in fact get inadvertently drawn into an exploitative whirlpool. The author is, however, for recognition and appreciation of women workers for their locally articulated responses; she argues that the paths that these responses trace cannot be derived mechanically from structural or gendered relations alone.

Crossing over to new economic spaces in the city of Kolkata in Chapter 10, Tanusree Paul's concern is with the technologically driven newly emerging sectors in the Information Technology (IT), information technology enabled services (ITES) sector, business process outsourcing centres (BPOs) and the knowledge process outsourcing centres (KPOs) as well as organized retail in shopping malls and franchise outlets. These sectors have been portrayed as representing a modern, egalitarian and secular world with respect to gendered constructs. The central question that the author is interested in is – to what extent the technologically driven 'modern' sectors have been able to provide a level-playing field to women by redefining traditional gender roles or do they continue to use/reinforce the prevailing socio-cultural strictures? The chapter critically examines the presumptions that the contemporary women are the privileged users and beneficiaries of technologies in the private as well as in the public spaces.

In some ways, the knowledge economy of the new generation jobs provides women with an enabling working environment; the salaries are relatively high and the work environment modern, undoubtedly imparting a certain sense of confidence and reasonable economic independence. And yet, the author observes that the interplay between work in the modern sectors and women's subjectivities are underlain by nuanced subtexts of covert subordination. For example, in the IT sector, the roles critical to the functioning of the business are appropriated by men, while the enabling services, although important, are secondary and therefore are earmarked for women. In the ITES sector, women are largely employed in the voice-call processes, dealing with clients and customers, while men do the more 'crucial' back-end jobs. This is also the case in the retail sector where the front-end male staff deals with floor operations, electronic goods and appliances, sports goods, etc. while women handle mainly the ladies' and children's sections and customer services. In both the ITES and organized retail sectors these front end tasks are perceived as more tedious, and less lucrative which is reflected in the fact that most of the respondents in these jobs want to change to the back end jobs in their respective sectors. In the traditional sector, women are concentrated in the Humanities/Arts departments while Science and Commerce streams appear to be male dominated in both colleges and universities. Although women have gained access to liberating spaces and opportunities, their increased access to public spaces has not been able to deconstruct their culturally architected identity as 'women', which continues to be essentialized around their sexualities and reproductive roles.

Chapter 11 is by Supriti Bezbaruah who looks into gender equality, work and employment in the banking sector in India's National Capital Region (NCR). Drawing upon a questionnaire-based survey, the chapter aims to move beyond the media hype of select celebratory icons and questions whether there has been any significant change in gender relations in the Indian banking sector. According to the author, although women in the banking sector have undoubtedly benefited from the expansion of employment opportunities since economic liberalization in the early 1990s, particularly in managerial positions, local cultural discourses on femininity that emphasize respectability and the need to prioritize family, remain a strong influence on gender relations in the workplace. Respectability, a crucial concern of middle-class Indian women, highlights the simultaneity of both gender and class identities for determining women's lived experiences in the banking sector and illustrates the importance of acknowledging how gender intersects with other identities such as caste and class.

Even in this modern and formal sector of employment, familial context is the paramount driver shaping women's decision-making in the workplace, and the nature of gender inequalities in the workplace (also see Chapter 9). For example, when issues pertaining to career progression based on performance-linked promotions and achievement of targets came up, women who had taken maternity leave did face setbacks; that this could have resulted on account of their legitimate absence from the office was never mentioned. As women opt for motherhood, the possibility of moving up in the occupational hierarchy is thus stalled. The framing of gendered location within the familial fold not only has implications for women's reproductive choices, it even hinders their job prospects; many had to refuse career advancements because they entailed transfers from one place to another!

However, while women continue to have the conventional responsibilities in the domestic sphere, there are emerging signs that there is space for change and negotiations. While the centrality of the family in women's working lives underlines the importance of the inter-connectedness of the public and domestic sphere, there is now greater focus on how women's work can influence their position in the household. Furthermore, this research shows that the family can play a major role in influencing women's position in the workplace. The interface between work and home is thus mutually constitutive.

Chapter 12 is by Winifred Poster on women body screeners and the securitization of space in the Indian cities of Hyderabad and Delhi. The chapter describes how the growth of the security industry is drawing women into new jobs in Indian cities. Occupations in body screening at public and private checkpoints represent more than an emergent employment sector though. They reflect the changing nature of the city itself, which is reorganizing to accommodate militarization, surveillance, and technology. They also reflect an emergent field of cybersecurity and how it is incorporating women globally.

Security scanning has provided many opportunities for women in India. Many of the recruits – men and women – are from the villages where income-earning jobs are scarce and families are impoverished. Moreover, the industry offers chances for upward mobility in terms of better emoluments than the previous jobs, particularly to women who are often concentrated in beauty industries and retail trades. Some women are earning not only for the first time, they sometimes receive higher wages than their male colleagues. This may be due to the current shortage of women entering into this niche, in combination with the high demand for women guards. The wage differential may swing back towards men after women enter the job in bigger numbers. Given the present scenario, many women are experiencing empowerment with respect to their familial, social, and economic situations.

In an interesting take, Poster questions the overarching framework of patriarchal structures that seem to be present in the world of women's work. According to her, the technologically-endowed field of cybersecurity creates a new and perhaps undefined role for the women workers. They are neither hyper-feminized as victims of male violence, like the other women in the city who are seen as passive and agentless, nor are they hyper-masculinized as male military personnel who are seen as domineering and aggressive. Instead, women guards are intermediaries in the gender continuum.

* * *

Defining and accounting for 'work' that women do appears to be so commonsensical as not to require much attention and still it is an extremely complex and difficult concept to expand and apply univocally and simply and continues to invoke intense debates and discussions. Equally contentious is the issue whether or not (formally defined notion of) work brings liberation to women. There are impressive expositions supportive of the proposition that it does while some as forcefully question the straightforward links. Given the overall social structures and encoded behavioral norms still prevalent for most women in India, the authors in this book maintain that their liberation takes place within restrictive confines of gendered ideologies. The limits do get stretched and expand now and then; we encounter occasional sparks of resistance and strategic negotiations, but how profoundly they have been shaped by implicit and explicit ideas about gendered subordination to dominant (patriarchal) discourses, and how real are the changes, is the question that lingers on!

Endnotes

[1]   Interestingly, the regional distribution pattern of women workers in EPZs follows the general pattern of regional distribution for women workers as a whole. For example, in EPZs of Santa Cruz (Maharashtra) and Madras (Tamil Nadu), women workers constituted 70–80 per cent of the workforce whereas in NOIDA, Uttar Pradesh, their share is only 30–35 per cent (Khan 2012).

[2]   According to Standing, with the spread of low wage jobs, more women tend to enter the labour market, an occurrence that he describes as 'feminization', which include two processes – a rise in female labour force participation in the face of a fall in male participation rates and the feminisation of certain jobs that were traditionally performed by men, i.e., the substitution of men by women. The concept of neo-liberally induced 'flexible labour' has also been associated with this process. Not everyone is in agreement with the 'feminisation of labour' thesis. Diane Elson has pointed out that although many countries might have shown the increase in women's share of total employment, this need not necessarily imply feminisation. It could be the disappearance of jobs traditionally done by men at the cost of the expansion of jobs that women did (Elson 1991; also Banerjee 1989; Mahadevia 2002a). A recent paper by Raju (2011) suggests a similar process whereby, better educated men in developed states of India are moving to nearby urban centres in search of non-agricultural jobs while women occupy the vacated slots in agriculture.

[3]   It has been argued that the informal component of labour has always been predominantly present in the Indian labour market whereas the employment in the formal sector has shown stagnation. Breman (1996) associates the emergence of formal sector employment to the late colonial era when a legal framework was introduced on the labour regime in enclaves of modern industrial production. According to him, this trend was followed by post-independence policies in order to bring the social organization of capital under control. Quoting Gordon (1972), he sees the division between formal and informal labour historically rather than technologically arising. The informalization that usually gets associated with neoliberal developments thus can only be seen as an accelerated process contingent upon the opening up of newer job opportunities in general and for women in particular. Moreover, as Chapter 2 would elaborate, much of self-employed home-based work that goes hand-in-hand with informalization is in fact interlinked with the formal sector. These peculiarities question a neat formulation of the 'globalization-informalization nexus' paradigm.

4 According to one estimate of occupational sex segregation in India, earlier a very high proportion of the women (62.2 per cent in 1999–2000) were employed in typically female or integrated occupations. However, the decade of 1990s saw a decline of 9–14 per cent in sex segregation levels with significant regional/district level variations, particularly in urban areas – this period coincides with trade liberalization in India. The author attributes the observed fall in gender segregation in labour market to rising levels of educational attainment, increasing presence of feminism, changing cultural and traditional mores, changes in industrial and occupational structure and presumably declining gender prejudice in the work environs (Kapur Bakshi, undated). Downloaded http://www.isid. ac.in/~pu/ conference/ dec_11_conf/Papers/ShilpiKapurBakshi.pdf, dated 2 July 2012.

5 For example, Chhachhi (1999) sees the term 'flexibility' as widely contested. According to her, on one hand, the term is associated with the revival of neo-classical economics which equates flexible labour force with dynamic free market economy while on the other it may signify a dualism in the workforce indicating a new form of capitalist control – the neo-Fordist response to the crisis of Fordism (Pollert 1987). She contends that in the absence of regulatory framework for majority of workers, Indian labour has always been flexible.

6 Withholding the broad generalization, northern Indian social space is relatively more patriarchal and feudal as compared to south India having a bearing upon women's mobility and spatial interactions thereby, along with other aspects, restricting their access to work (Rahman and Rao 2004).

7 Erasure of geography, etc. – See, Raju 2007.

8 Raju demonstrates how the garment export and InfoTech boom in India is linked to global commodity chains and how gender, caste, and class combine in different ways to create 'regional patriarchies' that define capabilities and choices for women and men who enter the lower end of the occupational hierarchies of these industries (Raju 2006).

9 As pointed out by Kelkar and Nathan, in some cases, particularly in more competitive areas of the industry such as multinational companies or large Indian firms where poaching is common, employers seem to prefer married women with children, as they are not too mobile and would be willing to stay in 'a boring job' for domestic reasons. Women were viewed as 'efficient in the work and do not leave the company as soon as they get better opportunities' (2005: 13).

10 The South Indian social regime is supposed to be relatively more gender egalitarian and yet the labour market dynamics are not free from the caste system and the marital role in women's life in determining their career options; in this case entrepreneurship in spite of their intention to become entrepreneurs (Reddy and Christopher 2012).

11 See Chapters 7 and 8 in this volume.

12 According to a Thornton International Business Report survey 2012, covering both listed and privately held business, only 21 per cent of senior management roles are globally held by women – a miniscule change from 2004 when the percentage was 19. In Russia this percentage is as high as 46 per cent followed by Botswana and Thailand. The country with lowest proportion of women in senior management is Japan (5 per cent) followed by India and United Arab Emirates with 14 and 15 per cent respectively. Women currently hold 3.4 per cent of *Fortune* 500 CEO roles and 3.6 per cent of *Fortune* 1000 roles. (Catalyst April 2012, quoted in Maheshwari K. 2012).

[13]   Radhakrishnan elaborately brings out the tension that is generated because of the long and erratic hours of job requirements in the IT sector vis-à-vis women's responsibilities towards home and family. Although the divide between work and home blurs under such conditions, questions regarding priorities arise. Her research suggests that women rarely privilege career aspirations over family life (D'Mello 2006).

[14]   If stable salaried government jobs and globalized workers are only signifiers of middle class, it is of interest to note that about 15 per cent of workers in India are privy to salaried jobs and slightly more than 2 per cent account for IT induced employment. Radhakrishnan is careful to treat her samples as 'symbolic' rather than 'representative' (2009, 199).

[15]   In supporting our discussion as to how certain constructs continue to bind women across from different classes, the case of home-based workers in Delhi can be cited. In a Delhi survey, over half the home-based women could work at their homes only due to social and ideological considerations by family or community.

 While child care did act as a real deterrent in taking up employment outside the home which could bring in better incomes, social restriction emerged as the single most important of other reasons – the combined influence of what Mazumdar calls 'domestic patriarchy'. Child care does not emerge as an issue of concern in official discourses. In fact, home-based work is seen as providing working women time to go about their domestic duties along with income-generating work (Mazumdar 2005, 47).

[16]   In his 'The Limits to Capital', David Harvey (1982) has theoretically integrated the production of space with the accumulation process in order to illustrate how capital must create particular 'spatial fixes' in the landscape at specific times to allow accumulation to proceed. According to him, spatial fixes are integral to the circulation of capital. More significantly, they constitute the very basis for the uneven development of the geography of capitalism.

[17]   Labour geographers have been criticized – often by themselves – for tending to conflate worker agency with trade union agency (Coe and Jordhus-Lier 2010).

[18]   Patel (2010) cites a contradictory example of how class/mobility–morality intertwines with the 'middle class' location of women employees in the call centres when compared to bar dancers. Both have unearthly working hours, but in case of call centres' employees, the organizations make arrangements for their transport, the latter escape such a concern.

[19]   Bangalore had a long tradition of trade union activism. However, given the political position regarding the space of activism, an organization solely concerned with workers' interest (in garment industry) had to camouflage their intent by calling itself an NGO rather than a trade union (Roy-Chowdhury 2005, 2252). The most recent attempts at labour reforms have been critiqued as curbing the freedom of workers (Times of India, 18 October 2014).

 In her study of silver chain makers in Bengal, Soni-Sinha (2011, 117) talks about 'contestations and disruptions' whereby some women used the discourse of men as breadwinners and constructed their own earnings as 'pocket money' to have control over their wages and use them for personal expenditure.

[20]   Despite being one of the fastest growing work categories in urban India generating recent debates within the framework of the 'decent work' paradigm, cleaners are often equated with what Adam Smith initially referred to as 'non-productive' personal care services.

[21] According to data from the 2009–10 National Sample Survey Organization (NSSO), just 8 per cent of women above the age of 15 in urban Delhi are in the workforce, compared to the national average of almost 20 per cent. The corresponding numbers for men are close to 75 per cent both in Delhi and nationally. Moreover, this number has been steadily declining for women; in 2004–05, it was 8.8 per cent for Delhi's urban women. One of the major contributing factors, as identified by the International Labour Organization (ILO) economists Steven Kapsos and Andrea Silberman, is the concentration of women in areas of the economy where there is little job growth, which according to them explains more than half of the fall in female participation in the labour force between 1994 and 2010 (Times of India, 16 March 2013).

References

Appadurai, A. 1996. *Modernity at Large: Cultural Dimensions of Globalization*, Minneapolis: University Minnesota Press.

Andrea Cornwall, A., and J. Edwards. 2010. 'Introduction: Negotiating Empowerment', *IDS Bulletin*, 41(2): 1–9.

Banerjee, A., and S. Raju. 2009. 'Gendered Mobility: Women Migrants and Work in Urban India', *Economic and Political Weekly*, 46(28): 115–23.

Banerjee, N. 1989. 'Trends in Women's Employment, 1971–81: Some Macro Level Observations.', *Economic and Political Weekly*, 24(17): WS10–WS22.

Banerjee-Guha, S. 2009. 'Contradictions of Enclave Development in Contemporary Times: Special Economic Zones in India', *Human Geography*, 2(1): 1–16.

Bradley, H. 2000. *Myths at Work*, Cambridge: Malden, MA: Polity Press.

Bremen, J. 1996. *Footloose Labour Working in India's Informal Economy*, Cambridge University Press: Cambridge, UK.

Chatterjee, I. 2012. 'Feminism, the False Consciousness of Neoliberal Capitalism? Informalization, Fundamentalism, and Women in an Indian City', *Gender, Place and Culture: A Journal of Feminist Geography*, pp. 1–20, downloaded http://dx.doi.org/10.1080/0966369X.2011.649349, dated 26 June 2012.

Chhachhi, A. 1999. 'Gender, Flexibility, Skill, and Industrial Restructuring: The Electronics Industry in India', *Gender Technology and Development*, 3(3): 329–60.

Coe, N. M., and D. C. Jordhus-Lier. 2010. 'Constrained Agency? Re-evaluating the Geographies of Labour', *Progress in Human Geography*, 35(2): 211–33.

Corbridge, S., and J. Harriss. 2000. *Reinventing India*, Polity Press: Cambridge.

De, I. 2012. 'Emerging Spaces and Labour Relations in Neo-Liberal India: A Review Essay', downloaded, www.mcrg.ac.in/pp49pdf, dated 25 June 2012.

Deshpande, A. 2007. 'Overlapping Identities under Liberalization: Gender and Caste in India', *Economic Development and Cultural Change*, 55(4): 735–60.

Deshpande, S. 1992. 'Structural Adjustment and Feminization', *Indian Journal of Labour Economics*, 35(4): 349–57.

————. 2003. *Contemporary India: A Sociological View*, New Delhi: Viking.

D'Mello, M. 2006. 'Gendered Selves and Identities of Information Technology Professionals in Global Software Organizations in India', *Information Technology for Development*, 12(2): 131–58.

Elson, D. 1991. 'Male Bias in Development Outcomes' in Elson D. (ed.), *Male Bias in Development Process*, Manchester: Manchester University Press.

Freeman, K. 2001. 'Is Local: Global as Feminine: Masculine? Rethinking the Gender of Globalization' *Signs*, 26(4): 1007–37.

Gordon, D. M. 1972. 'Theories of Poverty and Underemployment: Orthodox, Radical and Dual Labor Market Perspectives'. Lexington, Massachusetts: Lexington Books.

Groves, J. M., and K. A. Chang. 1999. 'Romancing Resistance and Resisting Romance: Ethnography and the Construction of Power in the Filipina Domestic Worker Community in Hong Kong', *Journal of Contemporary Ethnography*, 23(3): 235–65.

Harvey, D. 1982. *The Limits to Capital*, Oxford: Basil Blackwell.

Hayter, T., and D. Harvey. 1993. 'The Factory and the City: The Story of the Cowley Automobile Workers in Oxford', Brighton: Mansell.

Himanshu. 2011. 'Employment Trends in India: A Re-examination', *Economic and Political Weekly*, 46(37): 43–59.

ILO, 2010. 'Decent Work for Domestic Workers, Report IV (1)', http://www.ilo.org/wcmsp5/groups/public/@ed_norm/@relconf/documents/meetingdocument/wcms_104700.pdf. Accesses with downloaded, 10th August 2015.

————. 2014. 'Transitioning from the Informal to Formal Economy, International Labour Conference', 103rd Session, downloaded, http:// www.ilo.org/wcmsp5/groups/public/---ed_norm/relconf/documents/ meeting document/wcms_241897.pdf. Accessed 10th August 2015.

Jessop, B. 2001. 'Institutional (re)turns and the Strategic-Relational Approach'. *Environment and Planning A*, 33(7): 1213–37.

Kabeer, N. 1995. 'Targeting Women or Transforming Institutions? Policy Lessons from NGO Anti-poverty Efforts', *Development in Practice*, 5(2): 108–16.

————. 2000. *The Power to Choose. Bangladeshi Women and Labour Market Decisions in London and Dhaka*, Verso: London.

Kannan, K. P., and G. Raveendran. 2012. 'Counting and Profiling the Missing Labour Force', *Economic and Political Weekly*, 47(6): 77–80.

Kapoor, R. 2014. 'Creating Jobs in India's Organised Manufacturing Sector', Working Paper 286, *Indian Council for Research on International Economic Relations* (ICRIER), New Delhi, pp. 1–30.

Katz, C. 2004. 'Growing up Global: *Economic Restructuring and Children's Everyday Lives*', Minneapolis, MN: University of Minnesota Press.

Kelkar, G. and Nathan, D. 2005. 'Gender, Livelihoods and Resources in South Asia', *Fifth South Asia Regional Ministerial Conference*, Celebrating Beijing Plus Ten Islamabad, Pakistan, 3–5 May.

Kelkar, G., Shrestha G., and N. Veena. 2002. 'IT Industry and Women's Agency: Explorations in Bangalore and Delhi, India', *Gender, Technology and Development*, 6(1): 63–84.

Khandelwal, P. 2004. 'Employment in Organised Sector in 1990s: An Analysis from Gender Perspective', *Indian Journal of Industrial Relations*, 40(1): 17–38.

Khan, C. A. 2012. 'Women Employment in the Export Processing Zones in India: A Theoretical Framework', *Zenith: International Journal of Multidisciplinary Research*, 2(3): 133–41.

Krishna, S. 2001. 'Race, Amnesia, and the Education of International Relations', *Alternatives*, 26: 401–24.

Mahadevia, D. 2002a. 'Changing Economic Scenario: Informalization and Increased Vulnerability', (Kundu, A. and Mahadevia D. ed.) *Poverty and Vulnerability in Globalizing Metropolis Ahmedabad*, New Delhi: Manak, pp. 30–39.

————. 2002b. 'Communal Space Over Life Space: Saga of Increasing Vulnerability in Ahmedabad', *Economic and Political Weekly*, 37(48): 4850–58.

Maheshwari, K. 2012. 'The Glass Ceiling Impact on Indian Women Employees', National Conference on Emerging Challenges for Sustainable Business, downloaded, Deakin University, 28 June 2012.

Maringanti, A. 2008. 'The Devil in the Details: SEZs and State Restructuring in India', *Human Geography*, 1(1): 54–58.

Mazumdar, I. 2005. *Vulnerabilities of Women Home-based Workers*, Approach Paper, Centre for Women's Development Studies, New Delhi.

————. 2007. *Women Workers and Globalization: Emergent Contradictions in India*. Stree: Kolkata.

Mazumdar, I., and N. Neetha. August 2011. 'Gender Dimensions: Employment Trends in India, 1993–94 to 2009–10', Occasional Paper No. 56, *Centre for Women's Development Studies*, New Delhi.

Mehrotra, S., Gandhi, A., Sahoo, B. K., and P. Saha. 2012. 'Creating Employment in the Twelfth Five-Year Plan', *Economic and Political Weekly*, 47(19): 63–73.

Mirchandani, K. 2004a. 'Practices of Global Capital: Gaps, Cracks and Ironies in Transnational Call Centres in India', *Global Networks*, 4(4): 355–73.

————. 2004b. 'Webs of Resistance in Transnational Call Centers: Strategic Agents, Service Providers and Customers in R. Thomas, A. Mills and J. Helms Mills (ed.), *Identity Politics at Work: Resisting Gender, Gendering Resistance*, London: Routledge, pp. 179–95.

Mirza, A. M. B., and N. Jabeen. 2011. 'Gender Stereotypes and Women in Management: The Case of Banking Sector of Pakistan', *South Asian Studies*, 26(2): 259–84.

Mohan, R., and S. Dasgupta. 2005. 'The 21st Century: Asia becomes Urban', *Economic and Political Weekly*, 40(3): 213–23.

Mullings, B. 1999. 'Sides of the Same Coin? Coping and Resistance among Jamaican Data-entry Operators', *Annals of the Association of the American Geographers*, 89(2): 290–311.

Neff, D., Sen, K., and V. Kling. May 2012. 'The Puzzling Decline in Rural Women's Labor Force Participation in India: A Re-examination, GIGA Research Unit', Institute of Asian Studies, No. 196.

Ong, A. 1991. 'Gender and Labor Politics of Postmodernity' *Annual Review of Anthropology*, 20: 279–309.

———. 2000. 'Graduated Sovereignty in South-East Asia', *Theory, Culture and Society*, 17(4): 55–75.

Oza, R. 2006. 'The Making of Neoliberal India: Nationalism, Gender, and the Paradoxes of Globalization', New York and London: Routledge.

Qayum, S., and R. Ray. 2010. 'Male Servants and the Failure of Patriarchy in Kolkata (Calcutta)', *Menand Masculinities*, 13(1): 111–25.

Patel, R. 2010. *Working the Night Shift: Women in India's Call Center Industry*, Palo Alto CA, Stanford University Press.

Patel, R., and M. J. Parmentier. 2005. 'The Persistence of Traditional Gender Roles in the Information Technology Sector: A Study of Female Engineers in India', *Information Technologies and International Development*, 2(3): 29–46.

Parikh, P. P., and S. P. Sukhatme. 2004. 'Women Engineers in India', *Economic and Political Weekly*, 39(2): 193–201.

Pearson, R. 2010. 'Women's Work, Nimble Fingers and Women's Mobility in the Global Economy' in Sylvia Chant (ed.)', *The International Handbook of Gender and Poverty: Concepts, Research, Policy*, Edward Elgar, Cheltenham: UK, pp. 421–25.

Pollert, A., and A. Charlwood. 2009. 'The Vulnerable Worker in Britain and Problems at Work', *Work, Employment and Society*, 23(2): 343–62.

Pollert, A. 1987. 'The Flexible Firm: A Model in Search of Reality (or a Policy in Search of a Practice?)'. Warwick Papers in Industrial Relations 19, Warwick University.

Radhakrishnan, S. 2009. Professional Women, Good Families: Respectable Femininity and the Cultural Politics of a 'New' India, *Qualitative Sociology*, 32(2): 195–212.

Rahman, L., and V. Rao. 2004. 'The Determinants of Gender Equity in India: Examining Dyson and Moore's Thesis with New Data', *Population and Development Review*, 30(2): 239–68.

Raju, S. 2006. 'From Global to Local: Gendered Discourse, Skills and Embedded Labour Market in Urban India' in S. Raju, M. Satish and S. Corbridge (eds.), *Colonial and Post-Colonial Geographies of India*, New Delhi: Sage, pp. 99–119.

―――. 2011a. 'Mapping the World of Women's Work: Regional Patterns and Perspectives', ILO, New Delhi Office.

―――. 2011b. 'Reclaiming Spaces and Places: The Making of Gendered Geography of India' in S. Raju (ed.) Gendered Geographies: Space and Place in South Asia, New Delhi: Oxford University Press, pp. 31–59.

―――. 2011c. (edited) *Gendered Geographies: Space and Place in South Asia*, New Delhi: Oxford University Press.

―――. 2013a. 'The Material and the Symbolic: The Intersectionalities of Home-Based Work in India', *Economic and Political Weekly*, 48(1): 60–68.

―――. 2013b. 'Women in India's New Generation Jobs', *Economic and Political Weekly*, 48(36): 16–18.

Ramaswamy, K. V. 1999. 'The Search for Flexibility in Indian Manufacturing. New Evidence on Outsourcing Activities,' *Economic and Political Weekly*, 34(6): 363–68.

Rangarajan, C., Padma Iyer Kaul, and Seema 2011. 'Where is the Missing Labour Force?' *Economic and Political Weekly*, 46(39): 68–72.

Razavi, S., Arza, C., Braunstein, E., Cook, S., and K. Goulding. 2012. 'Gendered Impacts of Globalization: Employment and Social Protection, Gender and Development', Paper No. 16, United Nations Research Institute for Social Development, UNRISD, Geneva: Switzerland.

Reddy, B. S., and P. Christopher. 2012. 'Identifying the Variable that Affects the Development of Women Entrepreneurship in India with Special Reference to Scio Cultural Factor', *Online International Interdisciplinary Research Journal*, 2(1): 21–26.

Roy Chowdhury, S. 2005. 'Labour Activism and Women in the Unorganised Sector: Garment Export Industry in Bangalore', *Economic and Political Weekly*, 40(22–23): 2250–55.

Saunders, P. 1986. *Social Theory and the Urban Question*, London: Routledge.

Sen, S., and S. Raju. 2012. 'Interfacing Women's Work with Development in ICT: An Exploratory Exposition', Paper presented at the Workshop entitled 'New Spatialities and Labour', 6 – 8 July, 2012, IGIDR, Mumbai.

Sen, S., and B. Dasgupta. 2009. *Unfreedom and Waged Work: Labour in India's Manufacturing Industry*. Sage: New Delhi.

Singh, S., and G. Hoge. 2010. 'Debating Outcomes for "Working" Women: Illustrations from India', *Journal of Poverty*, 14: 197–215.

Soni-Sinha, U. 2009. 'Flexible Work, Gender and Globalised Production: A Study of the Jewellery Sector in North India'. *Contributions to Indian Sociology*, 43(3): 381–409.

———. 2010. 'Gender, Subjectivity and Agency: A study of Workers in Noida Export Processing Zone, India', *Global Labour Journal*, 1(2): 265–94. Available at: http://digitalcommons.mcmaster.ca/globallabour/vol1/iss2/3.

Standing, Guy. 1999. 'Global Feminisation Through Flexible Labour', *World Development*, 17(7): 1077–95.

Stiglitz, J. E. 2004. 'Globalization and Growth in Emerging Markets', *Journal of Policy Modeling*, 26(4): 465–84.

Tacoli, C. 1998. 'Rural-Urban Interactions; A Guide to the Literature', *Environment and Urbanization*, 10(1): 147–66.

Tara, S., and Ilavarasan. 2011. 'Work: A Qualitative Study of Unmarried Women Call Center Agents in India', *Marriage and Family Review*, 47: 197–212.

Taylor, P., and P. Bain. 2010. 'Across the Great Divide: Local and Global Trade Union Responses to Call Centre Offshoring to India' in McGrath-Champ, A. Herod and A. Rainnie (ed.) *Handbook of Employment and Society Working Space*, Edward Elgar Publishing Ltd.: UK, pp. 436–56.

Unni, J., Bali, N., and J. Vyas. December 1999. 'Subcontracted Women Workers in the Global Economy: Case of Garment Industry in India', Ahmedabad: Gujarat Institute of Development Research and Self Employed Women's Association.

2

Women Workers in Urban India and the Cities

Saraswati Raju and Debangana Bose

Introduction

Early 1990s is somewhat of a watershed in terms of Indian economy, which had seen rather unprecedented trade liberalization in India in response to internal and external impulses. Following the rise in fiscal deficit, negative industrial growth, enhanced inflation and political uncertainties, structural reforms were introduced in industrial and import licensing sector for microeconomic stabilization. One of the impacts was the changing employment and wage pattern in the labour market. Outward looking policies aimed at greater participation in international economy and increased export were supposed to favour labour surplus countries. Such globalizing processes, accompanied by macroeconomic changes also led to an integration of the different labour markets on the one hand and rising segregation and segmentation within, on the other. Whereas labour has become relatively more mobile and tied with contact-based migration, the segmentation of labour markets has been due to rising concentration in certain sectors and types of economic activities (Paul and Raju 2014). Overall, such processes have brought the informality in the labour markets to the limelight. While some call this informality and globalization linkage as a new phase in capitalism, others contend it to be unique in itself.

The emergence of the 'new economy' is characterized by an enhanced engagement of women labour as a cheap source of maintaining the 'standards of capitalism' and 'reserve army of labour' by making them act as a support system of the economy. This is widespread in almost all developing countries and more so in India where the rise of women's employment is usually accompanied by rise in distress in the Indian economy. However, women display a high presence in the informal employment as casual labourers and self-employed and also in domestic labour as regular salaried.[1] Export-oriented growth, which is becoming extremely competitive despite remaining committed in principle to collective interests at some social cost, not only reconfigure the existing social and gendered constructs to serve the interests of few and marginalize many, women are usually less likely to be highly mobile and their access to resources and human capital remains limited (Raju 2013). As Arora (2012) points out, India has a continuously rising import/GDP ratio since 1990–1991 and yet the trade openness may be illusory when women workers are brought in.

In general, urban existence, particularly cities, are supposed to lend the inhabitants a certain sense of anonymous identities that overcome the socio-cultural barriers posed by caste, ethnicity, religion and gender, etc. in accessing job opportunities. We are often confronted with talks about the expanding new generation employment avenues of work for women and the recent official discourses eulogizes about rising incidences of employment amongst urban women. They have also been conceived as spaces of transition from traditions to modernity. And yet cities' supposedly linear trajectories have long been questioned and contested. Indian cities, for example, continue to display an ambiguous mix of both – the so-called modern trends existing in close proximity with traditional values and anchoring. Much of the available literature suggests that global capitalism, while providing new job prospects to women, not only exploits the prevailing gendered stereotypes, but also rearticulates them. Given this, an intriguing question to ask is – in what ways women workers may simultaneously be posing challenges to such claims. Do city locations alter the working conditions for women or their gendered locations continue to align with women's exclusions and relegation within the job markets? That women also make up largely for the pool of cheap labour, one of the hallmarks of capital accumulation for which metro cities seem to offer congenial spaces, is hinted at in the course of our discussion on the gendered nature of the workforce, although it remains as a sub-text.

The present chapter interrogates some of these issues.   The chapter is divided into five sub-sections. Subsequent to the introduction, the first section deals with the often debated and contested formal/informal nature of labour market in India and also tries to link the concept of 'informality' to 'gendered informality'. The second section visits the characteristics of labour markets in general. As far as the overall quantum of women's work in cities per se is concerned, the published statistical data, however, do not offer much systematic information. The following third section therefore reviews specific case studies with particular reference to post-liberal informalization of women's labour, which have received significant academic attention in recent times. The fourth section attempts at a comparative empirical analysis of the million-plus cities (or the metro cities) and the non-million plus cities (or the rest of the urban centres), in terms of their labour market outcomes using unit level National Sample Survey (NSS) data. The last section concludes the discussion.

Informal/formal nature of labour market

It may be pertinent at this juncture to briefly talk about the informal and formal nature of the labour market. Earlier known as 'traditional sector' to mark unregistered, low-income and unprotected, outside-the-legal-framework jobs mostly in the developing world, the 1970s saw it replaced with the term 'informal sector'. However, by the late 1990s, scholars began to see that it is not a sector per se in terms of specific industries that one is concerned with; it denotes a whole range of diverse economic activities, workers and enterprises. The term 'informal economy/work' came into vogue. There are several schools of thoughts and innumerable definitional attempts to define it (see, http://wiego.org/informal-economy/history-debates, cited in Rosaldo, Tilly and Evans 2012). With the dominant presence of market that thrives on competitive impulses and therefore on cheaper labour, the informal economy is now being seen as an inevitable as well as a growing component of the labour market.

It has also been increasingly recognized that the informal economy is significantly linked with the formal economy as a share of the latter's work is now being undertaken within the folds of the informal economy/work. The urban informal sector is thus at times not seen as a distinct entity, separate from a formal sector; it is seen as a continuum, a variation. Such an overlapping also suggests that the informal economy encompasses enormously heterogeneous and complex forms of work – although manufacturing continued to be the most important branch of economic activity for the employment of both women and men home-based workers, one observes a shift from earlier tobacco, textile and wood products to food and beverages, wearing apparel and other manufactured products (Raveendran, Sudarshan and Vanek 2013).

Fields (1990, 49–50) argues that even if the distinction between 'formal' and 'informal' is a matter of 'degree' and not 'kind', the terminology needs to be refined in the light of more recent developments.[2] Alluding to these two sectors as distinctly separate, he draws attention to the heterogeneity within the informal sector.[3] He maintains that the presumably homogenous nature of the informal sector may have been true in early 1980s but a decade and half later, the differentiated nature of the informal sector is more a reality. He thus suggests distinguishing between, what he calls, 'easy entry informal sector' of those who has a low-paying agricultural job or no job in land-scarce economies joining the urban informal sector and the 'upper-tier informal sector', which can consist of one who may have been working for a long time in the formal sector, albeit at the lower end of the occupational hierarchy, and may not want to continue in the formal sector. By virtue of skills, experience and money (that might have been accumulated over the years), the workers may move to set up their businesses, which may be small, unregulated and with or without a fixed place of work. Fields provides examples of taxi-driving, street vending and backyard industries as representing 'easy entry' activities, whereas small manufacturing entrepreneurs may belong to upper-tier informal sector.[4] It is true that informal activities could be quite diverse from one end of the occupational hierarchy to another, reflected through women workers in ITC driven sectors on one hand to home-based petty producers and unpaid family labour on the other (Mohan 2011).

It would be of interest to examine Fields's ideas when women workers are included in his analytical framework. As Fields suggests, educational levels of workforce can be a good reflector of intersectoral mobility. The in-depth account of workforce composition and placements of workers in different components of work, when interfaced with educational, attainments, clearly indicate that given the overall skills and educational levels of women workers, miscellany for them is quite curtailed and limited. Coupled with social and cultural barriers and prevailing gender constructs, their disproportionate bunching in specific jobs seems to be a distinct reality (Raju 2010; Klasen and Pieters 2012; Paul and Raju 2014).

Rodgers (1994) also highlights the two types of segmentations in the labour market namely the horizontal segmentation and the vertical segmentation. The former refers to the separation in types of enterprise or industry of work and the latter implies segmentation in the type of occupation, a hierarchical arrangement. These are not mutually exclusive and in most of the cases both exist simultaneously. As the subsequent discussion would reveal, women are not only disproportionately represented in the informal sector and as home-based workers within the informal sector (Raju 2013), the formal sector also witnesses women placed at the lower end of production chains and lower rungs of earnings. In this regard, the concepts of 'segregation' and 'concentration' are useful. They are not synonymous, although often used simultaneously; while 'segregation' measures the tendency of men and women to be employed in different occupations, 'concentration' measures the proportion of one gender, usually women, in a single occupation or a set of occupations (Anker 1998). In case of women workers, these two are intrinsically and deeply associated, although they may signify two very different processes and phenomena.

One of the most familiar arguments that has been put forward to explain the gender inequalities in the labour market is gender-differentiated investments in human capital endowments, which privileged women's role in biological reproduction over their involvement in the labour market. Feminist scholars have talked about the futility of this argument by pointing out that even with comparable levels of education/experience, etc. women are disadvantaged on account of the gendered identities. Neo-classical economics has tried to explain the inequalities in terms of individual choice and structural constraint approaches. Both have, however, converged over the years. As Kabeer observes, it was acknowledged that individuals and groups may opt for choices and exercise agency, but they operate within the confines imposed by the resilient, often institutionalized, structural norms. Affective over the life course, distinctly defined masculine/feminine constructs assigning specific roles to men and women operate in a given society. She terms these 'intrinsically gendered', whereas market (and state) institutions that reconfigure and rearticulate such norms to their benefit are 'bearers of gender' (Kabeer 2012, 12–13) – a framework that we have broadly adopted in the present work to decode the gendered dynamics of the labour market in India. Many of the norms are faced by men as well, but women's gendered locations seem to cut across other axes of differentiations.

Revisiting the Indian labour market

Significantly, it is extremely problematic to directly compare various data sets and the same data set temporally because of changing definitions and reference periods and so on. The NSS data, which we use for the present analysis, is not free from such a difficulty. The problems get further compounded by the age-cohorts, categories – rural/urban, formal/informal, absence/presence of census-adjusted figures, and selection of the initial of the base year and so on with the result that the interpretations can slightly differ even if they are derived from the same data sets. Moreover, temporal workforce participation rates get impacted by intermittent natural and economic events. And yet, several broad features of the labour markets can be discerned and that is what we attempt drawing upon various NSS Rounds on employment and unemployment. Although the NSS data on employment and unemployment are available since 1973, we focus on the period from 1983 onwards to capture pre and post liberalization phases as well to have a more contemporary sense of labour market changes. Admittedly, we do not involve ourselves with technical details embedded in the data, but look for broader trends.

It is well known that the Indian labour market has shown oscillating trends in the overall workforce participation rates in general and that of women in particular. One of the much talked about features of the subsequent employment situation (2004–2005) has been the overall increase in women's workforce participation rates. This has almost been a worldwide as well as an Asian phenomenon with varying degrees (ILO 2007). Of course, the work participation rates are still low by international standards in India – out of 131 countries, India ranks 11th from the bottom (ILO 2013); they reflect substantial variation across space. Overall, this increase has been variously interpreted as putting the 'jobless growth' syndrome of the 1990s to rest and as expanding opportunities for women in the labour market (Kabeer 2004). However, scholars were wary about considering this growth as a positive feature. In the Indian context, the issues being raised were about the nature and quality of employment (Kundu 1997; Kundu and Mohanan 2010). While the 2004–2005 NSS data were lauded for having shown an increase in the workforce participation rates of women, the most striking feature of the recent data for 2011–2012 is the significant overall fall in work participation rates since. The general drop is mainly due to the decline in the women's labour-force participation rate, which has decreased by about 12 percentage points from 2004–2005. This decline in turn can be accounted for by a much steeper decline of the rural women's workforce (14.7 percentage point) as compared to those in urban areas (3.9) (Table 2.1). Both as principal as well as subsidiary workers, women seem to have lost ground in recent years (Mazumdar and Neetha 2011). Incidentally, the signs were already visible for such a decline in the mid-quinquennial survey of 2007–2008 as well.

Table 2.1 Labour force participation rates in India
(usual principal and subsidiary status, age-group 15–59)

	1993–1994	1999–2000	2004–2005	2009–2010	2011–2012*
All India	67.1	64.5	66.6	59.6	58.3
Women	45.2	41.6	45.4	34.5	33.1
Men	88.0	86.6	87.1	83.7	82.7
Urban India	55.8	53.8	56.2	52.3	52.7
Women	25.2	22.2	26.1	21.0	22.2
Men	83.2	82.2	83.4	80.9	81.0
Rural India	71.2	68.7	70.6	62.6	60.9
Women	52.0	48.7	52.5	39.9	37.8
Men	83.2	82.2	83.4	80.9	83.5

Source: Adopted from Neff, Sen and Kling (2012)
*   Based on authors' own calculation using unit level data from NSS 68th Round. We have subtracted the subsidiary workers who are looking for work as principal status workers.

There are several explanations for the decline. Some attribute the 2004–2005 increase in women's workforce participation rates to the peculiar distress conditions[5] during that year, which if ignored as aberration, would see the decline in 2009–2010 in keeping with the secular trend of declining workforce rate amongst women in general (Abraham 2009; Himanshu 2011; Rangarajan *et al.* 2011). The decline has also been attributed to increased presence of girls/women in educational institute (Mehrotra, Gandhi, Sahoo and Saha 2012) – a proposition that has been contested as untenable as the decline in women's workforce participation is not in the age-cohorts that can be enrolled in educational institutes (Kannan and Raveendran 2012). Others argue that despite an increase in the number of urban women receiving education, there is no accompanying decline in their labour-force participation rate (Neff, Sen and Kling 2012). The elitist urbanism acting as an informal social check on poor people's move to the cities (Baviskar 2003; Kundu 2009), the pro-environment lobby and pushing up of (polluting) industries to rural peripheries (Kundu 2010), fastest growing industries in India with low employment potential within the 'formal' labour market are some of the other explanations on board for the latest labour market changes.

Like most developing countries, India's labour market is characterized by very low formal sector employment. Although already present, the post-liberalization phase is particularly marked by the enhanced growth of the informal sector. It was partly because of the export-oriented manufacturing, which tend to push subcontract production to informal producers much of whom are less skilled labour with women, on average, comprising a relatively disproportionate share (Dev 2000; Kalpagam 2001).

The upswing in women workers seems to because of the increase in their weekly and daily statuses signaling the growth in short-term employment which essentially characterizes the informal sectors. That the short-term part-time informal work is on rise in urban areas is borne by yet another observation, i.e., the reduction in urban unemployment rates for women who are classified as workers by daily status. Although the decade is marked by casualization of employment in general, urban women do not seem to be affected by this phenomenon whose share as regular/salaried had 'gone up at the cost of self-employed workers'. Kundu attributes this feature to '... a significant change in the organization of work and emergence of a new subcontracting system in the urban informal sector' (Kundu 1997, 1402; Deshpande and Deshpande 1998).[6] The interlinked impact seems to be on the declining share of manufacturing in urban areas, which according to Kundu, suggests increase in subcontracted manufacturing through smaller units that are usually placed at the household level. It is quite possible that such manufacturing activities are classified under 'services' and eventually under the tertiary sector. Under these circumstances, it is not surprising that urban women did not show the signs of stalled manufacturing sector that characterised the sectoral distribution of workers during the period under review (Kundu 1997, 2003).

The declining or almost stagnant trends in employment generation with a few exceptions, such as urban women workers, continued in the late 1990s. The period from 1993–1994 to 1999–2000 saw the overall rural employment increased very marginally (by only 0.66 per cent per annum) whereas urban employment increased by 2.27 per cent per year, which in the succeeding year rose to 3.22 per cent. However, as Ghosh and Chandrasekhar (2007) note, this recovery (in urban areas) was below the rates of employment expansion achieved in the period 1987–1988 to 1993–1994.

Although, as indicated earlier, the workers can broadly be categorized as wage workers and self-employed (a classification the ILO uses), the category of self-employed workers needs problematizing. In countries such as India, this dichotomy does not capture the complexities of home-based workers; all self-employed workers are not necessarily home-bound and all home-based workers are not compulsorily self-employed. Theoretically, home-based workers can range from high-tech professional workers to petty producers as well as piece-rate workers. And yet, the Indian workers who are based at home are not autonomous and self-contained individuals as assumed in the Western constructs. From the gendered perspective, this is an important issue because the recent years show that the proportion of home-based workers amongst the self-employed is overwhelmingly skewed towards women. In 2004–2005, about 46 per cent of usual status women workers in the age-group 15–59 in urban India were self-employed out of which 69 per cent were home-based. Slightly less than half of the urban self-employed workers were unpaid (family workers). The contribution of unpaid workers to the overall quantum of women workers is such that Mazumdar and Neetha (2011) see an uncanny (positive) association between unpaid labour amongst self-employed and women's workforce participation rates, both following a common trajectory.

Regular salaried work is often seen as occupying the top position in the occupational hierarchy. Although salaried workers in non-agricultural activities had shown some increase, particularly by urban women, it was essentially in subsidiary status indicative of informal part-time employment with low productivity and low wages at the cost of disappearing formal or full-time jobs (Unni and Raveendran 2007; Raju 2010; Chen and Raveendran 2012). The most significant increase was in self-employment.

Notwithstanding the discussions on the fluctuations and a complex dynamics that characterize labour market outcomes, it is significant to note that a higher percentage of urban women workers than their men counterparts have always been informally employed. As opposed to the earlier years, particularly 1999–2000 and 2004–2005 when self-employment had overtaken the wage employment in the informal sector, the year 2009–2010 saw an evenly divided informal employment between self-employment and wage work. For urban women it was the informal employment in manufacturing and non-trade services such as domestic workers. The relative decline in home-based manufacturing activities has been attributed to the decline in export-induced manufacturing in recent years. Chen and Raveendran have a striking point to make. In 2004–2005, three times as many urban women workers as men, both in the total and the informal workforce, were in four groups of informal workers– domestic, home-based, street vendors and waste pickers. By 2009–2010, however, we see a shift for 1.5 times as many men as women were in these occupational groups – these activities are largely home-based. According to them, it is the loss of self-employment amongst urban men that prompted them to take over these venues of work. They substantiate their argument by pointing out the significant increase in home-based work for urban men between 2004–2005 and 2009–2010 by 12 percentage points with a corresponding decline of 17 per cent for urban women (Chen and Raveendran 2012, 17).

Social and cultural constraints continue to have an effect on women's work even in urban context.[7] Despite the opening up of job opportunities for women in recent years, the participation of women in the labour market thus may remain curtailed. We have seen in the first chapter that even the relatively better educated women workers in more progressive sectors cannot escape their framing within the stereotypical sphere of domesticity.[8] That women have multiple locations is known. The caste/class and ethnic overlap may push women to further marginalization. In India, the abiding institute of caste clearly reveals that social stratification has been impeding the entry of certain marginalized sections of population into particular employments. It is not surprising therefore to see women of upper castes appropriating the benefits of the liberalizing processes (Deshpande 2007).

In sum, the implication of gendered location of women workers in India's evolving global capitalism and labour market leads us to think through about the interplay of a whole range of parameters with localized structural constraints in addition to 'the role of a global economy in creating new forms of feminized work' – work in which women's unequal social statuses are crucial to their constitution as 'workers'. Together, the changes are fraught with tensions between subversive 'patriarchal authority' and 'quintessentially modern aspirations and tastes' (Lessinger 2002, 13, 15). In an intensive theoretically oriented exposition, supported by empirical evidences, Esteve-Volart (2004) looks at how economic development impacts women workforce participation rates in India. It is seen that despite having a disastrous economic consequences, social norms continue to contain women's participation in India's labour market – regional developmental status withholding.

Workers in urban centres: Review of case studies

The almost stagnant or painfully slow increase in employment amongst men accompanied by relatively faster growth in workforce participation rates amongst urban women has already been commented upon. Although pre and post liberalization phases in terms of their impact on labour market outcomes is not our direct focus, the post-liberal increase in urban women's participation in the labour market, more so as in intermittent, casual and part-time work has also been noted (Deshpande and Deshpande 1998) as is the impact of the development of export industries during the 1990s on the growth of women's employment in most of the countries of the South, including India, a change that cannot be doubted.

Using the NSS data (1993–1994) and other surveys, Mahadevia (2002) has compared the urban workforce data for Gujarat vis-à-vis the city of Ahmedabad to point out how the city women workers have grown at a much higher pace when compared to women workers in the state whereas the men workers in the city had lagged behind the corresponding growth in the state. She attributes the relatively higher growth of women workers in the cities responding to a situation in which men were being pushed to casual and low-wage work because of massive closures of textile mills in the later eighties through the early nineties. The mills have traditionally been the backbone of the city's economic growth.[9] Given the generally low levels of education and skills of women and the structural inability of the labour market, these women could enter the paid work largely through home-based activities or self-employment (Gopal 2007). Klasen and Pieters captures the situation aptly and we quote – "rising female labour-force participation then reflects the erosion of men's position in the labour market, rather than an improvement in women's opportunities" (2012, 6).

The informal nature of women's work in Ahmedabad and associated exploitative structures has been critically addressed by Unni (2000, also Breman 2002). Home-based work, which incidentally makes up for substantial part of self-employed women insecure, routine and marginalized in the labour market is too well known by now to obviate a further discussion here. There may be situations that a particular craft is carried out in small unregistered and unrecognized enterprises, which primarily employ craftsmen who appropriate the factory spaces as regular workers whereas women who contribute to the production are at home-bases, effectively kept out of the orbit of training outlays or access to infrastructural facilities, as reported from peri-urban areas of Lucknow for Zardosi work (Sudarshan, Venkataraman and Bhandari 2007).[10]

Women in factory situation do not manage particularly better. Ready-made garment industry is a case in point. As against home-based and piece-rate work that characterizes the ready-made garment industries in Delhi and Mumbai, Bangalore can boast of well-organized factory based production in this field. And yet, the women workers are deprived of legally stipulated minimum wages. Security remains evasive as the women's services are terminated prematurely so as to avoid several provisions such as gratuity (Roy-Chowdhury 2005). Another example is that of Tiruppur, a city in South India known for its hosiery production. Although the export boom of the 1990s had drawn extensive women labour to the industry, they remain concentrated in the lowest paying activities occupying highly invisible part of value chain as home-based workers (Singh and Sapra 2007). Incidentally, the industry is not free from rather primordial caste relations. As Harriss points out, sub-contracting relations in Tiruppur are mediated through tight networks of caste whereby the locally dominant agrarian castes have effectively blocked the entry of the outsiders in the cluster (Harriss-White 2010)

The essential framing of women workers has been commented upon extensively in Chapter 1. What is disturbing is the continuation of such framing even in million-plus cities of India although the case here is about slum women in Mumbai who would have their workplace closer to their homes, at times compromising with lower wages, so as to carry out the paid work along with their regular housework (Deshpande 2001; also see Chapter 4 in this volume.). In general, such compromises are not uncommon even for those who are placed at relatively higher jobs (Patrick 2001).

Mitra (2005: 291) brings in yet another dimension when he talks about the difficulties Delhi women in informal sector face in accessing diversified activities, which tend to be located in specific geographic areas. Apart from social and economic barriers that prevent job diversification of women, physical segmentation of market, he argues, 'perpetuate[s] forces that entrap women workers in low-income situation with worse outcomes than those of their male counterparts' who do not face as much restrictions in terms of physical mobility.[11]

Workers in million-plus cities and rest of urban centres

So far we have tried to get an overview of how the cities treat their women workers from individual case studies. The following empirical discussion is based on NSS data for all cities. Until the 55th Round (1999–2000), the data had provisions to extract information on three size classes of cities – large cities (>1000000 population), medium cities and towns (50000–1000000 population) and small towns (5000–50000 population). Unfortunately, 61st Round onwards (64th Round 2009–2010; 68th Round 2011–12), the data can be extracted to identify only the two size classes of urban centres. They are million-plus cities (>1000000 population) and rest of the urban centres (5000–1000000 populations). The 68th Round provides a list of 27 million-plus cities for which data can be scrutinised by using the stratum variable in the estimation procedure.

A glance through the patterns of employment of urban workers in general clearly shows that the processes and outcomes of labour markets have been altering; as pointed out earlier, the most important process is informalization owing to sub-contracting and changing structure of employment induced by the 'new economic order'. However, the question remains whether this is happening ubiquitously – a common characteristic in all the urban centres or is confined to metro cities? Simply put, we are asking if the large (million-plus) cities are differentially placed, as compared to the rest of the urban centres in case of women workers and their attributes.

The following discussion is organised under three sub-heads – first, the characteristics of labour markets and the employment pattern between the million-plus cities and rest of the urban centres are presented; this is followed by a discussion on the component of informality within the realm of regular salaried workers. The third sub-section deals with a specific issue of domestic labour.

The work participation rates have remained almost unaltered in both million-plus cities and rest of urban centres among men as well as women over the years 1999–2000 to 2011–2012 (Table 2.2). Interestingly, regular salaried workers, both men and women occupy the major chunk of workers in metro as well as non-metro locations followed by self-employed. At the outset, the dominance of salaried workers in the employment structure looks promising. However, when this category is further disaggregated, one can see that most women are involved in services rendered at private households as maids and domestic workers, particularly in the metro cities. In non-metro cities, most women are engaged in activities related to education sector while manufacturing attracts most of the regular salaried men workers. We return to the category of 'salaried workers' in the later part of the chapter.

It is well known that self-employment has become a major avenue of labour absorption in recent decades, which is interlinked with outsourcing/ flexible production regimes of globalizing context in general. Both men and women have this component grown in 2012. As compared to men, a very large chunk of these self-employed women are home-based – a defining feature which is circumscribed by the traditional notions regarding women's place in domestic sphere (Raju 2013).

Table 2.2 Population and employment structure of all workers (UPSS) 1999–2000 and 2011–2012

	Million Plus Cities				Rest of the Urban Centres			
	Men		Women		Men		Women	
	1999–2000	2011–2012	1999–2000	2011–2012	1999–2000	2011–2012	1999–2000	2011–2012
Population (Aged 15–59 years)	53.6	68.18	46.4	67.07	52.2	64.60	47.8	65.93
Workers	78.01	79.01	18.51	21.02	78.65	78.16	21.72	20.96
Employment Status								
Self Employed	29.19	31.02	20.90	23.40	33.45	34.63	24.43	26.54
Unpaid Family Labour	5.83	5.48	13.95	11.89	8.33	7.61	22.20	18.54
Regular Salaried	52.16	56.16	52.97	58.93	39.44	39.43	29.13	37.60
Casual Labour	12.83	7.34	12.17	5.77	18.78	18.34	24.23	17.33
Total Workers	100	100	100	100	100	100	100	100

Source: Unit Level data, NSS 55th and 68th Rounds

Table 2.3 Top four shares of regular salaried workers (UPSS) 2011–2012

Ranks	Men in Million-plus Cities	Women in Million-plus Cities	Men in Rest of the Urban Centres	Women in Rest of the Urban Centres
1	Manufacturing (32.4%)	Activities of Private Households (24.0%)	Manufacturing (24.4%)	Education (32.9%)
2	Transport Storage, Accommodation (20.9%)	Education (17.9%)	Transport Storage, Accommodation (16.9%)	Manufacturing (12.7%)
3	Wholesale & Retail Trade (10.3%	Manufacturing (12.9%)	Wholesale & Retail Trade (13.2%)	Activities of Private House-holds (10.3%)
4	Public Administra-tion (8.4%)	Transport Storage, Ac-commodation (9.4%)	Public Administra-tion (11.9%)	Health (9.8%)

Source: Computed from unit level of 68th Rounds

As already indicated, while majority of the regular salaried women workers are in the education and domestic work in million-plus cities, the education sector and manufacturing sector employ majority of the women workers in the rest of the urban centre (Table 2.3). Unlike million-plus cities, rest of the urban centres display a more or less stagnant share by employment statuses. Manufacturing holds the major proportion of both men and women workers in million-plus as well as non-million plus sites. However, as Table 2.4 shows, the growth in the manufacturing sector has either been stable or sluggish over the period under observation.

Table 2.4 Top four shares of workers (UPSS) 1999–2000 and 2011–2012

Ranks	1999–2000		2011–2012	
	Men	Women	Men	Women
Million Plus Cities				
1	Manufacturing (27.6%)	Manufacturing (21.1%)	Manufacturing (27.7%)	Manufacturing (25.6%)
2	Wholesale and Retail Trade (25.1%)	Education (15.9%)	Wholesale and Retail Trade (19.7%)	Activities of Private Households (15.6%)
3	Transport Storage, Communication etc (15.6%)	Wholesale & Retail Trade (14.8%)	Transport Storage, Communication etc. (18.9%)	Education (12.9%)
4	Administrative and Supportive Services (8.2%)	Activities of Private Households (10.3%)	Construction (7.7%)	Wholesale and Retail Trade (9.2%)
Rest of Urban Centres				
1	Wholesale & Retail Trade (25.9%)	Manufacturing (23.8%)	Wholesale & Retail Trade (22.7%)	Manufacturing (30.0%)
2	Manufacturing (20.5%)	Agriculture and Allied (22.7%)	Manufacturing (19.7%)	Education (14.3%)
3	Transport Storage, Communication etc (13.1%)	Wholesale and Retail Trade (13.7%)	Transport Storage, Communication etc (14.8%)	Agriculture and Allied (14.2%)
4	Construction (9.7%)	Education (10.9%)	Construction (12.3%)	Wholesale and Retail Trade (9.9%)

Source: Computed from unit level of NSS 55th and 68th Rounds

As mentioned earlier, one of the reasons has been the recent drive towards removal of large industrial and polluting units outside the city boundaries, partly the impact of the environment lobbies in big cities that have campaigned against them, a process that has been termed as 'elite capture' of the globalizing cities. It would be of interest to disaggregate manufacturing activities further in order to see what men and women are exactly doing (Table 2.5).

Table 2.5 Top four activities of all workers within the manufacturing sector (UPSS) 2011–2012

Ranks	Men in Million-plus Cities	Women in Million-plus Cities	Men in Rest of the Urban Centres	Women in Rest of the Urban Centres
1	Custom tailoring (7.9%)	Custom tailoring (24.8%)	Custom tailoring (7.9%)	Custom tailoring (21.8%)
2	Manufacture of all types of textile garments and clothing accessories (7.5%)	Manufacture of all types of textile garments and clothing accessories (11.8%)	Weaving, manufacture of cotton (4.5%)	Manufacture of *Beedi* (16.6%)
3	Working of diamonds and other precious and semi-precious stones (5.9%)	Embroidery work and making of laces and fringes (9.8%)	Manufacture of furniture made of wood (3.5%)	Weaving, manufacture of cotton (4.7%)
4	Embroidery work and making of laces and fringes (4.7%)	Zari work and other ornamental trimmings (5.2%)	Manufacture of jewelry (3.1%)	Embroidery work and making of laces and fringes (3.7%)

Source: Computed from unit level of NSS 68ᵗʰ Rounds
Note: The categorization is based on the NIC 5 digit classification, 2008.

Manufacture of all types of textile garments and clothing accessories are concentrated in million-plus cities in contrast with other urban centres. Custom tailoring emerges as the major activity. However, while about one-third of women are engaged in this activity, men's share is less than one-fifth. Despite being carried out at different scales, most women, be in the million-plus cities or living in smaller urban settlements, are engaged in some activities related to textile and garments. In smaller urban settlements, weaving and *Beedi* rolling are the activities which keep women occupied. At the risk of digression, it may be suggested that while the million-plus cities emerge as the surplus-accumulating in the process of fine-tuning the textile/garment products, the smaller urban centres appear to be the providers of processing and semi-processing of raw material invoking and recalling what Lefebvre calls an instrumental view of (urban) space whereby large cities act towards maintenance of capitalism (Merrifield 2002). That women workers should occupy relatively large segment of the work, should not come as a surprise if the logic of profit maximization inherent in capitalism is kept in mind. Table 2.6 offers a still more refined classification of workers in manufacturing sector as it gives the occupations of workers.

Table 2.6 Top four occupational avenues for all workers (UPSS) in manufacturing sector 2011–2012

Ranks	Men in Million-plus Cities	Women in Million-plus Cities	Men in Rest of the Urban Centres	Women in Rest of the Urban Centres
1	Textile, Garment and Related Trades Workers (14.2%)	Textile, Garment and Related Trades Workers (37.4%)	Textile, Garment and Related Trades Workers (16.5%)	Textile, Garment and Related Trades Workers (36.3%)
2	Directors and Chief Executives (12.9%)	Directors and Chief Executives (18.6%)	Directors and Chief Executives (11.9%)	Food Processing and Related Trades Workers (18.2%)
3	Textiles, Fur and Leather Products Machine Operators (9.6%)	Textiles, Fur and Leather Products Machine Operators (6.4%)	Manufacturing Labourers (6.4%)	Directors and Chief Executives (11.7%)
4	Other Machine Operators and Assemblers (5.4%)	Manufacturing Labourers (4.1%)	Metal Moulders, Welders, Sheet Metal Workers (5.5%)	Manufacturing Labourers (6.4%)

Source: Computed from unit level of NSS 68th Rounds
Note: The categorization is based on the NIC 3 digit classification, 2004

Informality of regular salaried workers

It can be recalled that the largest section of workers in both million-plus cities and in the rest of the urban centres are in regular salaried work (Table 2.2). 'Regular salaried worker' is a category which needs deconstruction. Admittedly, this category can be perceived as the most desirable category sitting at the top of the occupational hierarchy located within the formal sector. The picture gets somewhat messy when intercepted with educational levels even for salaried work. The available evidences suggest a very small section of women accessing the higher occupational echelon, whereas a majority of women remains confined to low level jobs as also bunched in fewer occupations – cities seem to offer no significant exceptions.

Above three-fifth of the regular salaried workers, irrespective of their being men or women and type of urban location, have no written job contracts (Table 2.7). More than half of the workers in all categories of regular salaried employment do not have access to social security benefits (Tables 2.8). Slightly more than half of the men and women workers are eligible for paid leave. This highlights the informal ways the formal sectors, such as within the regular salaried sections, are being run. The million-plus cities and non-million plus urban centres do not behave differently in this matter nor are there disparities in terms of men and women.

Table 2.7 Job contract of regular salaried workers 2011–2012

Type of Job Contract	Men in Million-plus Cities	Women in Million-plus Cities	Men in Rest of the Urban Centres	Women in Rest of the Urban Centres
No written job contract	66.5	67.0	62.1	64.6
For 1 year or less	4.7	3.1	3.0	4.5
For more than 1 year to 3 years	4.1	4.6	2.6	2.1
More than 3 years	24.7	25.4	32.2	28.8
All	100	100	100	100

Source: Computed from unit level of NSS 68th Round

Table 2.8 Eligibility for paid leave of regular salaried workers 2011–2012

Eligibility for Paid Leave	Men in Million-plus Cities	Women in Million-plus Cities	Men in Rest of the Urban Centres	Women in Rest of the Urban Centres
Eligible for paid leave	48.3	50.3	52.6	52.2
Not eligible for paid leave	51.7	49.7	47.4	47.8
All	100	100	100	100

Source: Computed from unit level of NSS 68th Round

Tracing labour market discrimination

Labour market discrimination may be traced in two ways. Firstly, by capturing the job market discrimination and secondly, unravelling the wage-market discrimination (Anker Richard 1998). It has been proved time and again, that the former causes the substantial part of the labour market discrimination as it also directly affects wage-market discrimination. To explicate, if there are job market discriminations and hence some sections of the workforce get absorbed in more remunerative jobs with the same levels of education and skill, the wage discrimination will also be high. Clear traces of labour market discrimination on the basis of gender are found in both million-plus cities and rest of the urban centres, more so in urban centres other than million-plus cities. (Table 2.9).

Table 2.9 Social security benefits for regular salaried workers 2011–2012

Social Security Benefits	Men in Million-plus Cities	Women in Million-plus Cities	Men in Rest of the Urban Centres	Women in Rest of the Urban Centres
Only PF/pension	6.2	5.5	10.2	7.3
Only gratuity	1.4	1.7	0.8	0.7
Only health care and maternity benefits	2.7	2.4	1.0	2.2
Only PF/pension and gratuity	3.5	1.9	3.2	1.5
Only PF/pension and health care and maternity benefits	4.8	6.4	2.6	3.3
Only gratuity and health care and maternity benefits	2.1	3.7	1.3	1.3
PF/ pension, gratuity and health care and maternity benefits	19.6	20.1	26.7	25.5
Not eligible for any of above social security benefits	56.0	55.7	50.7	55.6
Not Known	3.7	2.5	3.4	2.6
All	100	100	100	100

Source: Computed from unit level of NSS 68th Round

About 31 per cent men with post graduate and above education are in high-end occupations such as legislators, senior officials and managers while the corresponding percentage is around 14 per cent for the women counterparts in million-plus cities. The picture remains unchanged in the rest of the urban centres with similar discrepancies although the levels differ. It can be seen that slightly less than half (46.4 per cent in million-plus cities and 40.8 per cent in rest of the urban centres) of women workers are illiterate and are in elementary occupations (Tables 2.10 and 2.11).

Table 2.10 Home-based workers by levels of education 2011–2012

Educational Levels	Men in Million-plus Cities	Women in Million-plus Cities	Men in Rest of the Urban Centres	Women in Rest of the Urban Centres
Illiterate	10.2	24.2	8.3	39.0
School Educated	9.5	40.3	10.7	44.5
Diploma and Graduate	4.8	12.0	7.9	16.5
Post Graduate	4.7	6.9	6.5	8.2
Total	8.2	27.5	9.7	35.7

Table 2.11 Workers across NCO categories based on educational levels, 2011–2012

Educational Categories	Men Workers					Women Workers				
	ILT	SCH	DG	PG	Total	ILT	SCH	DG	PG	Total
Million-Plus Cities										
Legislators, Senior Officials and Managers	6.4	18.1	24.9	30.7	19.7	6.8	16.8	10.1	13.7	13.1
Professionals	0.3	2.4	23.5	37.6	9.6	0.0	5.4	33.7	59.8	16.4
Technicians and Associate Professionals	0.2	3.5	12.7	15.8	6.3	0.8	5.5	24.1	7.5	9.0
Clerks	1.3	4.1	11.8	5.2	5.8	0.5	3.6	22.6	15.9	8.6
Service Workers and Sales Workers	13.2	15.3	13.3	5.8	14.0	19.8	16.5	2.6	2.4	12.6
Skilled Agricultural and Fishery Workers	2.5	0.6	0.4	0.4	0.7	3.6	0.8	0.7	0.0	1.2
Craft and Related Trades Workers	36.5	22.2	7.0	1.0	18.3	19.3	21.1	4.2	0.7	14.9

Plant and Machine Operators and Assemblers	14.2	19.4	5.3	3.6	14.6	2.7	5.3	0.8	0.0	3.3
Elementary Occupations	25.3	14.3	1.2	0.0	11.1	46.4	25.0	1.2	0.0	21.1
	100	100	100	100	100	100	100	100	100	100

Source: Computed from unit level of NSS 68th Round

Note: ILT: Illiterate; SCH: School educated; DG: Diploma and graduate; PG: Post graduate and above.

Gendered spaces and women's work

Initially women's workforce participation drops as per capita monthly consumption expenditure (MPCE) rises although women in higher expenditure households have higher educational levels (Fig. 2.1). The curve follows the well-known U shape curve with high workforce participation at the lower and the upper ends. Interestingly, at the highest end, all urban centres including million-plus cities seem to follow an identical path.

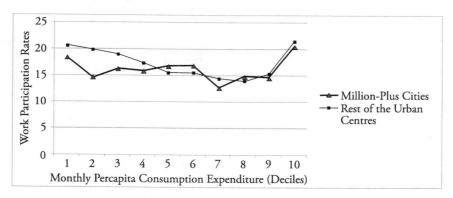

Fig. 2.1 Work participation of women aged 15–59 years by urban location, 2011–2012

Source: Computed from unit level data, NSS 66th Round

The emergence of new forms of work such as BPO and IT sectors and enhanced participation of women in these high-end activities has been well-documented in the literature.[12] This coupled with phenomenal increase in paid domestic work led us to interrogate one of the less explored, at least in the Indian context, phenomenon of 'replacement of one class of women with another' – whether these two are interlinked? That is, whether with more women participating in outside paid work, especially those at the high-end, the 'vacuum' created in the homes by their absence and consequent household work is being filled by the hired domestic labour, which predominantly consists of women or by the reconfigured division of labour among the members of the household? We have not analysed the division of household chores between members, but the existing literature suggests that the domain inside homes still remains the responsibility of women and in very few instances men cross their domain to assist even if both men and women in the same household are home-based workers. The time disposition and work clock of men and women home-based workers corroborate this observation (Mohan 2011).[13]

This is an absorbing proposition that warrants a detailed probe; not within the purview of the present discussion, we, however, offer an overview.

The NSS unit level records provide some leads – in million-plus cities women workers in IT and BPO have risen from 0.92 per cent to 4.68 per cent between 1999–2000 and 2011–2012. However, there has been a four-fold rise in women domestic workers in the same urban locations, from close to 4 per cent in 1999–2000 to 14 per cent in 2011–2012. Added to this, is significant rise in work participation of women aged 15–59 years, having children in high-end occupations during the same time span and in the same urban locations (Fig. 2.2) suggesting at the outset that there is some association between the two, increase in high-end women workers on one hand and the domestic workers on the other.

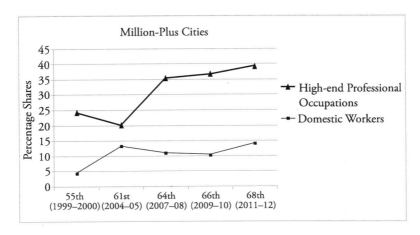

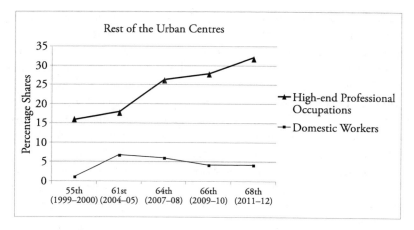

Fig. 2.2 Participation of women workers in two sets of work

Source: Computed from unit level data, NSS 66th Round

In contrast, there is stagnancy in IT/BPO jobs and that of high-end occupations among women in the rest of the urban centres accompanied by somewhat stable growth in women domestic workers. It seems that the 'replacement of one set of women with another' features only in million-plus cities and not in the rest of the urban centres.

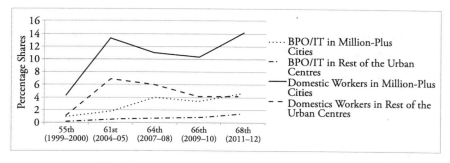

Fig. 2.3 Shares of BPO/IT and related workers and domestic workers to total workers by principal status (15–59 years) among women by urban location

Source: Computed from unit level data, NSS 66th Round

Conclusion

All urban settings are not similar and they do differ in deployment of labour. As several chapters in this volume reveal, shifting labour relations and sexual economies are accompanied by caste, religion, gender inter-sectionalities in diverse ways complicating the labour market outcomes. And yet, the perceived role of cities, particularly that of metros as reconstructing and liberating the social world of women is fraught with doubts. Apart from a few differentiating attributes, women workers across the urban settlements share a few comparable trends and patterns. With a few exceptions, most working women are confined to restricted domains of work, are largely illiterate and work under the most regressive and exploitable working conditions. The informal sector itself is differentiated, questioning the perception of the informal sector as a 'residual category' that lacks its own internal structuring. Although the million-plus cities seem to harbour the new generation jobs for women as compared to the rest of urban centres, majority of women workers continue to confine to the lower rungs of occupational hierarchy.

Although metro and non-metro settings differ in finer details, a gendered location of workers aligns with women's exclusions and marginalization. Gendered ideologies coupled with local social hierarchies and relationships contribute substantially to the concrete reality of work settings, labour relations, and gender statuses. Moreover, the productive/reproductive divide continues to re-echo through the conception of women labour influencing labour relations; women's autonomy and power is not synonymous with entry into the workforce in greater numbers. There seems to be, in any given location, little substantial change in women's status or social condition arising from a restructured labour market. In a nutshell, assumptions about the nature of globalization and claims of progress concerning women's employment and empowerment needs to be challenged; paying attention to local contingencies is critical.

The chapter concludes that women are not construed as workers separate from their existing status as structurally unequal citizens. Even as employment goes up for women, this does not in itself result in overwhelmingly positive outcomes. The much-vaunted increase in 'new generation' jobs is restricted to the giant metropolises, but everywhere, women are more likely than men to have more unstable and unrewarding jobs.

Endnotes

[1] Incidentally, self-employment is the main component of the labour market and both men and women equally share the phenomenon (Unni 2001). However, more women than men are home-based (Raju 2013). In 1999–2000, women home-based workers were 33.1 per cent of all women non-agricultural workers and in 2004–2005 the proportion increased to 36.7 per cent. However by 2011–2012, women home-based workers were

only 31.7 per cent of all women employed in non-agricultural work. By contrast, among men non-agricultural workers the proportion of home-based workers was much smaller, specifically 10.8 per cent in 1999–2000, 10.7 per cent in 2004–2005 and 11.0 per cent in 2011–2012 (Raveendran, Sudarshan and Vanek 2013). The overwhelming presence of women in home-based work brings upfront the gendered nature of informality.

2   Informal employment rather than informal sector is how one can see the continuum if there is one – since in addition to informal workers in the informal sector, there are informal workers in the formal sector (NIEUS; Sudarshan, Venkataraman and Bhandari 2007).

3   See, Chapter 8 in this volume.

4   The contemporary emphasis on self-employment in the policy discourses may have in fact added to the emerging 'bulge' of informal sector in the Indian economy in recent years.

5   The growing demand for women in the labour market can have a negative side – the 'distress sale' of labour in situations of overall falling earnings particularly that of male earners due to unemployment, underemployment and retrenchment, etc.

6   At this juncture, the distinction between 'informal work' and 'informal (unorganized) sector' needs to be made. Keeping with arguments made by the National Commission for Enterprises in the Unorganised Sector (NCEUS 2007), it is by and large the nature of work rather than its placement in a particular sector that makes work formal or informal. Thus, the organized (formal) sector can have workers who are employed under non-secure work conditions characteristic of the unorganized (informal) sector.

7   Of those aged 15 years and above and engaged in household work as usual activity, 55 per cent in rural areas and 58 per cent in urban areas were compelled to be at home because there was 'no other member to carry out the domestic duties'; another 20 per cent women in rural areas and 18 per cent in urban areas remained outside the formal work sphere because of 'social and/or religious constraints' (NSSO, 2004).

8   It is not surprising that according to 2004–2005 data, 33 per cent of rural women and 27 per cent of urban women aged 15 and above who were usually engaged in domestic duties but were available for 'work' wanted it on the household premises. Of them, about 72 per cent in rural areas and 68 per cent in urban areas preferred only 'part-time' work on a regular basis, while the percentages of such women preferring regular 'full-time' work were 23 and 28 in rural and urban India respectively.

9   The willingness of women to join the workforce and the inability of the labour market to absorb the surge could be seen in the increase of unemployment rates for all statuses of workers (Mahadevia 2002).

10 Incidentally, *Zardosi* households had the highest proportion of women workers as also extremely high retailers' share. The authors speculate that this may be because of the involvement of men at the core areas which might add to raise to return.

11 See Chapter 4 in this volume.

12 See Chapter 10 in this volume.

13 It is a socially well-accepted reality in most Indian households, even where both spouses are working, that women end up handling most household chores. Now there are data to confirm it. The average Indian woman spends more time on household chores than women anywhere else in the world. Man's contribution to household work is among

the lowest world-over. Those were some of the findings according to the study on gender disparities in 29 countries by the Organization for Economic Co-operation and Development (OECD). Indian women, the Paris-based group found, spend about six hours a day on unpaid household work such as cleaning, cooking, shopping and child care. Their male counterparts spend less than an hour, or 53 minutes, a day on those activities, only behind Korean men, who spend 45 minutes a day helping around the house. India and Portugal are the only countries on OECD's list to have government statistics only dating to the 1990s. Almost all others have data over the past decade; the U.S., for instance, has statistics from 2010, while the U.K. from 2005. More recently in 2010, the International Center for Research on Women, a U.S.-based non-profit surveyed men across six developing countries and found that in India, men said they pitched in with less than a quarter of the total housework. In the other five countries – Brazil, Chile, Croatia, Mexico and Rwanda – men said they divided household chores equally (http://timesofindia.indiatimes.com/india/Indian-men-spend-a-mere-19-minutes-a-day-on-housework/articleshow/31636967.cms).

References

Abraham, V. 2009. 'Employment Growth in Rural India: Distress Driven?', *Economic and Political Weekly*, 44(16): 97–104.

Anker, Richard. 1998. 'Gender and Jobs Sex Segregation of Occupations in the World', Geneva: International Labour Office.

Arora, R. U. 2012 'Gender Inequality, Economic Development, and Globalization: A State Level Analysis of India', *The Journal of Developing Areas*, 46(1): 147–64.

Baviskar, A. 2003. 'Between Violence and Desire: Space, Power, and Identity in the Making of Metropolitan Delhi', *International Social Science Journal*, pp. 89–98.

Berta, E. V. 2004. *Gender Discrimination and Growth: Theory and Evidence from India,* LSE STRICERD Research Paper No. DEDPS 42, downloaded http://sticerd.lse.ac.uk/dps/de/dedps 42.pdf, 14 July 2012.

Breman, J. 2002. 'An Informalised Labour System: End of Labour Market Dualism', *Economic and Political Weekly*, 36(52): 4804–21.

Chandrasekhar, P., and J. Ghosh. 2007. 'Recent Employment Trends in India and China: An Unfortunate Convergence?', *Social Scientist*, 35(3–4): 19–46.

Chen, M., and G. Raveendran. 2011. 'Urban Employment in India: Recent Trends and Patterns, WIEGO Working Paper No. 7. Downloaded 1st

August 2015, wiego.org/.../wiego.../Chen-Urban-Employment-India-WIEGO-WP7.pdf.

Deshpande, A. 2007. 'Overlapping Identities Under Liberalization: Gender and Caste in India', *Economic Development and Cultural Change*, 55(4): 735–60.

Deshpande, S. 2001. 'Impact of Emerging Labour Market on Women and their Households: A Tale of Three Slums in Mumbai', in Kundu A. and A. N. Sharma (ed.), *Informal Sector in India: Perspective and Policies*, New Delhi: Institute of Human Development and Institute of Applied Manpower Research, pp. 331–48.

Deshpande, S., and L. Deshpande. 1998. 'Impact of Liberalization on Labour Market in India: What do Facts from NSSO's 50th Round Show?', *Economic and Political Weekly*, 33(2): L 31–L 39.

Esteve-Volart, B. 2004. Gender Discrimination and Growth: Theory and Evidence from India, London School of Economics and Political Science. London: UK. Downloaded, 6th July 2015. http://eprints.lse.ac.uk/6641/1/Gender_Discrimination_and_Growth_Theory_and_Evidence_from_India.pdf.

Fields Gary, S. 1990a. 'Labour Market Modeling and the Urban Informal Sector: Theory and Evidence', Cornell University, ILR School, DigitalCommons@ILR, downloaded 15 July 2012.

———. 1990b. 'Labor Market Modeling and the Urban Informal Sector: Theory and Evidence', in The Informal Sector Revisited, Paris, OECD.

Ghani, Ejaz, Goswami, Arti Grover, and R. Kerr, William. April 6, 2012. 'Is India's Manufacturing Sector Moving Away from Cities?', Harvard Business School Entrepreneurial Management Working Paper No. 12–090. Available at SSRN: http://ssrn.com/abstract=2035478 or http://dx.doi.org/10.2139/ssrn.2035478.

Gopal, M. 2007. 'Revisiting Gendered Home-based Work in the Context of Reforms' in Banerjee, D. and Goldfield M. (ed.) *Labor, Globalization and the State: Workers, Women and Migrants*, Routledge: Hoboken, pp. 237–47.

Harriss-White, B. 2010. 'Globalization, the Financial Crisis and Petty Production in India's Socially Regulated Informal Economy', *Global Labour Journal*, 1(1): 152–77. Available at: http://digitalcommons.mcmaster.ca/globallabour/vol1/iss1/9.

Harvey David. 1989. *The Urban Experience*, Oxford: John Hopkins University Press.

Himanshu. 2011. 'Employment Trends in India: A Re-examination', *Economic and Political Weekly*, 46(37): 43–59.

Horn, Zoe Elena. 2009. 'No Cushion to Fall Back On: The Global Economic Crisis and Informal Workers', Synthesis Report, Inclusive Cities Study led by WIEGO. WIEGO, Manchester.

ILO. 2007. 'Labour and Social Trends in ASEAN 2007: Integration, Challenges and Opportunities, International Labour Office, Regional Office for Asia and the Pacific'.

———. 2013. http://www.ilo.org/global/about-the-ilo/newsroom comment analysis/WCMS_204762/lang--en/index.htm, downloaded, 2 December 2014.

Kabeer, Naila. 2004. 'Globalization, Labor Standards, and Women's Rights: Dilemmas of Collective (in)Action in an Interdependent World', in *Feminist Economics*, 10(1): 3–35.

———. 2012. Women's Economic Empowerment and Inclusive Growth: Labour Markets and Enterprise Development, *Centre for Development Policy and Research*, SOAS, Discussion Paper 29/12, pp. 1–70.

Kalpagam, U. 2001. 'Globalization, Liberalization and Women Workers in the Informal Sector' in Kundu, A. and Sharma A. N. (ed.) *Informal Sector in India: Perspectives and Policies*, Delhi: Institute of Human Development and Institute of Applied Manpower Research, pp. 310–30.

Kannan, K. P., and G. Raveendran. 2012. 'Counting and Profiling the Missing Labour Force', *Economic and Political Weekly*, 47(6): 77–80.

Klasen, S., and J. Pieters. 2011. 'Push or Pull? Drivers of Female Labor Force Participation During India's Economic Boom', IZA Discussion Paper No. 6395, Available at SSRN: http://ssrn.com/abstract=2019447, downloaded 17 July 2012.

———. 2012. 'Push or Pull? Drivers of Female Labour Force Participation during India's Economic Boom', IZA Discussion Paper No. 6395, pp. 1–36.

Kundu, A. 1997. 'Trends and Structure of Employment in the 1990s: Implications for Urban Growth', *Economic and Political Weekly*, 32(24): 1399–1405.

————. 2003. 'Urbanization and Urban Governance: Search for a Perspective beyond Neo-Liberalism', *Economic and Political Weekly*, 38(29): 3079–87.

————. 2010. 'Urban System in India: Trends, Economic Base, Governance, and a Perspective of Growth Under Globalization', in Ahmed, W., Kundu, A. and Peet, R. (ed.) *India's New Economic Policy: A Critical Analysis*, New York, London: Routledge, pp. 57–77.

Kundu, A. Kundu, Debolina. 2010. 'Globalization and Exclusionary Urban Growth in Asian Countries', Working Paper // *World Institute for Development Economics Research*, No. 2010, 70, ISBN 978–92–9230–308–2.

Kundu, A. 2009. 'Exclusionary Urbanisation in Asia: A. Macro Overview', *Economic and Political Weekly*, 44(48): 48–58.

————. Mohanan, P. C. 2010. 'Demographic Transition, Employment Structure and MDG Goals: Focus on Child Population in Urban India', *IHD – UNICEF Working Paper Series Children of India: Rights and Opportunities*, New Delhi: UNICEF.

Lefebvre, Henry. 1991. *The Production of Space*, Oxford: Blackwell.

Lessinger, J. 2002. 'Work and Love: The Limits of Autonomy for Female Garment Workers in India', *Anthropology of Work Review*, 23(1–2): 13–18.

Mahadevia, D. 2002. 'Changing Economic Scenario: Informalization and Increased Vulnerability', in Kundu, A. and Mahadevia, D. (ed.), *Poverty and Vulnerability in Globalizing Metropolis Ahmedabad*, New Delhi: Manak.

Mazumdar, I., and N. Neetha. 2011. 'Gender Dimensions: Employment Trends in India', 1993–94 to 2009–10, Occasional Paper No. 56, Centre for Women's Development Studies, New Delhi.

Mehrotra, S., Gandhi, A., Sahoo, B. K., and P. Saha. 2012. 'Creating Employment in the Twelfth Five-Year Plan', *Economic and Political Weekly*, 47(19): 63–73.

Merrifield, Andy. 2002. *Metromarxism: A Marxist Tale of the City*, New York: Routledge.

Mitra, A. 2005. 'Women in Urban Informal Sector: Perpetuation of Meager Earnings', *Development and Change*, 36(2): 291–316.

————. 2007. 'Women in the Urban Informal Sector: Perpetuation of Megre Earnings', Development and Change, 36(2): 291–316.

Mohan, Tanisha. 2011. 'Interrogating Temporal and Spatial Negotiations: Home as the Gendered Site for Working Women in Delhi'.

National Institute of Urban Affairs (NIUA). 1991. 'Women in the Urban Informal Sector', Research Study Series 49, New Delhi: National Institute of Urban Affairs.

NCEUS (National Commission for Enterprises in the Unorganised Sector). 2007a. *Conditions of Work and Promotion of Livelihoods in the Unorganised Sector*. Government of India. New Delhi: Academic Foundation.

—————. 2007b. *Report on Conditions of Work and Promotion of Livelihoods in the Unorganised Sector* (New Delhi: Government of India).

Neetha, N. 2013. 'Crisis in Female Employment: Analysis Across Social Groups', *Economic and Political Weekly*, 49(47): 50–59.

Neff, D., Kunal Sen, and V. Kling. 'Puzzling Decline in Rural Women's Labor Force Participation in India: A Re-examination', GIGA Working Papers, No. 196 in Co-operation with: GIGA German Institute of Global and Area Studies, www.econstor.eu, downloaded 12 July 2012.

Patrick, M. 2001. 'Unorganized Women in an Urban Setting: Opportunities and Challenges' in Kundu, A. and Sharma, A. N. (ed.) *Informal Sector in India: Perspective and Policies*, New Delhi: Institute of Human Development and Institute of Applied Manpower Research, pp. 349–60.

Paul, Tanusree, and Raju, Saraswati. 2014. 'Gendered Labour in India: Diversified or Confined?', *Economic and Political Weekly*, 49(29): 197–208.

Raju, S. 2010. 'Mapping the World of Women's Work: Regional Patterns and Perspectives', ILO, New Delhi Office.

—————. 2013. 'The Material and the Symbolic Intersectionalities of Home-Based Work in India', *Economic and Political Weekly*, 48(1): 60–68.

Rangarajan, C., Iyer Kaul, P., and Seema. 2011. 'Where is the Missing Labour Force?' *Economic and Political Weekly*, 46(39): 68–72.

Raveendran, Govindan, Ratna, M., Sudarshan, and Joann Vanek. 2013. 'Home-Based Workers in India: Statistics and Trends.' WIEGO Statistical Brief No. 10. Cambridge, MA, USA: WIEGO. Downloaded, 6th July 2015, http:// wiego.org/sites/wiego.org/files/publications/files/Raveendran-HBW-India-WIEGO-SB10.pdf.

Rodgers, G. 1994. Workers, Institutions, and Economic Growth in Asia, Conference Proceedings, Geneva: International Institute for

Labour Studies, downloaded 6th July 2015, http://trove.nla.gov.au/people/1115862?c=people.

Rosaldo, M., Tilly C., and P. Evans. 2012. 'A Conceptual Framework on Informal Work and Informal Worker Organizing', *UCLA Institute for Research on Labor and Employment*, http://www.irle.ucla.edu/research/documents/EOIWConceptualFramework-Rosaldo-Evans-Tilly-03.12.pdf downloaded 1 December 2012.

Roy Chowdhury, S. 2005. 'Labour Activism and Women in the Unorganised Sector: Garment Export Industry in Bangalore', *Economic and Political Weekly*, 40(22–23): 2250–55.

Singh, N., and M. K. Sapra. 2007. 'Liberalization in Trade and Finance: India's Garment Sector', in Harriss-White B. and Sinha A. (eds) *Trade Liberalization and India's Informal Economy*, pp. 42–127, New Delhi: Oxford University Press.

Sudarshan, R. S. Venkataraman, and L. Bhandari. 2007. 'Subcontracted Homework in India', in Mehrotra, S. and Biggeri, M. (ed) Asian Informal Workers Global Risks, Local Protection, Routledge: London and New York, pp. 173–209.

Unni, J., and G. Raveendran. 2007. 'Growth of Employment (1993–94 to 2004–05): Illusion of Inclusiveness?' *Economic and Political Weekly*, 42(3): 196–99.

Unni, J. 2000. 'Urban Informal Sector: Size and Income Generation Processes in Gujarat, Part I', SEWA-GIDR-ISST-NCAER, Report No. 2, National Council of Applied Economic Research, New Delhi.

————. 2001. 'Gender and Informality in Labour Market in South Asia', *Economic and Political Weekly*, 36(26): 2360–77.

3

Gendered Vulnerabilities
Work-life Trajectories of Female Domestic Workers in Jaipur

Kaari Mattila

Introduction

Of late, the gains and pains of paid domestic work have received much scholarly attention. Most studies are, however, located in a transnational context, exploring paid domestic work performed by migrant workers from poorer countries in wealthier countries in East Asia (Constable 1997; Lan 2003; Keezhangatte 2004; Dannecker 2005; Cheng 2006), Europe (Anderson 2000; Chang 2006; Näre 2010) and North America (Bakan and Stasiulis 1995; Hondagneu-Sotelo 2001; Parreñas 2006; Romero 2002; Chang 2006). While the structures within which domestic labour relations are established differ significantly in terms of legislation, welfare systems and gendered divisions of labour, the literature shows striking similarities in practices and attitudes towards workers across the board.

Paid domestic work is part of the societal reproduction system (Romero 2002). Households are fundamental units of social organization and domestic activities and relations have great political and economic significance, and are inseparable from the relationships and processes that make up the 'public domain' (Hendon 1996, 47–48). In India, paid domestic work has witnessed phenomenal growth in recent years, particularly in urban India; it is essential to the functioning of the Indian middle class households (Dickey 2000a; Ray and Qayum 2009) and their gender dynamics (Mattila 2011). A very large number of Indians are directly or indirectly involved in paid domestic work – as members of an employing household, as workers, or as family members of a domestic worker. While previous studies on India have provided rich analyses on how paid domestic work is organized on class, gender, and caste lines, age and life stages as governing tools in the market and their influence on employer preferences have received little attention.

Based on an ethnographically oriented study among local and migrant domestic workers from different ages in Jaipur, Rajasthan, this chapter places female domestic workers and their life courses and vulnerabilities within the framework of socio-cultural norms related to gender. These norms in turn lay a range of expectations, limitations and opportunities to working women and girls and heavily shape their employment trajectories. It is argued that in order to understand the meaning of paid employment in the urban female workers' lives, one must explore their life course as daughters, wives and mothers, since understanding the parameters set by these roles are necessary for understanding their labour market decisions.

The chapter brings into discussion the role of girls in the working class families' household economy and shows how work is transmitted from working mothers to daughters – one of the manifestations of an implicit intergenerational contract between daughters and their parents. The chapter also illustrates the intra-familial survival strategies of the poor working class families. It is seen how despite the daughters' significant contributions to the household economy, the restrictions on their mobility in the urban space shape their employment trajectories.

Finally, the chapter situates urban domestic workers on a continuum of vulnerability where one's position is heavily influenced by the above mentioned social hierarchies, with a particular focus on gender and life course.

The setting–an informal but structured domestic labour market

Aiming for a balance of worker and employer perspectives

The study draws on my doctoral work (Mattila 2011) – the fieldwork was carried out during 2005–2006 and 2007.[1] About eighty qualitative interviews with employers and domestic workers were conducted. While both the employers and employees were interviewed, I purposefully interviewed employers and workers from different geographical locations[2] in order to understand its complex realities. Moreover, interviewing employers and workers within the same household would have severely limited both groups' willingness to share their experiences and could have potentially been harmful to them – workers in particular. Moreover, while I interviewed employers of both part-time and live-in workers, I chose not to interview current live-in workers, excepting some pilot interviews in Kolkata in 2004. However, several girls and women whom I interviewed had previously worked as live-in workers, which allowed me to explore how both live-in and part-time works are manifested in the female workers' work–life trajectories.[3]

The employers, which included both housewives and women in full-time work, lived in three different middle class neighbourhoods in Jaipur. Majority of them were Hindus (14), nearly all of high caste such as Brahmins and Rajputs, three were Sikhs by religion. Most employers lived in wealthy middle class residential areas in single houses both in joint (extended) and nuclear families. Men from all ages in these families typically had a university degree and although women were clearly less educated, many had graduate and post-graduate degrees – children in these families went to private schools.

Domestic workers in India and elsewhere can roughly be divided into two main groups – workers who work and live at the employers' house (live-in workers) with varying degree of isolation and part-time workers who live in their own homes. The term 'part-time worker' hardly reflects the fact that most work long hours every day – 'self-employed worker' might be more accurate as a term to describe a cleaning person who also manages her or his own established business but it would not appropriately reflect the acute dependency of the Indian domestic part-time workers on their employers (see Baruah 2004). Workers include different occupations – cooks, drivers, washerwomen/men, gardeners, child caretakers, sweepers (to take out garbage, sweep the yard and in some houses to clean toilets) and maids. In keeping with the overall trend in India, maids are the most numerous group of domestic workers in Jaipur and among the part-time workers it is an all-female group in Jaipur.

This chapter is based mainly on several encounters with thirteen Rajasthani and six Bengali women and girls who all worked as maids (in Hindi *bais* or *kamwali bais*). Both groups lived in central Jaipur in their own homes and their work consisted of mopping and sweeping the floor and washing dishes for several houses per day. They usually visit each employer's house twice a day, once for the cleaning and twice for the dishes. Sikhs by religion, the Rajasthani girls were all born in Jaipur and their mothers, originating mostly from rural Rajasthan, had lived in Jaipur for most of their lives since they got married (at a very young age). At the time of our encounters, the daughters' ages varied from around nine to eighteen years, although neither the mothers nor daughters knew their exact ages. The Rajasthanis lived in a small colony or *basti*, sandwiched between wealthier neighbourhoods in central Jaipur. Their one-room homes had electricity but no running water; water was fetched from a nearby well and they prepared food on gas stoves outside their one-room accommodation. The families in their community were mostly joint families and most homes housed around ten people from three generations. The housing security for both groups was weak and housing rights non-existent. The Bengalis who rented a room in an apartment building had to fear arbitrary dismissal and the Rajasthanis who had built their own concrete houses feared demolition by the authorities. Despite this, especially older Rajasthani women said that their living conditions were clearly better than, say, twenty years earlier, especially after the installation of electricity.

The Bengali workers had come to Jaipur in search of work from the district of Cooch Behar in north-eastern West Bengal some years ago (from one year to about ten years at most). They were Brahmin Hindus by caste and religion. They rented tiny rooms in a large apartment building with a shared tap in the bottom floor. The Bengali workers were aged between (approximately) eleven and forty five; the youngest was unmarried, the others were married. Both groups included members of the same kin and there were mothers and daughters and even a grandmother from within the same families. This allowed for a better understanding of the importance of female family members in the female work-life trajectories.

After the initial hesitations of our first meetings the workers spoke quite openly during subsequent interviews about their work, challenges with employers and their family problems[4], for example, the frequent violence they faced from their husbands or the inability of husbands to provide income for the family.[5]

Commodified and stratified labour market

Maids and other domestic workers are a very common sight on the otherwise quiet streets of the middle and upper middle class Jaipur neighbourhoods. Typical middle and upper middle class families employ at least two to three domestic workers to perform specific tasks – a maid for cleaning and dish-washing, a sweeper for sweeping the outside of the house (and to clean the toilets) and a washerwoman/man. Depending on the income level and the size of the house, they may also employ a driver, a gardener or a cook, and more seldom, a child caretaker. They may employ only part-time, task specific workers or both live-in and part-time workers, in diverse combinations.

In Jaipur, as elsewhere in India, part-time work is today the more common of the two main work arrangements – part-time and live-in. The increase in part-time work has not meant the disappearance of the live-in arrangement, which continues as rearticulated merging of the traditional patron–client relation and the commodified relation (Mattila 2011). In Jaipur, live-in work thrives among the upper middle class, in particular those of high caste. The live-in workers can be seen as embodiments of Goffman's (1959) non-persons, as ever-present shadows illustrated by the local idiom of '24-hour workers'. In contrast with the situation when current employers themselves were children, the employers today have only one or two 'all-in-one' live-in workers or a combination of one generic and one task-specific worker such as a cook.

One reason that urban Indian employers prefer part-time workers is the smaller size of most homes today. Hiring live-in workers, at least adult workers, may also be too expensive for the average middle class. Hiring part-time workers is also related to the growing proportion of middle class women in paid employment outside the home (Neetha 2003; Fernandes 2006). Interestingly, in Jaipur, households with a working wife and those with a housewife employ equal numbers of domestic workers. But only families with someone at home during the day, in most cases, a 'housewife', would employ live-in workers as employers, for safety concerns, did not want to leave a worker in their home without their presence (Mattila 2011).

Paid domestic work, and the part-time work in particular, can be perceived a commodified market where the employers outsource domestic tasks to several task-specific workers, organized on the basis of gender, age, caste, ethnicity and religion. Following market logic, the work has become increasingly divided into narrow tasks and outsourced to cater for the employers' individual needs, schedules, and socio-economic standing (Mattila 2011). One of the employers' repeated phrases – "Finding a good servant is so hard" – promptly captures this, since what employers mean by this is that in principle finding a worker is easy, but it is more difficult to find a worker with the right combination of social attributes.

Even though managing workers' schedules and tasks takes considerable time, the system enables the middle class to live to the expected standards of domesticity with relatively little cost and effort. It also appears to halt transformations in household gender division of labour given that the cheap labour of workers enables women to outsource several tasks, while men largely continue not to take part in household work, except in occasional child care among the younger men. Being able to employ domestic workers in Jaipur is an important classificatory practice and a sign of having achieved middle or upper-class status.[6]

Researchers have emphasized the unique patterns of domestic labour relationships related to its location in private homes (Rollins 1985; Dickey 2000b; Romero 2002). Although domestic labour relations are increasingly commodified, capitalist relations of selling and buying labour, they are not straightforwardly contractual (Anderson 2001, 31), and they have a tendency to retain certain non-market features such as personalized relations and maternal benevolence, and rituals such as gift-giving, sometimes purposefully maintained by one or both parties in the relationship as shown both in India (Dickey 2000a; Ray and Qayum 2009) and other contexts (Rollins 1985; Romero 2002). Numerous studies have shown the employers' persistent use of the notion 'part of the family', which serves to obscure the fact that the relationship is essentially one of employment (Anderson 2000; Shah 2000; Romero 2002; Ray and Qayum 2009) and should be perceived as such.

Caste, gender and other boundaries

While work in the informal sector in India is largely unregulated, it is far from unstructured. It is organized through a kind of matrix based on social institutions or hierarchies such as class, caste and gender and urban domestic workers are no exception to such a highly stratified division of labour (Lingam 1998; Raghuram 2001; Mattila 2011). These societal structures are too overlapping to untangle the influence of the particular attribute needing an intersectional approach (Crenshaw 1989; Brah and Phoenix 2004; Yural-Davis 2007).

While class difference between employers and workers is self-evident for both sides, other social hierarchies – gender, caste, age and life-stage, ethnicity and religion – play a more complex role, and are shortly described next. The employer preferences related to these social categories vary considerably depending on the employers' own background and status and on whether the female employer herself works outside the home or not, as well as upon the existence of daughters in the employing household.

Research on paid domestic work in other Indian cities has shown gender intersecting with other hierarchies, especially class and caste (Dickey 2000a, Froystad 2003). The caste system in Rajasthan has been perceived as particularly rigid, but as everywhere, it is in transition.[7] While the pollution barrier is an enduring legacy for high and low-caste people, the principal division in India today is between the *dalits* (Scheduled Castes) and other castes (Bayly 1999 quoted in Iversen and Raghavendra 2006: 316). This was also the situation in Jaipur. The interviewed employers took up questions of caste, although most of them played down the significance of caste. It is politically incorrect in contemporary urban India to be openly discriminatory on the basis of caste but as Froystad (2003) notes, one needs to take seriously the disparity between discursive frameworks and everyday practices when analysing social distinctions in India. No doubt, in spite of the employers' declarations, caste continued to shape domestic undertakings in Jaipur, too. While most employers first claimed that they have no caste bar when recruiting a new worker, all except one later told that the *dalits* were an exception and they would not employ 'an SC'.[8] But apart from this essential division, the relevance of caste for the employers depends upon whether a particular task is considered polluting or not.

For the employers in Jaipur, caste concerns are central regarding occupations related to substances of the human body and to food, the sweepers and cooks being the two occupational groups of the lowest and highest status among workers. When cooks were employed, (upper middle class) Hindu employers in Jaipur invariably would have preferred them to be high-caste, although they could not always find one. The sweepers, the *jamadars* (male) and the *jamadarnis* (female) who clean the front of the house, and in some houses the toilets, were invariably *dalits*.

Caste and class status do not always correlate – caste is not automatically a sign of a person's economic status. Thus, in India today there are poor Brahmins, especially in the rural areas, and rich and successful *dalits*. Withstanding, the group of Bengali maids whom I met were Brahmins.[9] Labour migrants from poor, rural Cooch Behar, had come to Jaipur knowing that they would work as domestic workers, although such work contrasts starkly with their caste standing. Paradoxically, employers upheld the caste lines when it served their purposes and needs, but not even a high caste would prevent domestic workers from stigmatization. Given their low class status as uneducated poor, the Bengali maids' Brahmin caste neither helped them in the labour market nor protected them from humiliating treatments.

Gender and caste hierarchies intertwine in several ways. Cooks in Hindu homes were traditionally, Brahmin men, since women are considered impure during menstruation and childbirth. In Jaipur, cooks are no longer necessarily Brahmins, and another compromise is that women are today employed as cooks, albeit less than men. This can be seen as a sign of the restructuration of caste–gender nexus in paid domestic work and the loosening of purity rules. However, while even Brahmin girls from poor rural areas may end up as a maid, Brahmin men mainly remain in the occupations of relatively higher status such as cooks or drivers.

Employers world over have a tendency to rank workers into a hierarchical order and to reproduce stereotypes on the basis of nationality or race (Anderson 2000; Hondagneu-Sotelo 2001). In Jaipur, ethnicity was increasingly important as a recruitment criterion. The political correctness that was evident when discussing caste was absent when we discussed ethnic preferences. Open prejudice of certain ethnic groups thrived, related to dishonesty, cleanliness, laziness and so on. This illustrates the human tendency to homogenize social categories such as ethnicity, and to treat all who belong to a particular social category as sharing particular natural attributes (Yural-Davis 2007, 199). The ethnic hierarchy of each employer was shaped by experiences with previous workers and by the micro-cosmos of paid domestic work in each neighbourhood. While some portrayed the Bihari workers as 'hard-talking' and 'too clever', or even 'dangerous', others felt the same way about the Bengalis. In addition to negative stereotypes of both female and male workers, there were also more pragmatic reasons behind these ethnic preferences. Those who employ live-in workers usually prefer migrant workers since, among other reasons, they do not demand to go home on weekends and they are more willing to accept whatever working conditions are set upon them.

There has been little discussion on the role of religion as a recruitment criterion for paid domestic workers in India. The employers had strong opinions on this; most Hindu and Sikh employers explicitly said that they would not employ a Muslim worker, whereas Hindu employers had nothing against employing Sikh workers and vise versa.[10] On their scale of avoidance, Muslim workers seemed equal to Hindu *dalit* workers.[11]

Life course, gendered expectations and working girls

In every single discussion with female domestic workers, work was portrayed through and framed within the broader lives of women and girls. For them, poor working conditions are inseparable from other insecurities and vulnerabilities in their lives. Despite poor wages, lack of regular leaves and discriminatory practices, paid domestic work provided a relatively steady and secure income amidst other insecurities for poor women and girls.

As discussed above, gender organises paid domestic work in multiple ways. However, it is important to also juxtapose gender with *age* and *life course,* which barring a few exceptions remains a rather unexplored arena.[12] According to Elder (1994, 4) *life course* is 'a multilevel phenomenon, ranging from structural pathways through social institutions and organizations to the social trajectories of individuals and their developmental pathways'. The concept encapsulates some of the central threads that emerged from our conversations, such as the impact of marriage and reproduction on wage work.

This section explores how the life stages and reproductive roles interrelate with their work and employer requirements with focus on how the participation of mothers and daughters in paid domestic work intertwines through the 'implicit, intergenerational contract', which Kabeer (2000, 465) refers as 'a shared understanding between family members as to what each owes and can expect from others in the family'. Such implicit contract has been less explored in the literature than the more explicit and pronounced intergenerational contract, the filial respect and old-age support of sons for the parents. (Croll 2006)

Work runs in the family

In Jaipur, paid domestic work runs in the family. All female domestic workers in both Rajasthani and Bengali communities had several female family members working in the same occupation for two or sometimes three generations. Both Rajasthani and Bengali girls started working in houses early, typically when they were around eight to ten years old. Work was transmitted from mothers to daughters, from elder to younger sisters, and sometimes from other female relatives such as cousins, nieces and so forth.

Let us look at Deepa, a Rajasthani woman, and her two working daughters, Radha and Kamala, aged around thirteen and eleven when I first met them. Deepa, around thirty, had six children. Four were her biological children and two had come to live with her after their mother, Deepa's sister, had committed suicide. Her husband and in-laws included, there were ten people in the joint family. Deepa had worked as a maid for years and still worked for one house. Her daughter Radha started to work alongside her mother when she was about ten. First, they had shared the work. During that time, Radha still attended the nearby public school and worked only during the weekends and evenings. However, gradually she took full responsibility for one employer's house while her mother looked for a new one. When Radha began to work independently, she stopped going to school altogether. Later, Radha was offered another house to work in. Since she already worked for several houses by then, her younger sister Kamala, then around eight years old, entered the market, as she said, "so that my mother could pay different bills, it could be a help to her." Now, it was Kamala's turn to learn the trade from her mother. Eventually, she also started working independently, and stopped going to school at the second grade.

The work trajectories of Deepa, Radha and Kamala were typical in many ways. Most girls are introduced to the work by first working alongside their mothers, elder sisters, or other close female kin and gradually start working independently. Initially, they try to combine school and work but eventually many, just like Radha and Kamala, stop going to school. This is related both to the working families' own financial aspirations, but also to the employers' needs.

One reason for the casual labour households' vulnerability in the South Asian context is the irregularity and unpredictability of the income flows (Kabeer and Mahmud 2009). Thus, having several members of the family in relatively steady paid employment may act as a shield against economic insecurities (Srinivasan 1997). Even if one family member loses a job, falls ill or gets married, the family still has a pool of workers, a kind of labour reserve within the family.

Since parents are sending their children to work in houses, and since the labour authorities are hardly in a position to monitor children's work in Jaipur, at least some of the ethical reasoning and responsibility lies within the employers. The employers of part-time workers were generally less specific about the worker's age than those who hired live-in workers, although many preferred unmarried young women as maids. Indeed, they have less to worry about, since workers do not live on the same premises and have less intimate contact with them. Several employers of part-time workers explicitly said they would not want to employ very young children because 'children should be at school'. Notwithstanding, it was common for the maids' daughters to substitute for their mothers and, as we have seen, to take over the full responsibility when still very young. Hence, even if some employers spoke out against employment of children, in practice most were ready to accept them, at least as substitute workers.[13]

The employers of live-in workers lacked the moral stance of the part-time employers, and emphasized parental responsibility in deciding whether children work or not. Malti, who had one son and no daughters, elaborated her preferences and the question of children's work.

See caste I don't bother much but the man or whomever I keep should be clean, neat and tidy, that's all. I prefer that. Regarding the age [of a worker], if the parent is ready to make him work so I employ the person. If the parent says no, my kid is small, I don't want him to do this work then I say ok, this is your wish. If the parents themselves are sending them to work, then what's the matter, they must be needy of something, then, they need money because they are sending.

Yet, all those who employed live-in workers were of the view that children cannot perform quite the same tasks as adults. Within child labour studies, it is commonly agreed that the lower wages and children's obedience are among the reasons to choose children instead of adults. In addition, the assumption that children are easier to control and less likely to 'cause trouble' continued to be expressed by those who employed live-in workers. Life stage also mattered. The employers were reluctant to employ married live-in workers, since they might want to bring their families along or might demand leaves more often, in order to visit their families.

Girls as income providers

The literature on gender and development, particularly relating women's economic contribution, largely focuses on adult women (and men) and omits children's economic roles. I argue that such a focus does not capture the situation in the workers' communities in Jaipur, since children, and girls in particular, have a substantive role in the gendered income generation.

In the families in Jaipur, the daughters often had the highest income in the family, higher even than that of their domestic worker mothers, or brothers and fathers, who worked on daily contracts in construction work and were sometimes unemployed for long periods. The daughters' income was used almost entirely for living costs and for dowries. This reflects what economists have called the altruist motivations behind generational transfers, assumed to at least partially motivate generational transfers (Collard 2000). The mothers recognize the daughters' economic contributions and the gendered nature of the intergenerational contract involved. Some compared the lazy, unhelpful sons to the diligent dutiful daughters, but none of the girls or mothers explicitly complained of this situation. The daughters 'understand the needs of their parents', unlike the sons, 'who are not considerate for the needs of their family' was the common refrain.

The fathers' role in the daughters' employment seemed to range from passive to ambivalent. Although my findings are based only on the accounts of women and girls, not the fathers, the Rajasthani mothers and daughters raised the issue, and the mothers noted that even if fathers opposed the idea of the daughters' work in principle, they quietly accepted it. Girls, however, were worried about the shame their work caused to the fathers. Some said that their fathers were not even aware of their involvement in paid domestic work. For example, Mahi, a fourteen year old girl who had recently stopped school and started work, assumed that her father did not know about her work. Mahi may have believed that her father did not know about her work but her mother later told me that he was well aware of it. This reflects how sensitive the question of having female family members in paid work is for the pride of some fathers amidst the cultural expectation of father being the main bread winner, and their own inability to provide regular income. Moreover, as shown in many other studies, the men spent much of their income on their personal needs, such as alcohol, whereas women and girls spent practically all their income on household needs.[14]

In the previous literature, Iversen (2002) showed that boys in rural Karnataka often decided autonomously to migrate to Bangalore for work, sometimes against their parents' wish, and there was an element of adventure in their decision. In the same vein, Nieuwenhuys (1994) found that in Kerala girls too persuaded their fathers to allow them to move to the city for work, despite the loss of status this caused for them. But the girls I met in Jaipur entered paid domestic work first and foremost to help their parents overcome economic hurdles, not to gain experience nor for adventure. It is very difficult to fully isolate the girls' own agency in deciding to enter wage work from that of their mothers. The girls do participate in the decision-making but their decisions are heavily informed by the explicit or implicit pressure to support their parents.

The economic pressure for families to have daughters in paid work is strongly related to dowry. Dowry was outlawed in India in 1961 and yet, dowry demands and payments have increased everywhere in India, across boundaries of economic status, caste, ethnicity, or religion (Kapadia 1995; Ray 2000a; Aura 2008; Sheel 2008; Tenhunen 2008). Among the poor families in Jaipur, the dowry had a significant impact on the girls' labour market participation and their educational level.

Working mothers saved a large part of their own wage for their daughters' dowries but in addition, working daughters were expected to contribute for their own dowry. Ironically, the girls often left school so that they could work to finance their forthcoming marriages, thus providing the income their fathers could not. Some had spent incredibly high sums corresponding to around one's ten years' salary as a maid. Huge dowry sums often resulted in an increased economic dependence on their employers, since it was not uncommon for the women and girls to borrow money from their employers, to be deducted from their salaries. For example, one family borrowed 10,000 rupees from their eldest daughter's employer for her dowry. When this daughter quit the job upon getting married, her younger sister took over the job and was now working to pay off the debt. Once the elder sisters' debt would be paid, the family would start to save for the younger daughters' dowry, and so the cycle continues. I argue that the dowry system has severe implications for female labour market participation and contributes to the vicious circle of lack of education and poverty and should be carefully analysed in any development, educational or labour policy related to girls' rights or children's work.

Wage work, marriage and motherhood

The logic of female work relates to marriage in many ways. In essence, marriage and motherhood shape female work–life trajectories and frame female labour market participation. The gender structure and division of labour in Rajasthan have been considered as conservative compared to most other Indian states. The historical legacy of patron clientism, combined with political patriarchy, continues to influence the lives of women in all groups (Rajagopal 1999). However, since more women in all groups participate today in paid employment, the high caste Hindu ideology that married women should not work outside home is being renegotiated. A contrasting trend, however, is the strengthening of this ideology in lower caste and working class communities (see also Kapadia 1995; Lindberg 2001).

It is extremely difficult for poor working class women to uphold to this ideology in Jaipur or elsewhere, but it was reflected in the domestic workers' encounters. Many Rajasthani women and girls were first reluctant to admit that married women in their community had to work. Especially the young girls first blatantly told that "married women do not work" or "Mother stays at home, we do not let her go out to work". They explained that they themselves worked so that their mothers could stay at home, as culturally appropriate, but it later turned out that the mothers of all these girls also worked for wages.

In contrast, the Bengali workers were far less concerned with the housewife ideology and none of them concealed the fact that all women in their community were working; after all wage work was their main purpose in migrating to Jaipur.

Having children also has implications for work. Since there were no public child care facilities and private crèches are way beyond poor families' capacity, mothers had to organize the child care in some other way. Both Rajasthani and Bengali women typically left their children under the surveillance of female kin or their own older children. Work as a maid was pragmatic compared to other jobs, since it could be found near home, thus facilitating the combination of wage work and child care and other domestic responsibilities. Moreover, work in two shifts made it possible for women to move easily back and forth between home and work. (see also Lingam 1998; Dickey 2000b; Palriwala and Neetha 2009). The women and girls were responsible for virtually all household work in their own homes, a reason for bitterly comments which resembled those of their middle class counterparts.

Becoming a mother decreases job security and tenure. Middle class employers told that out of their several domestic workers, they are particularly dependent on maids. Thus, employers are reluctant to hold a job for a worker who conceives a baby and domestic workers typically have to give up their jobs towards the end of the pregnancy. Sometimes, their female family members took over the position or substituted them but workers typically had to look for new houses when returning to work. As said, many employers preferred unmarried girls or young women as maids, although most did not want to employ very young children.

Safety concerns and anxiety over family honour

If a close work location facilitates the combination of work and child care for married women, it is also important for safety reasons. Compared to other potential jobs, paid domestic work makes it easier for the parents to watch over their girls, at least theoretically. Surveillance of their daughters is especially challenging for the parents of working girls who move outside their home environments daily, especially in unsafe urban areas. This influenced the parents' choice of the girls' work in Jaipur as both mothers and daughters often referred to safety concerns in our conversations. Married women did not seem too worried about their own safety but they were highly concerned about their unmarried daughters – any inappropriate behaviour such as talking to strangers, i.e., boys or men, physical contact or even rumour of sexual contact – could damage their marriage prospects.

In the absence of fathers for most of the day, the mothers were responsible for keeping an eye on the daughters. They constantly warned them about perils and dangers and reminded them of the family honour. Such warnings about the potential for sexual victimization are a central feature of women's socialization in different contexts (MacMillan *et al* 2000). While mothers gave various instructions such as to avoid the sun, their main advice was to never talk to strange men or boys on their way to and from work. One proudly told how her daughter had once taken her slipper and hit a man who had tried to harass her, just as she had advised her to do. Another explained that her daughter had thrown a stone at one man in a similar situation.

Safety concerns also influence working schedules. Women fear the night and it is less acceptable for women to be seen out after dark. Women were reluctant to work in the evenings or to let their daughters do so, even if employers often asked them for the same. When they did agree, they tried to get an employers' family member to escort them home.

If streets are unsafe, there are risks in the employers' houses too. It seems that the parents have to choose between two bad options – part-time work and the risks in the public space or live-in work and the risks within the employers' house. Both Rajasthani and Bengali mothers worried for the safety of their girls but the two communities had adopted different solutions – the unmarried Rajasthani girls worked as part-timers, the unmarried Bengali girls were mostly in live-in work before they got married.

In contrast to the streetwise local Rajasthani workers, the Bengalis found the employers' home safer than the road in an initially unfamiliar city. Vibha, a Bengali woman in her forties, explained why she preferred her daughter to be in live-in work before she got married – "It's not good for them to work as (part-time) maid and roam from door to door". Her daughter had started to work as a live-in worker and although the wage had been very low at that time, the mother valued the relative safety of the arrangement.

Even if the Bengali parents may hope the employers take some responsibility for the girls' protection, the potential risks involved in the live-in arrangement was a cause of concern. One Bengali woman, Kajal, first described rather euphemistically her younger sister's situation, comparing it to her own situation as a married woman.

> We are no longer girls. We are married so for us this life (part-time work) is better. But for my sister it is better to work for 24-hours because you cannot trust anybody nowadays. You can be teased or molested on the road so it is safe for her to work in a single house. Now my sister is their responsibility. So we are satisfied that she is being treated like their own daughter.

But when our discussion evolved, Kajal told that her sister had already left two former employers' houses. In the first, the employers had given her only four *chapattis* per day to eat and she had not been allowed to meet her own family. Moreover, the employer had said she would not be paid for the first two months. The second employer also prevented her from meeting her own family. Now, Kajal's mother had selected a third house and they were satisfied – "They keep her very well. Now my mother says it's okay, she pays less but our daughter is well there".

Kajal's youngest sister Kalpana had also faced problems as a live-in worker, since another older live-in worker had forced the young girl to perform all the work. As Kajal summarized it, the safety of the live-in arrangement is relative – "It is very risky". But the recently arrived migrant families have little choice but to hope for the best and trust their instinct. Moreover, the Bengalis lived in very small rented rooms and putting daughters into live-in work meant one person less to accommodate or to feed.

The responsibility for the daughters' respectability and the task of arranging their marriage lies heavy on the mothers' shoulders. They fear that someone would harass their daughters and also, that the girls themselves would get into close contact with boys or men. Moreover, their husbands seem to consider it the mothers' fault if something goes wrong. One Rajasthani mother, whose husband regularly assaulted her physically, described in an agonized tone her fear of how her husband would react if something would happen to her daughters at work or on the way to work.

> They (daughters) are very tired (of work). And I am also fearful that they may run away one day. Their father will kill me if it happens one day. He will say that it was your decision to employ them. So many times I accompany them to their work places.

A common reason for violence against women in their homes is the suspicion over the wife's sexual laxity or infidelity. Working women are at a special risk for such accusations and escalating abuse, since they cannot avoid coming into contact with unrelated men on a daily basis (Vatuk 2006).

Had some of the girls been sexually abused on the road or in the employers' homes? Dickey (2000b, 477) notes that fears about sexual transgression between employers and workers are almost never mentioned, since merely talking of this could cause great damage to the reputation of the family or its women. None of the workers I met told any personal experiences of sexual harassment or abuse in their employers' homes but even if they had faced this, they probably would not have mentioned it. Instead, women told that they knew "something happened to girls we know" or to girls in other communities.

Employer anxieties over sexuality

Workers and their families were not the only ones with concerns over sexuality. The employers, too, had worries and anxieties related to sexuality and domestic workers, which centrally influenced their recruitment decisions. First, employers feared for the safety of their unmarried daughters. If the employing family had daughters in the house, they would only employ female live-in workers.[15] Thus, the Bengali working girls whom I encountered had worked as live-in in employing households with daughters.

However, if employers had no daughter, they preferred male workers, most preferably unmarried boys or young men. Why boys and not girls? First, many high caste families of the employer class in Jaipur adhere to the restrictions on women's mobility, enhanced by the class notions of not having to move unnecessarily because of menial tasks. Thus, the female employers of live-in workers preferred to send their live-in workers to run errands for them. And this is easier for boys or young men, as emphasized by every single employer of live-in workers.

As discussed above, even allegations of inappropriate sexual behaviour could be disastrous for a girl's marriage prospects and for the family honour. Hence, whilst the parents place their daughters to work for wealthy families, the responsibility for the daughter's sexuality partly shifts to the employers, a responsibility that most employers preferred not to take.

In line with this, those who do employ female live-in workers (because they have a daugther themselves) often find it difficult. One employer with a daughter explained the problem with having a young female worker in the house – "We had to pay complete attention to her, she was in her teen years and was slowly getting inclined towards the neighbourhood male worker. For hours, she sat on the terrace aimlessly". To solve both these problems, she dismissed the young girl who had worked for the family and hired a widowed woman in her fifties instead.

The employers make considerable efforts to ease their concerns related to male sexuality and their own safety. Meetu, whose husband travels for long periods, had two male live-in workers. Since she did not want to be alone with the boys in the house, she had employed a third worker, an adult woman, as a cook. She actually paid this woman who stayed in the house from morning until about 6 p.m. more than the live-in workers. She was aware that this was higher than the local standard but she was paying not only for the cooking and washing of the dishes but also for her sense of safety.

There is also the question of female employers' anxiety over sexual contact between their husbands or sons, and female domestic workers. Although neither employers nor workers in Jaipur mentioned the potential sexual advances between male family members and female workers for fear of damaging the reputation of the families involved, female employers' anxiety over their husbands' or sons' sexual interest in the workers could be one additional reason for preferring male workers in families where there are no daughters.

Continuum of vulnerability

For many reasons, domestic work can be perceived as vulnerable employment.[16] In Jaipur, domestic workers lacked basic workers' rights such as right to a regular leave or to minimum wage, right to overtime compensation and so on. Since the labour relationships are totally based on oral agreements between employers and workers, in case of disagreement it is practically impossible for the workers to claim their rights.[17] But amidst this general situation, there are considerable differences among the workers in how vulnerable they are. In short, while all workers are structurally vulnerable, some are more vulnerable than others.

Efforts to conceptualize labour market vulnerability have focused on issues such as lack of appropriate employment legislation, lack of access to non-statutory benefits, lack of pension schemes, low salaries, and lack of stable employment (cf. Saunders 2003, 7–8). But as Pollert and Charlwood (2009, 354) note, when vulnerability is defined in narrow terms, the tendency is to look only at symptoms and characteristics associated with 'risks' of vulnerability, bypassing the underlying causes of the risks. Others have pointed out that a narrow approach to vulnerability, common in the agenda of development or women's rights organizations, may victimize the 'vulnerable' instead of empowering them (Ho 2008; Åsman 2008). Moors' (2003, 391) notion that domestic workers are neither passive victims nor active agents but to some extent both, is applicable also to the situation of domestic workers in Jaipur. However, one must take into account the high diversity among the workers where the most vulnerable ones have virtually no say over their life and work situation, work virtually as slaves and have highly limited opportunities of resistance.

Thus, a definition of vulnerability should be based on a diagnosis of the power imbalance inherent in the employment relationship, which means that 'the basis of vulnerability is in the fundamental asymmetry of the capitalist employment relationship between the individual worker and the employer' (Pollert and Charlwood 2009). I have suggested (Mattila 2011) that workers' vulnerability can be analysed through a 'continuum of vulnerability' with the least vulnerable on one end and the most vulnerable are at the opposite end.

In Jaipur, factors contributing to vulnerability are, at least, age and life-stage, gender, caste, one's ethnic background and language skills, degree of contact with one's family, and the familiarity with Jaipur (locals versus migrants). In addition, one needs to take into account of the diversity of work arrangements (e.g., live-in or part-time work) and the consequent influence on working conditions.

In Jaipur, those who are most vulnerable have no or very limited possibility to resist abuse or to claim their rights. Among them are the youngest workers, girls and boys, live-in workers who are isolated from their family members and, at worst, locked in the employers' house. Limited communication, as is in the case for recently arrived migrants, increase the vulnerability.

Girls and women, and also male workers, have different labour situations in different phases of their life course. As we have seen above, migrant girls are placed as live-in workers before they are married. Most parents of local girls, instead, prefer to have their daughters to work as part-time maids also before marriage.[18]

The situation of the young Bengali women, now in part-time work after getting married, had been much more precarious when in a live-in employment. They faced several problems tantamount to severe labour rights violations (if the sector would have been regulated) such as salaries left unpaid, or denial of the verbally agreed two hours biweekly free time. Risk of verbal, physical or sexual abuse was higher than when they lived with their own parents. Two Bihari girls whom I met had been literally locked inside the employers' house for two years with no contact with their families in Bihar. Their situation amounted to slavery and was at the other end of the continuum of vulnerability. Any possible potential for resistance was effectively cut by frequent violence one of the girls was subjected to by the female employer. These girls finally escaped their employer through a toilet window.

The Bengali and Rajasthani adult women working as part-time maids, instead, were in a much better position to negotiate with their employers and oppose their demands, e.g., for overtime or extra work. In the case of their daughters, vulnerability decreased when they gained more experience and matured. As very young workers – most of them started well before the age of ten – they had been more vulnerable. That is also why mothers have such a central role in guiding their daughters into work and aimed at handling the negotiations with the employers.

Although my focus in terms of workers was on female maids, the employers I met with also employed a number of males, especially live-in workers, cooks, gardeners and drivers. Among them, the same factors of age, isolation, lack of relatives nearby, lack of mutual language, increased vulnerability. Very young boys working as live-ins are highly vulnerable to exploitation and diverse abuse, as was evident in the accounts of the employers. Still, especially the adult men in specific professions of cooks or drivers are much less vulnerable than, say, the young female workers or both small boys and girls, trafficked to Jaipur through obscure deals between their parents back at home in the village in other states.

Whether the workers are able to resist their employers depends on their vulnerability and the level of dependency upon their employers, particularly influenced by gender, age and whether one is a local or a migrant worker. However, even young workers do try to resist their employers, even if in subtle ways. If there is no strong push from an organized workers' movement, though, workers' diverse positions vis-à-vis employers makes it challenging to form a collective identity as working class women. Also, the lack of collective identity creates situations where domestic workers from different ethnic backgrounds easily suspect other groups of dumping the salary level. Especially, migrant workers are easily blamed. The Rajasthani workers said that Bengali workers are to blame for the low salary levels since they thought Bengalis would accept very low salaries. However, this assumption was based on rumours, since they had actually not discussed this with any Bengali workers. In fact, the Bengali workers in Jaipur seemed to have categorically negotiated themselves slightly better deals with employers, especially in terms of having regular leave days every month.

In sum, to assess and to understand the vulnerability of domestic workers, one must take into account the age, the life-stage, gender, caste, ethnicity, language, religion and their intersectionalities as well as to analyse how these come together with the institutional setup of the work.

Conclusion

Of the many groups of different workers providing services for middle and upper-middle-class households, this article has explored the work–life trajectories of women and girls who work as maids in Jaipur. Based on research among local Rajasthani workers and Bengali migrant workers, the chapter has in particular highlighted the intergenerational aspects of paid domestic work as well as differences between local and migrant workers in their work–life trajectories.

The availability of cheap labour force allows the middle class to live to the expected domesticity standards, while the gendered household division of labour of the employing homes remains largely intact. The majority of middle and upper-middle-class families employ part-time workers to perform specific tasks such as cleaning and washing dishes, cooking or gardening, and the division of labour is based on an informal but structured division of labour based on caste, gender, ethnicity, religion, and age and life-stage. Following an increasingly market-like logic (Mattila 2011), the employers make their recruitment decisions not only based on their labour needs but also based on their views related to caste, gender and other social categories.

While the significance of caste in recruitment was played down by most employers, they still routinely excluded Dalits from all other tasks except that of the sweepers. At the same time, however, the caste-gender nexus in paid domestic work was being restructured and purity rules loosened, as exemplified by high caste employers gradually giving up their preference for Brahmin male cooks. Paradoxically, though, employers upheld the caste lines when it served their needs but a high caste did not prevent domestic workers from stigmatization, which became evident in encounters with Bengali maids of Brahmin caste.

While the employers in Jaipur preferred to hide, initially at least, their caste preferences or prejudice, they were often openly discriminatory in terms of ethnicity and the same applied to discriminatory attitudes of the Hindu and Sikh employers towards Muslim workers.

Focusing on mothers and daughters who work as maids, this chapter has shown how paid domestic is transmitted from mothers to daughters and shared among female kin. Girls were introduced to the profession by their mothers at a young age and at first they worked together. Upon learning the tasks of cleaning and washing dishes, girls started working in houses independently. Many first combined work with school but eventually stopped going to school altogether. As a result, children in general, but girls in particular, played a substantial role in the gendered income generation of working class families. The daughters often had the highest income in their family and it was used for living costs and as savings for their dowry. Increased dowry demands were reflected in the necessity of the poor families' daughters to work. It is argued that the dowry system has considerable implications for girls' work trajectories and to the vicious circle of very low educational levels and poverty.

The article has discussed how gendered expectations and norms shape female work-life trajectories. As we have seen, an 'implicit intergenerational contract' prevailed among working class families and this meant that unmarried daughters were expected to support their parents as long as they lived with them. At the same time, though, girls were concerned about the shame their work might cause to their fathers. More broadly, the high caste housewife ideology was reflected in the discourse of Rajasthani mothers and especially their daughters, while in practice they all needed to work to survive. On the contrary, migrant Bengali women did not hold to such ideology, not even on a rhetorical level, underlining the fact that the purpose of migrating to Jaipur was wage work.

Having children also influenced the employment opportunities and decisions. Children were typically left home for older children or other female kin to take care of. The short distance to employer households was seen as an enabling factor in combining wage work with child care and other domestic responsibilities. Since the maids' employment relations were totally unregulated, their job security was very weak and they typically had to look for new employers when returning to work after giving birth.

Short distance to work places(s) was also considered an advantage for mothers who worried extensively of their daughters' – and thus, the family's – honour. While local families preferred for the girls to live at home with their parents for, among others safety reasons, the Bengali mothers considered the relative safety of a live-in position a better option than the risks of the road. Moreover, there was one person less to feed and the Bengali mothers placed their daughters as live-in workers before they got married.

Questions related to sexuality and domestic workers were also a concern for the employers, especially for those who hired live-in workers. Whereas, employers with only sons clearly preferred male live-in workers, unmarried if possible; male workers were not hired if there were daughters in the family.

The chapter concluded by locating domestic workers on a continuum of vulnerability with the least vulnerable on one end, and the most vulnerable at the opposite end. Because of the lack of regulation and informality of the labour relationships, paid domestic work is a vulnerable employment. However, there are significant differences among domestic workers' vulnerability depending on age, life-stage, gender, caste, one's ethnic background, language skills and degree of contact with one's family. Very young children who are placed as live-in workers and have no family members in the city, and especially those who do not speak the employers' idiom, are particularly vulnerable. Their situation is made more precarious as the employers of live-in workers appeared to lack the moral stance towards children's' work as compared to those who only employ part-time workers. This was painfully evident in the work trajectories of the young Bengali women, which included conditions tantamount to sever labour rights violations. Despite of the precarious nature of paid domestic work the more experienced workers especially resisted employers, even if lack of collective identity makes resistance not only subtle, but also sporadic and invidualized.

Endnotes

1 Interviewed twenty-one domestic workers (all girls and women) and seventeen employers (15 women, two men) in Jaipur, most of them twice or thrice in consecutive years, and talked less formally with several others. All names have been changed to protect their privacy. Interviews with all workers and with nine employers were made in Hindi, with the help of a local assistant, and with eight employers in English. While the language did not become a major barrier, the scope for misinterpretation posed by the use of interpreter can never be fully mitigated. Fortunately, I knew enough Hindi to be able to more or less follow the conversation and comment on possible misunderstandings.

2 Froystad (2003, 90–91) interviewed workers and employers from within the same houses, which she felt led to an overemphasis of the employers' perceptions in her otherwise rich ethnographic analysis.

3 An obvious drawback of this article is that I last met with the interviewees in 2007.

4 All workers were first interviewed in groups and only after that as individuals or in pairs. Both Rajasthani and Bengali workers tended to give a sanitised account of their working conditions in our first meeting. However, if one worker in a group interview broke this pattern and started to talk about the employers in a critical manner, the others would follow and give a more critical view. My experiences underline the usefulness of the group interview during the early encounters with informants, as well as the importance of conducting more than one interview with each respondent.

5 Here my experience differs from Vatuk (2006) who notes that Indian women generally do not speak badly about their husbands to other people or mention private disagreements outside their homes. The way women spoke about all their problems could also be read as a means to establish agency and to preserve self respect and dignity (Bos 2008).

6 See Mattila (2011) for a broader discussion on the many implications of class in domestic–labour relations.

7 The Governmental system of positive discrimination towards Scheduled Castes and Tribes has had paradoxical consequences. These reservations have entrenched the importance of caste as an institution and have reinforced the caste-based segmentation, as well as making the reserved castes into an interest group, instead of dissolving caste differences (Harris-White and Gooptu 2000, 99).

[8]   A person belonging to the Scheduled Castes.

[9]   Their case is not unique. Tolen's (2000, 54) study in Chennai showed that there were Brahmins among domestic workers and anecdotal discussions with other scholars also refer to such situations.

[10]   Since studies on domestic work in India have so far concentrated on Hindu families, and to some extent discussed Christian and Sikh workers/employers (see Tellis-Nayak 1983) there is a lack of knowledge about domestic labour relations in the Muslim homes. My data indicates clear religious divisions on 'who works for whom', and it may be assumed that Muslim workers mainly work for Muslim employers (see also Ray and Qayum 2009, 75) but the question merits further examination.

[11]   It appears that Hindu employers in Kolkata, studied by Ray and Qayum (2009), were more willing to employ Muslim maids than employers I met with in Jaipur, at least in those Kolkata residential areas which were adjacent to Muslim *bastis*.

[12]   Among few examples of integrating work and life courses, see Hapke and Ayyankeril (2004) for a study on the gendered livelihood strategies of fishermen and women in South India and de Haan (2003, 202–203) for an analysis of the gendered experiences of male and female labour migrants in Calcutta.

[13]   In 2006 the Government of India amended the Child Labour Act (1984), prohibiting the employment of children under fourteen as domestic servants or in roadside cafeterias, teashops, hotels, and other hospitality sectors (Save the Children 2007, 2). The labour officials have taken the issue on the agenda with varying effort and children evidently continue to be hired as domestic workers in large numbers.

[14]   However, I take Vera-Sanso's (2008: 55) point that women's statements on not spending money on themselves should not be taken at face value, nor should it be automatically assumed that mothers are intrinsically more altruistic than fathers.

[15]   Similarly, Ray (2000b, 698) notes that in Kolkata nobody wanted a male servant in the house when there was a young daughter there.

[16]   See Saunders 2003; Bolton 2007; Pollert and Charlwood 2009 for conceptualizations of worker vulnerability and vulnerability at work.

[17]   Paid domestic work has until recently been a grey area in Indian labour legislation. A 'Domestic Workers (Condition of Services) Bill' was introduced as early as 1959 but it has not been enacted (Gothoskar 2005, 1). For years, civil society organizations have called for national legislation to regulate domestic workers' rights, as well as for the inclusion of domestic workers under the Minimum Wages Act (1948) and the Unorganized Workers' Social Security Bill (2008). Instead, state-level regulation has been enacted, at least in Karnataka, Kerala, Maharasthra and Tamil Nadu. The Government has not ratified the recently established ILO Domestic Workers Convention nr 189 for which Indian civil society organizations such as the National Domestic Workers Movement lobbied actively on an international and national level.

References

Anderson, B. 2000. *Doing the Dirty Work? The Global Politics of Domestic Labor*. New York: Zed Books.

———. 2001. 'Just Another Job? Paying for Domestic Work. In Caroline. Sweetman (ed.)'. *Gender, Development and Money*. London: Oxfam Focus on Gender Studies, pp. 25–33.

Aura, S. 2008. *Women and Marital Breakdown in South India. Reconstructing Homes, Bonds and Persons*. Research Series in Anthropology, University of Helsinki. Helsinki: Helsinki University Printing House.

Åsman, S. 2008. 'The Moral Order and Worries about Trafficking in Nepal', *Asia Insights* No. 1, 2008 June. NIAS Nytt. Copenhagen: Nordic Institute of Asian Studies.

Bakan, Abigail, B., and Stasiulis, Daiva, K. 1995. 'Making the Match: Domestic Placement Agencies and the Racialization of Women's Household Work', *Signs: Journal of Women in Culture and Society*, vol. 20, No. 2.

Baruah, B. 2004. 'Earning their Keep and Keeping What they Earn: A Critique of Organizing Strategies for South Asian Women in the Informal Sector', *Gender, Work and Organization*, vol. 11, No. 6, November 2004, 605–26.

Bayly, S. 1999. 'Caste, Society and Politics in India'. From the Eighteenth Century to the Modern Age. Cambridge University Press, Cambridge.

Bos, P. 2008. *Once a Mother. Relinquishment and Adoption from the Perspective of Unmarried Mothers in South India*. Ipskamp B. V.

Bolton, Sharon, C. 2007. 'Dignity in and at Work: Why it Matters.', in Sharon C. Bolton (ed.) *Dimensions of Dignity at Work*. Oxford: Butterworth-Heinemann. pp. 3–16.

Brah, A., and A. Phoenix. 2004. 'Ain't I a Woman? Revisiting Intersectionality', *Journal of International Women's Studies*. vol. 5 #3, May 2004. 75–86.

Chang, G. 2006. 'Disposable Domestics: Immigrant Women Workers in the Global Economy in Zimmerman', Litt and Bose (2006). *Global Dimensions of Gender and Carework*. Stanford University Press, California.

Cheng, Shu-Ju Ada. 2006. 'Rethinking the Globalization of Domestic Service: Foreign Domestics, State-Control, and the Politics of Identity in Taiwan', in Zimmerman, Litt and Bose (2006). *Global Dimensions of Gender and Carework.* Stanford University Press, California.

Constable, N. 1997. *Maid to Order in Hong Kong: Stories of Filipina Workers.* Ithaca: Cornell University Press.

Collard, D. 2000. 'Generational Transfers and the Generational Bargain', *Journal of International Development,* May 2000, 12(4): 453–62.

Crenshaw, K. 1989. *Demarginalizing the Intersection of Race and Sex: A Black Feminist Critique of Antidiscrimination Doctrine, Feminist Theory and Antiracist Politics.* University of Chicago Legal Forum, pp. 139–67.

Croll, Elisabeth, J. 2006. 'The Intergenerational Contract in the Changing Asian Family', *Oxford Development Studies,* vol. 34, No. 4, December 2006, pp. 473–91.

Dannecker, P. 2005. 'Transnational Migration and the Transformation of Gender Relations: The Case of Bangladeshi Labour Migrants', *Current Sociology,* July 2005, SAGE Publications, vol. 53( ): 655–74.

Dickey, S. 2000a. 'Mutual Exclusions. Domestic Workers and Employers on Labor, Class, and Character in South India', in Kathleen M. Adams and Sara Dickey (eds). *Home and Hegemony. Domestic Service and Identity Politics in South and Southeast Asia.* The University of Michigan Press, Ann Arbor.

———. 2000b. 'Permeable Homes: Domestic Service, Household Space, and the Vulnerability of Class Boundaries in Urban India', in *American Ethnologist,* 27(2): 462–89. American Anthropological Association.

Elder, Glen, H. 1994. 'Time, Human Agency, and Social Change: Perspectives on the Life Course', *Social Psychology Quarterly,* 57, No.1, 4–15.

Fernandes, L. 2006. *India's New Middle Class. Democratic Politics in an Era of Economic Reform.* University of Minnesota Press, Minneapolis.

Froystad, K. 2003. 'Master-Servant Relations and the Domestic Reproduction of Caste in Northern India', *Ethnos,* vol. 68: 1. pp. 73–94.

Goffman, E. 1959. *The Presentation of Self in Everyday Life.* New York: Penguin Books.

Gothoskar, S. 2005. *New initiatives in Organizing Strategy in the Informal Economy – Caste Study of Domestic Workers' Organizing.* Bangkok: Committee for Asian Women July 2005.

Haan de, A. 2003. 'Calcutta's Labour Migrants: Encounters with Modernity', *Contributions to Indian Sociology*. vol. 37 January–August, Numbers 1 and 2. pp. 189–216. New Delhi: SAGE Publications.

Hapke, Holly M., and D. Ayyankeril. 2004. 'Gender, the Work-Life Course and Livelihood Strategies in a South Indian Fish Market', *Gender, Place and Culture*, vol. 11, No. 2, June 2004, pp. 229–56.

Harris-White, B., and N. Gooptu. 2000. 'Mapping India's World of Unorganized Labour', in Leo Panitch and Colin Leys (eds.). *Working Classes, Global Realities*. Socialist Register, The Fernwood Press, Canada 89–118.

Hendon, Julia A. 1996. 'Archaeological Approaches to the Organization of Domestic Labor: Household Practice and Domestic Relations', *Annual Review of Anthropology*, 25: 45–61.

Ho, J. 2008. 'Asian modernity and its 'Gendered Vulnerabilities'', *Asia Insights* No. 1, 2008 June. NIAS Nytt. Copenhagen: Nordic Institute of Asian Studies.

Hondagneu-Sotelo, P. 2001. *Doméstica. Immigrant Workers Cleaning and Caring in the Shadows of Affluence*. University of California Press, Berkeley.

Iversen, V. 2002. 'Autonomy in Child Labour Migrants', in *World Development*, vol. 30, pp. 817–34.

Iversen, V., and P. S. Raghavendra. 2006. 'What the Signboard Hides: Food, Caste and Employability in Small South Indian Eating Places', *Contributions to Indian Sociology*, vol. 40, No. 3, Sept.–Dec. 2006. pp. 311–43.

Kabeer, N., and S. Mahmud. 2009. 'Imagining the Future: Children, Education and Intergenerational Transmisison of Poverty', in Urban Bangladesh. *IDS Bulletin*, vol. 40, No. 1 January, pp. 10–21.

Kabeer, N. 2000. 'Inter-Generational Contracts, Demographic Transitions and the 'Quantity-Quality' Tradeoff: Parents, Children and Investing in the Future', *Journal of International Development* 12: 4, 463–82.

Kapadia, K. 1995. *Siva and her Sisters. Gender, Caste, and Class in Rural South India. Studies in the Ethnogprahic Imagination*, Oxford: Westview Press.

Keezhangatte James Joseph. 2004. 'Indian Household Workers in Hong Kong: Emerging Themes on Migration and Social Relationships', *E-Journal on Hong Kong Cultural and Social Studies Programme*, Hong

Kong. http://www.hku.hk/hkcsp/ccex/ehkcss01/index.htm, (viewed on 6.8.2007).

Lan, Pei-Chia. 2007. 'Maid or Madam? Filipina Migrant Workers and the Continuity of Domestic Labor'. *Gender and Society*, vol. 17, No. 2 April 2003, 187–208.

Lindberg, A. 2001. *Experience and Identity. A Historical Account of Class, Caste, and Gender among the Cashew Workers of Kerala*, 1930–2000. Department of History at Lund University, Studia Historica Lundensia, Malmö.

Lingam, L. 'Migrant Women, Work Partcipation and Urban Experiences', *Indian Journal of Social Work*, vol. 59, Issue No. 3, pp. 807–23, July, 1998.

Mattila, P. 2011. *Domestic Labour Relations in India. Vulnerability and Gendered Life Courses in Jaipur*, Helsinki: Interkont Books 19.

MacMillan, R., Nierobisz, A., and S. Welsh. 2000. 'Experiencing the Streets: Harassment and Perceptions of Safety Among Women', *Journal of Research in Crime and Delinquency*, 37, 306–22.

Moors, A. 2003. 'Migrant Domestic Workers: Debating Transnatinalism, Identity Politics, and Family Relations. A Review Essay', *Society for Comparative Study of Society and History*.

Neetha, N. 2003. 'Migration for Domestic Work: Women Domestics in Delhi', *Labour and Development*, vol. 9, No. 2, December 2003. New Delhi: V. V. Giri National Labour Institute.

Nieuwenhuys, O. 1994. *Children's Lifeworlds. Gender, welfare and Labour in the Developing World*. London: Routledge.

Näre, L. 2010. 'Sri Lankan Men Working as Cleaners and Carers: Negotiating Masculinity in Naples', *Men and Maculinities*, 13(1): 65–86.

Palriwala, R., and N. Neetha. 2009. 'The Care Diamond: State Social Policy and the Market', Research Report 3 – India, UNRISD Project on Political and Social Economy of Care.

Parreñas, Rachel, S. 2006. 'Migrant Filipina Domestic Workers and the International Division of Reproductive Labor', in Zimmerman, Litt and Bose (2006). *Global Dimensions of Gender and Carework*. California: Stanford University Press.

Pollert, A., and A. Charlwood. 2009. 'The Vulnerable Worker in Britain and Problems at Work', *Work, Employment and Society*, 23(2): 343–62.

Raghuram, P. 2001. 'Caste and Gender in the Organization of Paid Domestic Work in India', *Work, Employment and Society,* 15(3): 607–17.

Rajagopal, S. 1999. *Designing Interventions for Girls' Education. A Case from Rajasthan.* Department of Sociology. Faculty of Social Science. University of Rajasthan.

Ramesh, A. 'UN Convention of Rights of the Child. Inherent Weaknesses', *Econmoic and Political Weekly,* Commentary. 2 June, 2001.

Ray, R., and S. Qayum. 2009. *Cultures of Servitude. Modernity, Domesticity, and Class in India.* Stanford: Stanford University Press.

Ray, R. 2000a. *Fields of Protest. Women's Movement in India.* Delhi: Kali for Women.

———. 2000b. 'Masculinity, Femininity, and Servitude: Domestic Workers in Calcutta in the Late Twentieth Century', *Feminist Studies* 26, No. 3, 691–718.

Rollins, J. 1985. *Between Women. Domestics and their Employers.* Philadelphia: Temple University Press.

Romero, M. 2002. *Maid in the U.S.A.* New York: Routledge.

Saunders, R. 2003. 'Defining Vulnerability in the Labour Market', *Vulnerable Workers Series,* 1. *Ottawa: Canadian Policy Research Networks.* http://www.cprn.org. Accessed 20 June, 2007.

Save the Children. 2007. *Child Domestic Work. A Study Report on the lives of Child Domestic Workers in Leh and Kargil.* London: Save the Children.

Shah, S. 2000. 'Service or Servitude? The Domestication of Household Labor in Nepal', in Kathleen M. Adams and Sara Dickey (eds.). *Home and Hegemony. Domestic Service and Identity Politics in South and Southeast Asia.* Ann Arbor: The University of Michigan Press.

Sheel, R. 2008. 'Marriage, Money and Gender. A Case Study of the Migrant Indian Community in Canada', in Rjani Palriwala and Patricia Uberoi (eds.). *Marriage, Migration and Gender. Women and Migration in Asia,* vol. 5, New Delhi: SAGE Publications.

Srinivasan, S. 1997. 'Breaking Rural Bonds through Migration: The Failure of Development for Women in India', *Journal of Comparative Family Studies,* Spring 1997, 28(1): 89–103.

Tellis-Nayak, V. 1983. 'Power and Solidarity: Clientage in Domestic Service', *Current Anthropology,* 24(1): 67–79.

Tenhunen, S. 2008. *The Gift of Money: Rearticulating Tradition and Market Economy in Rural West Bengal.* Modern Asian Studies, 42(5): 1035–55.

Tolen, Rachel. 2000. 'Transfers of Knowledge and Privileged Spheres of Practice. Servants and Employers in ad Madras Railway Colony.' In Kathleen M. Adams and Sara Dickey (eds.). *Home and Hegemony. Domestic Service and Identity Politics in South and Southeast Asia.* Ann Arbor: The University of Michigan Press, pp. 63–117.

Vatuk, S. 2006. 'Domestic Violence and Marital Breakdown in India', in Lina Fruzzetti and Sirpa Tenhunen (eds.). *Culture, Power, and Agency. Gender in Indian Ethnography.* Kolkata: Stree.

Vera-Sanso, P. 2008. '"Whose Money is it?": On Misconceiving Female Autonomy and Economic Empowerment in Low-income Houesholds', *IDS Bulleting,* Dec. 2008. Institute of Development Studies, 39(6): 51–59.

Yural-Davis, N. 2007. 'Intersectionality, Citizenship and Contemporary Politics of Belonging', *Critical Review of International Social and Political Philosophy,* December 2007, 10(4): 561–74.

4

Occupational Domestication in a Post-Resettlement Context
An Analysis of Women's Work in Kannagi Nagar, Chennai

Karen Coelho

Introduction

In outlining the concept of 'occupational domestication', this chapter adds a spatial dimension to the familiar analyses of 'women's work' as a socially constructed category. For over two decades now, scholars have examined this category as a product of patriarchy's intercourse with capitalism. Marxist feminists have tracked the significant contributions of women, especially poor women, to capital accumulation not only through their household labour but also by providing an important source of cheap labour in waged work (Henessey and Igraham 1997 (1972), Dalla Rosa and James 1997 (1972)). More recent analyses of labour arrangements in settings of transnational or global capital – e.g., in electronics assembly, export-processing zones, and even in Silicon Valley (Ong 1987, Mohanty 1997, Anandhi 2007) – have noted how ideologies of domesticity, gendered definitions of 'workers' and 'work', and labour markets segmented by gender, race, and caste come to constitute specific work as 'women's work', thereby meriting lower wages and poorer working conditions. As Mohanty (1997) points out, industries source cheap labour by deskilling production and using race, gender and ethnic stereotypes to 'attract' groups of workers who are more 'suited' to perform tedious, unrewarding and poorly paid work. For example, certain kinds of factory jobs in the U.S. are targeted at women of Latin or Filipino immigrant communities, drawing on the community's culturally defined ideologies of women's place (ibid). Closer to home, Anandhi (2007), Kapadia (2010) and others have studied the large-scale employment of dalit women in export industries – garment, leather, software and pharmaceuticals – in or near urban centers. In Anandhi's case study of workers in a pharmaceutical export factory near Chengleput in Tamil Nadu, it was only young, unmarried women who were hired (in contrast to Ong's 1987 study in Silicon Valley, where only older married women were hired); this ensured that women could perform physically arduous work for long hours, on contract basis for very low wages.

Thus, the notion of 'women's work' as low-wage, unskilled and supplementary is aligned with the construction of women of particular castes, races or ethnicities as an appropriate and cheap labour force, ensuring continuities between women's unpaid domestic labour and paid market labour, and revealing the link between the feminization of work and the feminization of poverty in the global economy.

What is missing in these accounts is an explicit examination of the role of urban spatial restructurings within these strategies of capital – in other words, how the creation of cheap 'reserve' labour through the mobilization of gender, caste and/or race ideologies within segmentated labour markets is facilitated by spatial politics in globalizing cities. In particular, the type of urban restructuring addressed here, a form that has been unfolding in all Indian megacities over the past two to three decades, involves the forced relocation of working class residents of city slums, en masse, to state-sponsored resettlement sites on urban peripheries, to make way for infrastructure, commercial, real estate or beautification projects.[1] It is well recognized that such displacements disrupt slum-dwellers' hard-won occupational and livelihood security in the city. Yet, scant empirical material exists on how resettled populations rebuild their work lives in their new habitats. This chapter explores what this marriage of social marginalization and spatial dislocation yields, in terms of new hybrid productions of 'women's work'. It describes how the spatial segregation – or ghettoization – of urban working class and low caste families into mass peripheral settlements produces a domestication of working women, even within the realm of paid work, a process that we refer to as 'occupational domestication' and will be elaborated later in this introduction.

The chapter reports on a study of work and livelihoods in Kannagi Nagar (henceforth KN), Chennai's largest resettlement colony, located 25 km away from the centre of the city, settled since 2001, and housing close to 15,000 families.[2] The study was carried out in 2011–2012, slightly over ten years after the first groups of slum-dwellers were settled there. It sought to explore the impacts of the forced relocation on the livelihoods of the urban working poor, the resulting ruptures and/or continuities in their work patterns, networks, skill-development and career mobility, the opportunities and challenges provided by the new settlement, and how these dynamics differentially affected groups of relocated people. Large resettlement colonies, it must be remembered, over time come to house not only those forcibly relocated by state programs, but also large numbers of working class families driven out of the city by steep hikes in urban housing costs since the 1990s.

What makes this study particularly interesting is the location of KN, just off Chennai's Information Technology (IT) corridor, which is a high-speed toll road connecting the southern part of Chennai to IT parks and industrial estates in the neighbouring Kanchipuram district, and hosting a range of high-end commercial, financial and manufacturing as well as IT-related enterprises. The corridor has also attracted numerous upscale residential developments, which have in turn spawned a proliferation of malls, showrooms and restaurants along its length.

In the early years after the resettlement, however, the corridor offered few opportunities to KN's residents, partly due to their lack of local networks and partly to the strong stigma associated with their address. More significantly, our study found that even ten years down the road, employment remained a precarious condition in KN, particularly for women. This was emphasized by the eagerness with which women asked us, during each of our visits, whether we had work to offer, whether we could find them jobs. It turned out that this did not, as we initially believed, point to a continuing dearth of jobs in the area. In fact, there had clearly been considerable occupational dynamism over the intervening years. People had tried different jobs, some had retrained themselves, many had established new networks, and a range of jobs for low-skilled workers, primarily women, had opened up in the factories, offices, commercial and residential establishments in the area, mostly in the nature of housekeeping, office or sales assistance, cleaning, helping or casual factory labour. Why, then, were so many women here seeking work so keenly and persistently? The answers lay, as our study discovered, in the poor *quality* of jobs available for KN's workers, especially for women. The gendered segmentation of labour in the formal sector establishments of the IT corridor ensured that the vast majority of jobs for women were casual, highly insecure and poorly paid, with physically taxing working conditions and scant opportunities for economic mobility. Compounding the disruptive effects of residential relocation, then, these working conditions contributed to a scenario of frequent job change as well as high levels of unemployment and underemployment among women in the settlement. It was not uncommon to find women from dalit and fishing communities, typically among the more economically active women, playing cards at midday in KN.

Studying work and livelihoods within the socio-spatial framework of resettlement on the urban periphery provided us a lens on the numerous structures that shaped the occupational realities of working class households, while also throwing light on the profoundly gendered impacts of such resettlements. The workers hardest hit by the relocation were those employed in wage work sectors, most of whom were women, as against self-employed workers or petty commodity producers (PCP), who were predominantly men. In particular, paid domestic work, the single largest employer of women both before and after the relocation, underwent a significant exodus as well as a restructuring of its conditions of possibility, wherein workers were forced to commute across the city to their old working neighbourhoods to access established networks and contacts for jobs, even 10 years after the move (see under section 'The "Flexibility Factor": Domestic Workers In KN' below for more on this).

Reading spatial issues from the perspective of relocated workers thus revealed how employment opportunities for informal workers are crucially conditioned by circumstantial factors such as location, distance, travel, timings and the travails of a resettlement site. For women, these factors tended to converge with and compound the constraints posed by their household responsibilities – in other words, challenges of balancing household and paid work were rendered particularly difficult in KN due to the logistics associated with distance, and due to the disruption of social support networks, in many cases forcing women out of the labour force. However, the spatial frame also allowed us to explore the choices that women exercised within the repertoire of job opportunities offered by their location, offering important insights into the considerations that determined workers' options and preferences. Our fieldwork taught us that women workers in KN made work decisions based on much more than income calculations alone. Health effects, relationships at work, the hardship level of the job, convenience of access, and most importantly, the flexibility of timings that would enable them to send their children to school properly fed and clothed – all these factored importantly into the workers' choices of taking, rejecting or staying on in a particular job.

This study, then, throws light on the new makings of urban working classes in Indian cities through a politics of space in which gender, particularly as it configures women's work, is a significant player. More specifically, it points to a dynamic of ongoing 'domestication' of working women in the contemporary urban context, a dynamic that is accentuated by the (continuing as well as emerging) occupational settings and conditions of women's work. This partly resonates with the observations of Kapadia (2010) and Anandhi (2007) who note a recent strengthening of patriarchal norms of female seclusion and subordination among the lower castes in urban areas of Tamil Nadu (largely in imitation of wealthier conservative Tamil castes), even as larger numbers of poor women become primary breadwinners for their families.

However, the concept of 'occupational domestication', which anchors the analyses in this paper, goes further by identifying processes of domestication even within the world of work, domestication here referring to the sequestering of women into spatial and social positions that are subjected to lower valuation, reduced mobility, and greater control and surveillance. In this paper, this concept is substantiated by three interlocked phenomena that mark and constitute women's work. First, the nature of women's work, defined as unskilled by certain mappings of skill in which, for instance, cleaning and assembly work are inscribed as unskilled and machine operation as skilled. Second, the settings of women's work, typically confined to realms of service in homes and establishments or behind counters and desks, with timings that are 'flexible', either through agreements with employers, as in domestic work, or, at the other extreme, through the absence of regulation, as in casual company work. Third, the working conditions that render women's foothold in the labour market tenuous, creating an ongoing traffic between employment and unemployment, between home and work. This concept of occupational domestication is elaborated in this paper through its workings in the two predominant sectors of women's employment in KN – domestic work and 'company work'.

Methodologically, the study comprised two parts. The first was a survey of working members in 726 randomly sampled households (roughly 5 per cent of the 15,000-odd tenements) in KN. The sample was stratified, using allotment data from the Tamil Nadu Slum Clearance Board, to capture variations by year of settlement and area of origin. The survey followed a 'before/after relocation' framework in exploring occupational shifts, unemployment, travel and associated costs, and difficulties in finding/keeping work. This was followed by a qualitative component, wherein a sub-sample of workers from specific occupations were selected for longer, open-ended interviews, which explored the arrangements and conditions that shaped different occupations, types of contracts, routes for advancement and mobility, workers' preferences among available jobs, market conditions in various occupations, and the implications of KN residence for each kind of job.

The paper proceeds as follows. The section '"Women's Work" and the Mapping of Skill in KN' discusses the concentration of women workers in 'unskilled' occupations in KN, and maps this against patterns of unemployment in the settlement. The next section 'The "Flexibility Factor": Domestic Workers in KN' discusses domestic work, the single largest employer of women in KN, and the section 'Segments and Ceilings: "Company Workers" in KN' focuses on 'company jobs', the second largest category of women's work; both sections track different modes through which the dynamic of occupational domestication operates in the resettlement site.

'Women's work' and the mapping of skill in KN

This section outlines the range of occupations that constitutes women's work in KN. It reveals that not only is such work primarily composed of manual unskilled jobs (domestic work, housekeeping, cleaning/helping in offices and restaurants, and casual factory labour), but that the portfolio of occupations designated as women's work, or available for women, is conspicuously limited in comparison to those available to men.

There were 1086 employed persons in the 726 households we surveyed, in which employed men numbered 784 – over twice the employed women (302). Similarly, the number of unemployed women (120) was double that of unemployed men (60). Interestingly, single female-headed households were the exception in our sample, contrasting with accounts of large-scale and increasing female breadwinner roles in urban contexts in general (Chandrasekhar and Ghosh 2007), and in Tamil Nadu in particular (Kapadia 2010). While over half the households in our sample (56 per cent) had only one wage-earning member, men were the wage-earners in 346 of the 407 single wage-earner households, and women in only 61.[3] Seen in tandem with our other data on work patterns in KN, these numbers also point to relatively low levels of female work participation and a set of special challenges that women face in finding and retaining work in the settlement.

Aside from issues of location, features of the resettlement housing may also contribute to this phenomenon. The tenement-style apartments, with a size of around 120–150 sq. ft., created a push toward atomized nuclear family households, allowing little scope for the spillover accommodation that tends to extend the household unit in urban slums, and undermining the neighbourly or extended family support systems for child care and household maintenance which tend to form in urban slums. Simultaneously, as the low cost of housing in KN made it possible for women to not work, pressures to keep women out of the workforce were intensified. Numerous unemployed women that we interviewed told us that although they wished to find a job and earn an income, their husbands were opposed to their taking on paid employment. The resettlement, then, brought about a re-domestication of women, both through the practical difficulties women faced in going out to work from KN, and as part of the reassertion of the modern patriarchal nuclear family household that the resettlement housing appeared to provoke.

Over 40 per cent of the sampled workforce in our study had no more than primary education, but 28 per cent had school-leaving certificates (SSLC, HSC), diplomas or higher levels of education. More than three quarters of the sample reported themselves as Hindu, 15 per cent as Christian and 6 per cent as Muslim. SCs formed the largest single caste category in the sample (55 per cent). SCs, STs and MBCs together accounted for over 70 per cent of the sample and non-backward castes accounted for less than 2 per cent, offering further evidence of the overlap between caste and class in urban settlements, and the persistent caste segmentation inscribed into the spatial arrangement of cities.

As Table 4.1 reveals, women workers in KN were clustered at the low-skilled end of the occupational spectrum, in jobs like domestic work, housekeeping and cleaning/helping, which together employed almost two-third of the women in our sample. In addition, 5 per cent were in unskilled construction, although this is a low figure, given that such work constitutes a common option for unskilled women workers in urban areas. Seen against the fact that it employs 15 per cent of men in our sample, this finding perhaps points to the enhanced costs (in terms of distance and time) of this type of informal labour for women. The other two occupations categorized here as semi-skilled, which reveal some presence of women, are factory work (8 per cent) and vending (6 per cent). Our study, however, revealed that the women employed in factory work were predominantly in unskilled positions.

Table 4.1 Gendered distribution of occupations in Kannagi Nagar

	Occupations	Number of workers		
		Total (%)	Men	Women
Low skilled	Domestic work	125 (11.3)	4 (0.5)	121 (39.16)
	Housekeeping	46 (4.1)	11 (1.4)	35 (11.33)
	Unskilled manual and construction	131 (12.1)	115 (14.7)	16 (5.3)
	Painting	118 (10.6)	117 (14.9)	1 (0.3)
	Cleaners/helpers	97 (8.9)	62 (7.9)	35 (11.6)
	Security	52 (4.7)	51 (6,5)	1 (0.3)
Mixed/ semi-skilled	Petty services	36 (3.2)	31 (3.9)	5 (1.6)
	Factory work	66 (6.0)	41 (5.2)	25 (8.1)
	Vending	41 (3.7)	22 (2.8)	19 (6.2)
Vocational skills	Driving	118 (10.6)	118 (15.0)	0
	Skilled construction and technical trades	91 (8.3)	90 (11.5)	1 (0.3)
Soft Skills	Office and sales assistance	68 (6.3)	43 (5.5)	25 (8.3)
	Business, trading	39 (3.5)	32 (4.1)	7 (2.3)
	While collar salaried	51 (4.7)	40 (5.1)	11 (3.6)
	Others	7 (0.6)	7 (0.9)	0
	Total	1086 (100)	784 (100)	302 (100)

A second clustering of women, albeit much smaller, is evident at the other end of the skills spectrum – 14 per cent were employed in soft-skilled or white-collared work, the majority here (8 per cent) in office or sales assistance. More significant, women appear to be all but absent from one section of the occupational spectrum – that of semi-skilled or technically skilled occupations like driving, carpentry, or plumbing. These occupations also often tend to be organized in self-employed or entrepreneurial modes, are relatively mobile, and fetch better earnings than those in the low-skilled category.

Women's work in KN, then, is found at two ends of the 'skills' spectrum, in low-skilled manual work, or soft skilled jobs, outlining the contours of occupational domestication, wherein women are predominantly confined to realms of cleaning or helping services in homes, offices and companies, or to service roles behind counters or desks in stores or offices.

In contrast, more than 40 per cent of men were found in more skilled occupations such as driving, skilled construction and technical trades, or in office or white collar jobs. While the two occupations accounting for the largest proportions of men were unskilled construction and painting (15 per cent each), these attracted significantly higher wages than women's unskilled work. Indeed, painting is an ambiguous category – while it requires no formal qualifications, training or experience at the point of entry, and the skill is learned on the job in a comparatively short period of time, it emerges as among the best paid jobs for men in the manual categories, comparable with driving or the skilled technical trades. Similarly, the 5 per cent of men in factory jobs were mostly employed in the skilled segments of production, typically as machinists. Thus, not only were more men working than women in KN, they were also in better jobs in terms of the skill-based hierarchy of work.

Unemployment

The occupational structure outlined above translated into gendered patterns of unemployment and underemployment in KN. As Table 4.2 reveals, overall unemployment was high in KN, and particularly among women. By the conventional definition of unemployment (persons not employed but actively seeking employment), 181 persons (120 women and 60 men and 1 transgender person who identified as a woman) from the 726 households we studied were unemployed, as against 1086 working members, yielding a ratio of 17 per cent of unemployed to employed people in the sample. Out of these, 122 persons had been previously employed and 58 were looking for their first jobs.

In addition, an additional 165 persons (125 women and 40 men) had worked before but were not offering themselves for work anymore. These workers had dropped out of the workforce at various points, many at the time of relocation, but most, some years after.

Table 4.2 Profile of unemployed workers in Kannagi Nagar

	Total	Men	Women	Transgender
No. of unemployed persons	181	60	120	1
Of the above, number previously employed	122	39	82	1
Number searching for first job	58	21	37	
People who had worked before but were not currently looking for work	165	40	125	

We also found through our post-survey qualitative fieldwork that employment was a tenuous, constantly shifting, and highly contingent condition, particularly for women; large numbers of people who had been working at the time of the survey had lost their jobs or quit working, often, again, temporarily. Given this interchangeability, it is worth analyzing the two categories of people who had lost or left work as a combined category, distinguished from the 58 workers who were first-time aspirants to the labour force.

Together, then 288 people who had worked before had either lost employment or abandoned working after moving to KN. Of these, 208 were women. The reasons that workers, and women workers in particular, gave for their unemployed status are summarized in Table 4.3. For women, it was domestic responsibilities above all that explained their inability to participate in the labour market. Yet, it became clear in our fieldwork that this constraint was heavily shaped by circumstances arising from the resettlement. First, locational issues such as distance, timings, and lack of transport facilities played strong roles in constituting domestic circumstances as a constraint to outside employment. These were compounded by the special challenges of running households and raising children in the resettlement site, particularly in the early years, when water supplies were irregular, local schools were lacking, and social networks absent. All this combined with the social atmosphere in the settlement, described by women as marked by drunkenness, fights and 'rowdyism', to effectively re-domesticate large numbers of women workers. Issues of health and age also played a strong role in constraining employment possibilities in KN – in many cases, even relatively minor ailments (dizziness, blood pressure, a small injury) made it difficult for workers to negotiate the crowded buses and long commutes to and from the settlement.

Table 4.3 Reasons for unemployment

Reasons for losing or leaving employment	All unemployed (%)	Unemployed women (%)
Problems related to location of KN (transport, distance, lack of suitable opportunities)	92 (31.9)	39 (19.7)
Accidents/illness/old age	76 (26.4)	44 (22.2)
Domestic responsibilities	48 (16.7)	91 (46.0)
Problems related to the job	31(10.8)	19 (9.6)
Personal reasons	11 (3.8)	5 (2.5)
No response	30 (10.4)	9 (4.3)
Total	258	207

Our fieldwork also highlighted a tension between these interlocked sets of constraints (including husbands or other family members not wanting/allowing women to take paid employment), and women's keen and repeatedly expressed desire to participate in the labour market. Those who had dropped out for family reasons in particular, expressed feeling tied down and frustrated; many tried to outline the kinds of jobs that would enable them to go to work for at least a few hours a day, both for the sake of autonomy and control over their own time and for the extra income.[4] In KN, as elsewhere, it is paid domestic work in particular that offers the kind of flexibility that allows women with significant household responsibilities to participate in paid labour for at least a few hours in a day; hence this occupation – often seen from the outside as demeaning and low-status – emerged as a highly sought-after and valued occupation by women workers.

Examining the occupational categories that unemployed persons had been previously engaged in (Table 4.4) revealed that occupations that were more vulnerable to locational disruptions mapped on strongly to categories

Table 4.4 Previous occupations of unemployed workers

Occupational categories	No.	%
Domestic work	70	24.3
Factory work	49	17.0
Office assistant/sales	32	11.1
Cleaners/helpers/peons	25	8.7
White collar work	21	7.3
Unskilled manual and construction work	20	6.9
Petty service provision	15	5.2
Housekeeping	12	4.2
Security	12	4.2
Skilled construction work	7	2.4
Vending	6	2.1
Car driving	6	2.1
Skilled technical trades (plumbing, carpentry, etc)	4	1.4
Business/trading/contracting	2	0.7
Painting	1	0.3
Other	3	1.0
Total	287	0.3

of women's work as identified above. The single largest category of work in which unemployed people had been previously engaged was domestic work, followed by factory work, office/sales assistance, cleaning/helping and white collar work, all significant employers of women – of the 49 factory workers that reported unemployment, 40 were women. These were also occupations based in fixed establishments, while those with greater locational flexibility (auto driving, construction, painting and skilled technical trades) were evidently less impacted by the move.

Table 4.5 Types of jobs sought by unemployed workers

	All looking for work			New Aspirants only		
	Total	Men	Women	Total	Men	Women
Domestic work	32 (17.1)	0	32 (26.6)	13 (20.7)	0	13
Housekeeping	12 (6.6)	2 (3.3)	10 (8.2)	4 (6.9)	0	4
Security	4 (2.2)	4 (6.7)	0	1(1.7)	1	0
Painting	2 (1.1)	2 (3.3)	0	1(1.7)	1	0
Unskilled manual work	8 (4.5)	4 (6.7)	4 (3.3)	3 (5.1)	3	0
Cleaner/helper/peon	3 (1.7)	1 (1.7)	2 (1.7)	2 (3.4)	1	1
Skilled personal services (beautician, baby care, nursing)	3 (1.7)	0	3 (2.5)	1 (1.7)		1
Driving (car)	4 (2.2)	4 (6.7)	0			
Skilled construction work or skilled technical trades (plumbing, electrical, mechanic, tailoring)	10 (5.7)	7 (11.8)	3 (2.5)	3 (5.1)	2	1
Office-based or company work, sales jobs	29 (16.0)	7 (11.7)	22 (18.3)	10 (17.2)	2	8
IT/ITES	8 (4.4)	4 (6.7)	4 (3.3)	8 (13.8)	4	4
White collar work (teacher, HR, supervisor, media etc)	11 (6.2)	1 (1.7)	10 (8.2)	2 (3.4)	0	2
Government job	3 (1.7)	2 (3.3)	1 (.8)	1(1.7)	1	0
Part-time work, home-based work	3 (1.7)	0	3 (2.5)			
Any work	49 (27.1)	22 (36.6)	27 (22.5)	9 (15.5)	6	3
Total	181 (100)	60 (100)	121 (100)	58 (100)	21	37

Figures in parentheses represent percentages of the column variables.

Occupations in which very few reported unemployment were trading, vending, skilled construction work, and skilled technical trades. This picture points to a distinction between waged work and self-employed occupations, with workers in the former clearly more vulnerable to losing work than petty commodity producers (PCP), independent and self-employed workers. For these and other reasons, male workers appeared to have weathered the shift better than did women. Of all the painters in the sample, only one was in the unemployed category, and auto drivers were completely absent from the unemployed list.

As indicated earlier, 58 workers were looking for their first jobs, of which over two-third (68 per cent) were women. Men who were looking their first job were all under 25 years, conversely, all the older people looking for work were women. Table 4.5 below shows the types of work sought by unemployed workers; the three columns on the right represent first-time job seekers only.

Ironically, given the high levels of unemployment in wage-work categories, it was these very categories that unemployed workers (more than 50 per cent) seemed to be after. Domestic work was the single most wanted work, sought by 27 per cent of unemployed women in general, and about a third of the first-time job seekers. The next largest cohort were seeking 'company' jobs in offices, shops or factories (16 per cent overall and 17.2 per cent from among first-time job seekers), followed by housekeeping and white collar work (10 per cent each).

Given this profile of women's work and these patterns of unemployment and aspiration in KN, the following two sections examine the dynamics of occupational domestication operating in the major sectors employing women, i.e., domestic work (explained in section '"Flexibility Factor": Domestic Workers In KN') and company work (explained in section 'Segments and Ceilings: "Company Workers" in KN').

The 'flexibility factor': Domestic workers in Kannagi Nagar[5]

If occupational domestication, or the set of processes and pressures that keep women hemmed in to narrow and disadvantaged spaces in the labour market, is predominantly a product of women's wage-earning pressures within the context of an unchanged household division of labour, this production is most clearly seen in paid domestic work. For women with low levels of education or marketable skills in the workforce, in other words for women of lower castes and disadvantaged communities, this is the only available work that fits the bill. Here, then, the segmentation of informal labour markets by caste, class and gender, formed partly by the nature of work (e.g., sweeping and cleaning), intersects with the patriarchal structure of household reproduction to create this category of 'women's work' in which the single most important condition of possibility is that of flexibility of timings. This flexibility represents an 'agreement', or a settlement (however asymmetrical in power terms), between employers – typically middle or upper class women – and workers, over the shared exigencies of women's household reproductive roles.

As seen above, domestic work was by far the largest employer of women in KN, accounting for 39 per cent of women workers. About 59 per cent of domestic workers in our sample were dalit, another 29 per cent were from other Backward and Most Backward Communities (BC and MBC), 10 per cent were from 'other' communities – Christian and Muslim, and only 2 per cent were from higher castes.

However, domestic work employed few workers in younger age groups; of the 125 domestic workers in our sample, only 10 were under 25 years and of all women workers under 25 years, less than 20 per cent opted for this work, compared to 43 per cent and 49 per cent in the two older age groups. Most domestic workers in our sample (over 70 per cent) had low levels of education; however, 35 women and 2 men who had secondary education or school-leaving certificates were also working in this occupation. Domestic work in KN, thus, remained a preference of women in their late 20s or of middle aged women, mostly with little education.

This finding is a reflection of two trends in occupational choice among low-wage working women, representing both pull and push factors for/ against domestic work. First, in terms of push factors, young unmarried women tended to opt for company-based jobs (housekeeping, factory, or sales/office assistance) as, largely free of household responsibilities in their own homes, they could afford to take full-time jobs with fixed timings. A second push factor was constituted by a dynamic of generational mobility – many working class families in KN, including those of domestic workers, had invested substantially in educating their children, and preferred that they move into white-collar jobs, or at least into formal sector jobs such as housekeeping or company work. To some extent, status considerations played into this; while the majority of domestic workers we interviewed did not consider their occupations demeaning, they did not wish to see their children in this profession. Younger workers with low levels of education also preferred to take up housekeeping jobs (which involved similar work, but in more official or formal settings), at least partly because of its more professionalized ethos. We also came across some instances where women had dropped out of domestic work because their children did not want them to continue in that occupation.

The most powerful pull factor for domestic work is that of flexible working hours and timings, which allowed working-class women to earn an income, however small, while continuing to fulfil their (largely unchanged) roles as primary caretakers of children and household. This feature emerged as the single most important consideration that weighted domestic work as an option against other possible occupations for unskilled women. This feature also explains the rising popularity of part-time jobs in this sector and the broad demographic character of the workforce in this occupation – married women with children, or middle aged women with significant household responsibilities, many of whom may have earlier worked full-time jobs in shops, tailoring units or export houses, but had to move to domestic work after marriage.

Yet, this framework was somewhat altered in KN, where the conditions of commute defining the landscape of domestic work compromised this crucial advantage of flexibility, forcing large numbers of women to give up domestic work after marriage and childbirth, and making it difficult for them to return for several years. In addition, the flexibility of timings that allowed domestic workers to service multiple homes and work multiple shifts was compromised to a great extent by the move to KN, as workers were not able to return to their worksites for a second shift. All of the above factors help to explain the high rates of unemployment as well as the frequent changes in jobs seen among domestic workers in KN. Large numbers of women had moved out of or into this occupation following the move to KN. Overall, 97 women had left this sector after the relocation, of which 69 had quit working altogether, and 30 had moved to other occupations. For the old-timers, the stakes in continuing this work after the move were raised significantly, as the majority were forced to travel daily back to their old neighborhoods to work, over distances ranging from 5 to 25 km. The costs involved in this commute, in terms of time and bus fare, were significant, even for those travelling to the closest city neighbourhoods, and bordering on the prohibitive for the areas further away. Why, then, did they do it?

Part of the reason lies in the differentiated nature of markets for domestic work across the city; many neighbourhoods in central parts of the city, from where large numbers of families had been evicted before being resettled in KN, offered better wages and working conditions than the newer, smaller apartments that were commonly found in residential complexes on the IT corridor. Domestic workers who returned to these areas earned between Rs 1500 to 5000 per month (or an average of about Rs 2200 p/m) depending on the number of hours and/or houses they worked, , which works out to about Rs 500/- more than those working in the newer areas closer to KN.

Yet, a good part of these gains was offset by the costs of travel and the reduced number of working hours available due to travel time. Essentially, then, the major explanation for the continuing tendency of workers to travel to the city for work lies in the difficulties of entry into domestic work markets, and the importance of using and maintaining already built relationships and networks.

Domestic work is commonly portrayed as work that entails almost no entry conditions (Neetha 2004, Roy 2002) because it requires few skills beyond those that women routinely employ in their own homes. This, however, does not mean that these jobs are easy to get. Domestic workers almost unanimously reported extreme difficulties in finding work, particularly in older settled neighbourhoods, where there was a saturation of workers. They also claimed that employers were reluctant to hire unless workers came recommended by somebody they knew and trusted. Strong recommendations and active networks were thus needed to access the jobs that became available. Here, again, living in KN posed special challenges, owing to the stigma attached to this address. Retaining strong contacts with local workers, maintaining relationships with employers, and sticking to known areas and networks was thus even more important for workers from KN.

The same factor (difficulty of entry) explains why new entrants into this sector tended to take jobs in the vicinity of KN – they did not possess the contacts and recommendations to access established markets and hence, struggled to build access to emerging markets closer to home. The lower wage rates offered in these areas were compensated for by the lower commute time and cost and the greater flexibility of timings that such proximate worksites entailed. Over time, there appears to be a shift in KN toward giving up the long-distance jobs and settling for jobs in local markets, to take advantage of the flexibility of timings afforded by these jobs.

To sum up, we reprise the finding (highlighted in section '"Women's Work" and the Mapping of Skill in KN'), that despite all the difficulties outlined above, domestic work continues to be the primary draw for women seeking work, even in KN. What this suggests is that, ultimately, beyond the preference factors described above, and the constraints posed by the context of resettlement, the option of domestic work is less a matter of choice than of a *lack* of choice. This study highlights the fact that for unskilled women needing to earn an income while fulfilling their own household responsibilities (and this primarily includes women of the lowest castes and disadvantaged communities), paid domestic work remains among the few available avenues, no matter where they live or the conditions under which they have to work.

Outside the domestic work sector, in firms, factories and offices, women's work remains, as the next section shows, no less hemmed in by labour markets structures that exploit gender, caste and class characteristics of workers, as well as the situation of an abundant supply of unskilled workers in KN, to create and maintain a cheap, casual and unprotected labour force.

Segments and ceilings: 'Company workers' in KN

The workings of occupational domestication can also be seen in the short circuits that run between 'women's work' in companies or formal establishments, and women's unpaid work at home, via the tenuous conditions of employment, high rates of job change and job loss, and low returns from work. This is illustrated in the case below.

Ponni, 30 years old, a single Dalit woman residing in KN, had just quit her factory job because her brother's wife had had a baby, and she was needed to take care of the child. She had worked in the quality control department of a manufacturing firm located on the IT corridor for 10 years, and was earning Rs 4500 at the time she left. She had remained a casual worker for all those years, through a special contracting strategy in her firm, wherein casual workers were terminated every six months and re-hired after a break of two weeks. As she described it, "After 2 years of work, some get confirmed, but not women". Working conditions were hard, "We had to stand for long. We had hourly targets to meet, and we could only meet those by working in a standing position". Her brother, 29 years old, was working as a machinist in another factory nearby, earning Rs 14,000 after 7 years of experience. His wife, the child's mother, was also in full-time employment.

It was evidently Ponni's factory job that was considered expendable enough to sacrifice for the family's childcare needs. This case highlights the conditions of work and the wage levels that were typical of 'company work' as described by workers in KN. A range of low-end jobs – including housekeeping, factory work, office or sales assistance, or cleaning/helping in restaurants and stores – had become available along the IT corridor, and offered an expanding avenue for young unskilled female workers to escape from low-status domestic work, as well as an alternative for older people who lacked the networks and contacts to obtain domestic work.

Table 4.5 reveals that the vast majority of female company workers were under 40 years of age. The 4 categories of company work covered here employed close to 60 per cent of all women workers under 25 years in our sample. In terms of caste, company workers were mixed, but predominantly from lower castes and minorities (MBCs, SCs and 'others' – mostly Muslims and Christians who did not provide caste identifiers). These groups accounted for 28 of the 35 cleaners/helpers, 21 of the 25 factory workers, and 17 of the 25 office assistants. The Table also shows that the majority of these workers had low levels of education – even among factory workers and office/sales assistants, the largest proportions, 38 to 40 per cent, were uneducated or had only primary education.

Table 4.6 Demographic profile of women company workers in Kannagi Nagar

		Housekeepers	Cleaners/ helpers	Factory workers	Office/Sales assistants	Total
AGE	25 yrs or less	3	6	10	12	31
	26–40 yrs	22	18	15	11	66
	41–65 yrs	10	11	–	2	23
Total		35	35	25	25	120
Caste	OC	1	1	1	–	3
	BC	15	6	3	8	32
	MBC	2	3	4	4	13
	SC	13	20	8	11	52
	Other	4	5	9	2	20
Total		35	35	25	25	120
Education	None/primary	17	21	10	7	55
	Secondary	13	12	9	6	40
	HSC/SSLC	3	2	5	6	16
	Diploma, degree	2		1	6	8
Total		35	35	25	25	120

These jobs were clear manifestations of the gendered segmentation of labour markets in formal sector establishments. They mostly involved unskilled manual work, even though many of the women employed had secondary education and some (13 per cent) even had school-leaving certificates (Table 4.6). Most company jobs apparently required no educational qualifications, and many of our female respondents claimed that having a 10th standard or SSLC level of education hardly made a difference to the kinds of work they got.

Housekeeping, a term used to describe janitorial services provided to companies, including cleaning, collecting trash, and serving snacks and tea, was a job largely reserved for women, although it did employ a few men – in our study the proportion was 75 per cent women to 25 per cent men. There were no permanent jobs in this sector – workers were usually employed by contractors, typically men, although the contracting and hiring arrangements varied widely, from informal individual contractors putting together ad hoc teams, to more formal contracting agencies. Housekeeping work provided limited opportunities for occupational mobility, the highest post a worker could rise to was that of supervisor.

Factory work revealed a strong gender segmentation, primarily in terms of the distinction between casual and permanent workers. In several manufacturing firms, machine operators, almost exclusively men, constituted a relatively privileged category of workers that entered permanent status with attendant wage structures and benefits. The majority, however, were casual workers, mostly women, who faced insecure tenures and back-breaking, often hazardous working conditions, for less than minimum wages. Like Ponni, several women workers reported the existence of a clear ceiling on upward mobility for women, with permanent positions reserved for male workers. This was typically explained in terms of skill, with machine operation designated as skilled work and women's work – in assembly, packing, or quality check – as unskilled. But the notion of skill appeared to be more a product than a cause of the segmentation. Most machine operators that we interviewed also had low levels of formal education and had entered factory work as unskilled helpers, steadily moving up the production chain to their 'skilled' positions. Women, on the other hand, remained confined to functions that involved low engagement with technology; in some industries they were also kept out of the more dynamic segments such as site work. A woman working in a furniture factory said, "Women are not allowed to leave a restricted area in the unit". Many women in our study had worked as casual workers for over 15 years within the same company.

Yet, hiring strategies as reported by workers also suggested that large companies, particularly in manufacturing, faced a pull between keeping workers casual to lower the overall wage bill, and retaining experienced workers. With increasing competition for experienced and competent workers, companies were forced to make small concessions, like raising wage rates slightly, and giving annual increments. On the whole, however, the availability of a large pool of low-skilled workers in the resettlement colony allowed companies to keep wages low.

Company jobs, particularly housekeeping, factory work and cleaning/ helping in restaurants were almost universally reported to be physically taxing, with long and usually inflexible shifts and scant provisions for leave. Housekeeping workers claimed that they had to service many floors in multi-storied buildings, and were often forbidden to use the elevators. Many factory jobs involve 9 or 10 hour working days, with sometimes an hour's travel in each direction. Many hotel and restaurant cleaners showed us severe skin ailments that they contracted from continuous contact with chemical detergents at work. A large number of company workers in our study had given up their jobs due to hard working conditions and effects on their health.

Wages in these jobs, particularly for women workers, were low, indeed no higher than those earned by domestic workers in shorter work shifts. Wages for casual workers in factory jobs ranged from about Rs 3000 at the bottom end, to about Rs 7500, with a mean wage of under Rs 5000, even for workers with many years of experience. In housekeeping, the average wage was Rs 3330. Benefits were absent in these jobs, except for the Provident Fund and ESI schemes. While most workers in our sample had PF contributions deducted from their pay, many were unaware about how to claim benefits from the scheme after termination of employment. One casual worker said, "The numbers keep changing because we are re-hired frequently. And the company contribution has not been paid. We have been fighting about this at work. Because of our struggles they are now saying they will stabilize our numbers". But the struggles she referred to were informal in nature, "There is no union in our company, they will fire us if we try to start one". We found no evidence of membership in any union among female company workers in our sample.

In general, then, company jobs in our study were marked by insecure and tenuous contracts, working conditions that permitted only able-bodied workers to remain for long durations, high costs in terms of the workers' own household obligations, and low wages. Unsurprisingly, several company workers, especially those in housekeeping, claimed that they would readily switch to domestic work if available.

In this landscape of poor quality jobs in the advanced industrial sectors of the IT corridor, women negotiated their need and/or desire to work in various ways. At one level, their insistence on going to work under these conditions was itself as assertion of autonomy and aspiration. Ponni herself declared that, despite the hardships, "I enjoyed working – I made friends there, and once I got used to it, everything became easier. Working allowed me to buy things for myself which I could not have otherwise". Almost across the board in KN, women had control over their earnings, and married women claimed that they received a substantial part of their husband's earnings for household expenses. Women with children declared that their wages were spent on giving their children better food, clothes and schooling.

Women typically tackled poor working conditions by opting out and seeking change. The high rate of job turnover found in our study was not only due to the insecurity of the work and unsustainable conditions of labour, but was a testimony to women's active exercise of their options and decision-making powers vis-à-vis their working lives. Women moved in and out of company jobs for a range of reasons, from health impacts of the job to inconvenient timings, thus playing out their side of the relation of cheap and dispensable labour in which they were embedded.

Conclusions

The concept of women's work encodes a web of social structures and ideologies – of family, domesticity and the household division of labour, of caste and class, all of which are mobilized by capital in its profit-maximizing strategies of tapping into cheap labour supplies. These strategies are supported by state policies of spatially massing workers into large low-cost housing projects or resettlement colonies in urban peripheries.

In KN, however, women were not simply subjected to these ideologies, but actively shaped and negotiated them, primarily through their participation in the labour market, and their constant traffic in, out and across it. Women in KN, almost universally, saw themselves as workers, even when they were not active in paid work. Even for those with significant household responsibilities or small children to care for, the world of paid work beckoned strongly, and they believed it was only a matter of time before they returned, often against the wishes of their husbands. For these women, the ideology of the housewife was not exclusive of the worker. In paid domestic work, the overlaps between the two identities was a source of skill, this was work they knew how to do. In this scheme, flexibility of timings was a pivotal enabling mechanism, built on the shared ideologies of domesticity and work between middle and lower class women. Yet, it was a costly mechanism, as all wage jobs with flexibility in our study were at the bottom end of the wage spectrum.

In the workings of occupational domestication, however, paid and unpaid (household) work, while finding continuities and overlaps, were not symmetrical or equally valued. For most women who found themselves having to negotiate the two roles, the role of mother/housewife clearly carried priority. Women in KN appeared, for the most part, to be strongly invested in the values of home, family, and most of all, of generational mobility, i.e., of giving their children a better life by investing in their education. Almost all the workers we interviewed, male or female, expressed strong hopes that their children would study and move out of manual work to office-based, white collar work. Women's working lives to a large extent subserved this goal – in some cases it domesticated them, and in others it sent them into the labour market.

Thus, in being subjected to and by ideologies of the housewife, the underclass and the worker, working women in KN not only imbued these ideas with new meanings, they also disrupted their coherence, exposed their contradictions and destabilized their certainties. As Willis (1971) showed in the case of working class boys in England, they became, in many ways, bad subjects.

Endnotes

1   Although political dynamics stalled this process in Chennai until the late 1990s (Raman 2011), Tamil Nadu has now fallen in line with national orthodoxies of eviction and peripheral relocation of the urban poor as the pathway to slum-free cities.

2   The study was carried out by the Madras Institute of Development Studies, in collaboration with Transparent Chennai, a program of the Center for Development Finance, IFMR. For further discussions of this study, see Coelho *et al.* (2012) on formal sector employment and Coelho *et al.* (2013) on domestic workers in KN.

3   An important caveat here arises from the high rate of alcoholism reported to exist among men in Kannagi Nagar. We discovered that several men who had been formally recorded as employed, hardly went to work at all and that women were in fact supporting the family with their earnings. In the light of this, our data probably significantly underestimates the number of de facto female-supported households in our sample.

4   This resonates with Anandhi's portrayal of the young unmarried dalit women workers in a Chengleput pharmaceuticals export factory, who, despite low wages, backbreaking conditions, and exposure to ongoing sexual and caste abuse, felt empowered by their earnings and their relative independence. While their status as earners/providers had actually led to an increased surveillance and control over their sexuality, e.g., by brothers who would go to the bus stops to monitor their movements to and from work, their own negotiations within the factory and outside had also created spaces of autonomy and empowerment through their mobility to the site of work, through their earnings and through their deployment of sexuality to negotiate harsh working conditions.

5   Substantial parts of this section are taken from Coelho *et al.* (2013).

References

Anandhi, S. 2007. 'Women, Work and Abortion, a Caste Study from Tamil Nadu', *Economic and Political Weekly*, 42(12): 1054–59, March 24, 2007.

Chandrasekhar, C. P., and J. Ghosh. 2007. 'Women Workers in Urban India', In *Business Line, The Hindu*, Feb 6, 2007.

Coelho, Karen, Venkat, T., and R. Chandrika. 2012. 'The Spatial Reproduction of Urban Poverty: Labour and Livelihoods in a Slum Resettlement Colony', *Economic and Political Weekly* (Review of Urban Affairs 4), 47(47 and 48), Dec 1, 2012, pp. 53–63.

———. 2013. 'Housing, Homes and Domestic Labour: A Study of Paid Domestic Workers from a Resettlement Colony in Chennai', *Economic and Political Weekly* (Review of Women's Studies), October 26, 2013, 48(43): 39–46.

Dalla Costa, Mariarosa, and Selma James. 1997(1972). 'Women and the Subversion of Community', in *Materialist Feminism: A Reader in Class, Difference and Women's Lives*, edited by R. Hennessey and C. Ingraham. New York and London: Routledge.

Hennessey, Rosemary, and Chrys Ingraham. 1997(1972). 'Introduction: Reclaiming Anticapitalist Feminism', in *Materialist Feminism: A Reader in Class, Difference and Women's Lives*, edited by R. Hennessey and C. Ingraham. New York and London: Routledge.

Kapadia, K. 2010. 'Liberalization and Transformation in India's Informal Economy: Female Breadwinners in Working-Class Households in Chennai', in *The Comparative Political Economy of Development*, edited by Barbara Harris White and Judith Heyer, Routledge, pp. 267–90.

Mohanty, C. T. 1997. 'Women Workers and Capitalist Scripts: Ideologies of Domination, Common Interests and the Politics of Solidarity', in *Feminist Genealogies, Colonial Legacies, Democratic Futures*, edited by C. T. Mohanty and J. Alexander. New York: Routledge.

Neetha, N. 2004. 'Making of Female Breadwinners Migration and Social Networking of Women Domestics in Delhi', *Economic and Political Weekly*, 39(17): 1681–88.

Ong, A. 1987. 'Disassembling Gender in the Electronic Age', *Feminist Studies* 13, pp. 609–26.

Raman, N. 2011. 'The Board and the Bank: Changing Policies towards Slums in Chennai', *Economic and Political Weekly*, 46(31): 74–80.

Roy, A. 2002. *City Requiem, Calcutta: Gender and the Politics of Poverty*. Minneapolis: University of Minnesota press.

5

Old Jobs in New Forms
Women's Experiences in the Housekeeping Sector in Pune[1]

Kiran Mirchandani, Sanjukta Mukherjee
and Shruti Tambe

Introduction

Neeta leaves her home every morning for her twelve-hour shift at 6.30 a.m. She walks for twenty minutes to get to her workplace. She is a housekeeper and her job involves dusting, washing dishes and cleaning washrooms in a large transnational firm. She is proud to be gainfully employed although she complains that she is paid Rs 700 less than her male colleagues. She does not have a bank account. She has heard that she is entitled to receive employer contributions to her PF (pension/provident fund) but does not know whether she has a PF account. Although she is proud to be employed and earning as much as her husband, her neighbours and relatives only know that she works in a company, as she has not told them the exact nature of her job. She dreams of providing higher education for her son and three daughters. Neeta, like other housekeepers working in transnational corporations, which have mushroomed in India, occupies the ambivalent position of privilege and precarity; she works in a place which is associated with the formal sector of the economy, while many of the terms of her employment remain informal (Agarwala 2013). Neeta's on-the-job learning involves not only understanding the tasks she must complete but also requires that she makes sense of the new social norms which define the gap between economically privileged white collar professionals and low wage women housekeepers like her. At the same time training is imparted in such a way that she learns that housekeeping is a new clean 'profession' and she has to be skilled to qualify as a professional. She is expected to move beyond caste-based stigmas that have been historically associated with cleaning jobs. As a contract employee, her employment relationship and place of work are not the same; she cleans the premises of a company with which she has no direct contract. This distance makes her job precarious as she can be immediately replaced. Yet, paid employment also allows her to challenge feudal relationships upon which domestic cleaning is based, and to see herself as a worker who knows about and evokes labour law. Neeta's experience suggests that 'new' sectors, such as professionalized housekeeping, which serves to maintain the 'global' nature of multinational firms in India with their 'western' codes of cleanliness and hygiene, both re-inscribe and challenge patriarchal gender norms.

In recent years, service work has become 'tradable across international borders' (Van den Broek 2004, 59), operationalized through the growth of software firms and call centres across the world generating significant media, policy and academic interest in the global service economy and its workers. India is no exception. IT related outsourcing has been celebrated by governments, global companies and the media as providing the opportunity to 'leapfrog' the country into a post-industrial service economy and resolve the problem of widespread unemployment' (Vasavi 2008). For example, the former Prime Minister Atal Bihari Vajpayee has remarked that 'IT has... given us a developmental tool powerful enough to banish poverty and backwardness and make India a land of opportunities for all...' (Mukherjee 2008). Some economists have predicted that the growth of the IT sector 'creates indirect employment opportunities for the less skilled and less educated' (Chanda 2005, 6). As Sassen notes, however, constructions of the global economy in terms of enabling technologies or transnational organizational structures mask 'the actual material processes, activities, and infrastructure crucial to the implementation of globalization' (2002, 2).

Unlike the visibility and veneration of IT professionals and their contribution to India's economic success, to date, there has been little ethnographic research on support workers who clean and maintain global companies and little is known on how they access their jobs, how class, caste, gender and ethnicity structure their lives, and how new subcontracting regimes heralded by neoliberal globalization affect their work and life. In line with this, the primary objective of this paper is to explore the work experiences of auxiliary workers (specifically housekeepers) who scaffold the transnational information technology (IT) industry in India.

The research for this paper draws on fieldwork conducted in 2010–2012 and is based on interviews with ten women housekeepers in Pune located in the state of Maharashtra in India (Mirchandani et al., n.d). Most but not all of these housekeepers belong to Dalit or other deemed 'backward' castes, and come from rural areas. These interviews were conducted as part of a larger project on auxiliary workers in India. In this paper, we discuss the ways in which the emergence of the formalized housekeeping services sector associated with the IT/ITES industry provides some new opportunities for women, but simultaneously facilitates the re-inscription of gendered hierarchies.

Service workers in global IT/ITES firms

IT/ITES spaces are notable for their high levels of cleanliness and extremely ordered physical environments with western architectural designs. Most transnational firms are heavily guarded and spruced up spaces. These workspaces are considered 'posh' – suggesting that they are dust free, full of light and completely air-conditioned. Workstations and washrooms are in pristine condition befitting international/western corporate standards, as are the recreational spaces. The workers and cleaning staff are required to present themselves as 'professionals' – uniformed (in case of cleaning staff), well groomed, decorous, disciplined. These new hi-tech spaces have thus introduced new standards of hygiene and cleanliness as well as created the demand for a new kind of subjectivity embodied by the 'professional' housekeeper. Housekeeping occurs round the clock with modern cleaning tools and supplies to uphold these new standards of cleanliness. These discourses of professional standards are reminiscent of industries and sectors, which are formalized. At the same time, as Aguiar and Herod (2006) note, cleaners inhabit a contradictory position in the global economy – traditionally small and informal cleaning companies have been replaced by 'professionalized' cleaning service firms, which subcontract services to large companies. Yet, these subcontracted firms still maintain some of the inequities long associated with this kind of cleaning work structured by specific class, caste, gender and other power hierarchies. In fact these inequalities are crucial to maintain the apparent deskilling of housekeeping jobs. Ironically jobs cast as repetitive, routinized and simple in fact require a complex set of skills, which workers have to learn. While these skill requirements do not translate into higher wages, they are used to imbue the work with certain attributes of professionalisation in the neoliberal context. In this paper, we trace the ways in which housekeepers' jobs are formalized and simultaneously infused with practices of informality (Agarwala 2013). Their jobs are defined as simultaneously 'low skilled' and professionalized.

In India, women (and men) in the housekeeping sector have traditionally occupied informal, poorly paid jobs. However, the demands of transnational software firms and call centres have dramatically altered this sector. These firms profess to hold completely different (and explicitly 'Western') approaches to hygiene and cleanliness. By drawing on their transnational connections these firms emphasize the 'professional' services they provide, redefining the nature of cleaning work and reconstructing associated skills that go along with it to create new kinds of embodied subjectivities. Firms market their workplaces on the basis of the clean, well-maintained environments they provide including their smart, uniformed, professional housekeepers. Maintaining such sanitized environments has however given rise to norms where cleaning is technologically defined and work and workplace behaviour is heavily scripted and monitored. Although the labour of housekeeping staff plays a major role in making the IT industry a 'booming' sector, contributing to shining India's growth story, their work is still devalued in terms of payment, and dignity of labour.

The proliferation of global firms in India has gone hand in hand with neoliberalism, and as a result, housekeeping activities and their management has emerged as a complex web of subcontracting relationships. In some cases, large, transnational cleaning firms have emerged, or European/American firms have expanded their business in India. These firms bid for cleaning contracts at IT/ITES companies in India and recruit and train workers, either directly or through smaller subcontractors. Many subcontractors have set up businesses within India and these subcontractors in turn hire local workers and train them to adhere to specific organizational requirements of the hi-tech sector. In some cases, local firms have redesigned their systems to meet the requirements of transnational firms; these firms, too, often have multiple subcontractors. In many cases, contractors or subcontractors have complex relationships with regional political candidates or with builders.

These factors form the broader political economy within which cleaning jobs are situated. It is through analyses of the relationships between subcontracting systems, discourses of professionalism and the locally and historically situated connections between caste and cleaning that sense can be made of the contradictory experience of privilege and precarity, which Neeta who was profiled at the beginning of this chapter expresses. We argue that these factors are key to understanding the changing nature of work in the transnational IT/ITES service sector and its attendant gender, class and caste based implications in neoliberal India. We explore these issues through a study of housekeepers in Pune. Pune has experienced amongst the highest growth in the IT/ITES sector and has, over the past several years, projected itself as a 'global city'. Technical educational institutions, corporate group head offices and the city leaders envision the city as the IT hub competing with Hyderabad and Bangalore. Its proximity to Mumbai and sure supply of water and electricity (with the initiative of Maratha Chamber of Commerce) make it a preferred destination for many investors (Forbes 2006). Accompanying the growth of Pune's IT/ITES sector is the need for low-wage labour to provide transportation, housekeeping and security services. Workers in these sectors are residents of Pune or migrants from neighbouring villages who have been adversely affected by the agrarian crisis.

Women and work in Pune and the emergence of house keeping as a sector

Pune is one of the emerging metro cities in Western India. As per the 2011 Census, it had a population of 3,115,431 lakhs (Census of India). As a centre of the British Army's southern Command and Air Force, Pune city has historically experienced certain 'modern' occupations being practiced alongside traditional caste-based occupations and allied services provided to the British (Kosambi 1980; Gadgil 1945, 1962). While this has reproduced the caste–occupation relationship, it has also changed the nature of these occupations. However, the so-called low castes attained modern education in Pune, as it was a centre of reformist ideas and movements since the advent of the British. Kosambi (1980, 212–213) explains that 'in the second half of the nineteenth century western education spread rapidly in Poona'. Deccan Arts College was started in 1857 and The Science College was renamed as the Engineering College in 1868 and was affiliated to Bombay University. In the early 1880s there were 24 government schools and 45 private schools with 2 separate training colleges for male and female teachers. Thus, the reproduction of caste-based skill sets and occupational practices coexisting with mobility continued, largely due to the British education. As Kosambi

(1980) points out, Pune's proximity with Mumbai was also one of the factors shaping its access to British modernity and education always emerged as one of the key areas in this transition to modernity.

After independence, Pune emerged as an important educational and administrative centre. The rural elite around Pune retained the reformist milieu and also consolidated caste-based alliances for democratic politics. It was during the 1960s that the city emerged as a major industrial centre; new industrial jobs were created in this period. Automobile, chemical engineering and manufacturing activities dominated this period alongside booming allied small scale industry. A few major Indian and international players started their plants in Pune. A number of public sector undertakings were also established in Pune including Hindustan Antibiotics. This attracted skilled and unskilled migrant workers from across India (Tambe 2010). Despite changes in occupational fields, the caste system, that historically has been regulating the stigmatized occupations such as scavenging and cleaning, continued to define occupational choices and practices of the lowest caste groups. Not only have certain occupations been historically considered low status and undesirable but the people practicing these occupations have been treated with condemnation as the bearers of inferior labour. In more contemporary context, the inter-linkages between caste and occupations have become more complex in the industrial and informational sector and yet caste and class overlap, compel certain people to work in the same professions as their predecessors. This explains why in the present study we found that many of the frontline housekeepers were from Dalit or other so-called lower castes, or at best from the intermediate castes (OBCs).

Cleaning also has a gender dimension, given women's assumed 'natural' inclination towards keeping house. Traditionally, cleaning jobs are considered appropriate for women (Moss 1997). Historically, women have been relegated to the domestic sphere and their caring work in the home has been the hallmark of their femininity. Women's biological ability to reproduce and assumed natural proclivity toward caring and nurturing has thus led to a gender division of labour, establishing men as the primary breadwinner. As a result, women's work outside the home is undervalued, low paid, accounting for their secondary status in the labour market. At the same time this is why occupational sex stereotypes have emerged, such that certain jobs are considered more suitable for women and others for men. Most caring jobs like nursing, cleaning, cooking have thus been feminized, and considered mere extension of women's domestic work. However, this argument gets more complicated when one takes into consideration how gender is mediated through race, class, caste, and other differences. For example, anti-racist feminists in the United States have long argued that in Anglo-American cultures, historically, poor and black women (and men) have worked (often enslaved or indentured) outside their own homes in the domestic spaces of white, middle and upper class women and men. In such conditions race further devalues the bearer of the labour, marking black bodies as inferior (Hill Collins 2000). Similarly, in India while domestic work has always been considered women's work, class and caste privilege has allowed some women to offload the burden of such work on women and men of lower class and caste status whose labour is devalued and deskilled. Nevertheless, men still predominate in cooking, cleaning and other such 'feminine' jobs when those are paid, and fall within the purview of the public domain in the catering, laundry, food and restaurant business; such jobs continue to remain off-limit to women given the caste/patriarchal ideology restraining women's wage work for maintaining their 'purity' and honour (Raju and Bagchi 1994).

Historically, women's performances as *lavani* (erotic dance form performed by Dalit women) dancers during Peshwa period are mentioned in literature on Pune and Maharahstra. Rege (2002) illustrates how famines in parts of Maharashtra led to migration of women from lower castes to Pune. Their labour was appropriated during the Peshwa rule either as prostitutes or as erotic dancers or as workers in various workshops.

In Pune, women worked as teachers in government schools with reformist initiatives during the colonial period. Although prostitution continued to be another area of women's work, some women entered teaching and nursing jobs during the British period. Others participated in large numbers in the informal labour market. They worked as florists, petty shopkeepers, vegetable vendors, and cooks in middle class families. In the post-independence period of the 1960s and 1970s, women's participation in the organized sector expanded slightly making them visible in the public sphere. Some joined industrial jobs as well.

Nature of subcontracting relations in housekeeping work

In the past decade, India has seen the revamping and unprecedented expansion of the housekeeping sector. Traditionally, cleaning jobs were performed by paid employees, who were an integral part of the industrial or professional service organization. Later direct employment was replaced by contracted jobs, wherein small contractors hired workers from the lowest caste for jobs, which were widely recognized as least desirable and most stigmatized. With the IT boom since the early 2000s, multinational full service property management firms have emerged. They offer a comprehensive range of services. Many IT companies hire such large corporations to take care of all their cleaning and property maintenance needs. They sign a 'service contract' annually. Companies provide building repairs, solve electrical problems as well as provide what is referred to as 'soft services' such as housekeeping. Housekeeping contractors' marketing brochures depict uniformed women and men in gloves, cleaning with modern and 'glamorous' cleaning equipment like vacuum cleaners, using the latest chemicals. This depiction of housekeeping exists alongside the stigma associated with cleaning work and the low caste people who perform it. Additionally, these jobs are poorly paid as they are seen as unskilled work. As a result, recruitment companies often have scouts placed in poor rural areas from where they recruit people offering them jobs and in some cases housing in the city. One recruitment company, for example, told us that they specifically target areas where rural poverty is high and then provide workers with incentives to migrate to cities such as the provision of food and dormitories.

Despite current efforts to professionalize the sector, lower caste people have been traditionally considered suitable for cleaning jobs. These jobs are condemned along with the workers who perform them. The normative frame of purity and impurity of various castes was the defining ideology. As a result, these are the jobs which are low paid and less desired by the higher caste and class workers. Under the caste system these occupations were hereditary and even today scavenging work is allotted on caste lines within government offices. The nature of the 'dirty' work allocated, performed and embodied by these marginalized groups historically worked to stigmatize them and perpetuate hierarchies that maintained the hegemony of higher castes in India.

Although housekeeping involves cleaning, which is considered to be women's work because it was established outside the confines of the home (which is the sphere of unpaid domestic work), in the wage economy, men predominate in it. But given the manner in which caste works in India, these housekeeping jobs are mostly performed by men from lower caste and class backgrounds. With the transformations in Indian cities fuelled by more new economy jobs like IT and financial services in recent years, which has allowed the expansion of the housekeeping sector, it is not surprising that over time poor and lower caste women have increasingly become part of this industry.

Narratives of women in Pune's housekeeping sector serving IT companies

An analysis of workers' narratives reveals that there are several ways in which housekeeping work is distinguished from long-established domestic service jobs, which also focus on cleaning. The notion of 'standards' pervades emerging cleaning industries, which gives the impression that there are universally established, scientifically determined methods of cleaning. In addition, gendered stereotypes of women's assumed 'natural' skills in domestic work are challenged through the introduction of technology and training. At the same time, notions of appropriate cleaning jobs for women and men are reinscribed.

In describing the nature of their work, women interviewed for this project frequently mention the use of chemicals and gloves in their work. Swetha, a 40 year old woman who works at a large IT firm describes her job in the following way – "First we dry mop the floor. Then we go in the pantry and then we clean the washrooms – commodes, mirror - for this they give us liquid; we get R6 and R2. We use R6 for commode and we use R2 for the floor". Similarly, Manjhu who works for a small company says that her supervisor trained her when she first started working. She notes, "housekeeping work involves dusting, dry mop, wet mop, toilet cleaning, cleaning tea machines and we have to work as per our supervisor's expectations". Cleaning jobs at companies are described as being different from domestic work performed in homes, and Manjhu who worked as a domestic worker before she got her housekeeping job says, "we have to clean the toilets, deep cleaning of toilets… every day [at home] we clean the toilet, but not in such a manner". The use of gloves and uniforms gives women like Manjhu a sense of pride in their work – "we have hand gloves, mask and a goggle while cleaning the toilet. Our safety is ensured. We get dusters from time to time. They take care of us. And I tell you one thing, no one behaves rudely with us. No one, not employees, big big bosses, neither our security supervisors, nor maintenance supervisors – no one. Our security, maintenance and staff, everyone is very nice",

While the use of gloves and uniforms are widely prevalent, the feeling of being 'taken care of' however is less common amongst the women we interviewed, particularly those working at large organizations. For many women, subcontracting chains result in significant work intensification as well as job uncertainty. Vijaya, who works for an organization with 500 employees, describes her work – 'At first there were three of us but then they dismissed the third person. I told our supervisor if you have dismissed that person then at least raise our salary but he didn't listen". As a result of her workload, she arrives half an hour early (without overtime pay) to complete her tasks. As scholars like Saini (2010) note, the contract Labour Act of 1970 is poorly enforced and the labour practices of firms remain largely unregulated. When asked about her salary, Vijaya reports that her "salary is not yet decided. My Madam told me you start your job I will observe your work and accordingly I will give you salary". It is the combination of job uncertainty and intensification, which makes women working as housekeepers extremely vulnerable in their jobs.

Ethnographic work conducted in Chile, South Africa, Canada and Australia reveals a similar trend towards the outsourcing of cleaning and the resulting vulnerability of workers. A study of janitors working in shopping malls and corporate skyscrapers in Chile, for example, reveals that workers' wages are depressed due to the significant growth of subcontracting cleaning firms, some of which are large foreign-owned multinationals. Workers have no unions and are employed on short-term contracts (Tomic and Trumper 2006). Campbell and Peeters similarly trace the ways in which the tender process (where organizations requiring cleaning services invite subcontractors to provide a bid for the provision of service) has led to fierce price competition between service providers in Australia. Given that capital costs for potential contractors is low, and labour costs are high, there is significant pressure to reduce wages and intensify work in order to win contracts (Campbell and Peeters 2008; Bezuidenhout and Fakier 2006 and Aguiar 2006).

While the subcontracting structure has an impact on all workers, women workers are particularly vulnerable. Gender-based stereotypes and wage discrimination was widely noted by all the women interviewed for our project. In a study of male and female cleaners, Coyle (cited in Aguiar 2006) notes that job titles are often different for women and men, and this serves to mask the similarities between cleaning jobs and support gender based wage differences. In a similar way, a study of office cleaners in Toronto shows that women's jobs are constructed as 'light' because they involve dusting, mopping and sweeping while men's jobs are seen as 'heavy' because they involve the use of machines in more public areas such as lobbies and corridors (Aguiar 2001). The largely unconvincing distinction between light and heavy work is used to justify wage discrimination. In a similar way, some women housekeepers in India reported that men earn more than women. This earning differential is explained in terms of the different work which women are expected to do, as Neeta summarize, 'Boys do night duty and women do the day shift. Men are paid INR 6,500 and women INR 5,800.' Aside from not being allowed to work at night, women are also not allowed to clean men's toilets or to clean employees' desks, since the latter is said to involve 'lifting computers'. Women housekeepers also note that the work of serving guests to the organization (often foreign clients) is often reserved for male housekeeping staff. These distinctions between appropriate men's work and women's work are linked to perceptions of the need for women's 'safety'. In the absence of a union or workers' association and in the context of the highly competitive job environment, there is little opportunity for women to challenge the wage discrimination they face.

Comparing housekeeping work to domestic services

In India, women working as housekeepers talk about the hazards of work intensification and job insecurity in the housekeeping sector in relation to the conditions of employment in the other sector in which most women have experience – domestic service in households. While some women note that as housekeepers they earn more than they otherwise could in domestic service, others report exactly the opposite. This suggests that wages in both the housekeeping sector and in domestic service are highly variable. Accordingly, women interviewed for this project ranged from [i] those that preferred housekeeping work, [ii] those who were engaged in both jobs, and [iii] those who preferred domestic work but faced family objections or were unable to get domestic jobs and were therefore employed as housekeepers.

Most women in housekeeping had been employed in private households in the past. Manjhu, who has a very long commute to work, explains her preference for her current job despite the amount of time it takes her to get to work – "I don't feel like doing that kind of work (domestic work). I do not have that kind of enthusiasm… Here facilities are nice. And when we work at home (as a domestic worker), the attitude of the owner of the house of looking at us, our work is different but when we work in the company, we work as a worker. We properly get paid for our work in the company. But if we work in the houses as domestic help, there are chances of this turning out to be autocracy…work in the houses as domestic help means you have to tolerate autocracy you have to follow their orders and fulfil their demands. In the company there is no autocracy. In the house, they say, don't do rotis, do some other work, then we have to that other work. Here, it is not like that in the company. We have to do our stipulated work".

Vijaya reports that she was employed as a 'cook' in two households. Her income was considerably lower than what she could earn as a housekeeper but she aspires to return to domestic work in the future. She explains that she would like to take "any type of job but I don't want to go in housekeeping … (when I was a domestic worker), at one place the owner of the house left Pune and at other place the lady of the house told me we can't afford to give your payment as there was some problem at their house. In this way I lost my job as a domestic worker". Women appreciate the job proximity as well as the opportunity to establish their own schedules, which can accompany domestic work, especially when they are employed as part-time workers in multiple households (Ray and Qayum 2009). Earlier research in Pune and other cities suggests that domestic labour market is segmented geographically, as most women obtain jobs through neighbourhood networks and their family situation demands that they devote time to family and work alternatively by ensuring vicinity from home (Tambe 2009). This greater control over their place and time of work in domestic work, however, also has a negative impact on women. Neeta explains that while she would prefer 'washing clothes and doing dishes in different houses' she cannot do this because "my husband doesn't like it… Because he can't trust me". While domestic work necessitates movement in the public sphere, her husband prefers the confinement in an organizational space, which a housekeeping job entails.

For some women, housekeeping jobs in fact supplement continued involvement in domestic work. Sangeeta describes her schedule – "At eight in the morning I go to Sanjay Park to work in a house and come home by 11:30. I leave home soon at 12 and walk to the company office in Viman Nagar. It takes me one hour to reach office. I arrive for duty on time at 1 p.m. I work from 1 p.m. to 9 p.m. and then go home". This also suggests that housekeeping job is not fetching enough money to handle family expenses in neo-liberal times. Women workers have to undertake additional jobs in domestic work sector for survival needs.

Caste-based stigma and housekeeping

While women compare their housekeeping and domestic jobs, many note the greater stigma associated with housekeeping. This is because of norms in domestic service that workers can sometimes insulate themselves with the more stigmatized dimensions of cleaning work such as cleaning toilets. Many women reported that they had to deal with both their own stigmas and those of others around cleaning toilets.

Swetha explains the process of coming to terms with her work – "I felt very bad, initially I cried when I was doing this work. I never did this kind of work but I just gathered courage and did this kind of work". Coming to terms with her work involves reconciling her own caste position and class aspirations with the traditional connection between cleaning and lower caste women. Many women report both wanting to challenge the stigma associated with toilet cleaning and the need to maintain social norms. Neeta notes "what is shameful about any job? Work is work and we do it for our children". At the same time, she does not tell her extended family members about her work and only reports that she is working in 'a company.' In describing her work, she notes with pride that caste and class barriers are not maintained in her workplace and she and her colleagues use the same toilets and canteen facilities as employees and managers at the firm. Thus, by crafting stories which highlight these workplaces as neutral territories devoid of some of the traditional patriarchal and caste based practices, women like Neeta negotiate the everyday challenges from patriarchy and caste hierarchy.

This does not mean that women are unaware of the manner in which such jobs are stigmatized. However, their narratives highlight that doing stigmatized work is justified and necessary in order to support their families. Many of the women interviewed had significant aspirations for their children, even though most of them also discussed these aspirations in conjunction with the many difficulties they faced and therefore their uncertainty about whether these aspirations were realistic. Neeta describes her children – "I want them to study well and stand on their own feet. I won't marry them off in a hurry… My only wish is that they should study. I will educate them on my own. He (husband) doesn't support me. He doesn't speak about education, he has no desire to. I paint dreams of education for my children. I work hard for 12 hours for you, I tell them". Vijaya similarly notes, "I feel that they should become someone good, but we cannot afford it. How can we do anything in this case? Not even a single rupee is left from the salary". Although it is clearly evident that housekeeping work allows women to support their families, the emergence of this sector in India does not seem to have made a significant impact on several structural issues, which significantly shape working women's lives. First, they are paid at or below minimum wage defined by the act and are not given social security benefits. This makes them very vulnerable as workers. Secondly, gender-based wage discrimination pervades the sector. Third, many women provide examples of the violence and harassment which they face at home. Swetha describes her husband's objection to her employment outside the home. She notes, "My mister (husband) used to drink a lot of alcohol. Sometimes he would come near the company gate. That was troublesome for me. He would come in the company and used to say things. I would feel awkward because there were 80–90 ladies, only my husband used to come till gate. That's not right. So I left the job". After a period of unemployment and extreme poverty, as well as the death of her husband, Swetha returned to housekeeping work to support her children. While in isolated cases the women we interviewed described how their waged work outside the home as housekeepers have led to a greater involvement of men in domestic work, most women report only minor shifts in the sharing of household work. As Aguiar's research (2001) with women office cleaners in Toronto reveals, women may repeat cleaning work three times per day – as housekeepers, as domestic workers, and as family members. Indeed many housekeepers have extremely long work days, as Vijaya describes:

> I get up at 4 o'clock. After bathing I first make tea and give girls tea and *Khari* then prepare breakfast for them, make their tiffin ready. My brother-in-law's daughter has morning school, that is from 7 to 12. They take tiffin with them and come home at 12.30. After that I cook for all of us and then I clean utensils, wash clothes, etc. Before going to office I finish all household chores... I leave home around 8.30 and reach office by 9 o'clock. My duty hours are from 9 to 5. After reaching home I again finish rest of the chores, make tea for everyone and start preparation of dinner. Around 11 o'clock I go to bed.

Conclusions

Given the demands of the new hi-tech economy, workers (both women and men) are being actively recruited from urban and rural areas for housekeeping jobs in India. Based on our interviews, it appears that most housekeeping companies proactively recruit from poor and depressed areas in and around Pune. This raises several questions – Does working in this new 'modern' hi-tech sector strip these workers of old stigmas based on caste? Communities and peoples considered 'dirty', 'unclean' or 'untouchable' are now finding employment in IT firms, symbolized by high standards of cleanliness and hygiene. Is this pattern of recruitment altering caste structure in India or is it reproducing it? Similarly, are these firms reproducing gendered practices of labour recruitment or are they contributing to the alteration of these?

Our study reveals that the housekeeping sector provides both promise and an entrenchment of gendered norms for women workers. Contractors promise regular salaries at the legislated minimum wage. Another factor luring women to join this sector is the supposed promise of rightful access to Provident Fund (pension) and subsidized medical services. Despite these promises, many of the workers we interviewed did not have access to these legally sanctioned benefits. There is little standardization of wages in the sector and women are sometimes paid less than men. Due to casualisation and subcontracting, housekeepers are deprived of many legal protections. To reduce attrition rates and control demands for pay hikes, employers treat pension (P. F.) cards as benefits provided to loyal and hardworking workers only. In other words, there is a double standard in the proliferation of transnational business norms – the 'international standards' apply at the level of disciplining the workers and maintaining flexible labour regimes for the companies, but do not help ensure social security benefits.

Nevertheless, the newly emerging recruiting networks, clean pristine work environment of prestigious IT firms, wearing of uniforms, acquiring new 'western' cleaning skills, working with modern electronic cleaning gadgets and supplies has also brought with it a new sense of pride and sense of achievement to the housekeepers. "Who doesn't want to work in a nice office?", remarked one of the recruiters. Most of the housekeepers interviewed have few other employment options, apart from domestic service.

The professionalisation of housekeeping services therefore brings several tangible advantages for workers. No longer constructed as 'outcast' jobs, cleaning has been discursively resituated as a key organizational function, which demands efficient and standardized management styles. Transnational corporations with financial means and an interest in maintaining the formality of their employment arrangements implement 'contracts', which are written to meet the requirements of labour law. Cleaning staff sometimes use the same washrooms as office staff, and eat in the same canteens, which is not common for workers historically employed in cleaning and domestic service work in India (Ray and Qayum 2009). In fact, this particular feature, that is who one eats with in a communal space has historically been a key marker of caste hierarchy in India. However, for some workers eating in the same canteen as company professionals was much more costly and they note that they would have preferred another arrangement. But for paucity of time allotted to eat they have to continue using the same canteen.

At the same time, a degree of work informality pervades the sector, and in fact, is further masked behind the veneer of professionalisation. Workers feel as though they are benefactors of and dependent on subcontractor goodwill, often reminiscent of older feudal relations, rather than treated as 'formal' wage earners. Informal hierarchies of work structured by caste and gender stereotypes continue to pervade the work. Workers receive training on 'tools' and 'machines' which do not recognize long standing patriarchal norms that have historically feminized these jobs due to women's gendered and racialized responsibilities for household and childcare work. Often men are preferred over women for night shifts (given that companies operate round the clock and they do not want to compromize women's perceived domestic responsibilities and safety). There is also evidence that women are paid less than men. It is impossible for workers to receive a clear breakdown of deductions. At the same time, some housekeeping women earn approximately the same amount as their husbands and they, as a result exert some influence over household decisions and the future of their children. Workers individually manage the 'shame' associated with cleaning work, and hide, rather than express pride in the nature of their work. In these ways, workers experience the emergence of housekeeping work as posing new opportunities as well as new challenges.

Endnotes

[1]   This project was funded by the Social Sciences and Research Council of Canada. (Grant # 410-2011-1901.) We would like to acknowledge the invaluable contributions of several research associates: Vandana Palsane, Vandana Kulkurni, Prashant Apte, Rahul Dalvi, Dhananjay Paigude, Rahul Paithankar, Swaroop Waghmare, Chintamani Dengale, Nilima Gawade and Nitin Thorat and all the respondents who spared their invaluable time to share their experiences. The names of the authors appear in alphabetical order.

References

Agarwala, R. 2013. *Informal Labor, Formal Politics, and Dignified Discontent in India.* Cambridge: Cambridge University Press.

Aguiar, Luis, L. M., and A. Herod. eds. 2006. *The Dirty Work of Neoliberalism: Cleaners in the Global Economy,* Malden: Wiley-Blackwell.

Aguiar, Luis, L. M. 2001. 'Doing Cleaning Work 'Scientifically': The Reorganization of Work in the Contract Building Cleaning Industry', *Economic and Industrial Democracy,* 22: 239–69.

Apte, D. P., and R. G. Pendse. 1956. Poona: *A Resurvey: the Changing Pattern of Employment and Earnings.* Gokhale Institute of Politics and Economics, Pune.

Bezuidenhout, A., and K. Fakier. 2006. 'Maria's Burden: Contract Cleaning and the Crisis of Social Reproduction in Post-Apartheid South Africa', In *the Dirty Work of Neoliberalism: Cleaners in the Global Economy,* edited by Luis, L. M. Aguiar and Andrew Herod. Malden: Wiley-Blackwell.

Campbell, I., and M. Peeters. 2008. 'Low Pay, Compressed Schedules and High Work Intensity: A Study of Contract Cleaners in Australia', *Australian Journal of Labour Economics,* 11(1): 27–46.

Chanda, R. 2005. 'Spreading the Benefits of BPO Growth', *The Financial Express,* April 5. Accessed December 19, 2013. http://www.censusindia.gov.in/2011census/population_enumeration. aspx.

Gadgil, D. R. 1945 and 1962. 'Poona: A Socio Economic Survey. Part I and II', Gokhale Institute of Politics and Economics, Pune.

Kosambi, M. 1980. 'Bombay and Poona: A Sociology–Ecological Study of Two Indian Cities –1650–1900', Stockholm: University of Stockholm.

Hill Collins, P. 2000. *Black Feminist thought: Knowledge, Consciousness and the Politics of Empowerment,* New York: Routledge.

Mirchandani, K., S. Mukherjee, and S. Tambe. nd. 'Hidden infrastructures of transnationalism: India's new auxiliary service sectors'. Unpublished manuscript.

Moss, P. 1997. 'Spaces of Resistance, Spaces of Respite: Franchise Housekeepers Keeping House in the Workplace and at Home', *Gender, Place and Culture: A Journal of Feminist Geography,* 4(2): 179–96.

Mukherjee, S. 2008. 'The Bangalore Brand: A City of Empowerment?', in *Producing the IT Miracle: The Neoliberalizing State and Changing Gender and Class Regimes in India.* PhD Dissertation. Syracuse University.

Poster, Winifred, R. 2007. 'Who's on the Line? Indian Call Centre Agents Pose as Americans for U.S Outsourced Firms', *Industrial Relation,* 46(2): 271–304.

Raju, S., and D. Bagchi. 1994. *Women and Work in South Asia: Regional Patterns and Perspectives,* London and New York: Routledge.

Ray, R., and S. Qayum. 2009. *Cultures of Servitude: Modernity, Domesticity and Class in India.* Palo Alto: Stanford University Press.

Rege, S. 2002. 'Conceptualising Popular Culture: 'Lavani' and 'Powada' in Maharashtra', *Economic and Political Weekly,* 11(37): 1038–47. (Mar. 16–22, 2002).

Sassen, S. 2012. *Cities in a World Economy,* (Second ed.). Thousand Oaks: Pine Forge Press.

Saini, Debi, S. 2010. 'Contract Law', *Indian Journal of Industrial Relations* 46(1).

Tambe S. 2010, Unpublished, 'The world of Informal Labour in Pune city', Report, DP Coalition, Informal Sector Economy and Occupations Project, Pune.

Tomic, P., and R. Trumper. 2006. 'Manufacturing Modernity: Cleaning, Dirt and Neoliberalism in Chile', in *the Dirty Work of Neoliberalism: Cleaners in the Global Economy*, edited by Aguiar, L. M. and Herod, A. Malden: Wiley-Blackwell.

Tikekar, A. 2000, *Shahar Pune*, Pune: Nilubhau Limaye Foundation.

Van den Broek, D. 2004. 'We Have Values: Customers, Control and Corporate Ideology in Call Centre Operations', *New Technology, Work and Employment*, 19(1): 2–13.

Vasavi, A. R. 2008. 'Serviced from India: The Making of India's Global Youth Workforce', *In an Outpost of the Global Information Economy: Work and Workers in India's Information Technology Industry*, edited by Carol Upadhya and A. R. Vasavi. Delhi: Routledge.

6

Persistent Inequalities and Deepened Burden of Work?
An Analysis of Women's Employment in Delhi

Neetha N.

Introduction

The capital city of Delhi with its neighbouring and growing satellite hubs such as Gurgaon and New Okhla Industrial Development Authority (henceforth NOIDA) offer varied and increasing possibilities for work, which is evident from the constant stream of in-migrants to the city. However, one of the most important trends, which has occasionally but casually been highlighted in the discussion on the city is the low participation of women in economic activities[1]. The statistics on this aspect itself is shocking, given the expansion of service-oriented industries in recent years, which are often assumed to attract a large number of women. The data also indicate much deeper issues – of the nature and the gendered specificities of employment created, reflecting the existing notions and understanding of women's work both within the family as well as at work places. Sectoral/occupational concentration of women is universal and given this, the changing structure of employment would undoubtedly define the workforce in terms of gender. Alongside gender, social and demographic factors are also critical in determining as to who gets employed in various sectors/occupations. Thus, even within the overall poor participation of women, there are sectors or occupations where women's shares are higher or lower, or where women from a certain section of the population are more, indicating the larger social and economic factors that determine women's entry into paid work. These concentrations also indicate the gendered stereotyping of labour markets, which in turn are often based on the patriarchal notions of women's work – highly anchored in their role in social reproduction.

In more contemporary context, the liberalized economic regime, underlined by the growth of modern service sectors with gendered notions of skills skewed in favour of women, has resulted in an expansion of women's participation in the labour market in many countries of the world. The education and skill characteristics of these workers are often assumed to have further enhanced the positive vibes in the labour market with better wages, working conditions and renegotiation of women workers rights. This economic attainment alongside their social capital could pose challenges to existing power structures, questioning gender relations both at the workplace as well as at the individual level.

The city of Delhi with its diversity in terms of women workers across different sectors provides an interesting site for examining some of these propositions. Factory work has been one major sector of women's employment in the city much before the growth of the service sector. Although gendered nature of work places in general is an acknowledged phenomenon, various occupations carry specificities of their own. However, it may be presumed that modern work places would be more gender-egalitarian as well as be domains of workers' negotiations, which continue to rupture the gendered codes. In this backdrop, the paper addresses women workers in factory work and in service sectors in a comparative framework in the city of Delhi in order to interrogate some of the central questions related to gendered nature of various work places and, the ongoing negotiations that destabilizes the existing gendered norms.

Both secondary and primary data have been used. Secondary data on employment from National Sample Survey (NSS) are used to provide an overall context of women's employment, sectoral dimensions and changes. Primary data used in the paper were collected as part of a study conducted by Centre for Women's Development Studies (CWDS) during 2008–2009.[2] A crucial hypothesis that the paper examines is the assumption of modern workspaces as more egalitarian and gender sensitive because of the profile of women workers, which constitute young and better educated women. The rest of the paper is divided into five parts. Following the Introduction, the section titled 'Low and Volatile Female Work Participation Rates', provides an overall pattern of women's employment in Delhi and its changes over time. Drawing upon the secondary data, this section discusses the sectoral profile of workers that contextualize some of the workplace issues. The next section 'Mirroring the Sectoral Shifts: The Micro-profile of Women Workers' provides an overview of women workers across prominent sectors of their employment, which brings the issue of labour market segmentation to the forefront. The section titled, 'Basic Labour Rights' explores the working conditions and employment relations across select sectors and provides a comparative picture of work relations in different sectors. Further, the discussion under 'Gendered Homes: Burden of House Work' picks up the issue of unpaid housework burden of women workers in different sectors, which suggests the prevalence of patriarchal divisions of work even with the changing profile of women workers which have implications for women's agency and empowerment. Finally, the last section summarizes the findings of the paper.

Low and volatile female work participation rates

The first and the foremost critical variable in the analysis of gendered labour markets is the participation rate of women in economic activity. Along with formalized gender discrimination, attitudes and behaviour on the part of employers can further curtail women's capacity to take advantage of economic opportunities (Kabeer 2012). Employers' preference for male workers, on the grounds that women have a weaker attachment to the labour market, evident in higher rates of absenteeism and turnover, affect women's employment adversely in many sectors (Anker and Hein 1985). On the other hand, preference for women workers marks labour-intensive export sectors. The availability of flexible cheap labour combined with docility explains such preferences (Ghosh 2002).

As per the Census 2011, female work participation rates in Delhi is just 10.6 per cent as against male participation rate of 53.1 per cent Though there is a marginal rise from 2001 when it was 9.4 per cent, the proportion of working women in the city possibility remains the least in the country.[3] The NSS estimates for 2011–12 for the city matches the Census estimates, which puts the female work participation rates at 10.7 per cent (in comparison to 52.7 per cent for males) showing an improvement from 2004–05 when the same was just 8.8 per cent. Such low work participation rates for women do not match the established understanding, as metropolis is often assumed to offer increased and diverse opportunities to women from various socio-economic categories.

A related trend, which is of concern, is the fact that, not only are the proportions of women workers low but the levels of female work participation have actually been highly volatile. As per the NSS data, the percentage of workers among women aged 15–59 moved forward from a low 13.2 per cent in 1993–94 to reach 14.7 per cent in 1999–2000 before making a sharp downturn to reach 11.2 per cent in 2004–05. The rate again showed an increase in 2011–12 to 14.9 per cent. What is particularly important is that this fluctuation in work participation is not just in terms of proportions but is also in absolute numbers. According to the NSS estimates, the number of women workers of all ages declined from 3,79,900 in 1999–2000 to 3,31,200 in 2004–05, which show an increase in 2011–12 to 5,69,678. Such a scenario of volatility with very low work participation rates obviously disturbs the prevalent assumptions regarding women's opportunities for employment in the city and invites serious consideration.

Figure 6.1 presents the trend across the three categories of employment status, namely among the self-employed, regular and casual workers in the female and male workforce respectively for Delhi. It may be seen that the proportions of casual workers in the female workforce declined sharply from 18.2 per cent of all women workers to 1.9 per cent over the decade, i.e., 1993–94 to 2011–12. The share of the self-employed, on the other hand shows considerable fluctuations with a long term decline from 24.2 per cent in 1993–94 to 20.9 per cent in 2011–12. This is reflective of the contingency driven character of self-employment and the risks and uncertainties associated with such employment. What is interesting is the increase in proportion of regular workers, almost consistently though the latest data, show a decline of about 2 percentage points. The share of regular workers increased from an initial 56.7 per cent in 1993–94 to account for about more than one-third (77 per cent) of women workers in 2011–12. This is quite in contrast

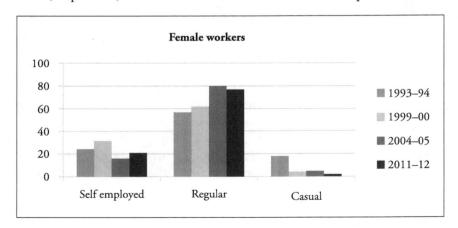

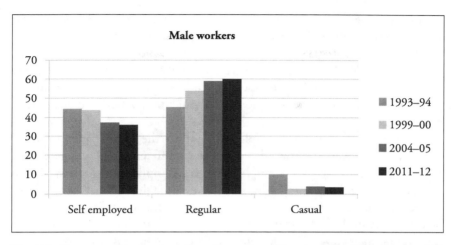

Fig. 6.1 Percentage distribution of usually employed female and male workers aged 15 and above across categories of employment status – Delhi (1993–94 to 2011–12)

Source: NSS employment and Unemployment data – Various Rounds

to the structure of employment in urban India, wherein the percentages of regular, self-employed and casual workers are 48.9, 36.6, and 14.4, respectively.

In a sense, this large scale movement across categories of employment confirms the proposition regarding volatility in women's employment. This becomes particularly clear when one compares it with that of male distribution. For women, in one phase when casual work came under pressure, many women seem to have taken to self-employment, though regular work was also sought for. In the second phase, when obviously self-employment did not offer adequate opportunities, there was a movement towards regular wage employment. The decline in the share of the self-employed, a reduced significance of casual work alongside an increase in regular employment is also noticeable among male workers. However, these changes are consistent and not sharp unlike the changes in women's employment.

It should be borne in mind that the employment categories used in the NSS surveys differ substantively from the legal definitions of permanent/ regular, casual, and contract workers. For example, the distinction between regular and casual workers in the NSS is merely based on the fact that regular workers receive salary or wages on a regular, weekly or monthly basis (i.e., not on daily or periodic renewal of short term work contract), whereas casual workers receive daily wages or occasional contract work. Thus, the picture of increasing shares of regular workers indicates the rising proportions of regular wage workers, but this does not mean increasing shares of better quality work or employment with greater levels of social security or rights and protections.[4] Further, it should be noted that casual piece rated wage workers working at home for employers under the subcontracting or putting out system are also placed in the category of self-employed, although they would also be a part of casual-piece rated wage workers.

Changes in the nature of employment affect the social composition of workers, as not everyone could be absorbed in different employments. Who gets absorbed in what kind of employment is a complicated issue determined by a host of factors. As much as, or sometimes more than human endowment of women determining their choice of employment, social and cultural factors are critical. Thus, sharp shifts in nature of employment are surely to disadvantage a section of the female population while benefiting some.

The structure of women's employment in Delhi

A closer look at the distribution of women workers by broad industry division gives some indication of factors and features involved in the fall and volatility in women's work participation rates. In Table 6.1 the NSS estimates of distribution of the men and women workforce for Delhi by broad industry divisions is given for comparison.

Table 6.1 Distribution of usually employed principal and subsidiary status workers aged 15 and above by broad industry divisions[i]

Year and sex of workers	Manu-facturing	Construc-tion	Whole sale and retail trade	Services (1)	Services (2)	All indus-tries given in table
1999–00 Women	18.9	0	8.7	59.4	5.3	92.3
2004–05 Women	10.9	3.1	8.0	55.9	19.6	97.5
2011–12 Women	9.6	0.5	20.8	60.9	7.9	99.1
1999–00 Men	27.4	8.7	28.6	21.6	1.8	88.1

2004–05 Men	28.3	8.1	27.0	21.7	1.6	86.7
2011–12 Men	22.4	4.8	24.1	41.3	1.27	93.9

Source: NSS employment and Unemployment data – Various Rounds

While most of the industry categories are self-explanatory, Services 1 covers the sub-categories of the National Industrial Classification (NIC) such as Education, Finance and related activities, business activities, computer related activities, public administration, health and social work, etc. These are services associated with the more advanced and mainstream forms of productive economic activity that contribute the major share of the GDP and may also be termed as a complex of mainstream or organized/institution/ company/firm/profession based services. The second category of services – Services 2 – are far more subsidiary in terms of contributing to the GDP, although they are significant in terms of women's employment. This sector comprises of private households with employed persons and includes all kinds of domestic personnel such as maids, cooks, gardeners, baby sitters and so on for women this largely means paid domestic work.

The most striking feature regarding changes in the share of different industries in women's employment in Delhi is the sharp fall in the share of manufacturing, especially between the years 1999–2000. The huge increase in the share of domestic work (the second category of services) marks this phase, which seems to have petered out in the later phase.[5] What is striking for the latter period is the huge increase in the share of trade, of which the share of wholesales is negligible.

It may be observed that the shift from manufacturing to paid domestic work or retail trade runs parallel to the shift of women workers from self-employment to regular work as discussed above. Thus, it seems that the most substantial increase in regular work for women in Delhi has been in the sphere of domestic work and retail trade. However, it is the fall in the share of manufacturing that distinguishes the changes in distribution of women workers in Delhi from that of the aggregate picture.[6]

The increased share of women in trade is reflective of the changes in the nature of retail business, especially in cities.[7] Most women employed in retail industry work in Non-Directory and Directory Establishments, which are distinguished on the basis of the number of employees – the former with at least one hired worker, but less than 6, and the latter with 6 and above.[8] Within retail, about half of the women workers are employed in smaller Non-Directory retail units. Of late, there has been a massive expansion of relatively larger modern retail trade with the coming up of corporate retail outlets – the shopping malls, which have led to the emergence of a new array of sales workers in Directory services. Women engaged in their own account retail trade establishments and therefore self-employed, is the smallest segment with roughly one-fifth of the total women workforce engaged in the sector (Neetha and Mazumdar 2010).

The stagnant share of the more white-collared services in women's employment is a worrisome feature, particularly since these services have long accounted for the overwhelming majority of women workers in the capital city. The expectations of globalization-induced growth of women-friendly new services leading to expansion of employment opportunities for women, appear to have been belied, or are perhaps of insufficient order to compensate for losses in the more traditional segments of organized services.

The changing industrial distribution of workers is more critical for women as apart from gender, stereotyping of occupations based on caste, migrant and regional statuses do exist which makes shifts across industries highly unlikely. Thus, expansion of a women friendly industry/sector may result only in the absorption of a given set of women. For instance, the growth of domestic work in the city, although has provided employment opportunities for a number of women, for many this does not appear as a choice at all. On the other hand, though employment in one sector may appear as a possibility for women, employer's preference for a sub-category of women may adversely affect opportunities for the rest. The known preference for young women in export manufacturing and also in customer oriented service industries explains the negligible presence of older women in such occupations (Ghosh 2002; Mazumdar 2007).

The composition of the more prominent industries and services in any given city, and the relative weight of the women dominated industries/sectors also determine the differences between men and women's work participation. There can be little doubt that gender based divisions in labour processes, related stereotypes of jobs that women can or cannot do or are better or less skilled, and gender based preferences of employers differentiated by perception of skills have increasingly become more standardized across cities (Mazumdar 2007).

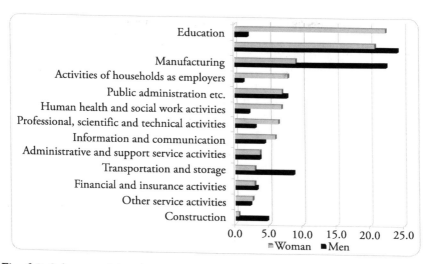

Fig. 6.2 Sub-sectoral distribution of men and women workers in Delhi – 2011–12

The detailed distribution of workers across industries[9] elucidates the gendered stereotyping of labour markets (Fig. 6.2). The first point that emerges is that education is the largest sector of employment for women in Delhi, employing about 22.4 per cent of women workers in the city (women's share of the sector is highest at about 66 per cent clearly showing the domination of women in education) followed very closely by trade with about 21 per cent. Education and trade together with manufacturing, account for slightly more than 50 per cent of women workers. Yet, another interesting pattern is the proportion of women in the category, 'activities of households as employers' who are largely domestic workers accounting for about 8 per cent of women in 2011–2012.

The sharpest difference in male and female patterns of employment is with regard to education, activities of households as employers (largely paid domestic work), manufacturing and construction. While the first two categories have a considerable share of women workers, the latter sectors, manufacturing (6.3) and construction (1.7), show very small proportion of women. The pattern clearly shows that while men's employment is much more spread out across various sub-categories, higher degree of concentration is noticeable in women's distribution, largely in occupations that are extensions of their traditional house work. Thus, the gendered definitions of skill across these occupations, which are extensions of a patriarchal understanding of women's and men's work, underlie these concentrations.

Mirroring the sectoral shifts: The micro-profile of women workers

It is evident that there is a sectoral shift in women's employment with increased concentration in certain sectors alongside absence of a large number of women from any sort of economic activity. Here, it needs to be noted that it is the influx of women into modern service sector and education which defines the overall sectoral change in women's employment.

Each of the sectors, given their specificities and demands represents a segment of women with well-defined social and economic profiles. The critical issue then is to identify or define the characteristics of women who are working in these segregated sectors. This would help in situating women's agency and status within changes in the labour market.

The discussions in the present as well as subsequent sections are based on the data collected during the CWDS study[10] and cover 75 factory workers, 75 live-out domestic workers, 57 teachers in informal employment, 48 sales workers[11]; 23 clerical workers and 10 public relations and customer care workers. In the subsequent discussion, the last 3 categories – managers, clerical workers and public relations and customer care workers – are combined together as 'modern service sector workers' as they largely share similar work profiles and working conditions.

The profile of workers across various sectors shows distinct patterns with respect to age, educational backgrounds, caste and migrant status. Age and marital status are found to play a critical roles in many women dominated sectors, especially at the lower end of the employment ladder where their presence is also the highest. The preference for young girls though is prevalent in many industries, sales and modern service sector represented one of the worst, with over representation of young women. All the workers employed[12] in the modern service sector industry belonged to the age group of below 35 years, of which, about 58 per cent were from the age group of 21–25. The largest concentration of young women was in 'retail sales' with about 62 per cent belonging to the age group of 21–25.

The predominance of unmarried women marked all jobs in the modern service sector, though the proportion of married women varied across jobs. Sales workers represented the highest skewness with 88 per cent being unmarried. The highly skewed pattern of age and marital status in these acclaimed sectors of service employment favouring unmarried girls are indicative of a lack of provisions for married women such as maternity leave, crèches and so on in these workplaces, which makes these jobs undesirable for many women. This alongside longer working hours and odd work timings could prevent married women from entering into these occupations. Further, the employers preference for unmarried women for known reasons of maternity and familial care responsibilities could have also adversely affected employment, resulting in fewer married women in these sectors (Neetha and Mazumdar 2010).

Teachers in private schools and in other private educational institutions, who did not have any fixed pay and other conditions of work also largely belonged to the younger age cohort, with 54 per cent in the age group of 25–30. Though the predominance of young women characterized this sector also, the marital status was clearly distinct from that of modern service sectors. A large section of young teachers were married. The presence of more married women among teachers could be related to the social acceptance of teaching profession as a suitable occupation for married women. Further, the timing of schools which allow women to combine employment with other household care responsibilities seem to play a critical role in the entry of women and their continuance with teaching after marriage (Kelleher, Fatimah 2011).

In contrast, domestic workers and factory workers show distinct patterns. A large section of factory workers and domestic workers belonged to higher age brackets with the prime age between 26 and 35, accounting for about 51 per cent of the factory workers and 58 per cent of domestic workers. There was a gradual reduction in the number of women workers with higher age cohorts with no factory worker above the age of 50.[13] Among domestic workers though there was a better spread, not many workers belonged to the older age brackets.[14]

Reflecting the social identity of different industries, the educational profile of workers varied across industries. On one hand, well over one-third of the factory workers were illiterate (39 per cent) and another 8 per cent were educated only up to primary school level; on the other, about 29 per cent had studied up to the secondary level, while just 7 per cent of the workers had continued upto senior secondary. Domestic workers, not surprisingly, were largely illiterate with no worker reporting education higher than middle school.[15] On the contrary, 60 per cent of modern service sector workers had education of at least graduation or above and another 12 per cent had education till 12th. None of them, even those who worked as sales workers, were illiterate and the minimum education was that of middle-school pass. Teachers, as expected were better educated though many did not have the prescribed qualifications for what they are hired for.[16]

Confirming to the pattern elsewhere, strict divisions and concentration of women across the sectors were found along the lines of caste and their local/migrant status (Jeyaranjan and Swaminathan 2012; Deshpande and

Palshikar 2008). However, the concentration was clearly striking, which one do not normally expect in the context of a metropolitan city like Delhi. Domestic work and factory work represented women from various caste groups, but one represented the counter image of the other. A large number of domestic workers were from marginalsied communities whereas the single largest group of factory workers were from the upper caste families (46 per cent), although women from marginalized communities were also present (20 per cent).

Domination of upper caste Hindus was very clearly visible in jobs which could be categorized as high-end service sector occupations such as managers, public relations and customer care and clerical work. The only category with a mixed pattern among such service sector work was that of retail sales, although here also the proportion of marginalized communities was small (less than 25 per cent). Most of the teachers were also from the upper caste Hindu households. There were only 3 women teachers from SC/ST background, which could be explained in terms of caste-based labour market discrimination and/or as a reflection of the poor educational background of the community that prevents them from competing for such jobs. The proportion of Muslims in all categories of work were negligible, possibly a reflection of the enhanced barriers to undertake wage work – either from the supply or the demand side (Das 2005).

A large section of teachers, sales workers and modern service workers were from Delhi who are largely children of earlier migrants. Women from nearby areas – from the states of Uttar Pradesh, Rajasthan and Punjab – were also present. In contrast, domestic workers and factory workers were largely migrants though many factory workers are now settled migrants. The question therefore remains as to whether employers prefer to hire larger numbers of migrants in categories of work that are assumed to be unskilled or are more manual in nature, or are the conditions of work in the factories as well as in paid domestic work so abhorrent to the more settled and perhaps more educated women of Delhi that they do not seek such work?

From the discussion so far, it is evident that each sector is marked by a distinct profile of women workers. However, on the basis of broad demographic and educational profile, differences can be observed between those represented largely by the young and educated versus the others in the traditional sectors. Thus, while sales workers, modern services sector workers and teachers would fall into the first category, factory workers and domestic workers represent the relatively older age-cohorts and are less educated.

The above pattern suggests that access to certain jobs is not only restricted by skills and human resource endowment, but also by a variety of social and demographic attributes of the aspirants. In some cases, the profiles and requirements of certain jobs make it less attractive for certain sections of the labour force. On the other hand, the existing stereotyping of jobs combined with employers preference for a category of workers are also important in defining the work force.

The increased presence of young and better educated women in the workforce with an enhanced presence of modern service sector is clearly the notable change, if the overall employment scenario is juxtaposed with the workers' profile. From the perspective of women's agency, the most important question is as to whether these changes have had led to the questioning or renegotiation of any structural constraints – be it at workplace or at the household level. At the workplace, these would be reflected in the nature of work, workplace relations, conditions of work and bargaining possibilities.

In the following section, employment relations and working conditions are examined to explore the relative situation of women workers across various sectors, which could suggest the prevalence of any positive change in gender relations in the workplace.

Basic labour rights

Modern work spaces are commonly perceived as relatively more democratic, which to a large extent is attributed to the presence of an educated and vibrant youth. Owing to the nature of work, and the gendered nature of skill required, women constitute a considerable proportion of workers in these sectors. Apart from some sporadic discussions, the conditions under which they work continue to go largely unnoticed and unchallenged. There are no secondary data available on the various categories of such employment in terms of total employment, the men/women share, wages and other conditions of work. Compared to the above group of workers, the exploitative elements of employment relationship in factory work and domestic work are better documented and acknowledged (Neetha and Mazumdar 2010).

The first mandated entitlement of all factory workers in Delhi (regardless of the size of the establishment or number of workers) is the statutory minimum wage, which includes a bi-annual variable dearness allowance. The Act also defines working time as well as overtime as minimum wages are fixed for daily hours of work. There are two other laws that set the tone for social security entitlements of workers, namely, the Employees' State Insurance Act

(ESI) and the Employees' Provident Funds and Miscellaneous Provisions Act (EPF).

Violation without awareness and resistance

Lower, erratic and differential wages is an issue that characterise all the sub-sectors of modern service sector. However, among all occupations, sales workers represented the worst given its profile of educated workers. Sixty-six per cent of sale workers reported a monthly salary of Rs 5000 or less with the maximum number of workers being in the range of Rs 3000 to 4000. Only 2 workers reported of having the monthly salary more than Rs 8000. The salary is inclusive of all incentives and the perks that they are eligible for. The wages of many sales workers are found to be below the legal minimum wage[17], taking into account their educational qualifications. Interestingly, only 2 workers received wages more than their eligible minimum wages. Unsurprisingly, even among other modern service workers, many (about 57 per cent) were found getting wages below their eligible minimum wage as per their qualifications.

More than the prevalence of poor wages, the fact that many workers were not aware of their right to minimum wages and eligibility for a higher wage was particularly striking in the context of new service sector workers given their educational and other social profiles.[18] Their ignorance of a statutory wage is reflective of a critical issue that marks the divide in the labour market. The differentiation was clearly visible between the less educated, manual, blue collared workers and that of the educated white collared service workers. Factory workers owing to their location in the traditional industry, marked by collective interventions and negotiations, was assumed to have the coverage of labour regulations at large. In contrast, modern workspaces as they are often made to appear distinct, with extreme levels of individual negotiations, the binding of a regulatory framework is often forgotten, which is clear from the poor levels of awareness on minimum wage regulation among such workers.

Nature of employment gives further insights into the employment relationship in these sectors. Though many workers reported their status as regular, they did not have appointment letters nor had any non-wage benefits such as provident fund, bonus, and maternity leave and so on. Thus, regularity means regular in terms of work duration; that they can work under the given condition till they decide to leave the job or till they are dismissed by the employer. Few workers were also on contracts, who were employed for a fixed period ranging from 3 months to 1 year. Once the contract period is over, normally, it is extended for a further period. About 30 per cent of sales workers were on contract, while in other modern service sectors the proportion was lower.

The actual working hours of these workers were prolonged, many in the range of 8–10 hours a day. A small proportion (10 per cent) had reported working for more than 10 hours. Though the actual working hours exceeded the agreed upon or legally defined working hours in context of many workers across sectors, payment for overtime was largely absent. Further, though many workers, especially those working as sales workers, had to stay back late in the evening till 9.00 p.m., there were no provision of transportation and the workers had to manage on their own to return to their place of stay.

As high as 65 per cent of workers, had no leave provisions other than a weekly off and off during one or two festivals. Only 4 workers in the new service sector occupations (3 in clerical job and 1 manager), reported of having maternity leave and that too of one month. The absence of maternity leave could explain the disproportionate presence of married women in these sectors. None of the workers surveyed had medical leave and situations of sickness were invariably met with loss of pay/break in service.

Increments based on performance was the prominent system found among women workers in all the modern service sectors, though 32 per cent reported of the absence of any provisions for increment. The reported period of performance-based incentives by most of the respondents was 6 months, though few workers had provision every quarterly. Even the performance-based increment was reported highly arbitrary depending heavily on the worker's relations with the managers/employers. Only 24 per cent of these workers reported of having provision for PF.

Owing to the adverse conditions of work, a large turnover was reported across all the sub-sectors and here also, sale workers topped the list. Close to 70 per cent of sales workers had work experience of less than a year in the present organization – suggestive of a high turnover rate and mobility across firms. This is further evidenced by the fact that 54 per cent of the workers had previous work experiences in similar work and had shifted jobs. The reasons for shifting jobs in many cases were for better employment prospects, though few (6 cases) were also due to better timing of work and/or transport facilities. Pregnancy and marriage, as reasons for change or quitting jobs, constituted for 8 per cent of modern service sector workers. Though this constitutes only for a small proportion of the total workers, it accounts for a substantial share of married workers (27 per cent) employed in the sector.

Maternity benefit provisions are clearly absent in the sector and this is clearly an important reason for breaks and or change in jobs among married workers. Most workers (except one) who took breaks for marriage or maternity had to change jobs. Only few actually changed their jobs 'voluntarily', as they considered their earlier work too demanding either due to increased travel or house work. The rest of the changes were in a sense forced on the workers, as employers perceived that the workers' commitment would not be the same as before. In many such cases workers were dismissed unilaterally.

Education sector also represented more or less a similar picture. Only 33 per cent of the teachers interviewed were receiving salaries as fixed by the government. For the rest, decisions on pay were matters of negotiation or in many cases unilateral decisions of the management. Other conditions of work were highly variable across teachers. Total working hours were more than stipulated; apart from actual lecturing and teaching, teachers were also undertaking a number of associated tasks such as maintaining registers, preparing charts and other teaching aids and materials, evaluation of students and so on. Leave provisions and access to social security benefits were the major areas of concern among teachers also. The major attraction of the sector that was pointed out by many teachers was the work timing, which accommodated their household work demands to a greater extent. In further discussions, it was indicated that teaching allows them to get back home early, most of the times when their children return from schools. It was highlighted that school admissions are relatively easier for their children and if the children studied in the same school as that of theirs, the possibility of getting fee concession and monitoring of the child's education exist. Many teachers shared that teaching has 'more morality' as a profession for women, as it helps in making the family more stable owing to its 'family friendly' nature described above.

Persisting exploitation: Better to worse; still better?

Factory work and domestic work also mirrored the above picture though the extent and intensity of the issue varied in these contexts. An important aspect that needs to be factored in the discussion on domestic workers is their exclusion from the coverage of all labour laws – even the minimum wage legislation.[19] It may be noted that The Minimum Wages Act is perhaps the single-most universal labour law and should be applicable to workers in the unorganized as well as organized sector. However, the list of 29 scheduled employments covered by the Act in Delhi does not include domestic workers.

The working conditions of part-time domestic workers were awful with wage settings, conditions of work and immensely flexible working hours among the part-time domestic workers. Wages varied across locations in the city depending on the economic and social characteristics of the employers and employees and the tasks performed. The wages received by domestic workers (which range from Rs 200–500 for cleaning to Rs 400–1000 for cooking) show that it is one of the lowest paid occupations with wide dispersion in wages between workers.

Long and irregular working time characterise this sector also, with the average working hours being 6.2 hours, which is only the time spent at doing the specified task at the employer's homes. In the broader sense, the working hours need to take into account the commuting time between households as well as other incidental time; this was roughly one and a half hours more than the average given above. Apart from the unduly hours of work required in domestic service, it was also noted that there was a total lack of standards regarding holidays, days off and sick leaves.

Part-time workers do not have any fixed number of leaves, though an average of 1–2 days leave in a month is a common practise. Extended leaves very often have the risk of losing wages and annual holidays are unknown to most of the workers. Added to these, job tenures are not fixed and are mostly left to the employer to terminate the worker at any point of time. Termination was reported to be the quickest and mostly a unilateral decision of the employers. The employee is also free to leave the job, but given the economic pressures and difficulty in finding fresh employers, employees do not tend to leave jobs. These clearly show a great deal of indefiniteness in employment relations in domestic service. The conditions of women factory workers, though far from ideal, were better off when compared to many modern service workers or domestic workers. The notified minimum wages per month of factory workers at the time of the survey were Rs 3,683 for unskilled workers, Rs 3,849 for semi-skilled and Rs 4,107 for skilled workers. Annual or other increments, although not statutory, are part of reasonable or negotiated practice. The study revealed that just over half the surveyed workers were paid the statutory minimum wage. The data revealed that denial of minimum wages spans all skill categories of workers, although the position of skilled workers appears to be better than the others. Eighty per cent of the skilled workers had the minimum wages in comparison to 68 per cent of the unskilled workers and just 3 per cent of the semi-skilled workers. The proportions of workers who were covered by ESI was just over half (51 per cent), while the proportion covered by Provident Fund was somewhat less at 47 per cent.

Most of the workers had a working day from 9 a.m. to between 5.30 and 6 p.m. or from 9.30 a.m. to 6.30 p.m. with a half hour lunch break and in some cases, a short tea break. While this is more or less the normal working hours, some 5 per cent of the workers were doing a longer shift from 9 a.m. to 6.30 and 7 p.m., i.e., their normal working day without any overtime wages was over 9 hours. Strangely, more than the extended regular time, the survey revealed that overtime work was not very frequently demanded of the workers. On average the number of days of overtime work for those who reported more frequent overtime (65 per cent) was around one or a maximum of two months in a year. Others who reported a few days of seasonal overtime on rare occasions, constituted around 29 per cent of workers. But it was clear that the majority of the workers were not given their legal due of double the normal hourly wages for overtime. 59 per cent of the workers reported same rates and only 27 per cent were given double rates for overtime work.

In the context of factory workers, the decline in manufacturing in general and the relatively higher decline in the number of women in the sector because of the relocation of many textile and garment units in the city, seem to be a central issue which has adversely affected women's conditions of work. As has been shared by old workers, many women workers who have lost work in these manufacturing units also represented a category of workers who were part of various labour struggles in the 1980s. Their participation and exposure to working class activism not only meant better working conditions, but also helped in creating an environment sensitive to the issues of women workers such as maternity and child care provisions. With the shifting of factories, the conditions of women factory workers were reported to have deteriorated in the city, owing to the increased competition among workers for limited employment inflated by the breakup of organized working class movements, a point taken up later.

Given the above broad scenario of wide spread violation of labour rights, an intriguing puzzle is of the young, better educated modern women, supposedly capable of questioning social norms and values, constituting an exploited yet voiceless work force. The small size of female workforce and their spread across various workplaces is an issue at the overall level, but even in sectors where their presence is striking, no discernible difference was noticed.

The observed profile of workers suggest that a large section of workers are not foreseeing themselves as permanent workers. Many unmarried women do not consider themselves in employment after marriage or child birth. Even those who want to remain in the labour force also do not anticipate themselves working in the same sector or firm on a long term basis, which explains to some extend, the indifferent attitude. The near absence of any collective organization or unions among workers in all the occupations studied, is another issue that needs special attention. No women workers, except for a few from factories were associated with or members of any unions. The informal nature of work with many workers being on contract and therefore easy to fire by employers, effectively ensures that workers do not raise their voices or organize themselves for fear of losing their employment.[20] The highly individualized negotiations on salary and other conditions of work add to their vulnerability. Each co-worker is thus seen as a competitor and not as a possible comrade in the joint struggle to achieve just conditions of work. The failure of the existing trade unions in the organization of informal workers, especially of those engaged in service sector occupations, is another factor that explains the complete absence of unions among this group of workers. Even in factories, with large scale contract employment, the number of permanent workers have declined, which has adversely affected the space for organized resistance. This, alongside a declining share of manufacturing employment in general, have indirectly contributed to the decline in organized space in the city. Thus, apart from the individual reasons, the larger climate of industrial relations with labour flexibility at the centre seems to have resulted in working class suppression in general and of women workers in particular. This is an issue which women factory workers with several years of work experience have also highlighted.

Though the nature of work and conditions of employment of women do not capture any evidence of empowerment, at the individual or personal level, access to income even if it is meagre gave many women resources of their own to fall back on. Though there are variations across categories of women, many women keep back some of their income for their own use. Most domestic workers and factory workers spend almost all their wages on basic requirements of the household such as food, education of children, etc. On the other hand, teachers and modern service sector workers, though also contributed to household budget, do invest a considerable proportion of the income on their clothes and other personal belongings. This varies considerably across age, marital status and household's economic position[21]. Has the access to income brought about any meaningful shifts in power relations between men and women within the household is an issue that needs exploration.

Gendered homes: Burden of house work

As discussed, an aspect that is critical in the understanding of women's agency is with regard to their position outside the workplace, especially at home. Burden and intensity of unpaid house work is clearly one indicator that could give insights into the overt and covert gender power realtions that exist in families. Married women were few or absent in certain categories of jobs, which was partly due to the employer's preferences again rooted in their care functions. Unpaid housework was the norm across all women workers though the intensity of the same varied. Unmarried workers in general were engaged in housework on an average 2–3 hours on a day across all sectors, irrespective of their paid work status. There were only few exemptions to this, but here again no one was out of the grip of housework. The average hours do mask the wide variation – few unmarried workers were also prime workers at home. This was especially when mothers were either dead or ill or disabled. The pressure of paid work and their perception of housework was such that many unmarried women did not consider themselves working after marriage or child birth. Even for those who wanted to remain in the labour force after marriage, also did not anticipate themselves working in the same sector or firm, given the work related demands.

Housework constituted an important activity of all married women across sectors, though total time spent and time spent across categories of household work varied. Many married workers who dared to enter the work force are found struggling to meet their social reproductive roles at the same time coping with hostile labour market requirements. Sales workers shared the worst stories with odd working hours. As compared to other modern service sector workers, the time spent on housework was higher among married sales workers. While the average number of hours spent on housework by married women engaged in modern service sector occupation were roughly 4 hours, the same for sales workers was 5 hours 30 minutes. The comparatively less time spent by the first category was not due to any sharing of house work by the spouse, but by depending on alternative arrangements/provisions. Many workers could sustain their participation in outside work because of the support from female family members or some could afford paid domestic workers. Since sales workers in general had low salaries, the possibility of hiring domestic workers as an option was out of reach of many. As such, these women had to labour for 13–14 hours every working day. For these workers, more than the actual working hours, it is the timing of work which needs attention. Largely, the working time was from 11.00 a.m. to 8.00 p.m., which is extended normally for another 1 hour. When travelling time of an hour one side is added to this, it would mean that workers are away from their households for more than 12 hours and are back only late at night. All the married sales workers had children upto 6 years old, i.e., their employment coincided with precisely that period in their lives involving concentrated responsibilities in child care. Though occasional sharing of house work by spouse was reported by few respondents, it was never the norm. Tensions around housework especially child care was the most talked about issue by these workers because of which some workers even shared that they are contemplating of changing/leaving jobs. However, not even a single worker identified child care issues as one that could be handled through workplace policies. Obviously, as the profile of workers clearly show a large section of workers who are not foreseeing themselves as long-term full-time workers.

As discussed in the previous section, most of the factory workers had a working day of about 8–9 hours. The average number of hours spent on housework was 4 hours 40 minutes. As such, these women had to labour for 12–13 hours every working day. Close to three quarters of the workers had children upto 10–11 years old, again reinforcing the demands of housework. Mandated creches were not functional in even one of the factories where the surveyed women workers were employed[22]. Though domestic workers were also equally troubled, the degree of tension around housework was comparatively less as they were working in different houses mostly close to their dwellings, which allowed some flexibility. Workers were found adding or deducting the number of tasks or employers according to household care demands. Matching the time schedules of different houses with the demands of own household chores, however, put pressure on these workers, especially when they cater to many employers.

From the discussion it is clear that the patriarcial demands and expectations on women prevail irrespective of their status in the labour market. However, labour market expectations on women are still based on the assumption that women are free to undertake and devote any amount of time at any time in the day in paid work. Thus, what is disturbing is the fact that there has been no acknowledgement of these pressures, as visible in the absence of any policy initiatives towards maternity leave, child care leave, creches, etc.

Provisions for maternity benefits and creches are provided for in the Factory's Act (1948); however, there is a complete violation of such rights even in industries that come under the Act, while a large number of enterprizes are left unregulated. Ironically, in sectors where young and educated dominate the work force these concerns are the highest, however, with no acknowledgement or resistance. The fact that the young dominate, also speaks of the selective elimination of those women for whom housework demands are critical. Overtime work, distance from residence and the civic situation in which women are expected to carry out their housework are all interrelated and inevitably linked to the income and wage levels of the class of women who have effected a marginal entry into paid work. Thus, it seems that married women who can afford to manage financially withdraw from the unfriendly labour market and those who remain are the ones for whom the income from paid work is central in the survival. Thus, domestic workers and factory workers represent a distinct class of workers for whom entry into paid work is not a matter of choice but compulsion. On the other hand, married teachers represents another class for whom the social acceptance of the job is the most favourable factor coupled with the timing of work that suits child care demands. The possibilities of engaging hired care workers are also open to these women who can afford such options.

Conclusion

While it is acknowledged that individuals and groups make choices and may exercise agency, they do so within the limits imposed by the structural distribution of rules, norms, assets and identities (Kabeer 2012). The paper provides distinct and yet overlapping evidences of women workers' subordination in the city. The low participation of women in employment is the central issue. Gender disadvantage in the labour market is a product of many constraints and could operate over the life course of individuals. The paper provides evidences to the contention that the degree of female work participation is influenced by the nature of existing opportunities for employment- skill requirement, timing of work, work-loads, levels of wage/ earnings, and more importantly protection during pregnancy, childbirth and so on. The pressure of child care and other housework alongside drudging paid work seems to influence women's decision to withdraw from the labour market if that option is viable which to a greater level explains the strikingly low work participation of women. Though women are certainly making some choices either not to enter or withdraw from the work force, it is problematic to attribute such decisions entirely to their priority to the well being of the family or children. The fact that many women enter the workforce for short periods/intermittently/or are in the look for jobs that meet their aspirations and requirements even though family and other patriarchal restrictions exist do indicate their desire to be part of the workforce.

Though there has been some diversification of women's employment with the emergence of newer sectors of employment, their confinement to select sectors/occupations is an issue. Gender based segmentation is not the only issue, as other social and demographic attributes are also central in such fragmentation. The understanding that newer and modern workspaces are more egalitarian and gender friendly when critically analysed, through an exploration of basic labour rights, reveals large scale of violation of women's workers' rights. The analysis reveals that the entry of the young and educated women workers has not resulted in much difference in workplace relations or conditions of work in general. The highly informalized work relations and the shrinking of organized space in the city that characterise current phase of employment, has been detrimental to women workers across all categories. Further, household work is still a constraining factor for many women workers though labour market expectations from women do not account for these and there has been no acknowledgement of such pressures at the policy level. In such a situation, the paper argues that the possibility of renegotiating existing gender norms, be it at workplaces or at homes, which would bring changes in the overall status of women is still a distant goal.

Endnotes

[1] An often highlighted, image of women in Delhi is one of victim to various crimes, which reached its peak after the incident of rape on 16 December, 2013. No attempt to highlight the issue of participation of women in work and its relation to overall status of women in the city could be seen even in a period of hyped interest on women's issues following this incident.

[2] The study was undertaken for the Delhi Commission of Women by the author jointly with Indrani Mazumdar. It covered 375 women workers from 4 sectors, namely, manufacturing, domestic work, education, and other services.

[3] As per 2004–2005 NSS data, Mumbai (26.7) and Bangalore (20.2) have nearly double the proportion of working women compared to Delhi.

[4] The National Commission on Enterprises in the Unorganized Sector (NCEUS) has pointed this out in its various reports, particularly in relation to women workers.

[5] The data for the year 2004–2005 is now acknowledged as an exceptional one.

[6] The fall in the share of manufacturing in Delhi is perhaps not surprising, since the period in question had witnessed large scale sealing of small scale industries in the background of the Supreme Court directives on closure of a range of manufacturing units in non-conforming areas of the city. However, as it is clear from the data, women workers have been displaced from manufacturing employment on a greater scale than men.

[7] In most urban centres, organized sales grew during the period of globalization, especially in the last decade with the emergence of a distinct segment of newly rich. The emergence

of the neo-rich class, the changing consumer mindset owing media proliferation, changing demographic mix, etc., there have been indicative of a transition from the traditional retail to organized retailing. For many new-generation urban households, the time constraint and the convenience of shopping with multiplicity of choice under one roof made organized retailing a preferred choice.

8   Neetha and Mazumdar, Report on the Conditions and Needs of Women Workers in Delhi, CWDS, Unpublished mimeo, 2010.

9   Agriculture is excluded, since the sector employs only negligible number of women such that when converted to proportion and adjusted for decimals gives 'zero'.

10 Though in the CWDS study, live-in domestic workers, teachers in the formal sector, security guards and house keeping workers were also covered because of the contrast in the conditions of work between other sub-categories and other sectors selected, these workers are not included in the paper.

11 Sales workers working in a range of retail outlets spread across the city was covered which comprised of those working in high value retail chains as well as food and grocery segment.

12 Since the sample respondents were not selected on the basis of any probability sampling method, it is possible that the results could be biased. However, special efforts were made in the selection of samples to include women with varied profiles such as age cohorts, and social and economic backgrounds. Even then, the fact that no women from older groups were found, shows the demographic characteristics of this workforce. For the sector as a whole, though the proportions may vary slightly, the overall picture would remain the same.

13 This ceiling of 50 may mean that either factories in Delhi do not keep women workers beyond this age or that the workers themselves get burnt out and are unable to continue.

14 This could be attributed to two divergent but yet related possibilities. Firstly, the reluctance on the part of the employers to employ workers who are in the upper age groups in the event of availability of workers from the younger age cohorts. Further, the physical and emotional demands of paid domestic work may have contributed towards pushing older women out of the sector.

15 This needs to be seen against the fact that average female literacy level of Delhi is 75 per cent in 2001.

16 Thus, many school teachers did not have the required teachers training certificate though they possessed a degree or post graduate degree in the subject.

17 Of all the existing labour laws, the Minimum Wages Act, 1948, which is designed to prevent employers from paying wages below a basic minimum wage, is applicable to all wage workers under the scheduled employment.

18 The notified minimum wages per month at the time of the survey were Rs 3,876 for non-matriculate workers, Rs 4,131 for non-graduates and Rs 4,443 for graduate and above workers.

19 Few states in the country have fixed an official minimum wage for the occupation.

20 A permanent worker can be removed from service only for proven misconduct or for habitual absence – due to ill health, alcoholism and the like, or on attaining retirement age. A contract worker has no such protection.

[21] Unmarried women without financial burden spent almost most of their income on personal expenses such as buying modern outfits, expensive gadgets such as mobiles.

[22] Factory's Act 1948 provides for creches for infant children of workers in every unit employing more than 30 women.

References

Anker, R., and C. Hein. 1985. 'Why Third World Urban Employers Usually Prefer Men', *International Labor Review*, 24(1): 73–90.

Census. 2011. http://www.censusindia.gov.in/2011census/B-series/B-Series-01.html, 'Population Enumeration Data', Data on workers, *Office of the Registrar General and Census Commissioner*, Ministry of Home Affairs, Government of India.

Das, M. B. 2005. 'Muslim Women's Low Labor-Force Participation in India: Some Structural Explanation', in *In a Minority: Essays on Muslim Women in India* edited by Zoya Hasan and Ritu Menon, New Jersey: Rutgers University Press, pp. 189–221.

Deshpande, R., and S. Palshikar. 2008. 'Occupational Mobility: How Much Does Caste Matter?', *Economic and Political Weekly*, 43(34): 61–70.

Ghosh, J. 2002. 'Globalization, Export-Oriented Employment for Women and Social Policy: A Case Study of India', *Social Scientist*, 30(11–12): 17–60.

Jeyaranjan, J., and P. Swaminathan. 2012. 'Resilience of Gender Inequities: Women and Employment in Chennai', in *Women and Work* edited by Padmini Swaminathan, Hyderabad: Orient Black Swan, pp. 262–84.

Kabeer, N. 2012. 'Women's Economic Empowerment and Inclusive Growth: Labour Markets and Enterprise Development', *SIG Working Paper* 2012/1, IDRC.

Kelleher, F. 2011. 'Women and the Teaching Profession: Exploring the Feminisation Debate', United Kingdom: Commonwealth Secretariat and UNESCO.

Mazumdar, I. 2007. 'Women Workers and Globalization: Emergent Contradictions in India', Kolkata: Stree.

Neetha, N., and I. Mazumdar. 2010. 'Report on the Conditions and Needs of Women Workers in Delhi', Unpublished Mimeo, *Centre for Women's Development Studies*, New Delhi.

7

Spare Change for Spare Time?
Homeworking Women in Banaras*

Amit Basole

Introduction

The overwhelming majority of women in the Indian informal sector are
home-based workers.[1] Eighty percent of homeworkers, that is home-based
workers who work for piece-wages rather than on own-account, are women
(Mehrotra and Biggeri 2007). Even after working for up to seven or eight
hours a day homeworking women only earn around Rs 30, far below the
minimum wage for unskilled workers (AIDWA 2010, Sengupta et al. 2007).[2]
Why are wages so low in home-based work? A recent study of homeworking
women in Delhi found that most of the women interviewed did not consider
themselves "workers" but rather "wives or mothers trying to make their little
contribution to the family income" (AIDWA 2010). Despite women's long
history of labour force participation in artisanal and other informal industry,
and despite several academic and policy studies, women's work is not

---

* I thank without implication, Mohan Rao, James Boyce, Nancy Folbre, Rajesh Bhattacharya,
   Sirisha Naidu, Smita Ramnarain, and Saraswati Raju for comments. Smita Ramnarain also
   suggested the title phrase. I also thank Sunil Sahasrabudhey and Chitra Sahasrabudhey
   for insights on women's knowledge and the concept of *lokavidya*. Finally, I thank Shilpi
   Suneja, Ehsan Ali Ansari, and Mohammad Aleem Hashmi for discussions and for their
   invaluable assistance during primary data collection.

considered "real work," but rather "spare-time work," "help," or "income-generating activity." Thus in addition to well-known factors such as a captive labour force resulting from social restrictions, lower fallback options, and low labour productivity, one hypothesis that emerges from the literature on home-based work is that the undervaluation of women's work can be linked to different values placed on women's as opposed to men's time. Since homework is seen as being performed in the time *left over* after housework responsibilities such as cooking, cleaning, child-care and other care work, have been discharged, it is described, by contractors, husbands, as well as women, as being performed in "free time." However, while references to this "spare-time discourse" are frequent, few studies have pursued the argument beyond anecdotes.

Drawing upon time-use surveys and interviews of women workers in the Banaras textile industry, I argue that women's time is undervalued in the market because it is seen as having a very low opportunity cost and their knowledge is undervalued because it is acquired informally and "free of cost." The result is that even when women spend a full working day on skilled work, they are paid wages half that men receive for manual labour. The majority of women surveyed and interviewed in the present study are poor Muslims from the Ansari community and are subject to varying degrees of restrictions due to purdah. They are thus located at the intersection of class, caste, and gender hierarchies.

During the course of conducting surveys among Ansari weavers in the city of Banaras (Varanasi), a renowned silk weaving center in eastern Uttar Pradesh, it became clear that women in weaving households, though they did not weave, made crucial contributions to the industry and to family incomes in two ways: as unpaid family workers in pre-weaving operations, and as paid homeworkers undertaking embroidery and other piece-rate work. Contrary to the perception in larger society and even in academic writing that women's work is invisible, Ansari men insisted on mentioning the contribution that women make to weaving, if only to point out that that piece-wages paid for weaving were too low considering that the entire family's labour was obtained in return for them. Not only unpaid work, but women paid work studied here is also thoroughly integrated into the Banarasi sari industry is two crucial ways. On the labour supply side, deteriorating incomes in the handloom sector have pushed women, who traditionally performed only unpaid work to undertake embroidery and other piece-rate work for direct payment. On the labour demand side, the rise of imitation "Banarasi" saris manufactured on powerlooms has brought with it an increased demand for post-weaving embroidery work intended to enhance the market value of cheap imitation saris.

Most accounts of the Banaras textile industry give only passing mention to women's work (Ahmad 2007, Kumar 1988, Varman and Chakravarti 2006). Only one recent study focuses specifically on Ansari women albeit more on gender and community identity than on women's work *per se* (Raman 2010). In this study I examine the labour process and the structure of the working day for home-based women workers in Banaras. I also estimate hourly wages and investigate the women's own perceptions of their work. Women's time use has of course received a lot of attention in recent years, both in OECD and developing country contexts. However, the bulk of this attention has been focused on unpaid housework work. Paid work performed at home and unpaid work performed for marketed goods has received less attention.

The remainder of this paper is divided into the following sections. First I present a theoretical framework to think about women's time and skills. The next section outlines the methods used in the study. Subsequently, there is a discussion regarding the gender division of labour and the putting-out system in Banaras. The last part presents the results of the time-use survey followed by the conclusion.

Women's time, women's knowledge

Roughly thirty years of political, academic and policy work have gone into understanding and improving the position of home-based women workers.[3] Some relevant insights that emerge from this work are the following. Even as their labour is set loose due to the destruction of artisanal industry and traditional agriculture (Fig. 7.1), patriarchal ideology restricts women, especially of the middle and upper castes, to working at home. The result is the production of a super-exploitable labour force where the opportunity cost of labour time is effectively zero and hence the minimum bound for the wage rate is only slightly above zero. On the labour demand side the attempts by firms to minimize labour costs, reduce the power of unions, circumvent factory legislation, and cope with market uncertainties (fashion trends, seasonal demands) generate demand for a flexible, home-based workforce (see Mehrotra and Biggeri 2007).[4] To these one may add technological factors such as vastly increased speeds of transportation and communication that allow dispersed production to become cost-effective (for e.g. de Neve 2005).

Most empirical studies of homeworking women conclude that wage-rates, regardless of the industry in question are far below any minimum wage norm. In a wide variety of occupations in our study, as well as earlier studies, women report earning around Rs 30–40 for a full day's work (AIDWA 2010, Sengupta et al. 2007). While gender-based occupational segregation makes direct comparison of male and female wages difficult, male wages, even in unskilled manual labour, rarely fall below Rs 80 or 90 a day. Several factors may act together to depress wages to such abysmally low levels. These include the existence of a reserve army of labour (excess labour supply), low bargaining power of workers, and low labour productivity. Here I consider two somewhat less emphasized reasons: the role of patriarchal ideology in devaluation of women's knowledge and women's time.

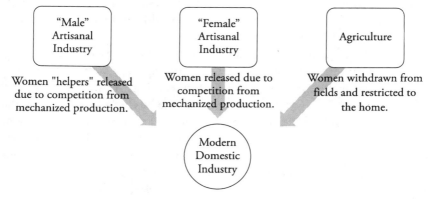

Fig. 7.1 Sources of labour-power for modern domestic industry

An important contribution of feminist scholarship as well as the women's movement has been the questioning of the concept of "skilled" and "unskilled" work. The central insight here is that not only can women be restricted to performance of low-skilled and hence lower-paid jobs, but that work can be classified as being low-skilled *because* it is performed by women (Kabeer 1994, Pearson 1998). The Sengupta Commission notes that jobs performed by women may be characterized as "low skilled" even if they involve "exceptional talent and years of informal training" (Sengupta et al. 2007, 84). Thus for example, in the textile industry, "Hand embroidery done by women was the most skill and time intensive, but paid the lowest wages, i.e. women's skills were systematically undervalued." (*ibid*) "Or similarly in the ceramic industry or in brick-kilns, preparation of the mud or clay is a skilled activity. If the consistency of this raw material is not correct, the pottery will disintegrate and the houses built of the brick would collapse. This work is done by women but is valued as one of the lowest" (*ibid*). Such examples clearly point out that only "human capital" based explanations of low wages wherein women are seen as being deprived of skills (Jacobsen 2003), are not sufficient and may even contribute to eliding the skills and knowledge women already possess.

One difficulty here is that informally acquired knowledge, whether of men *or* of women, has not been paid much attention in academic or policy literature. National Sample Survey data seem to suggest that 80–90 per cent of the informal workforce has received no training, formal or informal, for their work. This results in a common perception that the vast majority of the informal workforce is "unskilled." But case studies of informal occupations show that on-the-job training and apprenticeships are common. This *lokavidya*, a vast store of knowledge acquired outside of the formal education system, is the backbone of the informal economy.[5]

In case of craft communities such as the Banaras silk weavers, for men as well as women, growing up and learning work appropriate to their gender are indistinguishable processes (Basole, forthcoming). Boys can weave and girls can do preparatory yarn work as well as needle embroidery work by the time they are young adults. Thus, for the apprentice, the opportunity cost of training is effectively zero and there is no explicit price of the skill transfer process for either men or women. Community norms and institutions produce a skilled and disciplined labour force, ready for use by the capitalist economy, via the putting-out system. Via low wages, the artisanal sector, drawing upon family-based and other informal training systems, subsidizes knowledge (re)production, the benefits of which accrue to consumers as well as merchants. This argument applies to both men and women in the artisanal sector, but is accentuated in the case of women because their paid work is seen as a "natural" extension of their unpaid work.

Further, not only is women's knowledge available "free", so is their time. Since the woman's primary responsibility is for unpaid care work, time "left over" after the discharging of housework responsibilities is seen as "spare time" or "free time" which has no opportunity cost. In her groundbreaking study *The Lacemakers of Narsapur*, Mies (1982, 151) argues that "by defining women as housewives first, their labour power is treated as natural, freely available to their husbands, as well as to exporters. Their exploitation has therefore not only the character of the classical wage labour exploitation but also that of the exploitation of a natural resource (like forests) where the raw material appears to be free for all." Wilkinson-Weber (1999, 42) offers an example from the Chikan embroidery industry of Lucknow where merchants speak about women's embroidery work, a crucial part of the industry, as "a household task that is subordinated to domestic work," a "free-time activity" that is neither a priority for women nor a "real occupation." One merchant puts the matter succinctly, "They just sit around and they get work, and they get money. All in their spare time! I'm the one with all the headaches."

Low daily wage rates earned by women are also sometimes justified on the basis that women are not able to put in a full working day. Hence, the argument goes, hourly wage rate for women may in fact not be very much lower than prevailing rates for men. This argument can be sustained because hourly rates are in fact hard to determine for homeworkers. Various forms of putting-out or sub-contracting arrangements found in home-based work have generally been based on piece-wage contracts since these eliminate the need for supervision of work or keeping track of hours worked (Basole and Basu 2011, Marx 1867/1992) While hourly or daily wage rates are easily known and comparable across occupations, piece rates are industry-specific, not easily compared and are hard to convert into time-based rates if no records are available for hours worked.

Further it can be argued that piece-wages do not enjoy a *moral lower bound* as hourly wages might. That is, the effective hourly wages implied in piece-wage contracts may be far lower than if explicit hourly wage contracts were specified, because the conversion is not straightforward, particularly for women. Among workers as diverse as Iranian carpet-makers and Brazilian seamstresses, the important hurdle in estimating hourly earnings for piece rate workers is that it is difficult to determine the number of hours and days spent working because paid and unpaid work overlap and intertwine often unpredictable ways (de Paiva Abreu and Sorj 1996, Ghavamshahidi 1996, Rao and Husain 1987) The working day is composed of an interweaving of various tasks, the timing being determined by the needs of others, such as getting children ready for school or preparing three fresh meals a day. Unlike housework, market work does not proceed strictly by the clock, it is done as and when the woman has time "to spare." For these reasons, estimates of hours worked and hourly earnings are rare in the literature. Among the few studies that attempt to do this are Rao and Husain (1987) who use conventional (not time use) surveys to find that in the Delhi garment sector forty percent of women did at least six hours of piece work per day.[6] Mehrotra and Biggeri (2007) report that homeworking women in the *agarbatti, bidi* and *zardozi* (embroidery) industries work on average for 8.7 hours a day.

Direct evidence of the extent of women's participation in various activities comes from time-use surveys (TUS) that have become increasingly common in the last decade or so and have been very helpful in understanding the dynamics of unpaid work (Antonopoulos and Hirway 2010). However time-use surveys have rarely been applied to unpaid and paid work undertaken at home for production of goods and services sold in the market (one exception is a recent study by Floro and Pichetpongsa, 2010).

Methods

Time-use survey

Time-use data were collected from home-based women workers in Banaras from February 2010 to June 2010 as part of a larger project on the city's handloom and powerloom industries. Since most women's work is carried on in private (in purdah in case of the Muslim women) and no public lists are available, purposive and snow-ball sampling was employed to identify participants. Male weavers contacted for the weaving study were asked if their wives or other women in their household undertook paid work at home. Further, community contacts of a local non-governmental organization were used to identify women in the non-weaver localities of Banaras. Forty-two women engaged in preparatory yarn-work for weaving, embroidery, post-weaving processing of powerloom fabric and other miscellaneous work were surveyed in the following areas: Lallapura, Sarai Mohana, Ramnagar and several *mohallas* in Alaipura. Results are presented here only for the 32 women who undertook embroidery work or finishing of powerloom fabric. A subset of them also performed preparatory yarn work. The majority (20) of the 32 women in our sample come from weaving households. Five are from families where the traditional occupation is embroidery work and seven are from households with other backgrounds such as farming, informal service sector work and petty retail. The sample consists of 27 Muslim and 5 Hindu women. The women range in age from 16–45.

Time-use data were collected twice a day, using 12-hour recalls, for five consecutive weekdays. The five day period was chosen because fabric pieces (for example a sari) usually took somewhere between one and five days to finish. The intent was to capture the pattern of time use for the entire duration of time in which a woman worked on one piece, typically one sari. Due to low levels of literacy as well as time pressures, women could not be asked to keep their own time-use dairies. Instead female volunteers were employed to interview women twice a day. Primary activities were recorded at one-hour intervals and categorized as "yarn-work," "care-work," "market-work," or "leisure." "Yarn-work" refers to preparatory winding of yarn for weaving. The term "care-work" has been used to describe all non-market housework such as cooking, cleaning, and care of children, sick, and the elderly.[7] "Market-work" is any work undertaken for direct payment. "Leisure" includes personal time, sleep, and any other activity that one cannot pay another person to do. These categories were created on the basis of pilot interviews with three women who were subsequently also surveyed.

A binary code was utilized wherein the observer assigned the value "1" if a certain type of work was undertaken for the major part of an hour, and "0" otherwise. This method is rapid and therefore allows data collection over several days, but it suffers from two problems. First, only primary activities are recorded, potentially underestimating the work burden resulting from overlapping or simultaneous activities (such as embroidery and child-care carried out simultaneously). And second, activities that take up more than half an hour but less than an hour are still counted as a full hour. Despite these problems the method was employed so that surveys were brief enough to be administered to time-pressed women twice a day for five consecutive days. Interviews and field observations support the findings of the time-use survey.

Interviews

Semi-structured interviews were also carried out with twenty women who performed piece-rate work. Of these five were also part of the time-use survey. Interviews ranged from ten minutes to half an hour in duration and questioned the women on the type of work they performed, how long they worked, the wages they received, and how they prioritized different types of work. While an attempt was made to conduct interviews one-on-one, this was not always possible, since women often worked in groups, or were to be found in the presence of other family members. Under such circumstances, rather than stop the interview, it was accepted that the material would tend more towards a focus group than an interview. In instances when men started to dominate the conversation, they were requested to let the women speak for themselves. If this did not yield the desired results, the material was not used. In addition to the women themselves, one contractor and three middlemen were also interviewed regarding the organization of the putting-out process.

Gender, class, and the labour process in banaras

Banaras (also known as Varanasi and Kashi) is an ancient city on the banks of the river Ganga in the eastern part of the North Indian state of Uttar Pradesh.

Internationally known as the "holy city of the Hindus," it is on almost every foreign tourist's destination list. A somewhat lesser known fact is that at least 20 per cent of Banaras city's 1.5 million strong population is Muslim. The vast majority of Banarasi Muslims (over 70 per cent) belong to Momin Ansari or julaha (weaver) community and are the makers of the iconic Banarasi Sari.

In 2010 the weaving industry in Banaras was estimated to have around 75,000 handlooms and over 50,000 powerlooms but the exact size is not known, since the industry has been in flux for the past twenty years with a decline of handlooms and rapid rise of powerlooms (see Basole 2012 for varying estimates and their sources). Several allied industries such as dyeing, designing, and embroidery are also part of the cluster. The industry has an annual turnover of Rs 400 crore (DCHandlooms 2008). Traditionally Banaras weavers are best known for making the Banarasi sari, 5–6 meters long and 1 meter wide silk fabric with intricate woven embroidery. The vast majority of sari artisans in the city are Muslim. In the rural areas Hindu men (belonging to OBC and some *dalit* communities) are found weaving. Traders or merchants in the sari business have traditionally been upper-caste Hindu men (belonging to the Gujarati or Marwari community) though the past few decades have seen the rise of Muslim traders and exporters from the ranks of the Ansari community.

Given its size and reputation, the industry had until recently been the subject of surprisingly few studies. But in the last few years, in part due to an ongoing and severe crisis, a government-sponsored cluster study, an NGO report and two academic studies have been published, not counting several smaller reports and news articles (Ahmad 2007, DCHandlooms 2008, Raman 2010, 2013, Varman and Chakrabarti 2011). The foci of these studies are wide-ranging, from the overall structure of the industry, to the causes and consequences of its crisis, the condition of the weavers, communal and gender identity, and policy measures to support handloom weaving. However, none have focused on women's work that forms a crucial part of the industry.

Almost without exception, female labour in the Banaras textile industry is home-based. To convey an overall perspective of the different types of work involved, Fig. 7.2 schematically shows the steps in the production of saris or "dress material" (fabric meant for stitching *salwar kameez*). The black squares depict women's work and the gray squares men's work. In Banaras and surrounding rural areas women are almost never found weaving and are completely excluded from the class of masters and traders.[8] The weaving process, whether undertaken on handlooms or powerlooms, is a family labour process in which men, women, and children are involved. The completed fabric is returned to the merchant or master-weaver who has commissioned it. Powerloom saris must go through an additional step wherein unwanted yarn connecting design motifs is trimmed manually (locally known as "cutting"). After starching and finishing, saris may directly be sold to wholesalers from Banaras and other cities, or further work such as "patch-work," "*aari*-work," and "*naka-tikki*" may be undertaken to add value. All these activities are women's work, though men, may also undertake it for lack of other options. Finally, the merchant or master-weaver may also get embroidery done on the woven fabric using a computerized embroidery machine (usually operated by men in dedicated workshops).

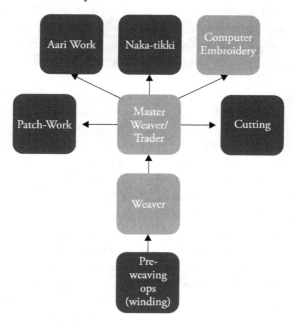

Fig. 7.2 Men's and women's work in Banaras
        Gray – Men
        Black – Women

Division of labour in an Ansari household

A "typical" Ansari household is a joint family consisting of a patriarch and his sons, each with his own nuclear family. Such a household may consist of four or five adult women depending on the marital status of the brothers. In Ansari households of Banaras, women are usually excluded from the public space of the weaving workshops and are restricted to the domestic space upstairs, known as the *zenana*. The organization of paid work mirrors the "spatial integration of women's work into kitchens and men's tendency to create workspaces away from children and from spaces dedicated to reproductive tasks" (Prugl 1999, 93): the looms are downstairs and embroidery, yarn-work or cutting work is usually done upstairs.[9] Household tasks such as cooking, cleaning, and washing clothes along with weaving-related work, and any paid work undertaken (such as embroidery) may be shared by women of the household, for e.g. one person doing the cooking for the entire household, while her sister-in-law does embroidery work. However, separate kitchens are also commonly found among joint families (Raman 2010).

Women from master-weaver households do not undertake yarn-work or paid market work. They may also observe purdah more strictly than women from working class Ansari households. Although the "culture of purdah is quite pervasive" (Raman 2010), it is equally true that the actual practice is highly variable with respect to class, family circumstance and the specific context of a male-female interaction. As an example of the last, the wife of my closest informant, Javed Bhai (name changed), practiced purdah in the sense that she was not seen downstairs or in public without a veil. However, as familiarity grew I was allowed access to the *zenana* upstairs.[10] There is also regional variation within eastern Uttar Pradesh. For example, it is interesting to note that the Ansaris of the town of Mau (about 100 km north of Banaras) display a different gender division of labour. Here women weave, mostly on light powerlooms (little more than mechanized handlooms). Men are found either weaving alongside women or dealing with procurement of raw materials and delivering finished goods. The way purdah is achieved in this case is by shuttering the windows of the workshop so that no passer-by can glance inside.[11]

Mehta (1997) has conducted a detailed anthropological study of the weaving labour process and its ritualistic significance among the Ansari weavers of the town of Barabanki in Uttar Pradesh. He argues that three generations of the family have defined roles in weaving. The roles of the father and the son in apprenticeship are described in detail for Banaras in Basole (2012, forthcoming). Here I note that, as in Barabanki, in Banaras also, women are responsible for winding and sizing operations that take place before weaving. The core of the work involves winding of weft yarn onto bobbins either manually or mechanically. Mechanized operations are common among powerloom-owning families while handloom weavers generally make do with manual techniques (since the consumption of yarn on powerlooms is much higher). It should be mentioned here that unlike the powerloom industries in Surat and Bhiwandi which are small workshop-based, in Banaras, powerloom weaving is also a home-based industry. The male weaver takes over after the pre-weaving operations are performed. The wife is usually responsible for preparing yarn for her husband's loom. Unmarried girls do not perform yarn-work, but are responsible for housework and often undertake embroidery or other paid work.

The smooth running of the family labour process is essential to keep production going. This is ensured through inculcation among women of a sense of duty towards their husband's work. The ability of the new daughter-in-law in the family to perform all work related to weaving is also essential to a successful marriage. Ansari girls are trained in this work (as in embroidery) by their mothers and grandmothers (or aunts and grandaunts) and most marriages occur within the community. This established system of training and labour extraction organized via the family provides merchants and master-weavers with a large, well-trained and disciplined workforce.

Even though women are paid directly for embroidery and cutting work, and are not paid for preparatory yarn work, we found that they usually considered unpaid work to be more important, since it is viewed as part of the wife's duties, along with taking care of the household. Echoing the division between *ghar* and *baahar* ("the home and the world") discussed by Raman (2010) in the context of north Indian Muslims, women distinguished between *ghar ka kaam* (house-work) and *baahar ka kaam* (outside work), with *ghar ka kaam* including not only care-work but also preparatory yarn work for weaving.

Outside work meant any work undertaken for wages. As a powerloom weaver noted when discussing his wife's allocation of time to various types of work, "Our main work is that one, downstairs [i.e. weaving]. That is the main thing, everything else is supplementary." (Field Interview, 2/11/2010) It is true that income from weaving exceeds income from women's homework by a factor of two or more; in this restricted sense the label "supplementary" is understandable. Unmarried girls, widows or separated/divorced women have different priorities and usually devote a large proportion of the day to homework.

The labour process

Unpaid work performed by Ansari women, viz. winding and sizing of yarn pre-weaving, has been briefly described earlier. I now focus on paid work. In my sample, women undertake two types of paid work at home: embroidery and cutting threads from woven fabric. The latter work is simple and self-explanatory, so I focus on embroidery in the discussion below. Two major types of embroidery work are found in Banaras today, viz. *aari*-work (also known as *zardozi* work) and *naka-tikki* (also called *tikki-sitara* or fancy work). These two have different techniques, histories and political economies.

Aari embroidery work has traditionally been performed by a distinct class of male artisans known as the *zardoz* and is found in several cities of North India and Pakistan. In Banaras, this work appears to be a few centuries old and male embroiderers often belonging to the Shia sect (Ansaris are Sunni Muslims) are found in the more high value-added activities in this industry (such as manufacture of items for export, including badges for US military uniforms).[12] Contemporary low-end *aari* work is performed by men and women of weaving as well as non-weaving Muslim castes. Typical *aari* embroidery is performed with a special curved needle called "*aari*." Gold thread (*zari*) maybe combined with sequins, beads, and other ornaments which are sown onto the fabric either in accordance with patterns already woven on the cloth or in areas where the fabric is plain.

The ornaments (beads and sequins) are sown with an ordinary needle. This is an example of *naka-tikki* work. Like *aari*, this work is also performed on saris and dress material woven in Banaras and in nearby towns such as Mau or Mubarakpur. Most studies of the Banarasi Sari industry either ignore or give brief mention to it. My experience suggests that *naka-tikki* work is performed overwhelming by women and young children. Adult males are rarely found doing it, except when no other employment is available or a consignment has to be finished on short order. According to Javed Bhai, a handloom and powerloom weaver, as well as middleman for embroidery work, *naka-tikki* work is of much later provenance than *aari*, having spread widely only in the last decade or two. According to him the rise of "fancy embroidery" is tied to the demise of the handloom Banarasi Sari. As powerlooms have begun to compete with handlooms in the sari market, various methods have been developed by powerloom weavers to mimic the woven embroidery of handloom saris. This is the demand-side for this type of labour. On the supply side, the declining fortunes of the handloom weavers have forced their wives to undertake any work available at home, in order to increase household incomes.[13] As weaver incomes decline, more and more women are desperate enough to work at this back-breaking, eye-straining and very low paid work. As Javed Bhai puts it, referring to embroidery work,

A: In the face of competition Banaras has maintained a niche, because even if the cloth comes from Surat or Mau or China, the decoration is done here. If this work was not there the Banaras weavers would be finished. When handloom saris declined, plain cloth came in and people started doing all this embroidery work, they closed down the looms.

Q: But the women we talked to said they didn't like *naka tikki* work...

A: They are helpless, what will they do? When handloom work was finished, people started doing *naka-tikki*, finishing of powerloom saris and so on. (Field Notes)

In both *aari* and *naka tikki* work, the fabric is usually stretched on a wooden frame. The worker sits on the floor and works on this frame. Work is labour intensive and demands high levels of concentration as well as attention to detail. Daylight or bright illumination is important for the work. Older women complained of failing eyesight and inability to perform the work due to eye-strain. Another hazard in the summer months is damage resulting from sweat. Since power-outages are common, women often cannot work in the night when it is cooler. Instead work usually proceeds in the afternoons under intense heat and humidity. Any damage to the fabric from sweat, water spillage or other reasons is deducted from piece-wages.

Embroidery work is well-known as being tiring and eye-straining. However, the monotony is somewhat relieved by the fact that it is often done communally. We frequently saw more than one person engaged on one sari, usually a mother with her daughters (or young sons) or sisters or daughters-in-law. Child-care also proceeds alongside this work as small children join in and contribute in whatever way they can or play in the vicinity.

Further, there is some room for creative input on part of the worker, especially when a new design is being tested or developed. While trusted and senior artisans are paid more to ensure loyalty, contractors are also able to take advantage of more mundane creative input from all artisans they trust. One mother-daughter pair who do *aari*-work described the design process in this manner:

Daughter: First, the good artisans (*acchhe karigar*) design the template and make the sample. Then they give the sample to artisans of average quality (*chalu karigar*) and tell them to make 50 saris according to it. So they look at the sample and mimic it. Or sometimes they [the contractor] will say "change this, its become too heavy, make it a little lighter next time."

Mother: Sometimes they also say, "Make something according to your preference."

Q: You mean if they trust the artisan?

D: Yes. If in the time you work for them, they feel she is a good artisan, then they might ask us to make something on our own (*apne man se*). Otherwise for those who are "local" (i.e. lower skilled artisans) they will repeatedly instruct them, do it like this or like that. (Field Interview 5/31/2010)

Finally, while clear data is hard to obtain, it does appear that hand embroidery is largely performed on low-end fabric, particularly machine-made saris for the mass market (selling to the consumer in the few hundred to few thousand rupees range), rather than handloom saris for the elite market. However, this obviously depends on the quality of embroidery.

A description of putting-out in Banaras

Ansari master-weavers or master-weavers-turned-merchants (known locally as *girhasts*) and traditional Hindu (typically Gujarati and Marwari) merchants (known locally as *gaddidars*) in the city are the key players in the putting-out system in Banaras. After a handloom or powerloom sari is returned to the master-weaver by a job-work weaver or is bought by a merchant, more work may be undertaken on it based on the market demand. The master or the merchant gives the fabric to a contractor who specializes in a certain type of work, say embroidery or patch-work. The contractor assumes responsibility for returning a fixed number of pieces with the work completed, within a certain time-frame. He then distributes them to home-working women via one or more intermediaries. The contractor may supply the materials (mainly thread and ornaments) or he may ask the worker to procure them from the market and pay for them later along with the piece-wage. In the latter case the relationship slides from a pure putting-out type to something that resembles an independent producer selling her output. However, the work is undertaken under specific orders from the contractor, and elements crucial to independence, such as control over design and over who to sell the product, are missing. Finally, in either of the two cases above, the equipment (needles, wooden mounting frame) and premises remain the worker's.

Figure 7.3 depicts a typical putting-out arrangement in Banaras. At least two persons separate the direct producer from the merchant who commissions the work and the chain may be longer in some instances. The merchants, contractors and middlemen are all men. I did not meet or hear of any women in these roles.

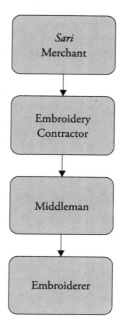

Fig. 7.3 The putting-out system in Banaras

While middlemen (sex intended) are often the key intermediaries who bring saris to women, in the Lallapura neighborhood we learned that the women-workers themselves also may do this. After finishing morning housework, women go to the *girhast*, deliver the previous day's work and take new work. To accommodate this, *girhasts* have a *gaddi* reserved for women. In several cases however, it is a male member, usually the husband (or the older son) who brings work home and returns the finished saris. This raises the question of who is the first recipient of the woman's wage. This varies from household to household and in many instances husbands or other male relatives who act as intermediaries are also paid the wages. But one respondent while confirming that her husband received the wage from the master-weaver, also confidently asserted that the money was delivered to her promptly and remained in her control (*paisa le ate hain to haath mein de dete hain*) (Field Interview 2/18/2010 #3).

The intermediary closest to the worker herself is often a male member of the extended family or a man from the neighborhood. For example, when interviewing one woman who undertook *naka-tikki* work along with her daughters, we also chanced upon their cousin, a man who supplied them with work. His role, as he defined it, was to bring the women saris from the *gaddidar* (the merchant who puts out the work), for which he received a margin of Rs 5 to Rs 10 per sari. He was a handloom weaver who had turned to this work after a decline in handloom demand and supplied work to around 15–20 women.

Homeworking women display a keen awareness of their vulnerable position and low bargaining power. In their analysis, wages are kept low by the threat of withdrawal of work, a credible threat given the rising number of women willing and able to do such work. Observing one respondent working very fast at her embroidering, the interviewer noted:

Q: You work so fast! You must be very practiced at it.

A: Yes! They [middlemen] tell us, make it quickly, we need to take it back [to the contractor]. If we take long, we won't get work, they will give it to someone else.

Q: Do you do housework also?

A: No, they [points to daughters] do the housework. They are all free, so they do it. I only do this. This needs to get done quickly. If we don't complete it in time, they wont give us work.

(Field Interview 2/11/2010)

Another worker identified the cause of low wages in competition among workers as follows:

Nowadays we have to work harder for lower wages. Earlier we could do work worth Rs 50–60 in four hours. Today we have to work the whole day for the same amount of money. There are people spread-out all over the place, even in the rural areas doing this work. Previously this work wasn't done in the rural areas. Now the wages for some work are say Rs 50, then someone will say I can do it for Rs 30. Then, people will go get the work done by someone who is charging only Rs 30, why would they go to one asking Rs 50? (Field Interview 2/18/2010)

Results of the time-use survey

The structure of the working day

A common expression used by women interviewed, to describe embroidery and other outside work undertaken for wages, was that it was undertaken in free or spare time, something they did after they were free from all work (*khali samay mein* or *sab kaam se khali hone par*). One simple question that arises here is, how many hours in a day do women actually spend doing embroidery or other market work? As noted earlier, several studies on homeworkers have documented piece rates as well as labour process but it has proved much more difficult to measure the number of hours spent doing this work, although one or two studies do provide estimates (without the benefit of a time-use survey). The major reason for the difficulty is that the women themselves see no need to keep track of their hours. Further the day is broken up by the rhythm of care-work. While they do see that a full day's work is earning them no more than a pittance, they cannot report hourly wage rates. This situation also suits the employers since it sustains the myth of spare-time activity and hides the actual hourly wage rate. A tailored time-use survey which allows us to bring together hours spent, work completed and piece-rate received is the only way around this problem.

The time-use survey reveals that women engaged in embroidery and cutting work spend 9 (+/– 3) hours in paid market work and 6 (+/– 2) hours in care work (N = 147 observations). Figure 7.4 (top) depicts the trade-off between care work and market work observed in the sample. We expect this labour budget constraint to be downward sloping and there is a cluster of data points around 9 hours a day of paid work and 6–7 hours of care work per day, as expected from the averages. The tempogram in Fig. 7.4 (bottom) shows the average time-use pattern of the same sample of 32 women over a 24-hour period starting at 5 a.m.

The working day is clearly split into three shifts of paid work structured around the rhythm of care-work. A typical day starts with two hours of care work that mostly involves cleaning the house and cooking breakfast as well as getting children ready for school. By 7 am there is a 50 per cent chance that market work has started. It continues till 11am or 12 noon at which point lunch must be prepared, dishes cleaned etc. From 2 pm to 5 pm is a second shift of market work, followed by preparation and eating of dinner. After dinner, electricity permitting some women put in a further two or three hours of work till 9 pm or 10 pm. Evening work often depends on deadlines to be met. The spirit of the tempogram is captured by the following respondent: "Whatever time I get after cooking three meals, I spend on this" (Field Interview 2/11/2010).

Although it has status equal to housework, yarn work typically takes much less time (three hours on average per day) because bobbins are wound everyday only in amounts necessary for one day's weaving. This figure of 3 hours per day that emerges from the time- use survey matches well with the results of an independent survey we performed of seven weaving households to get an estimate of the amount and value of women's labour in weaving (2.7 hours per day). Typically the wife undertakes this task the first thing in the morning after early morning housework responsibilities are done.

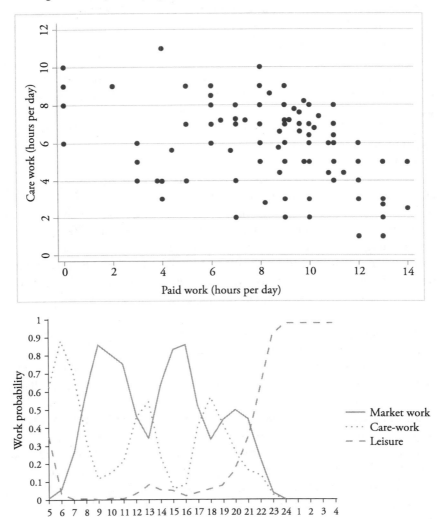

Fig. 7.4 Labour budget constraint and tempogram for home-working women in Banaras

Source: Time use survey

The long workday is sustained in part by economic necessity and in part by the ideology that women must always be productive and cannot be seen to be idle. These two aspects are intermingled in this mother's response:

> It doesn't look good if our daughters don't work and just sit around like others after studying. If there isn't work, it doesn't feel right, if there isn't a sari being worked on, it doesn't feel right. Even small children are at it. Prices are rising so fast, we can't make ends meet. And there are people even poorer than us. (Field Interview 2/18/2010)

And as a woman powerloom weaver in Mau noted,

> ...people will criticize a woman if she does not work. They will say, "his wife doesn't work, just lives off his earnings." They will criticize her mother saying she hasn't taught her daughter any skills. (Field Interview 4/21/2010)

Value of women's work

Unpaid work performed in home-based artisanal industry was included for the first time in the definition of home-based work by the Independent Group on Home-based Workers in India set up by the Ministry of Statistics and Programme Implementation in 2007 (Government of India 2008a), expanding the ILO–1996 definition. This work is widespread in informal industry and is largely performed by women. The National Sample Survey Organization collects data on number of unpaid family workers in its establishment surveys. However, it does not make any attempt to assign market value to their work. Since it is mostly women who perform this work, it is also viewed as an extension of the wife's duties to help her husband. Within the context of the putting out system what it means is that the entire family's labour can be purchased for the piece rate paid. This point is not lost on the weavers, who are quick to point out that Rs 100 a day that they earn is contingent upon the whole family's labour. While it is well-known that women's unpaid work is crucial to weaving and this fact is also readily accepted by male weavers, no studies have attempted to impute a wage-rate for this work. As Harris-White (2003, 116) notes, for sex-sequential labour processes, as weaving is, it is difficult to calculate separate male and female productivities.

An estimate can be made however, in a couple of different ways. One is to measure the difference between piece-rates received by job-workers who work at home and loomless weavers who work on an employer's loom in the employer's home. In the former case yarn work is performed by the weaver's wife and in the latter, it is not. This comparison is difficult to do directly because piece-rates vary from sari to sari and from master to master and the comparison would have to be done on exactly the same sari. Here I adopt the more indirect method of approaching job-work weavers and asking them what would earn for the same sari they are now weaving in they were to work in the master's workshop instead of at home. I then compare this number they offer to the piece rate they are receiving as job-workers. This method is not fool-proof, but does give us a start. A second method is simply to ask how much it would cost to get preparatory yarn work done outside the home, in which case it would have to be paid for.

In a sample of seven job-work weavers who own their looms (see Table 7.1), we discovered that if the weavers were to weave the same fabric on the master's loom in the master's house or workshop, they would receive 70 per cent of the wages they received for weaving in their own house. This difference, about Rs 210 in this case, represents payment for women's work as well as other costs incurred by the weaver, such as maintenance of the loom, electricity, rent, etc. How much of this amount could be imputed to be women's wages? Weavers reported that getting the same yarn work that their wife did, done outside would cost on average Rs 92 per sari. Thus approximately half of the premium in piece-rates that job-workers receive is accounted for by payment for women's work and half for other costs. If one takes this figure of Rs 92 as a proxy for the market value of women's unpaid work, then factoring in the number of hours spent on yarn-work, it amounts to Rs 3.6 per hour on average.

In interviews, women displayed that they were conscious of their exploitation by referring to embroidery work as *begaari* ("This work does not pay according to the effort involved. Its just *begaari* for sitting at home" said one woman.) *Begaari* historically referred to forced unpaid work performed by share-croppers and other tenants for their landlords. Today it is also used to refer to extremely low-paid work. But exactly how low is low?

Table 7.1 Estimating the value of unpaid work in weaving

Variable	Mean (SD)
Job-worker piece rate (Rs)	700 (81)
Loomless piece rate (Rs)	489 (55)
Job work minus loomless (Rs)	210 (43)
Market value of yarn work (Rs)	91.7 (14.2)

Note: N = 7
Source: Field Survey

It is easier to estimate wage rates for paid work as compared to unpaid yarn work described above, since piece rates that women receive are known. But there are other difficulties. As with unpaid care work, the women themselves see no need to keep track of their working hours, supporting the assumption that it is seen as time with no opportunity cost. As one home-based *aari*-worker in the Lallapura neighborhood notes when describing her daughter's work:

> She is a girl, if she just sits around she will only get bored. Its better, we think, just do whatever work you get. If we don't do it, we won't get any money, if we do something, at least we will get Rs 10. (Field Interview 2/18/2010)

The time-use survey allows us to partially circumvent these problems and calculate hourly wage rates for embroidery and cutting work.[14] The number of hours women reported working in a day are added over the number of days they reported taking to finish a piece (embroidery) or the number of saris they finished in a day (cutting). To this we add the number of hours of help they received on the sari from other family members (excepting children below 10 years of age). The piece-rate is then divided by the number of hours of labour input to obtain the hourly wage. Piece rates, hours per piece and hourly wages for the three occupations are reported in Table 7.2. Although *aari* embroidery work takes longer, it is also paid at a higher piece rate, such that hourly wages are higher in *aari* (Rs 5.6) as compared to *naka-tikki* (Rs 4.2). This difference is statistically significant ($p < 0.001$). Piece rates for cutting are much lower but it takes much less time to finish a piece since the work only involves sniping unwanted threads from between design motifs. Hourly wage rates were found to be the lowest in *naka-tikki* work, and indeed this work also has the reputation of being the least well-paid in addition to being very strenuous.

Table 7.2 Average (sd) piece rates in embroidery and cutting

Activity	*Naka-tikki* (N = 58)	*Aari* work (N = 21)	Cutting (N = 14)
Piece Rate (Rs)	71.0 (47.8)	134.3 (57.0)	18.5 (3.7)
Hours per piece	18.8 (12.9)	24.6 (9.0)	3.8 (1.6)
Hourly wage (Rs)	4.2 (1.4)	5.6 (1.8)	5.0 (1.6)

Source: Time Use Survey.

Similar figures are obtained for work as diverse as cutting vegetables for pickles, making *bindis*, fans and mats (data not shown). This figure is half the hourly wage rate that men receive for weaving and also far below the Uttar Pradesh State minimum wage rate for every occupation other than carpet weaving and glass bangle making.

Seeing such low wage rates, one may object that this is a result of overestimating the labour input. One source of overestimation could be that the hours of help provided to the main worker have been added without discounting them in any fashion. The quality of input will probably vary between an experienced worker and her daughter who may just be learning the work. To check for this possibility we calculated hourly wage rates separately for those women who did *naka-tikki* work by themselves. We obtain a figure of Rs 4.58, only marginally higher than that obtained for those who had help. Further independent corroboration that these estimates are correct comes from a contractor who puts out embroidery work to women via middlemen. He notes:

> To make [i.e. embroider] an ordinary sari it takes 2 days. We pay 60 rupees as wages. If he works hard for two days he can finish it, if he works for at least ten hours. Wages are very low in Banaras. People try to show that wages are high here, but that is not at all the case. (Field Interview 12/23/2009).[15]

Finally, though women usually claimed that they did not account for how many hours they worked, one *naka-tikki* worker during an interview did reveal her own estimation of how much she was able to earn– Rs 2 to 3 an hour. The following exchange illustrates how this woman had thoroughly monetized her conception of time.

Q: How long will you take to finish this work?

A: It will take 5–6 days. What can we do, things are so difficult.

Q: How much do you get for it?

A: Oh, just 150–200 rupees.

Q: How many hours a day do you work on this?

[She misunderstands the question as "How many rupees do you earn in a day?"]

A: Well, in one day maybe 20 or 15.

Q: 15–20 hours?

A: No, in a day. [i.e. she earns Rs 15–20 a day. She thinks she is being asked how much she earns per day, when we are trying to ask how much she works per day]

Q: How many hours do you work on this?

A: In an hour at most Rs 2–3, that is all.

[Again, she thinks she is being asked her hourly earnings.]

(Field Interview 2/11/2010)

The confusion in the above conversation results from the fact that even though the woman is being asked how much she works, she only answers in terms of how much money she makes. What emerges is the clear idea that the respondent has regarding the worth of her time. In fact she measures her time in terms of rupees earned.

Discussion and conclusion

In this final section, I reflect on the data presented above and place it in the context of the lived social reality of the women who are the subject of this article.

First, it should be noted that sheer economic necessity imbues even the paltry wages women receive with great significance for the family's well-being. In a household where weaving brings in Rs 100 a day, Rs 30 a day constitutes a 30 per cent increase in income. This importance of women's paid work is appreciated by women as well as men.[16] Further, while it is true that abysmally low wage rates cause women to work long hours, one should not neglect the important ways in which women make their own and others' life enjoyable and meaningful. The time-use data presented here suggests that women enjoy practically no leisure time but work is performed in groups, sharing stories, jokes, and gossip. Children are about, either working or playing. Thus work-time is also care-time mothers spend with their children and elder siblings with younger ones. As feminist economists have pointed out, such emotional labour is simultaneously tiring and fulfilling, being motivated by principles such as altruism, reciprocity, and obligation or responsibility (Folbre 1995).

The embeddedness of Ansari women in the family and community is striking and has been commented on by other observers of the industry (Raman 2010). The importance of the family as a support-structure is illustrated clearly by the challenges faced by women who have walked out of bad marriages, have been widowed, or have been forsaken by their natal families (ibid). It is tempting to conclude, within the dualism of the individual versus the family, that the family takes precedence in an Ansari woman's life choices. But note that such "other-regarding behaviour" can be the product of endogenous preferences produced by engaging in caring labour from a young age (in other words it need not be "natural" to women but a product of their upbringing). In fact we need not pose the individual against family, since as has been argued by feminist scholars in other South Asian contexts, women's subjectivities are *constituted within* family and social relationships (Leve 2009).

While such pro-social preferences enable women to equate their well-being with the family's, at the same time they create the myth of the "wife and helper" who is not a worker in her own right. As I have shown, unpaid work is given a higher priority than paid work because the artisanal family is seen, by both men and women, as an organic entity that functions together. As a result, even though women see themselves and men see them as productive workers, women's time other than that spent in housework and unpaid weaving tasks, is seen as "spare time." Employers do not regard them as "real workers," nor do the women themselves.

One purpose of undertaking this study is to destroy this myth of spare-time work and to produce evidence for effective agitation and advocacy at the political and policy levels. The subject population was chosen because it is understudied. Women workers in Banaras typically labour in the shadow of men's work in this famous industry. The time-use approach was chosen because careful documentation of actual hours worked and wages earned is vital to making the case for minimum wages. At the level of international policy, one achievement of organizations such as SEWA, WIEGO, and HomeNet has been the adoption by the ILO in 1996 of a Home Work Convention (C177) that brings homeworkers (but not own account home-based workers) within the ambit of labour legislation (ILO 1996).[17] By stating clearly that homeworkers are wage-workers and not self-employed, the ILO convention creates the legal basis to legislate minimum wages, working hours, rights to form unions etc. However, only ten countries have ratified the ILO convention as of October 2015 and India is not among these.[18]

The challenges to labour organizing for policy advocacy in such sectors are well known and need not be repeated. While there are several community-based weavers' organizations active in Banaras on various issues ranging from electricity supply, yarn supply, and government subsidies, to communal tensions, I did not find any organization taking up the issues of women workers. There are also several NGOs that work with weavers bringing them work and marketing their products, but again, as far as I could see, there were no NGOs that included women workers in their programs. However, interviews reveal that women display a keen awareness of the economic forces that create vulnerability and precarity and most women who were interviewed were very vocal about their circumstances suggesting that the issues can be raised if some organization displays interest. Since several types of piece-rate work are carried out in any given neighborhood, a neighborhood-based rather than occupation-based organization may be more effective.

At the ideological level, it is important to build awareness that women's *vidya*, their knowledge, skills, are neither non-existent, nor free. The extraction of labour based on this knowledge presently benefits both employers and consumers, since the knowledge itself is seen as a "natural" part of women's existence, rather than something acquired and scarce, and therefore, having an opportunity cost. Predictably, home-based workers account for a small fraction of value-added in most occupations (Khan and Kazmi 2003, Mehrotra and Biggeri 2007). While academic studies such as this have their place, this is a question of political assertion and the *lokavidya* perspective, alluded to earlier, can form a basis for such assertion.

Endnotes

The city officially known as 'Varanasi' is referred to by the local population, and in particular by the weavers who are the subject of this study, as 'Banaras.' Hence the term Banaras has been used throughout in preference to Varanasi.

[1] As the Arjun Sengupta Commission on the informal sector observed, "the conventional idea of a workplace is the office, factory or an institution" but "as little as one-third of the women workers worked in conventionally designated workplaces" (Sengupta et al. 2007, 79) The percentage of women working from home reaches well over 90 per cent for many manufacturing industries such as food processing and textiles.

[2] All values reported in the paper are nominal 2009–10 rupee values. AIDWA (2010) study notes that homeworking women in Delhi earned only Rs 32.54 per day while the minimum wage for unskilled workers in Delhi was Rs 140. The Sengupta Commission notes that:

> In Uttar Pradesh, home-based chikan workers on piece-rate can earn from Rs 20–25 per day to Rs 10–15 per day. In Ahmedabad, frocks were stitched for Rs 35 per day. Making of Agarbatti earns Rs 48–80 per day in Madhya Pradesh, but only about Rs 28 per day in Ahmedabad. Overall, piece-rate wages tend to be below minimum wage norms (Homenet South Asia and ISST 2006 in Sengupta et al. (2007, 91).

[3] See Bajaj 1999, Balakrishnan and Sayeed 2002, Beneria and Roldan 1987, Boris and Prugl 1996, Chen et al. 1999, Home Net 2006, Menefee-Singh and Kelles-Viitanen 1987, Prugl 1999, Sudarshan and Sinha, 2011. The Self Employed Women's Association (SEWA) of India, and HomeNet International, both founding members of Women in the Informal Economy: Globalizing and Organizing (WIEGO), have played a crucial role in bringing greater visibility to this workforce.

4   Also see Penington and Westover (1989) for a discussion of these factors in the context of homework in England in the late nineteenth-early twentieth century.

5   In Basole (2012, 2014a) I develop the concept of lokavidya (people's knowledge) as the knowledge-base of the informal sector, on the basis of work by Sahasrabudhey and Sahasrabudhey (2001).

6   And in a rare calculation of hourly wage rates Azid *et al.* (2001, 1115) offer the following details of homework in Multan, Pakistan:

> If a person gives 5 hour a day to one dupatta, than he or she will prepare it in 3 days it means they are spending 15 labour hours on one piece and getting Rs 3.5 against each labour hour (piece rate is Rs 50).

7   For debates surrounding the term "care-work" see Folbre (2006). A detailed discussion is outside the scope of this paper.

8   See Raman (2010) for a rare exception. The situation is different in Mau where women operate light powerlooms and also fly-shuttle handlooms.

9   A thorough examination of the practice of purdah is outside the scope of this study. See Papanek (1973) for an overview of the practice and meaning of purdah in South Asia. Kumar (1988) and Raman (2010) have dealt with this issue for the Ansaris of Banaras, while Mehta (1997) discusses family organization and kinship among the Ansaris of Barabanki (another town in Uttar Pradesh).

10   Raman (2010) offers the most detailed account available so far in the English language on the ways in which purdah is observed among the Ansaris, the restrictions it places and the ways in which women negotiate it or even utilize it for gaining access to the public sphere.

11   A convincing explanation of why women weave in Mau but not in Banaras is difficult to come by. A common response to the question was that women have always been weaving here (before powerlooms they wove on handlooms) and that the type of work done in Mau requires a lower amount of skill, which women are able to master more easily than the intricate work of Banaras.

12   In a bizarre turn of events, the Norwegian neo-Nazi Anders Breiwik, who murdered 76 people in a shooting rampage, got his crusader badge made from a zardoz in Banaras. See: http://www.thehindu.com/news/national/article2293819.ece?homepage=true (Accessed November 27, 2015).

13   The Banaras handloom industry has been in a prolonged recession since the late 1990s. Nominal wages for skilled weavers were around Rs 100 per day in 2009, and had most likely declined in real terms over the preceding five years. See Raman (2010) for a discussion of the causes of the crisis. See Basole (2012, forthcoming) for an economic survey of wage rates in this industry.

14   But an important supply-side factor that the survey lacks resolution to measure is that women engage in joint production of market and non-market goods, i.e. they are often engaged simultaneously in paid and unpaid work. Thus if one looks only at market measures of productivity one arrives at an incomplete understanding of women's productivity.

15   It is interesting to note, in passing, that the respondent uses the masculine gender to describe the worker, even though elsewhere in the interview he has mentioned that this work is performed overwhelmingly by women.

16 However, whether paid work strengthens the woman's bargaining position in the home was not investigated in the present study.

17 The ILO definition of homeworkers had one important omission, viz. unpaid workers in home-based industry (such as women who perform pre-weaving operations). The Independent Group on Home-based Workers in India set up by the Ministry of Statistics and Programme Implementation in 2007 has since broadened the definition to include this category (Government of India, 2008a).

18 The ten countries are Albania, Argentina, Belgium, Bosnia and Herzegovina, Bulgaria, Finland, Ireland, Netherlands, Tajikstan, and Macedonia.

References

Ahmad, Nesar. 2007. *Globalization and the Indigenous Artisan Economy: A Case Study of the Varanasi Silk Sari Industry*. Technical Report, All India Artisans and Craft-workers Association.

AIDWA. 2010. *Report on the Condition of Work of Home Based Women Workers in Delhi*. Technical Report, All India Democratic Women's Association.

Antonopoulos, Rania, and Indira Hirway. 2010. 'Unpaid Work and the Economy.' In *Unpaid Work and the Economy*, edited by Rania Antonopoulos and Indira Hirway, pp. 1–21. New York: Palgrave Macmillan.

Azid, Tauseef, Muhammad Aslam, and O. Muhamad, Chaudhary. 2001. 'Poverty, Female Labour Force Participation, and Cottage Industry: A Case Study of Cloth Embroidery in Rural Multan', *The Pakistan Development Review*, 40(4): 1105–18.

Bajaj, Manjul. 1999. *Invisible Workers, Visible Contribution: A Study of Homebased Women Workers in Five Sectors Across South Asia*. Women in Informal Employment: Globalizing and Organizing (WIEGO).

Balakrishnan, Radhika, and Asad Sayeed. 2002. 'Subcontracting: The Push-Pull Factor,' in *The Hidden Assembly Line: Gender Dynamics of Subcontracted Work in a Global Economy*, edited by Radhika Balakrishnan, Kumarian Press, pp. 15–34.

Basole, Amit. 2012. *Knowledge, Gender, and Production Relations in India's Informal Economy*. PhD diss, Amherst: University of Massachusetts.

———. 2014. 'The Informal Economy from a Knowledge Perspective', *Yojana Development Monthly*, October 2014.

Basole, Amit (forthcoming) 'Informality and Flexible Specialization: Apprenticeships and Knowledge Spillovers in an Indian Silk Weaving Cluster,' Development and Change.

Basole, Amit, and Deepankar Basu. 2011. 'Relations of Production and Modes of Surplus Extraction in India: Part 2– Informal Industry', *Economic and Political Weekly*, 46(15): 63–79.

Beneria, Lourdes, and Martha Roldan. 1987. *The Crossroads of Class and Gender: Industrial Homework, Subcontracting, and Household Dynamics in Mexico City*. Chicago: University of Chicago Press.

Bhatt, Ela. R. 2006. *We Are Poor But So Many: The Story of Self-Employed Women in India*. New Delhi: Oxford University Press.

Boris, Eileen, and Elisabeth Prugl. 1996. *Homeworkers in Global Perspective: Invisible No More*. New York: Routledge.

Chen, Martha, Jennefer Sebstad, and Lesley O'Connell. 1999. 'Counting the Invisible Workforce: The Case of Homebased Workers.' *World Development*, 27(3): 603–10.

DCHandlooms. 2008. *Diagnostic Study of the Handloom Silk Cluster, Varanasi (Uttar Pradesh)*. Technical Report, Development Commissioner of Handlooms, Ministry of Textiles, Government of India.

de Neve, Geert. 2005. 'Weaving for IKEA in South India: Subcontracting, Labour Markets and Gender Relations in a Global Value Chain', in *Globalizing India: Perspectives from Below*. New York: Anthem Press. pp. 89–118.

de Paiva Abreu Alice Rangel, and Bila Sorj. 1996. '"Good Housewives": Seamstresses in the Brazilian Garment Industry', In *Homeworkers in Global Perspective: Invisible No More* edited by Eileen Boris and Elisabeth Prugl. New York: Routledge. pp. 93–110.

Floro, Maria, S., and Anant Pichetpongsa. 2010. 'Gender, Work Intensity, and Wellbeing of Thai Home-Based Workers', *Feminist Economics*, 16(3): 5–44.

Folbre, Nancy. 1995. '"Holding Hands at Midnight": The Paradox of Caring Labour.' *Feminist Economics*, 1(1): 73–92.

Folbre, Nancy. 2006. 'Measuring Care: Gender, Empowerment, and the Care Economy', *Journal of Human Development*, 7(2): 183–99.

Ghavamshahidi, Zohreh. 1996. '"Bibi Khanum": Carpet Weavers and Gender Ideology in Iran', in *Homeworkers in Global Perspective: Invisible No More* edited by Eileen Boris and Eilsabeth Prugl. New York: Routledge. pp. 111–28.

Government of India. 2008a. *Report of the Independent Group on Home-Based Workers*. Technical Report, Ministry of Statistics and Programme Implementation.

Hahn, Jeanne. 1996. '"Feminzation Through Flexible Labour": The Political Economy of Home-Based Work in India', in *Homeworkers in Global Perspective: Invisible No More* edited by Eileen Boris and Eilsabeth Prugl. New York: Routledge. pp. 219–38.

ILO. 1996. *Homework Convention* (c177), International Labour Organization. Available at: http://www.ilo.org/ilolex/cgi-lex/convde.pl?C177.

Jacobsen, Joyce. P. 2003. *Women, Family, and Work: Writings on the Economics of Gender*. Blackwell Publishing.

Kabeer, Naila. 1994. *Reversed Realities: Gender Hierarchies in Development Thought*. London: Verso.

Kazi, Shahnaz, and Bilquees Raza. 1989. 'Women in the Informal Sector: Home-based Workers in Karachi', *The Pakistan Development Review*, 28(4): 777–88.

Khan, Shahrukh R., and Sajid Kazmi. 2003. Revenue Distribution across Value Chains: The Case of Home-based Sub-contracted Workers in Pakistan. University of Utah Department of Economics Working Paper No: 2003–04.

Kumar, Nita. 1988. *The Artisans of Banaras: Popular Culture and Identity*, pp. 1880–1986. New Jersey: Princeton University Press.

Leve, Lauren. 2009. Women's Empowerment and Rural Revolution: Rethinking "Failed Development", *Dialectical Anthropology*, 33(3–4): 345–63.

Marx, Karl. 1867/1992. *Capital: A Critique of Political Economy*, vol. 1. New York: Penguin Classics.

Mehrotra, Santosh, and Mario Biggeri. 2007. 'Subcontracting and Homework in the Value Chain', in *Asian Informal Workers: Global Risks, Local Protection* edited by Santosh Mehrotra and Mario Biggeri. New Delhi: Routledge. pp. 62–81.

Mehta, Deepak. 1997. *Work, Ritual, Biography: A Muslim Community in North India*. New Delhi: Oxford University Press.

Menefee-Singh, Andrea, and Anita Kelles-Viitanen. 1987. *Invisible Hands: Women in Home-Based Production*. New Delhi: Sage Publications.

Mies, Maria. 1982. *The Lacemakers of Narsapur: Indian Housewives Produce for the World Market.* London: Zed Press.

Papanek, Hanna. 1973. 'Purdah: Separate Worlds and Symbolic Shelter', *Comparative Studies in Society and History*, 15(3): 289–325.

Pearson, Ruth. 1998. 'Nimble Fingers Revisited: Reflections on Women and Third World Industrialisation in the Late Twentieth Century', in *Feminist Visions of Development: Gender, Analysis and Policy* edited by Cecile Jackson and Ruth Pearson. London: Routledge.

Penington, Shelley, and Belinda Westover. 1989. *A Hidden Workforce: Homeworkers in England,* Macmillan Education. pp. 1850–1985.

Prugl, Elisabeth. 1999. *The Global Construction of Gender: Home-Based Work in the Political Economy of the* 20*th Century.* New York: Columbia University Press.

Raman, Vasanthi. 2010. *The Warp and the Weft: Community and Gender Identity among Banaras Weavers.* New Delhi: Routledge.

———. 2013. *Entangled Yarns: Banaras Weavers and Social Crisis.* Shimla: Indian Institute of Advanced Study.

Rao, V. Rukmini, and Sahba Husain. 19870. Invisible Hands: Women in Home-based Production in the Garment Export Industry in Delhi in *Invisible Hands: Women in Home-Based Production,* New Delhi: Sage Publications. pp. 51–67.

Sahasrabudhey, Sunil, and Chitra Sahasrabudhey. 2001. *Lokavidya Vichar* (The Lokavidya Standpoint, Hindi). Varanasi: Lokavidya Pratishtha Abhiyan.

Sengupta, Arjun., Ravi, S. Srivastava, K. Kannan, V. Malhotra, B. Yugandhar, and T. Papola. 2007. *Report on Conditions of Work and Promotion of Livelihoods in the Unorganized Sector.* National Commission for Enterprises in the Unorganized Sector, New Delhi.

Sudarshan, Ratna. M., and Shalini Sinha. 2011. *Making Home-Based Work Visible: A Review of Evidence from South Asia.* WIEGO Urban Policies Research Report, No. 10.

Varman, Rahul, and Manali Chakrabarti. 2011. Notes from Small Industry Clusters: Making Sense of Knowledge and Barriers to Innovation, *AI and Society*, 26: 393–415.

Wilkinson-Weber, Claire M. 1999. *Embroidering Lives: Women's Work and Skill in the Lucknow Embroidery Industry.* New York: SUNY Press.

8

Gender, Work and Space
Home-based Workers in Garment Industry in Kolkata

Swati Sachdev

Introduction

In the current era of globalization, firms in order to ensure profits, reduce labour costs and introduce flexibility. The recent trends in the Indian labour market towards informalization have been in line with these global changes and have raised questions regarding watertight compartments between formal and informal sectors. Much of the formal activities are now being carried out in the informal settings through traditional putting-out system and its new guise, the sub-contracting practices leading to proliferation of home-based work, most of which are undertaken by women. This pattern of labor market development and incorporating and recognizing these women into the fold of paid work has been termed by scholars as 'Gender Reality' of employment growth (Chen, Sebstad and O'Connell 1999, 604). This reliance on women workforce is because their participation in labour market is considered as more flexible. Home-based work absolves unionization and saves labour costs because of minimum wages that can be paid without any social security benefits. In addition to such sub-contracting, the ensuing segregation of jobs makes the home-based work most exploitative.

As a consequence of the continuous clouding of formal-informal work, the traditional dichotomy of public and private gets replaced by the intertwining of both the spheres. The blurring of boundaries between home and work has varied ramifications for women. One can argue that urban contexts would be relatively more liberal and accommodating of women workers as compared to their rural counterparts. However, the available evidences suggest that informalization and gender segregation in urban India have not shown any significant decline and socio-cultural constraints for women continue to remain subtly effective.[1] Their manifestation are not as overt as is the case in rural India; they are nested within various layers, forms and conditions of work, creating gendered spaces within them.

It is within this framework that the chapter attempts to decode the nature of varied forms of work and gendered spaces that have evolved. It questions the often argued contention that access to employment would enable all women to be equally empowered and stresses that the occupational positioning in the labour market and socio-cultural factors such as marital status, generate differentiated gendered spaces as well as varied levels of empowerment. That is, the chapter tries to explore the dilemma as to whether home-based work provides women with a sense of self-reliance and improvement in their status within the household or does it act merely as a tool of surplus appropriation and ends up in increasing their workload and vulnerabilities.

The surveyed site is a clustered, predominantly Muslim location in the metropolitan city of Kolkata and the focus is on the textile and garment industry. It is argued that the invisibility of home-based women workers in urban West Bengal in general and Kolkata metropolitan city in particular, as shown in low workforce participation rates in official statistics, is a myth and the reasons behind the apparent invisibility is explored. The chapter seeks to examine the question of homogeneity vis-à-vis heterogeneity of the women within the home-based work (Thakur 1999; Sachdev 2004) arguing for a nuanced understanding of the nature of their economic and cultural environment that determine the exact type of home-based work and the degree of interdependencies, as the homogeneity of gendered spaces gets replaced by the plurality of workers and employment relations and varying levels of empowerment.

The chapter is divided into six sections. The first section deals with the physio-cultural regional specificities of the study area. Accordingly, they exhibit the clustering of home-based workers on account of historical factors and localization economies in the region. The next two sections position the home-based workers in Kolkata with reference to the labour market in India and West Bengal. The subsequent discussion examines the issue of homogeneity/heterogeneity of home-based workers in the city and argues for the greater vulnerability of certain segments even within the home-based workers, focusing on the role of marital status in differentiated gendered spaces. Furthermore, there is an examination of the organizational structure of the garment industry in the region and discussion in greater depth, of the gendered discrimination and segregation, explaining how the vulnerable position of women in the labour market hierarchy coupled with their societal identities determine the degree of gender discrimination and hence, the level of empowerment among women. The final section concludes the discussion.

Conceptual framework

This research seeks to analyse the social organization of space by trying to look at the spatial clustering of home-based manufacturing and arguing that regional specifications tend to differentiate the general impact of structural factors. Along the same line of thought, homogeneity is replaced by trying to identify the heterogeneity and plurality of workers, employment relations and hence, the terms of working even among home-based work. Such a deconstruction of labour helps to identify the discontinuities and disjuncture in the various categories of workers, which form a continuum (ILO 2002, 8; Unni and Rani 2004, 6).

Home-based work, it is argued, lies in between the informal and formal economy, with linkages with formal economy and characteristics more common with informal economy. Thus, there are various forms of home-based work at varying grades, reflected in the nature and intensity of employment relationships with the intermediaries and the employers (Carr, Chen and Tate 2000, 128). The research takes the stand that this position in the labour market governs and results in varying terms of work, varying vulnerability and levels of empowerment.

However, this heterogeneity of forms of home-based work is also a corollary of the heterogeneity of workers, which is a function of individual characteristics of workers, which include demographic factors (age, gender, marital status) as well as economic situation and household factors (social group, religion and household size) and socio-cultural milieu of the individual.

The role of gender in this nexus is of special significance, as the developments in the last century have resulted in feminization of the labour force especially in the informal sector. The chapter argues that even organized modern production relies on the informal labour relations and on women for its sustenance (Standing 1989; 1999, 584–586).

Very briefly, it may be recalled that there are several schools of thought regarding the cause of gender based occupational segregation. The first[2] and second[3] generation labour segmentation theories regard the role of capitalistic domination and patriarchy in relegating a subordinate position to women (Peck 1989; Jenkins 2004, 7–12). Third and fourth generation segmentation theories sought to incorporate the role of cultural factors like demographics to explain the exploitation of women (Jenkins 2004, 16–22; Hanson and Pratt 1995). Gender discrimination is thus variously seen as a function of patriarchy as propagated by some feminist scholars and modes of social reproduction as seen by social feminist (Peck, 1989). Alternatively, Marxist feminism sees it resulting from exploitation of neo-liberal system and patriarchy (Hanson and Pratt 1995, 5), whereas some argue that social institutions such as family and societal biases against women push them further within the poor (Bhat 2002, 5). Home-based workers, it is argued, lies at this juxtaposition of theories combining the influence of patriarchy and capitalist neo-liberal exploitation in the labour market (Thakur 1999; Jenkins 2004, 150–151, 163–164). While on one hand, flexibility suits women more as they need to balance household and workplace duties highlighting the role of patriarchy; on the other hand, they are compelled to do so due to household and societal norms.

The contention that underlies the discussion is that, although home-based work does provide women with some self-reliance, it is at a limited scale compared to women working independently and does increase their work burden. The socio-cultural family relations influence these gender dynamics in the labour market and garment industry as well (Flax 1987, 640–641; Gregson, et al. 1997; Laurie, et al. 1997; Bondi and Davidson 2005, 17–18) and space and place act as mediators in this context (Jenkins 2004, 155–169; Raju 2006, Raju 2011, 17, 39–40). These interconnections between space and gender are evident in the varying spaces they occupy in the labour market and household as a consequence of the patriarchal relations. The imposed invisibility of women workers together with the socio-cultural milieu in which they are placed, tend to reinstate traditional patriarchal structures and segregate women into specific occupations and compel them into the nature of employment that leaves little choices and in addition, underscores their importance in sustaining the family. In this nexus, the chapter explores the role of marital status, which it argues, has a direct bearing on their levels of mobility, recognition of their role in the family and their consequent empowerment.

Even within the garment industry, which is the focus of this study, the varied niches that these women occupy in the labour market and their multiple identities reflected in the gamut of the cultural and family relations, directly and indirectly govern the nature of home-based work resulting in varying levels of vulnerability and empowerment (Fig. 8.1).

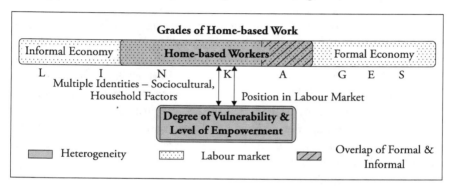

Fig. 8.1 Conceptual framework

Database

National Sample Survey (NSS) data on Employment and Unemployment, 2004–2005, 2009–2010 and 2011–2012 have been used to situate the home-based workers in the context of labour market and explore the reasons into their invisibility and assess the vulnerabilities and heterogeneity of workers. The analysis from NSS data is restricted to urban non-agricultural workers in the age-group 15–59 years only. It is to be noted that home-based manufacturing, as identified from the NSS data, is nearly identical with the concept of household industry as used by the census; hence, the chapter relies on the Census of India 2001, 2011 statistics to examine the clustering of the workers among Kolkata wards. The unit level data of National Family Health Survey – III (NFHS-III), 2005–06 have been used to address the issue of relation between employment and varying levels of empowerment. However, it is restricted to urban married women in the age- group 15–49 years[4] in Kolkata.

The study draws upon primary survey to examine how gender, space and place integrate in the readymade garment (RMG) industry in Kolkata. The wards 137 to 141 of Borough XV of Kolkata had the highest share of household industry workers and they are located in the Garden Reach/Metiabruz area situated at the western periphery of Kolkata Metropolitan Corporation. Besides, there is the presence of the Small and Medium Enterprise (SME) readymade garment (henceforth RMG) cluster[5] in these wards, which has vertical and horizontal linkages with both formal and informal components of the RMG industry in the region. The site is thus ideal for examining how the subcontracting linkages have influenced women's home-based work and their position in the labour market.

A sample of around 300 households was undertaken based on simple random sampling, wherein both men and women engaged in home-based work were surveyed. The questionnaire was canvassed at two levels – the 'household' and the 'individual' level'. In addition, four Focus Group Discussions (FGDs) and several interviews were conducted to trace the processes operating in the home-based textile and garment work. The FGDs were conducted among men and women home-based workers, the segment of men who had multiple roles, i.e., who were home-based workers and middlemen and the men 'Ostengars', i.e., the producer-traders who formed the link between the formal and informal segments of this garment industry. Each FGD had about 6–8 members and were conducted in the survey area in the backdrop of the garment cluster to situate and contextualize their roles in the labour market.

Physical, historical and socio-cultural setting and evolution of the study area

Garden Reach/Metiabruz industrial area lies in the western suburbs of Kolkata at the banks of Hugli River. Although the area is part of the Kolkata Metropolitan Corporation Borough XV, wards 133–141, it forms an independent niche in itself with its own socio-cultural economic and geographic setting within the city of Kolkata. The uniqueness is partly because of the presence of Kidderpore docks, which has resulted in Garden Reach Shipbuilding Industry and manufacturing units of other industrial plants such as Hindustan Lever, Cement, British Oxygen Company, Britania, Modern, Coca-cola, being located in its immediate vicinity. The adjacency to the industries, docks and ship building industries, not only provide employment to the workers in low pay unskilled jobs as labourers but also typifies the region, giving it its own character different from the gradually modernizing city of Kolkata.

The region was the domain of rich merchant princes in the Middle Ages; in 1856, during the British Period, Awadh's last Nawab, Wajid Ali Shah was exiled to Metiabruz. He imbibed the cultural customs, traditions, norms, modes of living and even some nobles and the courtroom amusements into this newly set up developing town. Even though, post his death in 1887, a number of changes had been introduced and old monuments were demolished by the British, a significant share of the population of the area continued to belong to the same cultural background. With the setting up of the shipbuilding and other industries such as several textile mills, a large number of migrants came over to work as labourers in these factories from adjoining states of Bihar, Orissa and even Uttar Pradesh. The closure of factories and the growth of the readymade garments industry in this region in the 1980's and early 1990's gave further impetus to the in-migration in this region, which already had a tradition of workers/artisans skilled in textile and related occupations (Chakravarty 2011).

This socio-cultural historical setting meant that majority of the population in this region were Muslims, a trend which is still persistent, a significant share being migrants. It is a close-knit community with limited cultural and societal interaction with the rest of Kolkata. A large section of this population is still engaged in the readymade garment industry. It is not surprising, therefore, that Metiabruz has been termed as 'mini Lucknow' by historian Chakraborty (Mazumdar 2008) and 'Kolkata's Choto Lucknow' by Tapadar (Tapadar 2002).

The continued clustering of home-based manufacturing work in the region can also be traced to the present economic scenario. Flexiblization and need to have a production system geared to 'just-in-time' work in order to serve dynamic markets, entails the homeworkers' location adjacent to the main firms as well as the market centers to save time (Barrientos, Kabeer and Hossain 2004, 1, 4). The closeness has its own perils; it is these workers who bear most of the risks of uncertainty in markets as contracts are cancelled without giving the home-based subcontracting workers due notice or compensation (Chen, Sebstad, O'Connell 1999, 607; Carr, Chen and Tate 2000, 8–9).

Overview of home-based workers in West Bengal

According to the NSS estimates, the workforce participation rates (henceforth WFPR) in urban areas for 15–59 years age-group have decreased from 54.3 to 50.8 for India and remained nearly stagnant from 53.3 to 53.6 for

West Bengal respectively from 2004–05 to 2011–12. While in India and West Bengal the WFPR for men is about 80 per cent,[6] for women it is just above 20 per cent. The sharp contrast between men and women workers is partly accounted for by the poor enumeration of women's work, which is not captured by the way the questionnaire is canvassed (Unni 2001, 2363; Unni and Rani 2003) and partly because of the cultural constraints that bar women's participation in the labour market or recognition of their contribution therein (Raju and Bagchi 1994, 182; Kundu 1997; Raju *et al.* 1999, 16, 30–31). Equally important is the urban context; it has often been argued that the women's participation tends to be lower in urban areas because the urban jobs, unlike rural ones, are more demanding in terms of time and distances (Kabeer 2003; Sethuraman 1998) dissuading them from working as they fail to balance their household and workplace responsibilities under such circumstances. Absence of disguised unemployment in urban areas compared to rural, wherein women assist in the farm, also decreases work force participation rates in the former settings (Raju *et al.* 1999).

Not only are urban women's WFPR rates lower, although increasing (21.3 to 23.8), a larger share among them is self-employed. This is more evident in West Bengal where nearly half (45 per cent) of the women workers, higher than the national level (40.1 per cent) and that of men (43.8 per cent), are self-employed. Amongst the self-employed women workers, nearly 23 per cent are unpaid family worker (henceforth UFW) as compared to the corresponding 12.6 per cent among men.[7] Not only are most women working as UFW, as high as 74 per cent of them (in West Bengal) are actually employed in unorganized sector[8]; 66 per cent men are in this category, with negligible social security. This plight in working conditions is more evident in manufacturing, which accounts for one-third share in the employment of women in urban West Bengal, wherein 85 per cent of women are in unorganized sector (compared to only 64 per cent men).

Within manufacturing, the textiles and garment sector accounts for the majority of male and female workforce, both unorganized and otherwise, at the national level and in West Bengal. The male–female disparity is even greater, as 57 per cent of women are engaged in the textiles and garment industry, which is almost entirely unorganized (86 per cent), while only about 44 per cent of men are employed in textiles and garment sector.

The extent of home-based work and the male–female disparity is more evident among home-based workers. While about 70 per cent of women are home-based workers in manufacturing in West Bengal, only 23 per cent of men report as home-based workers. Although there has been a significant decline in the share of women home-based workers in the State, from 82 per cent to 71 per cent from 2004–05 to 2011–12, a similar decline is not evident at the National level.[9] However, the cause for concern is that 80 per cent of these women work as homeworkers in West Bengal. Majority of these women are further concentrated in the lowest rungs of the employment ladder working as homeworkers entirely on a dependent basis and relying for even raw materials, credit, design or equipment on their employers[10] (Table 8.1).

Table 8.1 Select indicators of non-agricultural employment in urban India and urban West Bengal, (15–59 years), 2011–12

	India			West Bengal		
Percentage of Workers	**Male**	**Female**	**Total**	**Male**	**Female**	**Total**
Self-employed (SE)	39.0	40.1	39.2	43.8	45.2	44.1
Own account worker (OAW) among SE Workers	77.3	64.5	74.8	77.4	76.9	77.3
Employer among SE	6.4	0.8	5.3	9.9	0.1	7.8
Unpaid family worker (UFW) among SE Workers	16.3	34.7	19.9	12.6	23.0	14.9
Unorganised Sector (US)*	61.2	63.8	61.7	66.2	73.8	67.9
Manufacturing	23.5	32.0	25.1	29.7	33.1	30.5
US in Manufacturing	52.5	79.3	59.0	64.5	85.1	69.4
Textiles and Garments in US Manufacturing	37.3	57.6	43.9	43.6	56.9	47.5
US in Textile and Garments	65.1	83.8	71.9	69.6	86.1	74.6
Home-based in Textile and Garments	24.0	72.5	41.8	22.8	79.4	39.8
Home-based in Manufacturing	14.6	66.1	27.1	15.0	70.8	28.1
Homeworker in Textile and Garments Home-based Workers (SE)**	63.8	65.2	64.7	78	84.4	81.7
Dependent Homeworkers in Textile and Garments Home-workers**	64.1	78.2	72.4	71	88.7	81.6

*   Unorganised Sector has been categorised as per the NCEUS definition throughout the Chapter (NCEUS 2008).

** Data pertains to 2009–10 as these issues were not captured and canvassed in NSS 2011–12. Source: Computed using unit level data of NSS on Employment and Employment, 2009–10 and 2011–12.

In sum, almost the entire urban female workforce in West Bengal engaged in non-agriculture and manufacturing, is unorganized and operate as dependent homeworkers in textile and garments sector with vertical subcontracting arrangements under most exploiting and adverse terms.

Home-based workers in Kolkata: Examining their invisibility

The latest available detailed economic data at the district level confirms the above statement even for Kolkata Metropolitan Corporation (henceforth KMC). However, in KMC, main workers in household industries, both women and men, are mostly concentrated in textiles and garments along with recycling and tobacco. Within the textiles and manufacturing, majority of the workers are employed in tailoring (47 and 52 per cent men and women respectively), spinning/weaving and embroidery work and other textile products. Thus, manufacturing of textile and garments have one of the highest shares among household industry workers.

The ward-level data depict a clustering of household industry within KMC. The wards (137–141) which have such concentration are part of the SME RMG cluster in the region (Map 8.1). This cluster has vertical linkages and is of moderate size with more than 10000 units (MSME Foundation 2008; Government of West Bengal 2006).

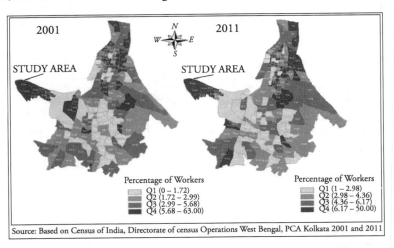

Map 8.1 Concentration of household industry workers in Kolkata, 2001 and 2011

Table 8.2 Profile of selected wards in Kolkata (M Corp.)

Ward	Sex Ratio	Literacy Rate			WFPR			Share of HHI to non-agriculture			Share of HHI to Kolkata (F)	Slum Popu-lation (%)
		P	M	F	P	M	F	P	M	F		
						Census 2001						
139	777	70.1	70.4	64.9	33.9	56.7	4.6	51.1	50.4	62.2	4.6	29.7
141	885	76.1	80.7	70.8	31.9	52.4	8.7	32.6	30.4	47.8	5.1	35.4
140	851	74.2	79.2	68.3	29.7	51.2	4.4	58.5	59.6	43.6	2.2	19.1
138	753	58.5	63.1	52.1	28.8	47.3	4.1	17.4	17.1	22.1	1.1	54.1
137	818	64.5	69.6	58.2	26.6	45.2	3.8	23.6	24.2	14.9	0.4	98.4
Kol-kata	829	80.9	83.8	77.3	37.6	58.1	12.8	3.1	2.9	4.5	100	32.5
						Census 2011						
139	890	77.6	80.6	74.1	35.7	57.9	10.9	42.1	42.3	40.6	4.14	NA
141	918	75.1	77.4	72.7	35.6	56.8	12.5	23.4	21.9	30.6	3.54	NA
140	898	79.9	82.9	76.6	38.5	62.8	11.4	44.2	44.2	44.3	3.43	NA
138	852	78.7	80.9	76.0	37.4	61.0	9.6	37.5	36.0	49.1	2.96	NA
137	845	79.2	81.8	76.0	32.2	52.9	7.7	16.4	16.4	16.4	0.43	NA
Kol-kata	908	86.3	88.3	84.1	39.9	59.9	17.9	3.9	3.4	5.6	100.00	NA

Note: P: Persons; M: Male; F: Female; HHI: Household Industry
Source: Computed using data of Census of India, Directorate of Census Operations, West Bengal PCA Kolkata, 2001, 2011

An examination of secondary data, pertaining to these wards, reveals not only a high concentration of household workers, but also some of the poorest development indicators (Table 8.2). These wards have the lowest sex ratios, lowest female WFPR, highest slum population and the highest share of female workers in household industry in Kolkata. The only redeeming feature is the moderate levels of female literacy. High share of workers in household industry in these wards co-exist with poor livelihood conditions.

Field observations reveal that majority of men and women in these wards are engaged in the textile and garment sector either directly or indirectly. In almost every household, at least some women in the household spend part of their time each day in these activities. Their presence in economically productive tasks belies the secondary data, which still reveal a WFPR of only around 10 per cent. Such gross underestimation of women workers can be attributed to a number of factors.

In order to comprehend the vast degree of underestimation, it becomes imperative to examine and to trace its roots in the physical and socio-cultural locale of these wards. The unique niche that the wards occupy within the specific historical–cultural setting, as discussed earlier, help to decode the high magnitude of underestimation of women's work force. Firstly, the fact that most of the garment industry work is carried out as home-based work in small workshops within the household premises/courtyard or in rooms adjacent to it, i.e., within the confines of their own homes, makes them invisible and inconspicuous in labour market (Singh and Viitanen 1987, Unni and Rani 2005, 1,56).[11] In contrast, home-based work for men in the region follows the broader concept of being either within the confines of their own home or even in an adjoining building or lane; also, men seen as the proverbial bread-earners are acknowledged and publicly visible.

Secondly, most of these activities are undertaken in conjunction with the household duties, wherein women throughout the day oscillate between their reproductive and productive roles. Although there is no fixed time allocated for the garment work, yet some part of each day is relegated to productive activities. Household chores and work related to garments and textiles intertwine and are carried out simultaneously; thus, hiding the visibility of the women in workforce and creating a double burden of work (Raju and Bagchi 1993; Kundu 1997; Unni 1998; Unni and Rani 1999).

Thirdly, the changing labour market with enhanced focus on subcontracting and increased flexibility has led to mushrooming of small household family-based enterprises, which take up these subcontracts. The larger firms tend to subcontract the work to them in order to fully exploit home-based cheaper and inexpensive labour, resulting in fragmented production. This also helps them to ensure flexibility to adjust to fluctuating markets. The family enterprises extract work from unpaid and underpaid workers, mostly women. FGDs carried out in the area expose how most women participate in the family enterprises/workshops as an extension of their household chores in order to assist their husbands in cleaning, trimming and even actively engaged in sewing on a regular basis especially during the six months of peak season. These women work and assist their husbands for long hours during afternoons and nights, even up to 8–10 hours in a day.[12] Others assist by organizing and delineating work on piece-rate basis among neighbours and kin. This phenomenon reinforces the thesis of housewifization as proposed by Mies (Mies 1982, Custers P 1997, 191–196; Dedeoglu 2004, 7, 10). Women in more than 90 per cent of households surveyed are involved in productive activity, either individually or as unpaid workers in the family.

The perception of these women themselves was succinctly summarized by one of the women Salma[13], (aged in early 40s with three children and living in a joint family) who when interviewed identified herself as a housewife and stated

> "The family sustains itself from the weekly money obtained by selling the products at the *haat* on Wednesdays and Sundays; thus, when there is more and 'tagdar' (urgent) work, it is my and my daughters' duty to assist in the cleaning, finishing of the garments even by working late at night if need arises. Otherwise, the delivery will be delayed and the agent will not provide work next time". She adds, "at such times I start the day early and finish my other household chores and then join my daughters who at such times only help in the 'haat work'."

Thus, women themselves perceive it not only as part of their household chores, but also as an obligation to assist their husbands. In addition, they themselves prioritize their work acknowledging indirectly that household work needs to be completed first. This further adds on to their work burden. In spite of the importance of their work in the sustenance, their roles as UFW itself results in enhancing their invisibility because of the merger of their private and public roles, making their situation similar to their counterparts engaged in agriculture in rural areas. Thus, they have a unique identity between the self-employed and the wage workers. That is, of being self-employment workers and yet working on contract often to a status similar to wage employees, resulting in their invisibility and falling outside the purview of most labour laws and their consequent greater vulnerability and exploitation.

The survey showed that nearly three-fourth of women, especially those not operating in family enterprises, enter into the garment industry by 'choice', as it not only requires little training but also provides additional income to support their family. However, in reality, it represents an element of compulsion, as this is the only work available in the region for women who opt for work.[14]

While on one hand, women prefer this activity in the absence of any other opportunities, on the other hand the socio-cultural set up of the areas prevents them from moving out of their homes.[15] It seems that women's confinement to limited spatial domain has implications for social and economic mobility. In such a scenario, home-based work remains the only recourse; however, this end up making them even more invisible. Not encouraging is the fact that women themselves regard their work merely as something to keep them busy between house work and term it as 'relaxation' or 'free-time activity' and fail to give due value to the activity (also, see Chapter 7 in this volume). Such self-efficacy further inhibits their being considered as part of the workforce (Custers 1997).

Heterogeneity within the socio-cultural environment – varying vulnerabilities

Within the apparent homogeneity that the home-based workers seem to have, there is an element of differentiation within them because of societal attributes and hence, their vulnerabilities vary (Sachdev 2004, 227). The NSS data reveal that in India, the middle aged men and women tend to be employed more in this sector as compared to young adults. However, in West Bengal young adult men and women too are employed in textile and garments sector. This is validated through the case study as well, wherein women from all age groups and across all stages of life tend to be working as home-based workers in garment industry. This may essentially be because most of such activities in Metiabruz are conducted at home.

Employment status and economic vulnerability

A significant share of the home-based women operate as own-account workers and more than 30 per cent are UFW (Table 8.3). However, the case study reveals that nearly 50 per cent of women are actually UFW. Most of these women work as dependent homeworkers at the lowest rung of the value chain. Incidentally, there is marginal discrepancy between the share of men and women working as unpaid helpers in the State in the garment and textile sector. There is a complete absence of women working as employers, as societal norms inhibit them from taking an active part in leadership roles as managers and organizers in this historical–cultural locale. Thus, women are relegated to work as own-account workers and unpaid workers in West Bengal. Talking to men in FGDs reveal that they cannot even conceptualize women (essentially their wives) working as employers and associate them with only reproductive roles.

Table 8.3 Demographic and social attributes of urban home-based workers (15-59 years), 2011–12

	Manufacturing Self-employed HBW						Textile & Garments Self-employed HBW					
	India			West Bengal			India			West Bengal		
	Male	Female	Total	Male	Female	Total	Male	Female	Total	Male	Female	Total
Employment Status												
Own account worker	64.7	69.1	67.3	75.0	76.5	75.9	65.5	71.4	69.2	71.9	69.6	70.6
Employer	3.7	0.0	1.5	0.7	0.0	0.3	2.7	0.0	1.0	0.8	0.0	0.4
UFW	31.6	30.8	31.2	24.3	23.5	23.8	31.7	28.6	29.8	27.3	30.4	29.1
Age Group												
15–29	34.1	36.3	35.4	34.9	31.2	32.8	39.5	39.8	39.7	40.7	38.7	39.6
30–44	40.8	46.8	44.4	35.5	49.6	43.6	35.3	45.6	41.8	27.9	40.2	35.0
45–59	25.1	16.9	20.2	29.6	19.2	23.6	25.2	14.7	18.5	31.4	21.0	25.5
Religion												
Hindus	61.4	69.4	66.1	46.1	76.8	63.8	52.6	68.7	62.8	35.9	85.0	64.1
Muslims	35.5	27.2	30.6	53.9	23.2	36.2	46.0	28.1	34.7	64.1	15.0	35.9
Educational Attainment												
Illiterate and Below Primary	26.6	38.9	33.8	25.9	41.4	34.8	29.8	30.9	30.5	16.3	31.5	25.0
Primary	21.0	16.6	18.4	28.7	23.2	25.5	21.2	13.1	16.1	33.9	24.3	28.4
Middle	22.6	21.2	21.7	30.1	26.6	28.1	24.6	25.6	25.3	40.9	36.1	38.1
Secondary	14.4	11.8	12.9	9.0	6.3	7.4	11.8	14.7	13.6	5.2	6.0	5.7
Higher secondary and Above	9.0	7.3	8.0	2.7	1.6	2.0	6.9	10.5	9.2	1.8	0.7	1.2
Marital Status												
Never married	27.9	20.4	23.5	28.7	10.7	18.3	32.6	21.8	25.7	34.1	12.5	21.7
Currently married	70.8	71.8	71.4	69.8	84.2	78.1	66.4	70.7	69.2	65.9	83.7	76.1
Widowed/ Divorced / separated	1.3	7.8	5.1	1.5	5.1	3.6	1.0	7.5	5.1	0.0	3.8	2.2
Monthly Per Capita Consumption (MPCE) Quintile Classes												
Lowest Two Quintile Classes	51.8	52.2	52.0	50.9	66.2	59.7	55.3	47.5	50.3	42.2	62.3	53.7

Source: Computed using unit level data of NSS on Employment and Employment, 2011-12

The relatively higher share of women having illiterate and below primary education may be an additional reason for the higher share of women still working as unpaid workers, as they are compelled to take up only routinely mechanical jobs even in the textile and garment sector as shall be discussed later (Table 8.3). Whatever basic education these women possess, it is considered by the local society only as a means to improve their probability of marrying well, hence neither is it a reflection nor a measure of their employability and labour market situation.

The lower educational attainment, higher share of unpaid helpers and absence of women employers point to distressing conditions, which is further accentuated by the fact that more than 62 per cent of women in textile (garments) belong to the lowest two quintile classes of the monthly per capita expenditure compared to only 42 per cent of men, indicating high levels of 'feminization' of poverty (Cagatay 1998, 9) amongst home-based women workers. A disturbing observation emerging from the FGDs with both men and women was that, while the earnings are shared between brothers in most family enterprises, no such distribution occurs among the women members of the household. Even if they help as unpaid workers, they are provided with just enough finances to conduct their household chores and they do not have access to even their own earnings.

Marital status

Despite homogeneity in their economic vulnerabilities, socio-cultural attributes such as demography and marital status create differentiated labour market for women. As mentioned earlier, women from all age-groups tend to operate as home-based workers. Majority of the women working as home-based workers are married.[16] However, a significant share of widowed/divorced/separated women work in this sector as home-based workers. In the study region too, marital status indirectly influence women's mobility and the extent to which they are framed by patriarchal biases. It is interesting to note that although both unmarried and married women are generally engaged in working on sequins and beads, cleaning and trimming, the reasons for selecting such activities or even opting for work and the control over their earnings do vary. The FGDs reveal that while most unmarried women from households having their own enterprises work only in order to while away their leisure hours or obtain some pocket money to spend on their toiletries, married women or women who belong to households that do not own household enterprises have to take recourse to work for bare survival or in order to substantiate their family income.

The pattern described so far also reflects the changes in the nature of mobility and societal perspective towards women with change in their marital status. In Metiabruz, women are still restricted within the confines of their homes; the restrictions are more stringent for unmarried women than married ones. Unmarried women largely work as homeworkers, on sequins and beads, only if their own or neighbouring households are engaged in the activities pertaining to garment sector. The survey also validates the above pattern and shows that all unmarried women who operate as home-based workers were either engaged in their own family enterprise and/or have neighbours/ relatives, having enterprises, who supply them with the piece-rate jobs.

The scenario is different in women headed households (mostly widowed/ divorced/separated), wherein dismal economic situation seems to override societal biases. Hence, in these households women and girls of all ages and marital status are compelled by their economic situation to undertake this occupation; but even under such circumstances, unmarried girls do not venture out to obtain the job-work. Ironically, however, their direct dealings with the agents, in the absence of men, expose them to more exploitative situations.

About half of the married women assist as unpaid family workers and a significant share works on job-contracts as own-account dependent homeworkers. However, unlike their unmarried counterparts they do venture out in search of work in their neighbourhood or get introduced to the adjoining communities. Although, more often than not it is the middlemen or some male member from the family who takes up the responsibility of obtaining contracts and delivering back the final products.

In general, while patriarchal norms limit women to the confines of home, having a bearing upon their mobility, changes in marital status somewhat lessen such constraints so that their (direct) dependencies and susceptibilities in the labour market are reduced leading to a certain variation in the situation and vulnerability of each women.

A logistic regression was undertaken for examining the factors that tend to make individuals more vulnerable and liable to become home-based workers, in manufacturing at the national level with home-based workers as the dependent variable. Three models representing all persons, women and men respectively, were run. Model 1 clearly reveals and reaffirms that women have significantly higher odds of being employed as home-based workers compared to men. Age is also a significant criterion, with increase in age resulting in higher odds of being home-based worker, especially among women as this tends to increase their household care work. Marital Status is significant only in case of Model 2, i.e., among women. As discussed earlier, married women have higher odds and have 75 per cent more chance of working as home-based workers (Table 8.4).

Although higher education does enhance mobility of men, education has no relevance and impact on women's home-based work and women from all levels of education are employed as home-based workers, which is validated through both regression analysis with macro data and field survey studies. Muslims among men and women both have higher odds of working as home-based workers, evident in the fact that almost the entire segment of population in the region engaged in home-based workers are Muslims.

Table 8.4 Dependent variable for logistic regression: Workers in manufacturing sector 15–59 years (1 = home-based worker; 0 = other workers)

	India	Female	Male
	Number of obs = 10605 LR chi2(27) = 3058.02 Prob > chi2 = 0.0000 Pseudo R2 = 0.2316	Number of obs = 2816 LR chi2(27) 267.1 Prob > chi2 = 0.0000 Pseudo R2 = 0.0771	Number of obs 7789 LR chi2(27)= 395.18 Prob > chi2 = 0.0000 Pseudo R2 = 0.0544
Gender			
Male *			
Female	11.736***		
Age			
15–29 *			
30–44	1,220**	1.095	1.363***
45–59	1.462***	1.512**	1.568***
Marital Status			
Never Married *			
Currently Married	1.138	1.756***	0.923
Widowed/ Divorced/ Separated	0.635***	0.758	1.353
Education			
Illiterate and Below Primary *			
Primary	1.158	1.360	1.085
Middle	1.139	1.275	1.069
Secondary	1.027	1.257	0.934

HS and Above (Diploma)	0.780**	1.053	0.708***
Social Group			
General ®			
SC/ST	0.888	0.710*	1.003
OBC	1.242***	1.160	1.295***
Religion			
Hindus ®			
Muslims	1.584***	2.045***	1.458***
Other Religions	1.204	0.986	1.319
MPCE Quintile			
Lowest Quintile ®			
Second Quintile	0.812**	0.658***	0.899
Third Quintile	0.772***	0.656**	0.827
Fourth Quintile	0.725***	0.688*	0.731**
Highest Quintile	0.569***	0.644*	0.528***
State			
Northern ®			
Southern	0.761**	0.571***	0.910
North-eastern	2.518***	2.386***	2.611***
Western	0.826	0.757	0.848
Eastern	1.148	1.223	1.103
Central	1.767	1.595	1.822***

Note: *** significant at 0.001 per cent ** significant at 5 per cent * significant at 10 per cent; ® Reference Category

Source: Computed using unit level data of NSS on Employment and Employment, 2011–2012

Economic vulnerability discussed in the previous section also has a significant impact. This too receives substantiation from both regression and field survey. Increase in economic stability lowers the odds of being employed as home-based workers more than 60 per cent times compared to the poorest of the poor segment. Thus, those belonging to the lowest Monthly Per Capita Consumption Expenditure (MPCE) quintile have maximum probability to be home-based workers. Region or space too plays an important role and in southern India, women have lower odds of working as home-based workers probably since the societal norms and patriarchal rigidities are significantly less there as compared to other parts of India, particularly the north. Thus, both macro-level regression analyses as well as field survey and FGDs bring out the gender rigidities in the labour market, which result in more women working as home-based workers. The nature of gender discrimination and patriarchal notions is such that even education fails to make a dent to improve the situation of women. Age group, marital status, economic liability – all tend to increase the women's household burden and increase their vulnerability in the labour market and bring about a differentiation in their labour market situation.

Gendered segregation and vulnerability of women

It has been discussed earlier that the recent trends depict increasing home-based work with a reliance on women. However, the manifestation of the gender rigidities in urban labour market is varied, though by no means less. In addition to such home-based sub-contracting, there is vertical segregation into jobs that are most exploitative. Besides, horizontal and occupational segregation are also evident; they are limited to specific industries and occupations. The tasks which are most mechanical and repetitive characterize those at the lowest rung of the job ladder and are often an extension of the work at home (Bhat and Nirmala 2000; UNIFEM 2002). The situation in Metiabruz is no different in terms of such gendered segregation as discussed below.

The organizational structure of the industry

It is necessary to digress and understand the organizational structure of the industry in Metiabruz in order to comprehend the nature and form in which socio-cultural attributes and labour market result in perpetuating and reinforcing gendered roles. The garment industry in the region has its own specificities. It relies on three interlinked production chains. The first production chain and seemingly the most local chain comprises of the local shops and weekly 'Haats' on Wednesdays and Sundays, largest and most famous being the 'Jabaar Haat' and 'ABM Haat', where the goods are sold by the producer traders, i.e., 'Ostengars'. Apparently local, the Haats' scale and magnitude defy the local conception, for the wholesalers and retailers drawn from all over the country (especially the metro cities) flock to these Haats to purchase and place orders. The second chain comprises of the producers, who obtain job-orders from the wholesalers in Burrabazar, Howrah and Park

Street areas in Kolkata or from other cities or malls and shops mostly in Kolkata or adjoining areas. The third chain comprises of the small segment of producers who obtain orders directly from wholesalers of other cities and hence, have a fixed clientele and are better off. Thus, the RMG industry of the region is influenced by market fluctuations all over the country. There is a complete absence of women at the top tiers of the production chains.

In all three production chains, there is primarily three strands of work – (i) zari/zardosi/'adda work', i.e., embroidery done with metallic threads on cloth stretched on a wooden frame, (ii) machine embroidery/'phool machine' and (iii) 'Silai', i.e., sewing or tailoring. Each of these segments include a series of occupations – designing, cutting, stitching/sewing, embroidery (or adda work), sequin and bead work/'tikkli-motti', cleaning, trimming, ironing and packaging. These are encompassed by the presence of middlemen who are present at each level in order to transfer products from one production cycle to another. It is interesting to note that the above series of production cycle represents a pyramid with jobs at the top being the most paid, prestigious with least number of workers employed. In contrast, the sequin and bead work, cleaning and trimming are the least paid, most repetitive, strenuous and employ the most and are overwhelming predominated by women.

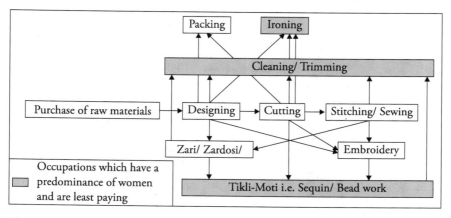

Fig. 8.2 Nested structure of home-based work in RMG industry in Metiabruz

The industry in the region is structured such that at the top are the 'Ostengars', who have their own 'Kharkhana'/'Dhalej'/workshops in the region and are at the top of the production chains in the region, have their own shops or sell in the Haats or obtain job-orders from the wholesellers/showrooms. These Ostengars thus are producer–traders at the top of the pyramid; they are the most prestigious lot in the region holding a place of prominence in the 'Dorji' community. They only undertake supervision of production in their own 'Dhalej', cutting work and designing and give out job orders to other OAW directly or through middlemen for stitching/sewing, embroidery, zari/ zardosi and sequin work. It is interesting to note that all the above series of occupations form a nested hierarchy, wherein job-works are given out for each stage by almost all other stages. Thus, not only do the Ostengars give out job-work, even the stitching, embroidery 'karigars'/workers put out job-work of stitched/ embroidered products for the next production cycle. This nested structure of home-based work (Figure 8.2) is partly responsible for perpetuating and reinforcing gender rigidities as shall be discussed later.

Although there is an overlap of occupations among men and an individual can undertake two roles in the hierarchy, women are confined to the sequin work, cleaning and trimming; more than 80 per cent of women are engaged in sequin–bead work alone, men do not undertake this activity at all (Figure 8.3). Some men do undertake cleaning and trimming themselves in case time permits, however this job is generally allocated to the apprentices who are mostly children or the women members and children of the household or other UFW.

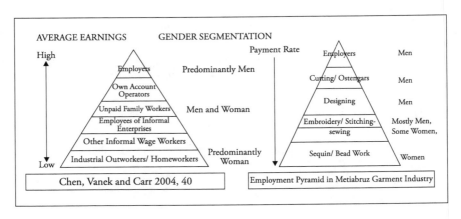

Fig. 8.3 The hierarchical positioning of gendered work

The argument for the overwhelming presence of women is that they do not need any training for stitching/ironing sequin and beads. Women themselves fail to give due recognition to these occupational skills as they are initiated into such work ever since their childhood and the training is imparted informally and transferred through generations. In their own perception, e.g., Nazma[17], who is a married women in early 30's with one child and living in a one-room squatter structure states that,

> "this is the easiest work which can be undertaken with the rest of the house-work, since we are used to sewing since childhood and do not require any training".

Another argument is that it is most conducive for women as they can combine this work with household chores; that they do not need to venture out to seek work as male members of the family/agents provide them with the work at their homes and also collect the finished products. There is, thus, a complete absence of women at the higher end of the pyramid as Ostengars, designers and embroiders. However, seen as convenient arrangement, the exploitative nature escapes women's scrutiny.

Economic scenario of home-based workers in garment industry in Kolkata

It is clear from the discussion so far that there is a nested hierarchy of workers and middlemen with women concentrated mostly at the lowest levels as home-based piece-rate workers. Apart from the hierarchy, other factors determining the gender-based segregation in garment industry is the number and nature of middlemen. Majority of women rely on a single fixed middleman for obtaining job-work, raw materials and collection of finished products. About 40 per cent of women rely on multiple middlemen. Men, on the other hand, rely more on multiple and variable middlemen, although a substantial share relies on multiple albeit fixed agents too. The high share of women homeworkers relying on single fixed agent is an indication of their restrictive mobility, which inhibits them to venture out into the market and they are forced to take recourse to social kinship networks to obtain job-work. This results in greater exploitation as they cannot bargain and secondly, in off-seasons they often remain underemployed in the absence of adequate work.

In case of men having access to multiple fixed middlemen (35 per cent) for obtaining job-work helps them in having better piece-rates through bargaining, avoiding underemployment in off-seasons; dealing with fixed agents ensures better relations and conditions of work (Table 8.5). Consequently, very few men compared to women are in the extremely exploitative condition of relying on single agents; whereas in several ways, women relegated to the lowest strands of the garment industry face the brunt of societal norms combined with lower mobility and resultant reliance on fixed single agents under more exploitative and stringent conditions. Thus, the nature of and the number of middlemen govern women's level of job security, conditions/

norms of work and bargaining capacity, which in turn are indirectly affected by patriarchal norms, which restrict the mobility of women.

Table 8.5 Gender-based differences in reliance on middlemen for job-work

Relying on single fixed middlemen	Relying on multiple fixed middlemen	Relying on multiple variable middlemen
More than 50% of women Less than 20% of men	About 25% of women About 35% of men	About 20% of women About 45 % of men

Source: Based on primary survey conducted on home-based workers in Metiabruz

In Metiabruz, the gaps in wages or earnings within the garment economy too are significantly high. While the piece rate for stitching/sewing ranges between Rs 5–30 and for embroidery it ranges between Rs 9–35, the piece rate for sequin and beads ranges from Re. 1 for extremely light work to Rs 10 for very heavy work. Consequently, while weekly income of men engaged in stitching/sewing and embroidery alone amounts to Rs 1000–2000 and Rs 3000–4000 respectively, for women working full time for all six days amounts only to Rs 600–1000. It is actually significantly lower if they are able to work part time, which is usually the case.[18]

The discrepancy of wages is also evident among the agents; women agents can provide and charge lower piece-rate than their male counterparts. Not only are the wages low for women, also very often, it is not paid weekly as is the norm in this region. Very often wages are only partly paid weekly and delayed considerably in case of both women and economically very poor men. Thus, lack of bargaining power exposes not only women, but also men to exploitation. This irregular pay becomes worse in this industry because of its inherent seasonal nature. There is a continuous oxymoron of over employment and underemployment. While in peak season, women work for eight hours or more in urgent 'tagadar' work, it is still reported as 'part-time' employment. On the other end, during lean seasons, delays in payments make sustenance a serious concern for most of the households' reliant on this work for day-to-day living expenses.

In sum, home-based work, instead of expanding women opportunities, reinforces the segregation or sexual division of labour which extends from the home into the work sphere and re-establishes the prevailing power structures of the patriarchal society (Flax 1987). The women in this region tend to be restricted to specific occupations, which are low paying and are traditionally considered for 'women', even within the textile and garment sector. This is evident by the fact that women are restricted to working on sequins and beads work, which involves only hand sewing, the knowledge of which most women in the region are expected by the local community to obtain in order to conduct their household responsibilities. They are not allowed to operate as either embroiders or stitching or as employers even within garment industry. It was observed that more often than not, their work is an extension of their husband's enterprises resulting in their ending up as unpaid family labour – a combined outcome of capitalism and patriarchy (Mies 1982; Prugl 1996, 119; Dedeoglu 2004, 17). Even women homeworkers who work independent of their household enterprises are forced by socio-cultural constraints to operate in similar niche occupations under more exploitative and dependent norms. Thus, household factors impose a constraint on women's time and cultural–behavioural patterns hinder their participation in work outside the household (Masika and Joekes 1996, 8–10) and consign them to segregated work spaces in the labour market and poorer terms of work, the degree of which varies and has an impact on their level of empowerment.

This varying impact of labour market participation on empowerment of women is validated by the fact that in Kolkata (based on NFHS-III data) the percentage of married[19] women, who had a greater freedom of movement[20] and final say (alone) on their own health, had a say in daily and large household purchases and on visits to the family were all higher for working women than non-working in Kolkata; although women working away from home have greater involvement in the decision making processes within the household than home-based workers. This implies that economic empowerment probably results in certain degree of empowerment in other spheres of life and that home-based work does provide women with at least some self-reliance compared to women not engaged in labour force; although, it does also increase their double burden and makes them more vulnerable. Thus, the nature of employment is an important determining factor in governing the level of vulnerabilities of women, as socially entrenched spaces have significant intertwining effects within the economic space.

Conclusion

The chapter thus concludes that the inherent invisibility of workers in Metiabruz (Kolkata) is a result of and accentuated by the physio-cultural locale, the forces of glocalization coupled with patriarchy and the socio-cultural-historical milieu of the region. This invisibility is further heightened as the women are concentrated mostly as unpaid family workers[21] in family enterprises within the confines of the home with little or no control over their earnings. These forces together result in relegating women to specific occupations, which are traditionally considered an extension of their household chores, are stereotypical and least paying and are situated at the lowest ring of the value chain. Women are further hampered by their lack of access to the labour market and excessive reliance on middlemen, which expose them further to exploitative conditions as they are compelled to work on poorer terms.

This nexus of invisibility-segregation results, on one hand, in obscuring and blurring the public and private space as the two intertwine and on the other hand, it results in additional burden for women, reinforcing the prevailing power structures within the homes and outside. As revealed through FGDs, the role of these home-based working women is indispensable for finishing the job-work within the specific time as market fluctuations result in sometimes very stringent deadlines. Ironically, despite their being so crucial, both for the garment industry and for the family/household survival, they are very often not paid their economic due[22] nor are they considered as part of the workforce.[23] Although home-based work does provide women with some self-reliance compared to non-workers; however it is limited and increases their double burden. The perception of women themselves and of the society at large needs to be modulated to address the issue.

The homogeneity of home-based women workers is somewhat deceptive, the stage in the life cycle, demographic characteristics, marital status, job hierarchies and economic susceptibility tend to lend a certain degree of differentiation even within the varying strands of gender based segregation as space mingles with place. The vulnerability of women is further accentuated because of lack of collective power as they are working in their individual homes. The Chapter thus displays how the public and private spheres of women's lives are intricately linked and impinge upon one another.

To conclude, the complex processes tend to expand the roots and dimension of informal sector into newer guises and strands by enhancing the informalization of the organized sector through the nested hierarchical glocal production chains, each of which has underpinnings that reinstates prevailing gender rigidities.

Endnotes

1   The intersectionalities that position women's place in labour market have been a matter of discussion in scholarly literature (Flax 1987; Raju 1993; Hanson and Pratt 1995; Jenkins 2004; Sachdev 2004; Raju 2013).

2 It was developed by Doeringer and Piore in the 1960's, who identified two separate sectors – primary sector, marked by high wages, secure, protected and safe work environment and the secondary sector, categorized by low wages, poor work conditions and insecurity of job (Jenkins 2004, 7–12).

3 It was proposed by the radical scholars who identified labour market segmentation as a means of the capitalists to maintain their control over the means of production and continue the process of surplus accumulation by surplus appropriation.

4 As NFHS data pertains only to women in the age-group 15–49 years.

5 These are of moderate size with about 10,000 units and employment between 10,000–1,00000 (www.msmefoundation.org 2008; West Bengal Economic Review 2005–06)

6 The WFPR for men was 78.4 per cent and 81.6 per cent for India and West Bengal respectively in 2011–12.

7 However, in this occupation in Metiabruz a substantial section of men too work as unpaid workers when they work in their family enterprises and the enterprise income is thus family income. However, the dynamics operating behind male and female unpaid family labour as discussed are entirely different – one with its basis in exploitation and domination and the other based more on mutual understanding.

8 Unorganized Sector has been categorized and identified throughout the Chapter using the NCEUS definition (NCEUS 2008, 47–50).

9 At the National level the share of home-based workers in urban manufacturing has remained nearly stagnant at 65 per cent between 2004–05 and 2011–12.

10 Home-based workers are most commonly categorized into the independent self-employment home-based workers (own account workers, employers and unpaid family labour) not working on contract and the contract workers working mainly or wholly on contract termed as homeworkers (Chen, Sebstad, O'Connell 1999; Sinha 2006; Carr, Chen and Tate 2000; Unni and Rani 2004; NCEUS 2007, 5). The homeworkers in turn may be categorized into the dependent workers who are dependent on the contractor for raw material or any other support and the ones who work on contract but independently. While the first category is said to have undertaken vertical sub-contracting, the latter is termed as undertaking horizontal sub-contracting (Unni and Rani 2004).

11 This extended connotation of home-based workers used in the primary survey includes not only those who work in their own homes but those working in the courtyard, same building or even adjoining homes, The argument for using the broader conception of home-based workers has also been elaborated in the report of the 'Independent Group On Home-Based Workers.' (GOI 2008, 9–10).

12 This is based on the survey undertaken in the selected wards.

13 Name changed to maintain anonymity.

14 In addition, kite making is also an occupation available for women in the region, however it too is a home-based activity and the piece rate wages for it are even lower.

15 In most of the Muslim families in the region, women are only allowed to move within the Metiabruz region and that too only on visits to relatives or with the family on festivals. Most of the relatives reside in the same neighbourhood and hence local visits suffice the purpose.

16   A micro level study of home-based workers in Ahmedabad textiles too reveals that married women have a higher likelihood to be in the sector, i.e., those who have household responsibilities (Kantor 2003).

17   Name changed to maintain anonymity.

18   Other studies in different cities validate the high levels of gender disparity in wages. A detailed study of the workers in Ahmedabad city in 1998–99 depict that 61 per cent of women were in informal employment and work from home. They get the lowest of wages and work on contracts due to resource and market constraints (Unni and Rani 1999). International studies by World Bank on homeworkers in Brazil, Ecuador and Mexico too concludes that the women home-based worker not only receives less wages per hour than men but also less compared to other non-home-based women workers (Cunningham, W. and Gomez, C. R. 2004, 15–20).

19   While for both married and unmarried women employment does lead to some empowerment; yet it has a greater impact for married women, e.g., while nearly 80 per cent of home-based married women have freedom to move out alone, only around 60 per cent of home-based never-married women have the right to move out alone.

20   Freedom to go to markets, health facility and places outside community alone.

21   Initially as the industry expanded with expanding markets during the colonial British period, more and more migrants settled in the region and became part of the industry. The joint family system sustained the viability of the production even at low prices. However, the gradual breakup of the joint family into nuclear ones have resulted in mushrooming of individual workers competing with each other for job-works resulting in lower prices and more difficulty in obtaining piece rate work. This has resulted in dire straits of the garment workers and their gradual impoverishment as real wages have been declining and they have been forced to rely on women unpaid labour for survival as they can't afford to employ workers. Some switch to or accompany home-based work with other industry work such as driver/labourers in ship-building to support themselves.

22   This further accentuates the feminization of poverty. 'Feminization of Poverty' was a term first coined by Diana Pearce in 1970s, where she referred to it as the 'concentration of poverty among women, particularly female-headed households'. It implies in simple terms that women are poorer than men. However, overtime its connotation has evolved to include not just economic aspects of poverty but also 'absence of choice, denial of opportunity and inability to achieve the goals of life' (Thibos, Lavin-Loucks and Martin 2007, 1).

23   More than 50 per cent of the women surveyed state that their work helps in augmentation of family income or increases the money at their disposal for supporting the family.

References

Barrientos, S., Kabeer, N., and N. Hossain. 2004. *The Gender Dimensions of the Globalization of Production.* Working Paper No. 17: 1–27. Policy Integration Department, World Commission on the Social Dimension of Globalization Geneva: International Labour Office. Accessed December 16, 2014. http://www.ilo.org/wcmsp5/groups/public/---dgreports/---integration/documents/publication/wcms_079121.pdf.

Bhat, K., Sham, and V. Nirmala. 2000. 'Gender-wise Determinants of Higher Occupational Scales in Service Sector', *The Indian Journal of Labour Economics,* 43(4): 883–96.

Bhat, R. 2002. 'Feminization of Poverty and Empowerment of Women – An Indian Perspective and Experience', Paper presented at the International Women's Conference, Townsville, Australia, July 3–7. Accessed November 12, 2009. http://www.adfvc.unsw.edu.au/Conference%20papers/TIWC/BhatRashmi.pdf

Bondi, L., and J. Davidson. 2005. 'Situating Gender', in *A Companion to Feminist Geography,* edited by Lise Nelson and Joni Seager. USA: Blackwell Publishing Limited. pp. 15–31.

Cagatay, N. 1998. *Gender and Poverty.* Working Paper Series 5. New York: Social Development and Poverty Elimination Division, UNDP. pp. 1–22.

Carr, M., Chen, M. A., and J. Tate. 2000. 'Globalization and Home-based Workers', *Feminist Economics,* 6(3): 123–42. Accessed December 8, 2007. DOI: 10.1080/135457000750020164.

Chakravarty, I. 2011. 'The Stately Pleasure Dome', *The Telegraph, Calcutta, India.* July 14. Accessed August 18. http://www.telegraphindia.com/1110714/jsp/opinion/story_14237607.jsp.

Chen, M. A., Vanek, J., and M. Carr. 2004. *Mainstreaming Informal Employment and Gender in Poverty Reduction: A Handbook for Policy-makers and Other Stakeholders.* Canada: Commonwealth Secretariat and International Development Research Centre. Accessed December 14, 2014. http://idl-bnc.idrc.ca/dspace/bitstream/10625/27817/21/IDL–27817.pdf.

Chen, M., Sebstad, J., and L. Lesley O'Connell. 1999. 'Counting the Invisible Workforce: The Case of Home-based Workers.' *World Development,* 27(3): 603–10.

Cunningham, W., and C. R. Gomez. 2004. *The Home as Factory Floor: Employment and Remuneration of Home-based Workers.* WPS 3295. Washington, D. C. : The World Bank. pp. 1–43.

Custers, P. 1997. *Capital Accumulation and Women's Labour in Asian Economies.* New Delhi: Sage Publications.

Dedeoglu, S. 2004. *Working for Family: The Role of Women's Informal Labor in the Survival of Family-Owned Garment Ateliers in Istanbul, Turkey.* GPID/WID Working Papers 281: 1–23.

Michigan: Michigan State University. Accessed April 14, 2014. http://gencen.isp.msu.edu/documents/Working_Papers/WP281.pdf.

Flax, Jane. 1987. 'Postmodernism and Gender Relations in Feminist Theory.' *Signs,* 12(4): 621–43.

Government of India. 2008. Independent Group on Home-Based Workers. New Delhi: Commission. Ministry of Statistics and Program Implementation, Government of India. Accessed October 23, 2011. http://www.unwomensouthasia.org/assets/Home-based-Workers-Report-india-unifem-pdf. pp. 1–87.

Government of West Bengal. 2006. West Bengal Economic Review 2005–2006. Kolkata: Development and Planning Department, West Bengal. Accessed February 5, 2008. www.wbplan.gov.in/docs/eco_05_06/Ch_6_CSS.pdf.

Gregson, N., Kothari, U., Cream, J., Dwyer, C., Holloway, S., Maddrell, A., and R. Rose. 1997. 'Gender in Feminist Geography', in *Feminist Geographies: Explorations in Diversity and Difference* edited by Royal Geographical Society and Women and Geography Study Group, The Institute of British Geographers. England: Longman. pp. 49–85.

Hanson, S., and G. Pratt. 1995. *Gender, Work and Space.* London: Routledge.

ILO. 2002. *Decent Work and the Informal Economy: Sixth Item on the Agenda.* 90th Session International Labor Conference, Report VI. Geneva: ILO. Accessed September 16, 2005. http://www.ilo.org/public/english/standards/relm/ilc/ilc90/pdf/rep-vi.pdf).

Jenkins, S. 2004. *Gender, Place and Labour Market.* United Kingdom: Ashgate.

Kantor, P. 2003. 'Improving Estimates of the Number and Economic Contribution of Home-based Producers in Urban India', *The Indian Journal of Labour Economics,* 46(2): 235–46.

Kabeer, N. 2003. *Gender Mainstreaming in Poverty Eradication and the Millennium Development Goals.* Canada: Commonwealth Secretariat, CIDA, IDRC. Accessed December 14, 2014. http://www.idrc.ca/EN/Resources/Publications/Pages/IDRCBookDetails.aspx?PublicationID=229.

Kundu, A. 1997. 'Trends and Pattern of Female Employment in India: A Case of Organized Informalization', *Indian Journal of Labour Economics*, 40(3): 439–51.

Laurie, N., Smith, F., Bowlby, S., Foord, J., Monk, S., Radcliffe, S., Rowlands, J., Townsend, J., Young, L., and N. Gregson. 1997. 'In and Out of Bounds and Resisting Boundaries: Feminist Geographies of Space and Place', In *Feminist Geographies: Explorations in Diversity and Difference* edited by Royal Geographical Society and Women and Geography Study Group, The Institute of British Geographers, England: Longman. pp. 112–45.

Masika, R., and S. Joekes. 1996. *Employment and Sustainable Livelihoods: A Gender Perspective.* Bridge Report No. 37. Sussex, United Kingdom: Institute of Development Studies, University of Sussex. Accessed December 12, 2014. http://www.euromedgenderequality.org/image.php?id=493. pp. 1–33.

Mazumdar, J. 2008. 'The Other Oudh', *Outlook India*. July, 7. Accessed May 4, 2011. http://www.outlookindia.com/printarticle.aspx?237870.

Mies, M. 1982. *The Lace Makers of Narsapur.* London: International Labour Organization.

MSME Foundation. 2008. 'Industrial Clusters in India', Accessed January 24. www.msmefoundation.org/sme_clusters.asp.

NCEUS. 2007. *Conditions of Work and Promotion of Livelihoods in the Unorganized Sector.* NCEUS. Government of India. New Delhi: Academic Foundation.

———. 2008. *Definitional and Statistical Issues.* Task Force Report for the *National Commission for Enterprises in the Unorganized Sector.* New Delhi: NCEUS, Government of India. pp. 1–242.

Peck, J. A. 1989. 'Literature Surveys: Labour Market Segmentation Theory', *Labour and Industry*, 2(1): 119–44.

Prugl, E. 1996. 'Home-based Workers: A Comparative Exploration of Mies's Theory of Housewifization', *Frontiers: A Journal of Women Studies*, 17(1): 114–35. Accessed December 12, 2007. http://links.

jstor.org/sici?sici=0160-9009%281996%2917%3A1%3C114%3AH
WACEO%3E2.0.CO%3B2-Z.

Raju, S. 2006. 'From Global to Local: Gendered Discourses, Skills and
Embedded Urban Labour Market in India', in *Colonial and Post Colonial
Geographies of India,* edited by Saraswati Raju, M. Satish Kumar, and
Stuart Corbridge, New Delhi: Sage Publications. pp. 99–119.

————. 2011a. 'Reclaiming Spaces and Places', in *Gendered Geographies:
Space and Place in South Asia,* edited by Saraswati Raju, New Delhi:
Oxford University Press. pp. 31–59.

————. 2011b. 'Introduction: Conceptualizing Gender, Space and Place',
in *Gendered Geographies: Space and Place in South Asia,* edited by Saraswati
Raju, New Delhi: Oxford University Press. pp. 1–28.

————. 2013. 'The Material and the Symbolic: The Intersectionalities of
Home-Based Work in India', *Economic and Political Weekly,* 48(1): 60–68.

Raju, S., Atkins, P. J., Kumar, N., and J. G. Townsend. 1999. *Atlas of Women
and Men in India.* New Delhi: Kali for Women.

Raju, S. and Bagchi, D. ed. 1993. *Women and Work in South Asia: Regional
Patterns and Perspectives.* London and New York: Routledge.

Sachdev, S. 2004. 'Heterogeneity and Employability of Workers in Informal
Sector in Urban India: Interface with Education', M. Phil Dissertation,
Centre for the Study of Regional Development, Jawaharlal Nehru
University.

Sethuraman, S. V. 1998. *Gender, Informality and Poverty: A Global Review.*
Geneva: The World Bank. Accessed December 14, 2014. http://wiego.org/
sites/wiego.org/files/publications/files/Sethuraman-Gender-Informality.
pdf.

Singh, Andrea Menefee, and Anita Kelles-Viitanen ed. 1987. *Invisible Hands
Women in Home-based Production.* Women and the Household in Asia –
vol. I. New Delhi: Sage Publications.

Sinha, S. 2006. *Rights of Home-based Workers.* New Delhi: National Human
Rights Commission.

Standing, Guy. 1989. 'Global Feminization through Flexible Labor', *World
Development,* 17(7): 1077–95.

Standing, Guy. 1999. 'Global Feminization through Flexible Labor – A
Theme Revisited', *World Development,* 27(3): 583–602.

Tapadar, A. 2002. *Kolkatar Chhoto Lucknow*. Kolkata: Subarnarekha.

Thakur, A. 1999. 'A Post – Modernist Enquiry into Women's Workforce Participation', *The Indian Journal of Labour Economics*, 42(4): 557–65.

Thibos, M., Daniele Lavin-Loucks, and M. Martin. 2007. *Feminization of Poverty*. Report for Joint Policy Forum on the Feminization of Poverty, Dallas, Texas, USA: The J. McDonald Williams Institute. Accessed November 12, 2009. www.dallasindicators.com/Portals/8/Reports/Reports_Internal/Feminization%20of%20Poverty. pp. 1–20.

UNIFEM. 2002. *Study on the Productivity Linkages of Indian Industry with Home-Based Women Workers through Subcontracting Systems in Manufacturing Sector*. New Delhi: United Nations Development Fund for Women.

Unni, J., and U. Rani. 1999. 'Informal Sector: Women in Emerging Labour Market', *The Indian Journal of Labour Economics*, 42(4): 625–39.

———. 2003. 'Gender, Informality and Poverty', *Seminar* 531: November. Accessed March, 2, 2006. http://www.india-seminar.com/semframe.html.

———. 2004. 'Home-based Work in India: A Disappearing Continuum of Dependence', Paper presented at EGDI and UNU-WIDER Conference on Unlocking the Human Potential: Linking the Informal and Formal Sectors, Helsinki, Finland, September, pp. 17–18. Accessed January 7, 2007. http://wiego.org/sites/wiego.org/files/publications/files/Unni-Rani-Home-based-work-India.pdf.

———. 2005. *Impact of Recent Policies on Home-based Work in India*. Discussion Paper Series – 10. Human Development Research Centre, UNDP. New Delhi: HDRC. pp. 1–76.

Unni, J. 1998. 'Wages and Employment in Unorganized Sector', *The Indian Journal of Labour Economics*, 41(4): 875–92.

———. 2001. 'Gender and Informality in the Labour Market in South Asia', *Economic and Political Weekly*, 36(26): 2360–77.

9

Labour Control and Responses
Women Workers in an Apparel Park in Kerala[1]

Neethi P.

Introduction

Prior to the 1970s, firms in the stable markets, essentially producing for masses, competed by improving productivity, decreasing costs, along with expanding market share within the existing markets (Benner 2002). However, of late, the ability of firms to adapt to changing market conditions, identifying new opportunities, and successfully meeting challenges, has gained importance for not just competitive advantage but also for economic survival. These changes have created an entirely different political–economic environment for workers around the world and the labour market has been radically restructured. More than simply reducing wages in a 'race to the bottom', there has been the apparent move away from regular employment towards part-time, temporary, or subcontracted work arrangements (Neethi 2008). Employers have cashed in on weakened union powers and pools of surplus (unemployed or underemployed) labour, advocating flexible work regimes and labour contracts; for regular employees, too, longer working hours during peak demand and shorter hours during periods of slack are becoming common (Milberg 2004). Workers are thus put at an immediate disadvantage in terms of bargaining power with the owners of capital and with respect to the State (Milberg 2004).

All these effects are doubly obvious when we consider the transformed role of women in production and labour markets. Not only do new labour market structures facilitate exploitation of the labour power of women on a part-time basis, and substitution of lower-paid female labour for that of more highly paid and less easily laid-off core male workers, the revival of subcontracting and domestic/family labour systems also permits a resurgence of patriarchal practice and home working (Harvey 1990, 1991; Harvey and Scott 1989).

A preference for women exists, as it brings with it reduced costs of production, reduced probabilities of the threat of unionisation, possibilities to avoid providing of minimal standards of decency and safety at work required by labour laws and to ignoring pay levels stipulated in minimum wage laws and prevention of access to social security (Harriss-White 2010). Women workers thus seem to stand at the trafficked crossroads of class and gender (Beneria and Roldan 1987). As a consequence, women are employed in simple, unskilled, labour-intensive tasks of assembly or finishing, requiring minimum use of capital or production tools. Also, women workers are concentrated in light industries producing consumer goods, ranging from, food processing, textiles and garments to chemicals, rubber, plastics and electronics (Momsen 2010).

It is within the hegemonic capacity of patriarchal norms to define women's labour as not only 'cheap' but socially and economically less worthy of equitable pay and other conditions, making female labour so crucial to the accumulation strategies of global capital (Wright 1999, 2001). Mills (2003) indicates how the literature has explained that in some cases it is women's status as unmarried and subordinate 'daughters' that makes them an attractively cheap and flexible a pool of labour; and in other contexts, it is their status as wives and mothers that justifies their lower wages and limited job security. Often, a female workforce is fully exploited by local capital, using its deep knowledge of local cultural norms about the roles women are made to play, and the docility that women are expected to practice in the family as well as the production unit (Chari 2004; Neethi 2012). Thus, around the globe, gender hierarchies are produced and maintained in relation to transnational circuits of labour mobilization and capital accumulation (Mills 2003).

It is against this backdrop that the present study enquires into the working lives of women workers in an export promoting apparel park (henceforth, the Park) in a major urban centre in southern Kerala, Kollur.[2] This study reveals how local labour markets develop their own forms of labour control, exploiting gendered stereotypes of women workers, making every effort to control them and reinforce gendered norms in the spaces of working and living of these workers. These are achieved by means of involving agents in the local communities and local religious bodies in the region, besides other strategies. However, the study also takes into account how these workers organized around a very local set of concerns and formed their own association to confront significantly the hegemonic limbs of local capital in the contemporary global economy. Such measures are not always clearly visible and may require something more than superficial enquiry to bring their salient features into view. Questioning global stereotypes on responses by workers, in this case urban women workers, to contemporary globalization, I argue that these workers can also be actively involved in the very process of globalization and the expansion of local capital, while being inadvertently drawn into an exploitative whirlpool.

The study is based on fieldwork undertaken in broadly two phases – June–July and October–December of 2008, and a few visits in April 2009. Information was collected mainly through recorded responses of respondents who were interviewed mostly individually but at times also in groups. Snowballing sampling was employed, since it was impossible to access lists of women workers in the Park from which to sample respondents for interviews. This was out of initial difficulties arising from both the workers and the managements.[3] It borrows partly from an ethnographic approach, and uses the 'Extended Case Method' (Burawoy et al. 1991; Burawoy 1998, 2009) as its main methodology.[4] Of different hierarchies of workers, discussed later on, the study focuses particularly on floor workers, which are primarily women.

The chapter is divided into four sections. The first section (see in 'Introduction' section) discusses, in short, the emerging workspaces in Kerala to commence the case study. The next section (see in 'Enquiries into emerging workspaces in Kerala') deals with general working conditions within the apparel park, bringing in further interesting revelations on labour control around women workers. Following this, the subsequent section looks at the women workers' response and further striking features and trends, before concluding in the last section.

Kerala state has been no less impacted by the turbulent changes in labour, particularly female labour. With social development overtaking economic growth, Kerala has for long been a paradox – on the one hand, social development in the state was universally acclaimed as a 'model' for poor states, while on the other hand, there was acute unemployment and low labour force participation (Gulati 1975; Mathew 1985; Kumar 1994; Mazumdar and Guruswamy 2006). Female labour force participation rates in Kerala have been among the lowest in India despite high education among women (Eapen 1992; Raju 2010), with currently a marked increase in casualisation of the female labour force, as reflected through the data. If we observe the work participation rate for women in Kerala versus that of an all-India level in the report on *Human Development in India* (Desai *et al.* 2010), we see a stark contrast – work participation of women in India stands at 47 per cent, whereas for Kerala, it stands only at 28 per cent (rural female work participation in India stands at 58 per cent , whereas for Kerala, this figure is a mere 33 per cent; urban female work participation is 20 per cent for India and only 14 per cent for Kerala).

Women in Kerala mostly occupy low-paid/low-status jobs, resulting in significant gender disparity in earnings (Eapen 1994 and 2001; Mitra and Singh 2006 and 2007), which in turn arise greatly from their limited mobility (Eapen 1994; Kumar 1994; Mathew 1985), and given the fact that decision-making and extent of participation is influenced by family and society. Even the uneducated have strong job preferences based on proximity to home, prestige, class consciousness, social status and the resulting inter-linkages in the social hierarchy (Devi 2002; Kumar 1994).

As far as trade union activity goes, in India, women's activities in trade unions (or the lack of it) have not received much attention, and when mentioned at all, the focus seems to be on their low level of trade union activity, allegedly due to apathy and a lack of interest in the literature (Menon 1992; Lindberg 2001). There is also an impression of a general submissiveness explained in terms of 'Oriental Docility', which Chakravarty (2007) reveals is not the docility of women that results in their low trade union activity, but the fact that mainstream trade unions prioritise the interests of permanent male workers, creating an impression of women having less to engage with the trade union activity. In Kerala's labour movements too, women workers played a secondary role compared to their male counterparts, though exceptions exist.[5]

Labour as an active social agent

The subjugated status of women workers, or for that matter, workers in general, are shared even by the meta-narratives of globalization. With the exception of studies of international labour migration, these meta-narratives usually portray 'the emergence of the global economy as capital's creation, the logical outcome of the expansionary nature of capital, and the new economic and political reality to which labour must respond' (Herod 2001, 131). Labour (especially female labour) as an agency of social progress has been replaced by pessimism that sees little prospect of them acting on their own behalf. Both national governments and organized labour are said to be powerless when faced with international marketisation, neoliberal deregulation, and global economic integration (Hirst and Thompson 1999). Castells (2000) mentions, "while capital is networked, labour remains 'switched off'". It closes its collective identity, becomes increasingly individualised in its capacities, working conditions, and its interests.

Claiming a different politics from neoliberalism, a parallel theoretical position towards globalization has been espoused (Herod 2003 a, b, c). Herod goes on to point out a sense of despondency and defeatism that has often pervaded much of the analyses of the position of workers in the global economy. Also, he observes an argument often seen in the literature that it is relatively pointless for local social actors, unless they develop global campaigns, to struggle against what are portrayed omnipotent and inevitable forces of global capitalism.

In view of such propositions, backed by Herod's observations, I contend that such a view is problematic for two interconnected reasons. Firstly, when talking about globalization, the literature often fails to portray that there are multiple varieties of this process, i.e., it doesn't come in a single flavour. Secondly, and more importantly, the literature shows the tendency to portray workers – particularly women workers – as structurally defenceless in the face of hypermobile, rapidly restructuring and globally organised capital; in a way they appear as bearers of global economic restructuring, not as active participants in the process. Instead, I argue for a much more active conceptualisation of women workers as engaged in the uneven development of capitalism. In doing so, my study stays away from the elusive assumption that workers might as well give up the struggle, especially at the local level, if they cannot develop connections at the global scale. It also argues that local balances between capital and labour may not be derived from generalizations easily and local responses might not often all be interpreted as outliers or deviations.

Another conceptualisation that must be brought in at this juncture is Burawoy's factory regimes. Burawoy's (1985) conceptualisation divides capitalist factory regimes[6] into two generic types – the despotic (based on coercive work) and the hegemonic (based on consenting work). With the mobility of global capital from advanced countries, Burawoy postulates (suggested in Xue 2008) that despotic factory regimes are most likely to be imposed in peripheral states, particularly in export processing zones where there is interplay between global capital and cheap labour. However, in a global production, both states and firms can develop new strategies and interventions to construct a more complex work organization and labour control than Burawoy imagined (Xue 2008). While Burawoy implied that the interplay was between global capital and local/cheap labour, in the present study, it is the *local capital* – pursuing cheap labour – that imposes a control over local labour catering to the needs of the global market.[7] Hence, when we deal with the despotic nature of capital, the distinction between local and global gets blurred since local capital makes use of the space created by the free mobility of global capital, imposing more or less similar control strategies over locally available cheap labour. Linked with this new spatial distribution of production is a restructuring of social relationships, in this case gender relations, as labour markets target a specific gender, besides specific ages, ethnicities, and religions (Momsen 2010). For example, in the Tiruppur hosiery cluster, feminisation of the workforce was pursued, not simply to benefit from the advantages of a female workforce as such, but also to carve the path towards a whole new set of social relations in production (Chari 2004).

With this in mind, I look into a model of worker organization, not on a global but a very local scale. I deal with the case of an apparel park in Kollur in Kerala.[8]

Enquiries into emerging workspaces in Kerala

Many state governments in India, over the decades, have established export promotion industrial parks in order to enhance export potentials. The industrial park in question in this study engages in apparel. In the apparel industry, changes in fashion over seasons – spring, summer, autumn, winter – are the first drivers of design and production.

Of the two firms under study in this case, one was originally owned by a proprietor who belonged to the same area and who was locally known, while the other was owned by a business group, also of Keralite origin, operating all over India. Both these firms neatly characterise 'local capital'. However, over the recent past, both were taken over by a large group, based out of Mumbai, that owned businesses internationally. These two firms were vendor factories for the latter large group, which caters only to export-market buyers. The *buyer* (the retail firm) and the *vendor* (who acquires the order) are the major players in the apparel production chain under the study. The head office of the vendor gets all the details from the buyer regarding the apparel product including details on style, fabric, measurement, and package. The vendors hand over this information to their factories, engaged in the actual manufacturing of the apparel products. The buyers, depending on their size, may have their own buying houses (mediators between the buyer and the vendor, whose main function is to look into matters such as quality assurance on behalf of the buyer). There is a renewal of order every six months, and if the vendor cannot maintain with the quality standards and compliances of the buyer, they lose the contract with the buyer. The sequence of production under study is given in Fig. 9.1. The sampled firms deal with buyers such as Wal-Mart, H and M, Van Heusen, American Eagle, Arrow, and so on. The raw materials for the production, such as fabric, threads, buttons, etc., are sourced largely from India, or in some instances imported according to the requirement of the buyer. Almost the entire production is for export to the United States, Europe, and the Middle East. Rejected items are sometimes sold in the local domestic markets after removing brand names.

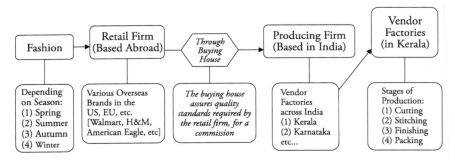

Fig. 9.1 Sequence of production
Source: Padmanabhan (2012)

To take advantage of the tide of the global apparel industry's interest in developing economies as potential hubs for good quality low wage manufacturing, the State agency involved with the Park uninhibitedly advertised itself, projecting a picture of its employees as 'highly skilled', 'cheap', having the 'shortest learning curve', 'disciplined' and its industrial relations 'cordial'.

Entry into the field

Since entry into the Park was restricted, interviews of workers and other agents were conducted outside the Park and outside working hours. I visited major 'labour pockets', situated around a major urban area, which had been identified during the course of the initial interviews. I was a passive participant in their union membership campaigns, but on one public occasion I did inform them of the academic and historical relevance of their campaign. These opportunities helped me establish enough rapport to conduct even a few telephone interviews and also directly interview the family and community members close to them. The first few sets of interviews were conducted of women workers in groups in an informal setting. I later interviewed them in their residences to gain familiarity with their living conditions and circumstances. The final set of interviews with the women workers was conducted in their family and community areas to seek more information on their socio-economic background as well as to facilitate interviews of family and kin. In this manner, the stages of interviewing moved from workplace, to their residences and finally, to their socio-economic background. Interviewees included the women workers, their families, their communities, religious bodies in their local communities, the local level government bodies and so on.

Working conditions and labour control

A major chunk of the women workers in these units were recruited primarily from surrounding areas, their families mainly engaging in fishing and coir-yarn production. Some workers hailed from other neighbouring districts. To secure an adequate labour supply at low pay levels these firms exploited workers' labour market dependence by recruiting mainly young, less educated and poor women (McKay 2004) who in turn responded positively to the employment offers, given the desire for some to be less financially dependent on their families or to support their kin. The apparel units under study consisted of three major sections – cutting, stitching, and finishing. Each section had its own strict hierarchical employment structure. The two units in total consisted of around 3000 female floor workers, ranging from 18 to 40 years of age. Figure 9.2 shows the hierarchical order under the stitching unit.

While the cutting and finishing units were segregated into different sections, the stitching unit grouped women workers into different batches of around 50 each. Each batch had a supervisor and line assistants. More than 80 per cent of the firms' workers were shop-floor workers consisting of operators and helpers (consisting *solely* of women workers), organized along the assembly line. While floor workers were mainly women, the upper half of this hierarchy, the supervisors, were male staff. When asked about why this was so, it was gathered from the management that this was a consciously undertaken differentiation; there were in fact a few instances when women were appointed supervisors, but this was not as successful in maintaining the discipline (and authority) as when men were in charge. More than being treated as 'women workers', they were treated simply as *women* who needed supervision, which was more easily maintainable by male supervisors on the shop floor.

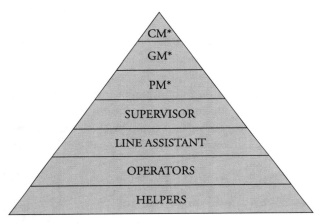

Fig. 9.2 Hierarchical employment structure under the stitching unit
Source: Padmanabhan (2012)

Women workers normally worked six, and often seven, days a week. Working hours started at 8.30 a.m. and end at 5.15 p.m., with a 15 minute break in the morning at 10 a.m. and a 30 minute break in the afternoon beginning at 12.30 p.m. Even a five minute delay required the women workers to get special permission to enter. A delay exceeding five minutes resulted in a 15 minute wage cut. Once inside the Park gate, exit even during free time was not permitted, except with special permission, which was usually a long procedure involving convincing the Batch Supervisor, the Production Manager and the General Manager, whose permission note had to be produced at the gate. While the supervisory staff was given a tea break before 5.15 p.m., floor workers were made to work continuously till the end of the day. A, an operator, says –

> ...once we enter the [Park] compound we are like slaves, with no control over ourselves from 8.30 a.m. to 5.15 p.m. It is just like a jail. Every morning we come into this jail; once we enter, we have no idea what is going on outside...

Production was based on piece-work but wages were not. There were line assistants to check the hourly efficiency of each worker in a batch, as well as the efficiency of each batch, marked on a scoreboard. Total production of that unit per day was calculated. Therefore, each worker in a batch was required to be consistent throughout the day with the efficiency she began with in the morning! Yet, their wages were not based on efficiency and were fixed, offered at the time of recruitment. B and C, two other operators, said, respectively –

> ...sometimes in the morning we will be able to offer good efficiency, but eventually we are tired and may not be able to meet the initial target, for which we face severe rebuke. So, we work even during the morning [15 minutes] interval to meet our target...and for half of our 30 minute lunch break. Yet, we prefer [working through intervals] than being reprimanded...

> ...we are rebuked whenever we can't meet the target...but if we exceed our target, not even a good word! Often they forget we are human beings, and they treat us only as machines...

Operators' remuneration varied from Rs 2100 to Rs 2175 per month, with an attendance bonus of Rs 100. Hence, an operator working the entire month, without taking any leave, was entitled to get a maximum of Rs 2275, but in reality, no one reported to have received more than Rs 2000 per month; from which Rs 250 was deducted every month for company-arranged transport and additionally for gratuity, Employees' State Insurance (ESI), and Provident Fund (PF). As a result, the maximum net amount they earned was less than Rs 1700 a month (or, in other words, merely Rs 60 per day). Even after five full years of experience, some workers received only Rs 2645 per month. It is interesting to note that the first six months were considered a 'training period'. However, while actual training lasted only for a month, wages were credited only five months later, despite contributing to production for the five months after recruitment. D, another operator, said –

> ...even if we don't take any leave we are supposed to receive Rs 1700 per month but we never receive even that amount. Our salaries are somehow reduced on the pretext of being 15 minutes late or having an extended lunch break on some arbitrary day. If we try to argue, we are rebuked even more...

Workers were paid on the 7th of every month, though there were many instances of delay reported. Experiences on the salary day were also intimidating. According to E,

...they pay us on the 7th of every month, on which they make us work more, alleging that workers are prompt in receiving money but are lax in working, completely disregarding the fact that we are paid for our work effort and drudgery...

During working hours the women workers were asked to wear a cap and a mask. Discipline in the shop floor was often harsh; once the work started it was forbidden to talk or even look at each other. Closed-circuit cameras observed their every movement. The women workers were sometimes forced to give explanations for even using the bathroom for too long, which was occasionally rather humiliating. Not more than ten minutes were allowed for rest in case of a headache or fatigue, and helpers and ironing staff were made to stand all day. F, a helper, says:

...the ironing job is so horrible that we can't sit even for five minutes. Because of the heat, girls sometimes faint, and at the end of the day our feet are swollen...

Getting a day's leave was also no easy task. Workers had to submit a leave application early enough to get permission. Even after returning from an emergency, they were obliged to explain to the Production Manager and sometimes even the General Manager, only after which they were allowed to return to work. Working overtime was also not uncommon.

The management and control of women workers' time and space beyond the shop floor was found to be helpful in maintaining flexible production and labour power (Xue 2008), which was quite evident in the case of those who are residents of the Park-run hostels. The living conditions in the hostel were reported to be below average and residents were required to get special permission from the company to go out or take leave. Permission to leave the hostels was required even during emergencies. Departure from the hostel without permission resulted in the hostel-resident women workers even being evicted from the hostel. Many instances were shared –

...a girl was informed that her uncle had passed away but the warden didn't permit her to go, and she had to approach the company for permission. By the time she got the permission it was already too late. Moreover, she was given only two days leave...

...another girl's own father passed away and her brother came to the company to take her home but he was not allowed to enter inside the gate. This resulted in a big fight with the security guard at the gate, with the administrative staff paying no heed...

Once inside, the Park compound workers were made to forget what leisure is, except for the 15 minute break in the morning and the 30 minute lunch break. G, an operator, complained:

> ...even if we finish before time we are not allowed to take rest. If they see us relaxing idle after meeting the target, we are asked to help others. They just don't like to see us resting...

This brings us to a discussion on temporality and the ways in which capital pervades time. Overtime is not the only means that capital uses. The line diving 'working' and 'non-working' hours, as well as weekdays and weekends, is blurry. All this is attempted by capital using various strategies, both threats as well as incentives, when coercive methods alone are not workable. Therefore, strategies such as informing the women workers of their easy substitutability, of the cruciality of deadlines and the fear of losing orders, are utilised. Workers are made aware that if they do not comply with overtime or weekend work, their services can easily be terminated and they can be replaced by new workers, since there is no dearth of labour, not only from the local region but also from neighbouring states. Moreover, they are made aware that losing orders is a grave concern to the company as well as the workers themselves, since a loss in future orders would threaten the very continuance of their jobs. It was easier to use these persuasive methods on hostel-resident workers since, unlike those women workers who resided with their families and commute from their native localities, the hostel-resident women workers had little in terms of family and other similar commitments to attend to on a daily basis. Interestingly, these commitments and engagements within family, otherwise viewed as social restrictions on women, are used by many native-locality-residing workers as shields to resist these strategies of capital. A hostel resident said –

> ...they take full advantage that we stay in their hostels and they have full control over every aspect of our lives, inside and outside of the Park. Whenever there is overtime work, they pick us up instantly, on the pretext that we have 'no family obligations every other day' and that we are 'hostel girls'...

Monetary incentives, in the form of payment rewards for regular attendance and compliance with overtime demands were also offered, apart from coercive and persuasive methods, to assist capital's attempts to structure time.

It is not surprising that the attrition rate in these units was quite high. Smaller firms faced greater difficulty in securing labour supply. However, these factories relied more on changing their hiring policy rather than improving working conditions to recruit enough workers because they were at the bottom of the production chains, and, as a result, their profits mainly came from minimising production costs, especially labour costs (Xue 2008). The management in the apparel firms here created strategies that included giving monetary incentives to those who brought a new worker to the company, usually at Rs 100 per worker.[9] Instances of workers shifting from one firm to another within the Park were also common. If the women workers were in need of money, say on occasions like marriage, they resigned from one unit so as to obtain monetary benefits, later only to join another firm within the Park.

Another interesting aspect was that 'skill formation' was completely absent in the case of these women workers because from the beginning they are trained to do only one type of work. A worker who was trained to stitch a collar was trained in no other skill; hence, she may have become an expert at collar stitching but not even a novice in producing any other part of a shirt! However, at times, this came to their advantage – workers tried to avoid overtime using the same token, saying that they cannot do any other work except the one they were trained in. Even workers' families seemed to have concerns about this. One family member mentioned –

> …we are not happy about the fact that our girl cannot do anything except stitch one part of a dress. What if she wants, or needs, to start a small tailoring unit for earning a living after her term at the Park is over? She will be stuck…

A 'native-place network' often played an important role in worker recruitment, as families and societies had a say in terms of decision making about work participation and work processes among these women workers. My discussions with the family members revealed –

> …in this area our religious committee had taken a decision against sending our girls for work especially to faraway places. However, in this firm's case, though the wages are less and the work schedule is hectic, they are 'safe'. All the girls from this region travel together by the van, which is arranged by the company and we don't mind paying for the van…

To reiterate a theme discussed earlier, the family and community are the decision-makers regarding whether or not these young women are 'sent' out to work. That is, the very decision to participate in the labour market is not within the ambit of the women workers' own choices, but a choice that is taken for them by community, family, and often even religious bodies – these bodies almost always consisting entirely of male members. Hence, despite being 'urban' or 'semi-urban' women, the very idea of working away from home was framed within patriarchal limits. This implied that since the decision to go out and work was not individual, the young women workers (though possessing the desire to be less financially dependent on their families, as mentioned earlier) did not feel a sense of being individually 'empowered' in terms of the work adding to their well-being. Another noteworthy aspect is the fact that while in several cases women workers shape decisions about work around primary concerns of family, in the case here, there were many agents (such as senior family members, community and religious heads, etc.) who ensured that the sense of 'well-being' of these young women workers already had family and relationships at the core.

As the women workers were treated as 'girls' who needed 'protection', outside of the shop-floor too, the community and religious heads were in authority. In one incident, local people in the community stopped the van, which came late in the evening due to overtime – consequently resulting in the stoppage of compulsory evening overtime. During my discussions with religious body members in the local community, one individual remarked –

> …but even if the van by itself is safe, we were not happy with bringing our girls late, especially after dark, because we too are responsible to their families regarding the safety of these girls…

> …we are proud that we could stop this van bringing our girls too late. Our efforts seemed to work well…

This can be interpreted as one instance where agencies within the 'local' influenced women workers' response. It is yet another instance where the community and family decided at what time it was 'appropriate that the girls get back home'; a decision which has significantly deep patriarchal connotations.

This incident resulted in the company making an effort to put the workers hailing from the same places in different batches to prevent any similar incidents, and any solidarity in general.

Labour response

This section deals with a confrontation that altered existing capital-labour relations within the two firms under study. The confrontation, having its foundations in long-standing grievances among the women workers, turned into a nine-day episode as a result of an issue surrounding promptness in payment.

A salary increase is due in April or May every year, in accordance with the rules, but this did not materialise in the April of 2008. On approaching supervisors, the women workers were informed that the increase would be distributed by June. Matters worsened when the increment did not materialise. With even Sunday added in as a salaried working day, workers complained of being made to work all week, in addition to the management's unconcerned attitude for over three months – in sum amounting to an erosion of workers' legal rights. Following this, some workers met their Production Manager who treated the matter as insignificant and asked them either to return to their respective work places, or leave the company. This choice – either quietly working or entirely leaving – was at this juncture taken up seriously by the workers, who took up a protest against the salary-increase delay by threatening to quit *en masse* until the salary increase was actually made. Upon realising that the workers could not be toyed around with this time, the management decided to reveal a major internal change that had occurred without the knowledge of the workers. The firms in question had been taken over by a 'giant' in the garment sector, who by virtue of having markets all over the world, had tugged the firms into a large apparel production chain. Despite the management and workforce composition remaining untouched, the ownership had changed as much as to render the management 'helpless' in matters concerning wages. In addition, the new owners were not in favour of this salary hike. Workers treated this matter as a grave offence, protesting –

> … without informing us, they sold us too, along with the company…

This information on the internal change fuelled the fire, giving workers enough reason and justification to encourage even their counterparts in the other acquired firm to join them in a strike. Thus nearly 3000 women workers participated in a strike, which persisted for nine days. The few discussions between the firm and the workers did not prove successful, the workers still remaining firm on their decision on the salary increase. While the company made it clear that workers could think about a salary hike upon first getting back to work, an experience in 2003[10] had taught workers to comply with the company's clarification if and only if their salary increase was materialised and made legal.

> …we were not going to fall for the same trick once more…so we were quite stern on our stand.…

Meanwhile, the company adopted various control measures that included police protection for shipment. At a later stage, workers were even threatened with the possibility of the company being locked forever. Yet, these measures did not change workers' stand. On the contrary, workers even strengthened their position by accepting support from various political and non-political organizations, local leaders of various political parties, Panchayat members, Kudumbashree[11] members, and so on. In the later stages, the issue reached right up to the District Labour Officer (DLO), who was presented a 14 point demand by the workers, covering salary hikes, code of conduct towards workers, illegal working days, compulsory overtime, etc. When the meeting with the DLO failed, the issue was then being sent to the Regional Joint Labour Commissioner (RJLC).

Discussions with the RJLC concluded with the decision that, except for the hike in the salary, the management was to seriously consider and act upon all other demands from the workers. With regard to the salary hike, a discussion between the management and the workers was imminent, in order for a quick solution. This time, however, the management relented on the issue of salary increase and the workers accordingly withdrew their strike. The nine-day strike thus succeeded, beside other amendments, in an agreement increasing workers' wages, doing away with compulsory overtime, increasing overtime wages and eliminating a salary-cut on *hartal* days. In general, treatment towards workers improved relatively, and more importantly, it led towards the formation of an apparel workers' association.

Formation of the worker association: An assessment

This confrontation reveals the new challenges facing labour as a factor of production due to the strategies adopted by capital to sustain the game of competition. Observations from the field, analysed in detail in the following section, question and disentangle the assumptions and preconceptions of capital–labour relations among women workers in Kerala.

The basics

As I have already discussed earlier, labour unions were central to the implementation of Kerala's model of development. Kerala's informal sector was typical of other Indian states with agriculture–worker dominance but its specialty was in the existence of state-specific informal sectors like toddy tapping, coir, cashew, etc., wherein a high degree of unionisation and mobilization has been noteworthy (Kannan 1998). This can be considered as the broad base of the labour movement in Kerala. Recognising the power of the unions and its ability in destabilisation, the State responded by actively intervening in the informal sector through a series of direct regulatory and informal reforms along with broader welfare measures (Heller 1999). This process of unionisation continued over the decades and is inextricably tied to Kerala's political process.

However, the form of the women workers' organization, as we see in the case study, barely resembles the mainstream and commonly understood trade unionism based on 'class struggle' and having the 'capitalist system' as its target.[12] Here, the women workers were unaware of seemingly simple information, for example, whom they were working for. Their knowledge of the company's workforce and relations extended only up to the supervisors and the production managers, i.e., those with whom they were in regular and proximate contact. There was literally a screen obstructing their view of what goes on beyond their immediate working environments. The response was similar on enquiring on details like the employee strength of the company, for which the answer was a vague 'many'. Workers seemed to be unconscious about the fact that the very awareness of these details is important and crucial, sometimes even dismissing these as 'unimportant details we need not know'. This is quite in contrast from the traditional scenario where workers, both male and female, were at times aware of wage legislation and prevailing wages even in industries besides their own (Heller 1999). These are starting points to show how, although knowledge on labour relations and consciousness of the workers on their placement within the production system was formerly fundamental, this awareness is now not featuring even at a basic level during labour confrontations.

'We have no politics'

The formation of the women workers' association here cannot be equated with the proletarian struggle usually synonymous to the Kerala experience, since unlike earlier, the formation of the association in this case was spontaneously sparked and carried on for the existence and survival of these women workers. Moreover, the workers' association here claimed no direct political support. Kerala's politics, specifically the dominance of a communist ideology in the mid 20th century, attracted the attention of a number of political scientists who treated it as a laboratory of communist politics within the broader liberal–parliamentary framework of India (Chander 1986; Nair 1965; Mankekar 1965; Jeffrey 2003, 2010). However, in the case seen here – with largely less educated women workers from economically vulnerable families – political backing seems to be kept at a distance.

...we have no politics...ours is an independent workers' association ... we don't want our association to be known as a 'trade union', which is why we call this a 'workers' association'...

There exists a small body of literature suggesting that there might be a new course in the working class history of Kerala, deviating from the long established path of 'multiple political parties and multiple trade unions' (Heller 1999), and a widely emerging threat of depoliticlisation and the attendant growth of public cynicism about all forms of politics (Devika 2007). Many workers' associations – like the one in this case – claimed to have 'no politics', an idea hinged upon the grievance that a politically strong group did not come to their aid. Though it cannot be immediately concluded and ascertained that the newly formed 'workers' association' in our apparel park is an example of this trend in Kerala, this body of literature is called to mind. A similar trend has been clearly described also in Devika and Rajasree (2012), in their study on widow associations in Kerala. They have described that although these widows also emphatically stated that 'we have no politics' (pp. 211), this was arguable since it was clear that they were not averse to accepting help from persons who were influential and had long experience in politics. This is the same case in our case study here too, which we see in the next point – mentors.

Mentors

The women workers' association was equally open to seeking help and advice from *mentors* who appear to have had considerable influence in political parties. These mediators were men of influence both in the civic community and in political parties. Association leaders argued that the presence of a well-educated, well-connected *man* was necessary to talk to the company on behalf of the workers and also, to secure state welfare benefits.[13]

However, the most interesting aspect in this help-seeking was that the leaders of the association stressed the fact that only the personality and support of the individual and not his political-party connections were sought after during confrontation. During an interview, the secretary of the association told quite distinctively that 'sir' was only guiding them, without imposing or mixing in his political ideology and connections. Their trust in him was un-diminishing mainly on this account. They sought his help only as a mediator between the company, the State, and themselves, and not as a political trump card. Affiliations with him did not automatically extend to affiliations to his political party, or for that matter any political party. Independence of their 'association' from any sort of mainstream political support was a virtue the workers wanted to sustain.

The new face of labour control measures

Along with the above interesting dimensions from the women workers' side, we can see equally interesting transformations in the labour control strategies by the firm, from recruitment of the labour to even the threat of terminating services. First, regarding recruitment – to begin with, allowing young girls to work outside the house was a decision taken collectively by the community, rather than a choice given to the individual woman, as observed while interviewing workers in their family environments. Most families I interviewed had mentioned –

> …we did not take this decision for our daughter based only on our instincts. We had long talks with neighbours and our other acquaintances who were also interested in sending their daughters. It was only after some sort of consensus was reached that we finally gave a 'yes' for our girls to go work there…

> …moreover, we don't want our girls to continue in the same jobs that we and our ancestors have been doing for long. This is much more respectable, and will only help them for their marriage…

Hence, the community decided in favour of the girls working for the firm largely due to the convenience of transport provided by the firm.

Also, the local governing body and religious bodies were used as vehicles by the company to win the faith of the community, who, as we have seen, would favour the girls working if placated enough with such incentives. The *Panchayat* office in this case gave wide propaganda on the vacancy in the company besides other benefits of working there, even going to the extent of allowing the firm's interviews to be conducted on the *Panchayat* office's premises.[14] A few members of the *Panchayat* office mentioned, during my interviews with them –

> …its true that we helped out by using the office premises for conducting interviews and gave propaganda on these vacancies. This is for their own good! Our aim was to help them get a good job, nothing more…

It is rather interesting to note that during recruitment, besides other identification, applicants were required to bring a group photograph of themselves with their family. The reason for this was to get a rough idea about the family and confirm that these potential recruits belonged to a 'proper' family, whom the company could approach in cases of an emergency.

After recruitment, during training, while workers were taught and made aware of their position in the production chain and the various implications that this brings, a sense of belonging to this position was not instilled. The importance of 'labour' as a factor of production and the 'workforce' as an entity in its aggregate was explained to them (using persuasive strategies discussed earlier in the discussion on temporality) but simultaneously, their easy substitutability as individual workers was also made well known. In other words, while their role in the production chain was evidently non-substitutable – and in that respect workers conceived of themselves as part and participle of the global economy – their easy replaceability as individuals divorced them from the conception of themselves as the *labour*, an invariable part of the firm's internal organization and its decision making processes. There was therefore a disconnection between the importance of their position – as labour – and the importance of each individual – the individual worker X or Y – occupying that indispensable position.

Returning to the strike, we note another interesting strategy – to offer high positions, rather than punishment, to those who were active in the strike. On interviewing two shop-floor workers who were very active in the strike, I was told that they had been approached by the company with an offer of promotion. This was an active effort from the side of the company to keep strike-leaders away from other workers, by promoting them to positions, which did not allow frequent interaction with floor workers.

During the association's membership campaign, the distinction in behaviour towards strike-leaders and other workers was noticeable. Towards the strike-leaders the firm was always soft and not on the offensive, even giving special offers and promotions as seen above. On the other hand, the firm was rather harsh towards not-so-active members of the association, using measures that included inculcating a sense of fear of deprivation of company benefits, closure of company, resignation of strike-leaders, and so on. One firm even announced that joining the workers' association was 'against the company', since the motive of this association was allegedly to close down the company.

> ...think about whether you need the company or the association...

More dramatic events happened on the day of the inauguration of the workers' association. Both firms declared this day a working day, in addition to spreading rumours of chances of a bomb explosion in the inauguration hall! Though these had reduced the attendance, a large majority of workers attended the function. When asked about the bomb rumours, I was told, rather sarcastically, that it would be better to suffer the explosion than succumb to a continuance of the firm's suffocating environment.

Conclusions

Capital and its agents have utilised various strategies to overwhelm women workers – patriarchy, pedagogy, perceived docility, familial ties and constraints, convincing a sense of 'security' and 'discipline' for the 'girls' in the work environment. It has also utilised forums permitted by local-government, religious bodies, and civil society agents. To reiterate, local capital has used the space – such as the shop-floor – which was already created by global capital, blurring the distinction between local capital and global capital. Women workers have thus been be trading somewhat contested domains, standing at a precarious crossroad between gendered norms and local capital control strategies. On one hand, their very entry and continuance in the labour market is regulated through socially architected gendered norms, while on the other hand, their identities as workers are shaped by local capital.

Herod (2003b, 219–220) observes that much attention is paid in the literature to 'how transnational corporations have "gone global", how institutions of governance have become supra-national, and how labour unions have sought to globalise their operations to match with those of an increasingly globalised capital'. These notions are countered by asking how we are subjected to the discourse of globalization and the identities (and narratives) it indicates to us, and *not* how the world is subjected to the global capital economy (Gibson-Graham 2002). Massey (2004), taking a step further, says that local identities created through globalization vary substantially, hence calling the need for taking care of local discourses. This study examined a specific site in the light of these arguments and showed empirically how local agencies 'engage in' and 'respond to' the process of globalization, and how this is important and relevant in the globalization literature.

The study raises the need for going against the grain by questioning global stereotypes with regard to expected economic responses to globalization, especially by urban women workers. Hence, contrary to the 'globalization thesis' – which posits that mobility of capital has been freed from the constraints of locations and localities – this enquiry contends that the expansion of capital remains in a tension-ridden and in an unstable relationship in each locale. The aim of this study was not to argue that labour is in any way 'successful' in conquering the overarching power of capital. Nor does it seek to push forward the argument that labour, as an entity, is becoming 'stronger' in opposition to capital. This study aims to recognise and appreciate the responses from the side of female labour at the local level and the paths that these responses trace, which cannot be derived mechanically from structural or gendered relations alone.

In line with this, the position this study seeks to hold is the assertion that labour has been actively involved in the very process of globalization itself. Although it would seem a simple proposition to suggest that working class people and their organizations affect the ways in which the landscapes of capitalism are made, until recently, there has been little work addressing this issue. This study contributes in this direction.

Endnotes

[1] This study forms a part of my completeld PhD work at the Centre for Development Studies (CDS), Trivandrum. An earlier version of this study has appeared as Padmanabhan (2012) in *Antipode*, which has been reproduced here with kind permission from Wiley. Acknowledgements are due to J Devika, KN Harilal, Andrew Herod, and Anant Kamath. I am indebted to the workers and their families I interviewed, as well as the staff of the firms I visited.

[2] This is a fictitious name to protect the identity of the actual site as well as that of workers.

[3] The first step was to meet workers outside the Park compound, after their working hours. I spoke to them casually, first about their recruitment and then towards general work experiences. Some apprehension was initially shown, but later due to advantages stemming out of my identity as a woman, being of almost the same age group, and a native of Kerala, it became easy to establish rapport with them. I attended a recruitment drive to understand, first hand, labour experiences from the recruitment stage onwards. This allowed me to gain entry into the Park, and make a few initial contacts. After this, I furthered my acquaintances among the workers. Apart from the workers, family-, community-, and religious-body members were also interviewed.

[4] For such a genre of enquiry, one has to look for causality and not pattern in explanation, inclining towards gleaning qualitative information. The extended case method, expanded upon by Michael Burawoy, is the application of reflexive science into ethnography in order to extract accounts of real events, struggles, and dramas that take place over space and time. It allows to dig beneath oversimplifying political binaries such capital-labour, city-periphery, and so on, that might hamper a realistic assessment of the events at the apparel park. It discovers multiple processes, interests, and identities, and recondenses these differences around 'local', 'national', and 'global', giving a more comprehensive explanation to the empirical phenomenon under question. Narrative interviews are employed, based on an intervention of the observer in the life of the participant, uncovering local processes.

[5] Lindberg (2001) observes that labouring women have failed to be identified as 'true' workers and 'true' radical members of the labour movement, having experienced a status of 'secondary worker', a victim of labour law violations and of unemployment. According to Lindberg, they have undergone, over the decades, a process of 'effeminisation' through which adherence to feminine norms have overtaken their worker status.

6 Factory regime, according to Burawoy, refers to the overall political form of production, including both the political effects of the labour process and the political apparatuses of production.

7 The work of Sharad Chari is noteworthy in this aspect. In his 2004 work, he gives a vivid account of the story of the Tiruppur hosiery cluster, where a local community, the Gounders, turned their decades-long 'toil' up the social ladder and transformed themselves into local capital. They are said to have successfully transferred the agricultural labour relations they had long-familiarity with, to the Tiruppur industry (Kapadia 2006, 73). Their main source of dominance and power was *fraternal* capital, which they altered in due course to act as *local* capital using a cheaply and locally available female workforce, catering to global export markets.

8 The degree to which rural and urban wage earning classes in Kerala have been politically and economically incorporated, was for long, in stark contrast to the disorganised and largely excluded condition of the depressed classes in the rest of India. Kerala's departure from the national pattern resulted from specific patterns of class formation and the institutional linkages that emerged from repeated cycles of class-based contestation and state intervention (Heller 1999). However, there eventually arose a 'realization', both by the government and the people, that redistributive strategies had reached their limits and, by the early 1980s, class struggle and redistributive demands were no longer at the centre of Kerala's politics (Heller 1999). Solutions to Kerala's crises followed a neoliberal economic development and an opening up of the economy. It is this depiction of disavowal of labour politics in Kerala that sets the stage for this study.

9 A similar trend was seen among information technology (IT) workers. Since inter-firm rivalry among the IT firms were very high, in some firms there was an employee referral scheme where the workers were encouraged to recommend friends and other acquaintances to the firm for employment. For each referral, workers were also rewarded monetarily. This was a common practice among IT firms all over the country (Abraham 2005).

10 One worker reported that the company, while witnessing a strike in 2003, had promised that a salary increase would eventually come if work resumed. The increase never came, allowing a common feeling of betrayal to spread among the workers.

11 Kudumbashree ('prosperity of the family' in Malayalam) is a women empowerment and poverty eradication programme adopted by the Poverty Eradication Mission of Kerala Government. It has been widely appreciated for its innovativeness and unprecedented coverage. Kudumbashree was conceived to be a state-centric civil society body, an autonomous body in the Panchayats. The village panchayat president was to be the patron (without much formal control beyond this) of the Kudumbashree apex body at the village panchayat level. See Devika *et al.* (2008) for further information.

12 This is not an entirely new phenomenon, as work by Lindberg (2001) and Waterman (1999) has shown that even traditional trade unionism was not always resorted to against any 'capitalist system' or 'class struggle' but simply for daily bread; having several of characteristics of new social movements. Waterman even introduces the concept of 'social movement unionism' for a new social movement within the unions' (Lindberg 2001, 220).

13 The fact that the workers' association needed a male mentor was again demonstrative of how strongly patriarchy was intertwined in their experiences, whether during recruitment, labour control, or in response.

[14] This became an issue for the firm to look into during the days of the strike. It was found that workers of the same Panchayat were familiar, allowing for easier cohesion. One measure to counter this was to increase heterogeneity in residences and the workspace, to make cohesion due to familiarity a little more difficult.

References

Abraham, Vinoj. 2005. 'Labour Productivity and Employment in the Indian Information and Communication Technology Sector.' PhD diss., Jawaharlal Nehru University, New Delhi.

Beneria, Lourdes, and Roldan, Martha. 1987. *The Crossroads of Class and Gender: Industrial Homework, Subcontracting, and Household Dynamics in Mexico City.* University of Chicago Press.

Benner, Chris. 2002. *Work in the New Economy: Flexible Labour Markets in the Silicon Valley,* Blackwell Publishing.

Burawoy, Michael. 1985. *Politics of Production: Factory Regimes under Capitalism and Socialism.* London: Routledge.

———. 1998. 'The Extended Case Method.' *Sociological Theory,* 16(1): 4–33.

———. 2009. *The Extended Case Method: Four Countries, Four Decades, Four Great Trasformations and One Theoretical Tradition.* Berkeley, Los Angeles, London: The University of California Press.

Burawoy, Michael, *et al.* 1991. *Ethnography Unbound: Power and Resistance in the Modern Metropolis.* Berkeley, Los Angeles, London: University of California Press.

Castells, Manuel. 2000. *The Information Age: Economy, Society and Culture,* vol. 3: *End of Millennium.* UK: Cambridge University Press.

Chakravarty, Deepita. 2007. '"Docile Oriental Women' and Organised Labour: A Case Study of the Indian Garment Manufacturing Industry.' *Indian Journal of Gender Studies,* 14(3): 439–60.

Chander, Jose. 1986. *Dynamics of State Politics Kerala.* Bangalore: Sterling Publishers.

Chari, Sharad. 2004. *Fraternal Capital: Peasant Workers, Self Made Men, and Globalization in Provincial India.* Delhi: Permanent Black.

Desai, Sonalde, Dubey, Amaresh, Joshi, Brij Lal, Sen, Mitali, Sharif, Abusaleh, and Vanneman, Reeve. 2010. *Human Development in India: Challenges for a Society in Transition.* New Delhi: Oxford University Press.

Devi, Lakshmy. 2002. 'Education, Employment, and Job Preferences of Women in Kerala: A Micro Level Study', Discussion Paper 42, Centre for Development Studies, India.

Devika, Jayakumari, and Rajasree. 2012. 'Widows' Organizations in Kerala State, India: Seeking Citizenship Amidst the Decline of Political Society,' in *Reframing Democracy and Agency in India*, edited by Ajay Gudavarthy, UK: Anthem Press.

Devika, Jayakumari., *et al.* 2008. 'Gendering Governance or Governing Women? Politics, Patriarchy, and Democratic Decentralisation in Kerala State, India', IDRC Grant Number: 102927–005.

Devika, Jayakumari. 2007. 'Fears of Contagion: Depoliticisation and Recent Conflicts over Politics in Kerala.' *Economic and Political Weekly*, 42(25): 2465–78.

Eapen, Mridul. 1992. 'Fertility and Female Labour Force Participation in Kerala.' *Economic and Political Weekly*, 27: 2179–88.

———. 1994. 'Rural Non-agricultural Employment in Kerala: Some Emerging Tendencies.' *Economic and Political Weekly*, 29(21): 1285–96.

———. 2001. 'Women in Informal Sector in Kerala: Need for Re-examination.' *Economic and Political Weekly*, 36(26): 2390–92.

Gibson-Graham, Julie. 2002. 'Beyond Global vs. Local: Economic Politics Outside the Binary Frame,' in *Geographies of Power: Placing Scale*, edited by Andrew Herod and Mellisa Wright. Oxford, UK: Blackwell.

Gulati, Leela. 1975. 'Sex Discrimination in Wages'. *Social Scientist*, 4(4–5): 155–60.

Harriss-White, Barbra. 2010. 'Work and Wellbeing in Informal Economies: The Regulative Roles of Institutions of Identity and the State.' *World Development*, 38(2): 170–83.

Harvey, David. 1990. *The Condition of Post-Modernity: An Enquiry into the Origins of Cultural Change*. Oxford, UK: Blackwell.

———. 1991. 'Flexibility: Threat or Opportunity.' *Socialist Review*, 21(1): 65.

Harvey, David, and Scott, Alan. 1989. 'The Practice of Human Geography: Theory and Empirical Specificity in the Transition from Fordism to Flexible Accumulation', in *Remodelling Geography*, edited Bill MacMillan, Oxford, UK: Blackwell.

Heller, Patrick. 1999. *The Labour of Development: Workers and Transformation of Capitalism in Kerala.* Ithaca: Cornell University Press.

Herod, Andrew. 2001. *Labour Geographies: Workers and the Landscapes of Capitalism.* London: The Guilford Press.

———. 2003a. 'Geographies of Labour Internationalism.' *Social Science History,* 27(4): 501–23.

———. 2003b. 'Scale: The Local and the Global,' in *Key Concepts in Geography* edited by Holloway, Rice, and Valentine, London: Sage. pp. 219–20.

———. 2003c. 'Workers, Space and Labour Geography.' *International Labour and Working Class History,* 64: 112–38.

Hirst, Paul, and Thompson, Grahame. 1999. 'Globalization: Frequently asked Questions and Some Surprising Answers,' in *Globalization and Labour Relations,* edited by Heisink, Cheltenham, UK: Edward Elgar.

Jeffrey, Robin. 2003. *Politics, Women and Well-Being, How Kerala became 'A Model'.* London: Macmillan.

———. 2010. *Media and Modernity: Communications, Women, and the State in India.* Ranikhet: Permanent Black.

Kannan, K. P. 1998. 'Political Economy of Labour and Development in Kerala.' Working Paper 284, Centre for Development Studies, Trivandrum.

Kapadia, K. 2006. 'A Tirupur Story.' *Frontline* 2 June. pp. 73.

Kumar, Rachel. 1994. 'Development and Women's Work in Kerala: Interactions and Paradoxes.' *Economic and Political Weekly,* 29(51–52): 3249–54.

Lindberg, Anna. 2001. *Experience and Identity: A Historical Account of Class, Caste, and Gender among the Cashew Workers of Kerala, 1930–2000.* Sweden: Department of History, Lund University.

Mankekar, D. R. 1965. 'The Red Riddle of Kerala.' Manaktalas, Mumbai.

Massey, Doreen. 2004. 'Geographies of Responsibility.' *Geografiska Annaler B,* 86: 5–18.

Mathew, P. M. 1985. 'Exploitation of Women Labour: An analysis of Women's Employment in Kerala.' *Social Scientist,* 13(10–11): 28–47.

Mazumdar, Sumit, and M. Guruswamy. 2006. 'Female Labour Force Participation in Kerala: Problems and Prospects', paper presented at the

2006 Annual Meeting of the Population Assocation of America, Los Angeles.

McKay, Steven C. 2004. 'Zones of Regulation: Restructuring Labour Control in Privatised Export Zones.' *Politics and Society,* 32: 171–202.

Menon. 1992. 'Women in Trade Unions: A Study of AITUC, INTUC and CITU in the Seventies,' in *Struggles of Women at Work,* edited by Sujata Gothoskar, New Delhi: Vikas.

Milberg, William. 2004. *Labour and the Globalization of Production: Causes and Consequences of Industrial Upgrading.* Basingstoke: Palgrave Macmillan.

Mills, Mary Beth. 2003. 'Gender and Inequality in the Global Labour Force.' *Annual Review of Anthropology,* 32: 41–62.

Mitra, Aparna, and Singh, Pooja. 2006. 'Human Capital Attainment and Female Labour Force Participation: The Kerala Puzzle.' *Journal of Economic Issues,* 40(3): 779–98.

———. 2007. 'Human Capital Attainment and Gender Empowerment: The Kerala Paradox.' *Social Science Quarterly,* 88(5): 1227–42.

Momsen, Janet. 2010. *Gender and Development.* New York: Routledge.

Nair, R. R. 1965. 'How Communists Came to Power in Kerala', Kerala Academy of Political Science.

Padmanabhan, Neethi. 2008. 'Contract Workers in the Organised Manufacturing Sector: A Disaggregated Analysis of Trends and their Implications.' *Indian Journal of Labour Economics,* 51(4): 559–73.

———. 2012a. 'Globalization Lived Locally: Enquiries into Kerala's Local Labour Control Regimes.' *Development and Change,* 43(6): 1239–63.

———. 2012b. 'Globalization Lived Locally: A Labour Geography Perspective on Control, Conflict and Response among Workers in Kerala.' *Antipode,* 44(3): 971–92.

Raju, Saraswati. 2010. *Gendered Access to Higher Education in Kerala.* Thiruvanthapuram, Kerala: State Higher Education Council.

Waterman, Peter. 1999. 'The New Social Unionism: A New Union Model for a New World Order', in *Labour Worldwide in the Era of Globalization: Alternative Union Models in the New World Order,* edited by Ronaldo Munck and Peter Waterman, UK: Macmillan.

Wright, Mellisa W. 1999. 'The Dialectics of Still Life: Murder, Women and the Maquiladoras.' *Public Culture,* 29: 453–73.

————. 2001. 'Desire and the Prosthetics of Supervision: A Case of Maquiladora Flexibility.' *Cultural Anthropology*, 16: 354–73.

Xue, Hong. 2008. 'Local Strategies of Labour Control: A Case Study of Three Electronic Factories in China.' *International Labour and Working-Class History*, 73: 85–103.

10

New Urban Economic Spaces and the Gendered World of Work in Kolkata

Tanusree Paul

Introduction

Scholars have suggested that industrial technology, being associated with bodily prowess, typically has had a masculine connotation.[1] However, with the emergence of the new knowledge economy in the contemporary era, the conceptualization of technology seems to have undergone a change from an essentially masculine perspective to a feminine one. It now refers to collection, processing and dissemination of intellectual knowledge and information. It has been set free from manual labour that constitutes the essentially masculine component and brought within the ambit of women. Industrial technology may have had a patriarchal character, but digital technologies, based on brain rather than brawn, on networks rather than hierarchy, herald a new relationship between women and machines (Wajcman 2010).

In contemporary times, women have been projected as the privileged users and beneficiaries of technologies in the private as well as in the public spaces.[2] In the latter sphere, the rise of the information and communication technology (ICT) based jobs in the wake of economic liberalization and the subsequent entry of women in this sector is a case in point. The main contention in this chapter is to understand how employment in these jobs have been affecting women's negotiations and resistances in the labour market given the fact that digital technologies have been posited as offering possibilities for destabilizing gender differences (Green and Adam, 1999; Kemp and Squires, 1998; Kirkup *et al.* 2000, also see Wajcman 2010). Scholars (such as Plant 1998, cited in Wajcman 2010, 148) argue that such technologies blur the boundaries between male and female, revalorise the feminine, providing the technological basis for a new form of society that is potentially liberating for women. In fact, professional women in the corporate sectors frequently feature the magazine covers, public hoardings, company campaigns etc. and 'usually stand in for broad societal change in a country conventionally thought of as particularly patriarchal' (Radhakrishnan 2009, 197). Thus, these professional women working in the new generation sectors are placed at the 'economic and cultural cutting edge of a rapidly changing urban India' (*Ibid.* 196).

That said, it is salutary to be reminded that "the possibility and the fluidity of gender discourse in the virtual world is constrained by the visceral, lived gender relations of the material world" (Wajcman 2010). It is these existential gender relations that affect the doing of gender even in the new economic spaces. As Banerjee (1999, 109) notes, gender relations, remain embedded in myriad institutions and are interdependent; the controls imposed within one are usually accepted and promoted as legitimate by the others (Banerjee 1999, 109). Given these complexities, the main objective of this chapter, which draws upon research carried out in Kolkata, is to understand whether the new economic spaces have been able to provide women with sites of resistances against archetypal gender relations compared to the spaces that have been occupied by women in the traditional sectors. The central question is to what extent the technologically driven 'modern' sectors have been able to provide a level-playing field for both sexes by redefining traditional gender roles or are they adapted to the existing socio-cultural strictures? This chapter argues that much of the disadvantages faced by women accrue from their framing within certain kinds of spaces–either physically or figuratively. Thus, although these sectors provide women with opportunities to work, in lucrative and high-end professional jobs and earn competitive salaries, women actually have to negotiate with well entrenched structures that subtly reflect unequal power relations in the society.

The chapter is organized into six sections. The introductory discussion is followed by a description of data and methods. The next section presents the gender differences in the choices and opportunities of work, which shows how women occupy a gendered position despite their belonging to different sectors of work. Further discussion looks into practising gender at work, which articulates through a) preferential treatments and ratings in favour of men as well as through sex typing of jobs, b) gendered career outcomes in terms of access to information and future aspirations, and c) the importance of engendered perceptions and stereotypes that in effect delimit their access to an enabling working environment. The study then explores the possibilities of progressive intercepts in terms of women's agency that working in the new generation sectors offer. The last section concludes the chapter.

Data and methods

The study draws upon the primary data derived from the field survey in Kolkata conducted during the year 2010–11. Data have been generated through questionnaire-based survey and short face-to-face interviews. In addition, published and unpublished research works have also been used to supplement the information obtained from the field survey. About 460 samples have been collected from men and women working in the new generation sectors as well as in the traditional sector. The former is constituted by the information technology and enabled services as well as the organized retail sectors[3] while the latter is represented through the academic sector in this study. About 100 interviews have been taken from each of the IT and organized retail sectors and about 70 from the ITES sector where the target of taking 100 interviews could not be fulfilled due to difficulty of locating contacts. Another 70 samples have been taken from the academic sector as a representative of traditional sector since teaching has been considered to be a traditional sector employing women. In addition, about 120 men, 30 from each of the four sectors have also been interviewed. Workplaces are the key sites for the enquiry, since they act as the institutionalised places for the production of identity and a sense of self.[4]

Respondents were asked to indicate their attitudes, perceptions, constraints they faced, etc., on Likert's 5 point scale.[5] Comparison of these mean scores between men and women and among women working in different sectors has been widely used in the analysis. The difference is then tested for determining the significance levels.[6]

Overlapping and differentiated choices and opportunities of work

Having restricted access to the public spaces, women lack access to structural and institutional sources of power which consequently robs them of their inner capability to negotiate and resist asymmetrical power and status relations. Scholars like Banerjee (1999) and Raju (2013) have argued that the free play of market processes fail to deconstruct the existential gender relations in the labour market operating within the society at large. It is in the context of the prevalence of such gendered spaces and power in the labour market that the concept of social capital plays an important role. Women's association with private space renders them noticeably powerless since information and resources are fundamental bases of social power (French and Raven 1968). Spain (1993) is of opinion that although women's status is a result of the culmination of a variety of factors viz. cultural, religious and socio-economic, the physical separation of women and men further perpetuates gender stratification by relegating women to inside spaces. As Massey (1994, 179) has put it, "the attempt to confine women to the domestic sphere was both a specifically spatial control and, through that, a social control on identity McDowell and Sharp (1997) argue that "[s]patial relations act to socialize people into the acceptance of gendered power relations–they reinforce power, privileges and oppression and literally keep women in their place" (cited in Dilworth and Trvenon 2004, 189). That such spatial framing of women impacts upon their career mobilities is perhaps easily understandable so as to obviate the need for further elaboration here. As Valk and Srinivasan (2011) note in their study on the women workers in the Information Technology industry that the societal role expectations, women's career ambitions, and the nature of the IT industry challenges the manner in which they attempt to strive for a work-life balance.

Hindrances to career development

The personal barriers encountered by women towards career development are undeniably reminiscent of their unequal position in the labour market since these limit the choices at their disposal at the very entry level. The women respondents from both the sectors were asked to cite how their gendered identities have affected their professional aspirations and developments and to rank the causes on a scale of 5.

Figure 10.1 indicates the reasons in the order of ranking. Lack of freedom of mobility has been reported by more than half of the women working in each of the new generation and traditional sector as a telling obstacle which hinges on their gender. Marriage and contingent array of responsibilities appear to be inhibiting the career of all women alike, particularly those working in the ITES and retail sector, perhaps because the erratic shifts and limited week-offs they have, make it extremely difficult to balance their professional and personal lives.

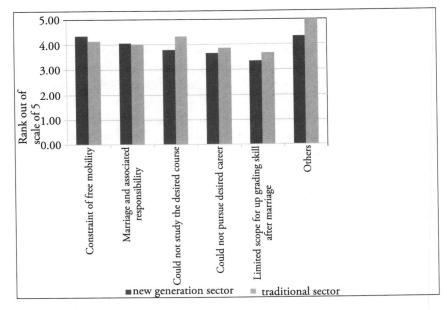

Fig. 10.1 Hindrances towards career development

Source: Field work in Kolkata 2010–2011

Limited scope for upgrading skill after marriage is also a major problem confronted by most of the women working in both the new generation and traditional sectors. Further, among the unmarried women, inability to study their desired courses followed by lack of free mobility have been posited as the major constraints. The factor marked as 'others' include time constraint, stereotypes of the employers that women always prioritize home and neglect work, lack of access to information and resources, a little amicability in the workplace is susceptible towards sending out the message that the woman is 'available', inability to take 'hard', i.e., robust career decisions due to responsibilities towards family, being extra conscious at the workplace during informal interaction with male colleagues, requiring to do multitasking that affect professional rigour, etc.

Choices, criteria for job search and career interruptions

Needless to point out that these personal barriers often pose as major impediments to professional development by affecting the choices that the female respondents make with respect to their career. The respondents were asked whether they had been able to pursue the career they desired for. Most of the women answered in negative and the reasons for not doing so clearly reflected their disadvantageous position in making career-related decisions (Table 10.1). It may be mentioned that in this regard the differences are more conspicuous between men and women rather than between and among women from the new generation and traditional sectors. On the one hand, lack of family support and appropriate contacts and information have been cited as the most important reasons for not pursuing the desired career by women; most of the men have replied that while they had to accept their present jobs due to compulsion to support family, they would pursue their desired career in future. One can argue that this indicates men's entrapment within the gender-ascriptive role of being the bread winner in the family. While such stereotypes indeed have compelled respondent men to immediately enter the workforce, it needs to be pointed out that their future aspirations have only been postponed and not curtailed. Less than 1 percent of the women and about one-fifth of the men working in the new generation sector reported that they would pursue their aspirations in future. Among other reasons, lack of concerted effort on the part of self, failure in qualifying entrance examinations, limited scope in Kolkata, inability to move out of current job and personal problems, etc., have also been reported.

Table 10.1 Reasons for not pursuing desired career

Reasons	Traditional Sector			New Generation Sector		
	Women	Men	Total	Women	Men	Total
Family does not encourage	22.9	2.6	17.6	7.7	9.1	8.1
Lack of appropriate contacts to venture into the job	10.1	0.0	7.4	0.0	18.2	5.4
Lack of required skill and no opportunity to acquire that skill*	7.3	2.6	6.1	7.7	0.0	5.4
Would require more time investment	2.8	0.0	2.0	19.2	9.1	16.2
Would require greater travelling/physical mobility	0.9	0.0	0.7	19.2	0.0	13.5
Would pursue in future	0.9	17.9	5.4	0.0	45.5	13.5
Male dominated profession/not suitable for women	0.9	0.0	0.7	3.8	0.0	2.7
Others	54.1	76.9	60.1	38.5	18.2	32.4
Total	100.0	100.0	100.0	100.0	100.0	100.0

Note: In the new generation sector, non-cooperation from the family and extra time
    involved in skill development interfering with domestic life was also mentioned

Source: Field work in Kolkata 2010–2011

The pre-conditions that women have when they look for jobs as well as the
reasons that prompt them to change their jobs also mirror their limited career
related choices vis-à-vis men. Table 10.2 indicates that among the workers
of the new generation sectors, salary structure is the most important criteria
for job search, although it has been reported by a higher proportion of men
compared to the women. Among other criteria, short/flexible working hours
in order to strike work-life balance, closer to residence to reduce travel time
and location of workplace in safe areas of the city have been reported by more
than one-third of the women in both the new generation and traditional
sectors. Among the men in the traditional sector, job satisfaction followed
by environment at workplace are the most important factors influencing job
searches. Women's concern for location of the workplace in safe areas perhaps
reflect their urge to adhere to norms of spatial legitimacy even as they routinely
engage with the masculine public spaces for paid work. Further looking for
jobs with flexible/short working hours imply that they consistently attempt to
be career oriented, but rarely at the expense of a family life. As the discussion
in this paper progresses, this point that primacy of family and relationships
continue to structure the professional choices and decisions made by women
would be further elucidated.

Table 10.2 Most important criteria for job search of men and women

Preconditions	New Generation Sectors		Traditional Sector	
	Women	**Men**	**Women**	**Men**
Salary structure	66.3	91.1	51.4	33.3
Environment at workplace rank	50.7	50.0	55.7	46.7
Short/flexible working hours/weekend offs so as to be able to manage chores rank	38.5	2.2	62.9	16.7
Job satisfaction, roles, responsibilities rank	37.8	38.9	32.9	63.3
Closer to residence to reduce travel time rank	33.7	26.7	47.1	20.0

Location of workplace in safe areas of the city	33.0	14.4	42.9	10.0
Brand name rank	13.3	17.8	1.4	3.3
Kolkata based location	6.7	5.6	0.0	3.3
Shift of the duty	6.3	6.7	0.0	0.0
Other considerations	3.3	5.6	8.6	0.0

Figures indicate the percentage of women/men out of total women/men in each sector. Since the same respondents have reported more than one reason, the percentages do not add up to 1000

Source: Field Work in Kolkata

The reasons for changing jobs also re-instate this argument. About one-third of both men and women working in the new generation sector have changed their jobs for better opportunity. What is interesting to note is that a higher proportion of men have changed their jobs for lack of job satisfaction and inadequate remuneration. Women are more likely to do so in response to personal problems like marriage, husband's transfer, changing sector in order to move from night to day shift, own education and health problems, etc (Table 10.3). The incessant struggle waged by these women to balance work and family life tacitly demonstrate some continuity with nationalist conceptions of women as the protectors and nurturers of Indian culture and celebrated signifiers of symbolic capital and respectable femininity (Radhakrishnan 2009).

Table 10.3 Most important reasons for changing job

Reasons	New Generation		Traditional	
	Women	Men	Women	Men
Better opportunity	30.9	31.3	20.8	15.4
Relocating to Kolkata	9.9	10.9	1.9	15.4
Inadequate remuneration	8.8	14.1	15.1	0.0
Inhospitable work climate	8.3	6.3	9.4	0.0
Personal problem	6.6	4.7	–	–
Marriage/husband's transfer/child birth	5.5	0.0	1.9	0.0
No job satisfaction	4.4	15.6	9.4	15.4
Timing problems	3.3	3.1	–	–

Family pressure	2.2	3.1	–	–
Too long working hours/too much work load	2.2	1.6	–	–
Workplace too far away from residence	1.7	0.0	3.8	0.0
Appraisal not transparent	1.1	0.0	–	–
Work too hectic and too much pressure	0.6	0.0	–	–
No proper holidays/no holiday on weekends	0.6	0.0	–	–
Stunted growth opportunities	1.1	0.0	–	–
Routine professional transfers	0.0	1.6	18.9	30.8
Other	12.7	7.8	18.9	23.1

Source: Field Work in Kolkata 2010–2011

Reflection upon interruptions in career and the reasons behind that is another important marker of disparate opportunities in career development. About 22 percent of the women and only 9 percent of the men have had breaks in their careers. Among the women, about 25 per cent of those working in the new generation sectors and 11 percent of those working in the academic sector have had such interruptions. The reasons for interruptions in career appear more nuanced when interfaced with marriage (Table 10.4). Among the married women working in the new generation sectors, husband's transfer, child birth and rearing are the most important reasons while pursuing own education followed by husband's job transfer have been reported by those in the traditional sector. Among the unmarried women in the new generation sectors pursuing own education, health related problems and 'other' reasons, which include personal problems, inhospitable work climate, etc., emerge as the most important. Among the men working in the new generation sectors, changing sectors and other reasons have been reported by more than half the respondents. Both the unmarried women and married men in the traditional sector have taken breaks for engaging with further higher studies, which indicate that marriage and the contingent array of family responsibilities bear different implications for men and women.

Table 10.4 Reasons for interruptions in career

Sector	Reasons	Women		Men	
		Married	**Unmarried**	**Married**	**Unmarried**
New Generation	husband's job transfer	16.7	0.0	nil	nil
	own education	6.7	38.7	0.0	12.5
	Health	0.0	25.8	0.0	50.0
	Marriage	26.7	0.0	nil	nil
	Others	16.7	32.3	50.0	37.5
	child birth and rearing	23.3	0.0	nil	nil
	Relocation	3.3	3.2	nil	nil
	shifting sector/changing job	6.7	0.0	50.0	0.0
	Total	100.0	100.0	100.0	100.0
Traditional	husband's job transfer	22.2	0.0	nil	nil
	own education	33.3	100.0	100	nil
	Marriage	11.1	0.0	nil	nil
	Others	11.1	0.0	nil	nil
	child birth and rearing	11.1	0.0	nil	nil
	Marriage and husband's job transfer	11.1	0.0	nil	nil
	Total	100.0	100.0	nil	nil

Source: Field Work in Kolkata 2010–2011

All these factors problematize the 'choice' that women exercise in deciding their career paths. These re-iterate that the choices women make are controlled by their familial responsibilities and by social and cultural conventions and sanctions imposed upon them, particularly when they make 'unconventional' choices (Dewan 1999). Thus, it may not be misleading to conjecture that although the new generation sectors do provide women with emerging spaces, some constraints hinged on their gendered identities continue to operate even within these sectors. This suggests that women as women occupy a certain space in the society, having access to entitlements upto a certain extent and no farther (Raju 2006).

Practising gender at work

The practising of gender at work appears to be non-reflexive, often shaped by the normative of action and behaviour legitimized by the society for doing gender (Martin 2006). The succeeding sub-sections discuss how gender is being practised in the workplaces in a number of subtle ways.

Engendered roles and professional growth

The new generation sectors are propelled by knowledge generation, information processing and sharing (Basant and Rani 2004) rather than manual labour. These sectors provide women with enabling working environment; support them with attractive salaries that can give them a certain confidence and reasonable economic independence, which may help them to withstand the gender discrimination that prevails in Indian society (Clark and Shekher 2007).

> Educated, English-speaking, urban middle-class women find in the high-tech sector not only an opportunity to improve their financial autonomy, but also a platform for greater mobility and larger social acceptance in a male dominated society. This can be considered as not merely a cosmetic change, but as a small beginning of a reversal of female devaluation among some educated segments of society a small beginning of a reversal of female devaluation among some educated segments of society (*Ibid:* 289–290).

Provision of a host of support services, mainly flexible work arrangements, crèches, canteens, etc., to facilitate women's participation have also been posited as a marker of the gender-friendliness of these sectors.

> An implicit mandate of the IT and ITES is a certain proportion of workforces as women which means you also have to cater to the needs of women, to have the support structures. Standard government rules like maternity leave are given. Besides, day cares, crèches, etc., at some companies are also given. You (a lady) will not be special person but you will be equal
>
> Shubhodeep Lahiri, Vice President, IT
>
> IT sector is suitable for women compared to other sectors like power-plants, mechanical engineering, etc., which are dominated by men.
>
> Sonali, 24, Unmarried, Software Engineer IT
>
> IT is conducive for women unlike mechanical engineering because here constraints like staying/working in factory environment do not apply. Jayati Chatterjee 39, Marrried, Senior Manager, IT

However, this should not be taken as indicative of a perfectly egalitarian work environment in the new generation sectors so far as gender constructs are concerned. This is because there exist several covert mechanisms, which exploit the disadvantageous social positioning of the women in the labour market, already discussed in the preceding sections. One such manipulative mechanism is the scope for subjective ratings and appraisals by the employers at workplace. Often, such ratings turn out to be biased against women since these are influenced by stereotypes about women—not only regarding their care and reproductive roles but also misapprehension regarding their commitment towards work. Overall, more than one-third of the women and about one-fifth of the men reportedly have received unjust ratings and appraisals in their professional life. Further, about 43 percent of the women working in the new generation sector have been affected by unscrupulous appraisals.

> Maternity leave caused six months delay in my promotions. I was away for just three months and despite putting in hard work for remaining part of the year, my being away for the leave made a difference.
>
> Jayashree Chatterjee39, Married, Senior Manager, IT.[7]

> Rating process is not transparent; women are often given unjust ratings because they remain invisible. Men stay till late night, smoke, socialize and have higher interaction with PL (project lead), TL (team lead). Women also work hard but are often overlooked.
>
> Sonali 24, Unmarried, Software Engineer, IT.

> Visibility is a problem. I could not publicize my work. Indian women especially are more shy and submissive. They have to stick to decorum, Mimi Kanungo 41, Married, Deputy Manager, IT.

> A woman cannot devote as much time as a man. He would come at 9 a.m. and stretch back till next day, and when he is giving so much time he is bound to succeed. I cannot stay overnight at the office and that affects my growth. Debamitra 23, Unmarried, Software Developer, IT.

Thus, the lack of visibility in the workplace seems to be a key problem faced by women in the new generation sectors particularly those working in the IT and retail, leading to unjust appraisals for further promotion. The key reasons for such lack of visibility, in turn, are very many being unable to stretch for long hours in the office due to domestic responsibilities, absence from the workplace for pregnancy and child birth, inability for late hour socialization in parties and other events organized beyond the office hours.

These eventually result in a glass ceiling that blocks women's professional growth.

> The IT sector is all hunky and dory because we are working in a global platform. Yet there is a certain glass ceiling, a certain gendered equation.
>
> Rajeshwari 34, Married, Senior Content Developer, IT.

> At the senior level, employees are expected to travel frequently, attend seminars, clients, which call for greater bandwith. Therefore, many women opt out of it which creates an invisible glass ceiling.
>
> Jayati Chatterjee 39, Married, Senior Manager, IT.

Failure to accept a work profile that entails a physical mobility also affected ratings for women working in the retail sector. Among those working in the academic sector, only about 8 percent of women have suffered from biased appraisals, the primary reason for which is ambivalent to most of them. It may, however, be conjectured that less incidence of unscrupulous practices in the academic sector are-firstly because the working environment is not as competitive as in the new generation sectors and secondly due to the fact that teaching is customarily seen as a feminine field while the technology-based new generation sectors are discursively premised around biased social strictures. However, it is not to suggest that women are especially targeted and their career paths thwarted in these new sectors. As the NASSCOM (2008: 18) report on gender inclusivity suggests,

> A woman professional must also know that, at the top, life is very demanding and very desexed. It is just not possible to become an Indra Nooyi, Naina Lal Kidwai, Mallika Sarabhai or Vasundhara Raje Scindia by trying to juggle work, home, husband, mother-in-law and making pickle. The other part is that to get to the top, whether you are a man or a woman, you must travel a lot, sometimes work weekends, network outside the workplace, learn on your own initiative, engage continuously and finally, give an awful lot more than you get"
> Subroto Bagchi, Co-founder, MindTree Consulting.

It is true that work environs in new generation sector presuppose certain responsibilities, which both men and women have to carry out were they to excel. The irony is that given the socially encoded roles as child/family carer, women have less time than their male colleagues leading to their invisibility in the workplace. Thus, despite no explicit glass ceiling, certain strictures do operate that are discursively based on the situational reality of women. As put by the Vice President of a leading IT giant,

There is no glass ceiling as such. What I have been able to analyze is that upto a certain point, you work and grow within the organization as a junior, then you move to the middle, then to the senior level, then you become executive and then you move onto very senior positions. What happens is around the age of 35, 37, 38, that's when you actually break from the regular progression for the next 7–8 years, when if you exert, you move into the senior position. For women, usually at that stage, that's when your kids have moved to class X, class XI like that, that's when they need you. You move away from professional world to take care of your home for those 6–7 years. So, you lose out your career. That's the most vital part you know, when you have attained a certain level and you want to move onto the next level in career That's the prime time.... its very important that you are involved. Unfortunately...I would not say unfortunately, because that's your choice that you make, when you come back into mainstream again, that time lagging behind. In India, personal involvement is a yardstick and women cannot give 100 per cent personal involvement when she is taking care of kids and family.

Shubhodeep Mandal, VP, IT.

Soft options in hard lives: Occupation segregation and gender

Witz (1992) points out that segmentation of occupations are underlain by gendered take-over, exclusion and occupational closure that are detrimental to women and beneficial to men (cited in Guillaume and Pochic 2009, 17). Typically, the technical and more complex of jobs have been appropriated by men leaving a narrow band of occupations available for women. Notwithstanding the recurring rhetoric about women's opportunities in the new knowledge economy, men continue to dominate technical work. Men are more likely than women to be found in jobs that involve complex and advanced computer or computerised equipment use.[8] According to the NASSCOM report (2008, 10), technical functions traditionally are 'all-male bastions', although the proportion of women in this domain has registered an increase in the last couple of years. Field observations corroborate this fact; about one-third of the women respondents and about two third of the men in the IT sector work in core technical and software development. Even within this department, men are primarily engaged in coding while women in testing softwares, the former being more technical in nature. Beside this, women are clustered in 'softer' departments or the 'velvet ghettos' (Guillaume and Pochic 2009: 19) viz. consultancy, learning and development, content management, quality assurance and human resource; while men in the process and tools, delivery and operations.

In the IT sector, there are two kinds of work which are valued most – the delivery role and the sales role. These roles are the core ones in the functioning of the business of the company and are constituted by 99.99 per cent men employees. To enable these core functions we have different roles like learning and development, quality assurance, human resource, recruitment. Resource management, travel group, facilitator of research and development groups, etc., which are not really in the focus area and are dominated by women. Women mostly are employed in the non-challenging clerical roles.

Nayanika 41, Married, IT.

To think in terms of the spatial binaries of the public and the private, the roles which are critical to the functioning of the business can be considered as the primary driving force, therefore appropriated by men, while the enabling services, although important, are secondary and therefore earmarked for women. In the ITES sector, women are largely employed in the voice-call processes dealing with clients and customers while men doing the more 'crucial' back-end jobs. This is also the case in the retail sector where most of the human resource managers are constituted by women while other back-end services are carried out by men. The front end retail staff dealing with floor operations, electronic goods and appliances, sports goods, etc., are constituted by men; women remaining mainly in ladies' and kids' sections and customer services. In both the ITES and organized retail sectors these front-end tasks are perceived as more tedious and less lucrative, which is reflected in the fact that most of the respondents in these jobs want to change to the backend jobs in their respective sectors. In the traditional sector, women are concentrated in the Humanities/Arts departments while the Science and Commerce appear to be male dominated (Fig. 10.2) in both colleges and universities.

This seemingly incidental segregation of occupation is underlain by subtle stereotypes of gender roles and perceptions which have become evident from the informal discussions with the store managers, HRs and high-level officials. It arises out of certain assumptions about women being nurturing and perseverant and men being aggressive and fierce achievers. Such assumption and consequent occupational segregation eventually perpetuates a form of gender hierarchy within the organizations.

Women and men are employed according to their generic nature in IT. Women are mainly employed in negotiation and persuasion oriented tasks, while men are better go-getters. In IT, some departments are women dominated so it is not difficult to access information and resources in these. In other departments, there exists glass ceilings at higher levels, there competing with men is difficult because women cannot go onshore always, can't do late nights.

Suchismita 28, Married, Learning Consultant, IT.

In retail sector, you know, people have to stretch themselves. We usually look for people who are inclined to stretch, who are aggressive. For female employees, whether they would be able to stretch, whether their families would allow them to work on Sundays, these kinds of questions arise.

Chaity 32, Married, HR, Future Group.

This clear-cut occupational segregation of women into lower and mid-level positions[9] and to less challenging roles reflects subtle ways in which gender is practised at work which, according to Martin (2006, 267), is indicative of '… power where men hold most of the most powerful positions and most women are subordinate to men in the formal authority structures and relative to gender.' As Radharishnan (2009, 145) puts it, these sexual divisions in the labour market are proving intransigent and mean that women are largely excluded from the processes of technical design that shape the world we live in.

Information Technology

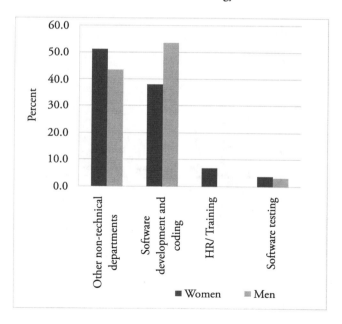

Information Technology Enabled Services

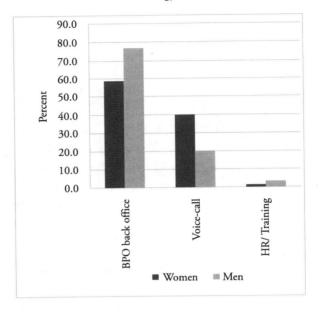

Organised Retail

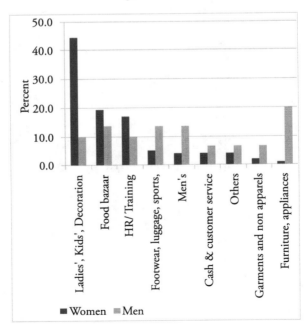

Academics

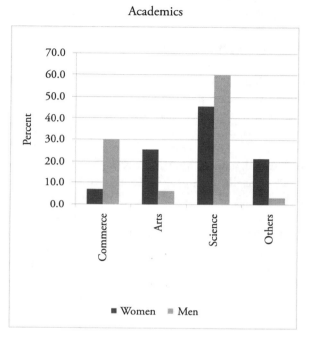

Fig. 10.2 Occupation seggregation by sector

Labour market economists tend to explain such sex segregation in terms of differences in human capital, domestic responsibilities that fall disproportionately on women, and employment discrimination (Radhakrishnan 2009). Feminists, however, have pointed out that the problem does not lie with women (their socialization, their aspirations and values) and that we need to address the broader questions of whether and in what way techno–science and its institutions can be reshaped to accommodate women (Radhakrishnan 2009).[10]

And yet, the present study indicates that such intractable scenario cannot be addressed through mere gender friendly company policies alone. Part of the problem also lies with women's unequal gender positions with respect to opportunity structure, as discussed earlier. For instance, according to an HR manager in an IT company, women are not preferred for delivery of project related job profiles because one has to stretch till late night, sometimes more than 24 hours. Thus, family roles have been discursively sited as a reason behind the clustering of women in certain profiles and lack of them in the others. Slow professional growth or absence of women from senior levels has been explicated through the persistence of mid career guilt or a choice that women make to prioritize families–a point which would be returned to later in this chapter.

The implications are somewhat subtle yet must not be undermined. In examining the interface between skills and labour market outcomes, Raju (2006), while looking at the lower end of the employment opportunities, notes that women are framed within a stereotyped skill set premised around their domestic roles, to the effect that often the work they do in the labour market is really an extension of what they do at home; the scenario in the upper echelons of the same becomes a little more nuanced. Although the well-paid professional women in these technology-driven modern sectors do possess highly complex technical skills, akin to men, there seems to exist some form of bunching of the work actually done. Often, the tasks allotted to women are assumed to be requiring greater perseverance and care. The logic behind employing women in such tasks is that they are perceived as embodying these qualities better than men and in representing women as inherently nurturing and pacifist, these modern sectors tend to reinforce an essentialist view of sex difference (see Wajcman 2010, 146). Further, such stereotypical interfacing of the intrinsic human qualities with labour market opportunities is a potential site of intersection of the global and the local. As Raju (2006, 103) puts it, gendered discourses continue to inform the labour market opportunities which 'on the one hand aim for an international reach, but on the other hand remain firmly embedded in the local/national contexts in which labour and skills are produced and institutionalized'.

Women as leads and engendered perceptions

In addition to the scope for subjective appraisals and bunching of jobs, the experiences women have as team/project leads are also indicative of the deeply entrenched patriarchal structures that they have to negotiate in the workplaces. The respondents have been asked to indicate how, according to them, a man occupying leading positions in the team/group/organization is different from a woman (Table 10.5). This question returned a multitude of responses ranging from gender-ascriptive perceptions to practical problems.

Table 10.5 Constraints faced by women in attaining lead positions

Sectors	Time Constraint	Male ego	Unequal access to information and resource	Difficult for women to reach top
IT	16.7	27.3	46.7	40.9

ITES	18.8	15.2	20	27.3
Retail	56.3	39.4	20	18.2
Academics	8.3	18.2	13.3	13.6

Figures indicate percentage of women returning each response. Since same respondent have given more than one reason, the total does not add upto 100 per cent.

Source: Field work in Kolkata 2010–11

Time constraint has been cited by more than 50 per cent of those working in the organized retail sector. About 40 per cent of the women working in the retail and about 30 per cent of those in the IT sector were of the opinion that a woman lead has to confront ego problems from subordinate men who fail to accept women at a commanding position. Further, about half the women in the IT sector and about one-fifth of those in the ITES and organized retail maintain that a woman lead does not have as much access to information as their male counterparts. Given these constraints, about 40 per cent of the women in the IT and about one-third of those in ITES felt that assuming the position of a team/department lead itself is extremely difficult, also because of women's personal commitments.

> The nature of team spirit and team building is different. Women-headed teams are closely bound, fellow feeling is intrinsic. Men are more professional and their teams are marked by clearer demarcation of work, more clarity in terms of yes and no. Mahua Seth 43, Married, Senior Manager IT.

> When a woman leads a project, there are certain sexual innuendos. If she takes a stand against wrong ratings, there is no promotion, professional life gets miserable Aditi Mukherjee 43, Married, Senior Instruction Designer, IT.

Reluctance on men's part in accepting women bosses has been cited by women in both new and traditional sectors.

Future career aspirations

The unequal position of women and consequently disparate opportunities available to them, gender biasness, gender role stereotypes and biased promotional practices manifest in ambivalent future aspirations and career ambitions. Women fail to take robust career decisions and seem to be unsure of what they hope to accomplish out of their careers. Men appear to be possessing greater zeal in pursuing their career, aspiring to excel in their present job, without much difficulty. Most women describe themselves as 'not too ambitious,' and view a career as something supplemental to a married life with children.

The nature of the ITES and organized retail, with the erratic nature of shifts and limited number of holidays, is such that it is difficult for women to aspire for a stable career or strike a work-life balance therein. While those working in the former intend to shift sector or move to day shifts, those in the latter sector intend to move to government job or simply quit working (Table 10.6).[11] About 40 per cent of the women and 80 per cent of the men in retail want to continue in the sector. Few would prefer the more secure government jobs, but as they are hard to come by, they want to stay in retail as long as possible.

Table 10.6 Future career aspirations of men and women by sector

Future aspirations	IT		ITES		Organized retail		Academics	
	Women	Men	Women	Men	Women	Men	Women	Men
Better position in the same sector	74.0	100	50.7	76.7	39.0	80.0	81.1	70.0
Better position in a different sector	8.0	0.0	13.0	0.0	16.0	6.7	4.3	0.0
In government service	0.0	0.0	0.0	0.0	6.0	3.3	0.0	0.0
Do not know	13.0	0.0	8.7	0.0	16.0	0.0	1.4	0.0
Non voice process in day shift/back office job	0.0	0.0	20.3	0.0	1.0	0.0	0.0	0.0
Quit working for family care	2.0	0.0	2.9	0.0	4.0	0.0	2.9	0.0
Business	1.0	0.0	0.0	3.3	5.0	10.0	0.0	0.0
In equivalent role but higher position in any corporate	0.0	0.0	0.0	0.0	12.0	0.0	0.0	0.0
Move to academic sector for work life balance	0.0	0.0	4.3	0.0	1.0	0.0	0.0	0.0

Do better research and evolve as a researcher	0.0	0.0	0.0	0.0	0.0	0.0	10.1	30.0
Total	100	100	100	100	100	100	0.0	0.0

Source: Field work in Kolkata 2010–11

Thus, organized retail sector has provided opportunity to those young people who have little human and financial capital and would have otherwise found it difficult to get job. Besides giving access to income that would help them strengthen their position within the family, is another important dimension associated with this sector. Many of the respondents seem to be deeply enchanted and contented with the—

> architecturally distinctive, western style edifices as their workplace, a physically comfortable, modern working environment that is a far cry from traditional retail in markets and bazaars; smart, westernized corporate clothing and English as the medium of communication with their customers whenever possible as status enhancing features (Gooptu 2009, 51).

Working in this sector, thus, provides the employees with the opportunity to be associated with ritzy first-world working conditions and freer life and consumption. Nevertheless, more than half the women in the new generation sectors compared to about 37 per cent of those working in the traditional sector have reported high work pressure and difficulty in managing domestic responsibilities as one of the major demerits.

The respondents have also been asked how easy or difficult it would be for them to satisfy their career goals. Needless to mention that the responses returned by the women are reminiscent of the unequal structural positions they occupy in general and the ways gender is being practised in the organizations in particular. These have been discussed at length in previous sections to obviate further mention at this juncture. However, it must be noted that the women working in the traditional sector appear to be rather contented with their jobs, desire to stay in their present job and do not consider prospering professionally as any difficult. On the other hand, their counterparts in the new generation sectors perceive it to be extremely difficult due to shortage of time at their disposal and biased appraisals etc.[12] There is 'a belief that commitment is represented by working full-time, — including being in early and staying on late; that personal circumstances should not impinge upon work' (Palmer, 1996: 140; cited in Guillaume and Pochic 2009, 29).

Even if she is contributing more than a man, it is typically perceived that she is a woman and she must be having family problems, babies, etc., She comes in the morning by 9 a.m. and leaves at 6:30–7 p.m. due to her family commitments. Her intention is how quickly she can finish her work and go home. However, a man stays back till long, take 4–5 breaks for smoking and socializing. People perceive woman as a constraint. They are often not given a fair chance.

Nayanika 41, Married IT.

Further, the study notes that about 13 per cent of the women and only 3 per cent of the men do not have any clear idea about their future aspirations. Table 10.7 presents the socio-economic characteristics of those who do not have any definitive career ambition. About two-thirds of this fraction, surprisingly, is constituted by professionals, and about one-third of them have B. Tech and M.B.A. degree. Therefore, lack of human capital in terms of skill and education is not the reason behind such ambivalence. These are the women between 25–34 years of age and mostly unmarried–women who are unsure about their career in view of the immanent circumstantial possibilities that might befall them due to marriage and associated responsibilities. Martin (2006, 260) puts it succinctly, "people routinely practise gender without being reflexive about it and without consciously intending to do so. They know they are doing something but often they are less than fully aware of the gender in their actions."

Table 10.7 Socio-economic characteristics of respondents who are ambivalent about future career aspirations

Characteristics	N	Percent	Characteristics	N	Percent
Sex			*Education*		
Women	36	90	Graduation general	18	45
Men	4	10	Graduate diploma	1	2.5
			Graduate technical	5	12.5
Age			PG general	9	22.5
<24	6	15	PG technical	6	15
25–34	23	57.5	PG law	1	2.5
35–49	11	27.5			

Marital Status			Sector		
Married with children	10	25.0	IT	13	32.5
Married without children	6	15.0	ITES	10	25
Unmarried	22	55.0	Organized Retail	16	40
divorced/ separated/widowed	2	5.0	Academics	1	2.52
Household Type			Occupation		
Nuclear	26	72.2	Other service worker	10	25
Joint	7	19.4	Professionals	24	60
Others	3	8.3	Senior officers and managers	6	15

Source: Field work in Kolkata 2010–11

Access to work-related information and job search methods

Shade (1998, 33) maintains that universal access to communication and information services must be recognized as an essential human right for maintaining basic democratic values. Indeed, information and resources are fundamental bases of social power (French and Raven 1968). Moreover, integrated access to information and resources endow individuals with higher levels of empowerment. However, this study notes that men and women do not have equal access to information related to work. Table 10.8 presents the chief sources of information for job opportunities as reported by proportion of men and women working in various sectors. Women in the new generation sectors appear to rely more on newspapers, consultancies and digital web for accessing information related to job vacancies (see also, Raju and Baud 2007). Online job portals like the Naukri.com and similar other websites provide them with the necessary information in case they are looking for job change. However, men tend to derive such information from their friends and colleagues in the present as well as earlier workplaces. This is also true for those working in the traditional sector. One can argue that this is suggestive of the universal construct of men as bread-earners and the society at large assuming a self-imposed responsibility towards providing for its realization. This observation also foregrounds the importance of informal networking in accessing information in these sectors, a point taken up at length earlier in this chapter.

Table 10.8 Sources of information for job opportunities

Sector	Gender	Present workplace	Newspaper and internet	Friends and colleagues	All
IT	Women	5.3	63.2	15.8	15.8
	Men	7.7	23.1	23.1	46.2
	Total	6.3	46.9	18.8	28.1
ITES	Women	0.0	92.3	0.0	7.7
	Men	27.3	9.1	63.6	0.0
	Total	12.5	54.2	29.2	4.2
Retail	Women	4.5	63.6	27.3	4.5
	Men	5.6	44.4	33.3	16.7
	Total	4.8	58.1	29.0	8.1
Academics	Women	0.0	85.7	0.0	14.3
	Men	22.2	44.4	0.0	33.3
	Total	12.5	62.5	0.0	25.0

Source: Field Work in Kolkata 2010–11

Sociologists, namely Granovetter (1974, 1995), Lin (1999, 2001a, 2001b) argue that using job contacts enhances the career success as well as prestige. This may result in a snowball process of advantage wherein contacts in one job provide access to contacts in other jobs (Granovetter 1995, 153). Among those who derive information related to work from personal contacts, non-kins, rather than kins, constitute the most important sources even for women. However, the average number of non-kin contact in this regard is significantly higher among men compared to women across all the sectors.[13] Further, the average number of male contacts among women's peers in supplying work information is much less compared to that of men across all sectors and across all designation in the organizational structure (Table 10.9).[14]

Table 10.9 Average number of contacts for work-related information

Sector	Gender	Total volume of contacts	No. of kin	No. of non-kin	Total volume of male contacts	No. of male kins	No. of male non-kins
IT	Women	7.5	0.7	6.8	4.0	0.7	3.3
	Men	14.8	1.0	13.8	10.7	0.3	10.4

ITES	Women	6.7	0.4	6.4	3.9	0.3	3.6
	Men	5.8	0.1	5.8	5.1	0.0	5.1
Orga- nized retail	Women	5.4	0.5	4.9	2.9	0.5	2.5
	Men	8.3	0.1	8.2	7.5	0.1	7.4
Academ- ics	Women	4.3	0.6	3.8	2.4	0.4	2.0
	Men	9.1	0.1	9.0	6.6	0.0	6.5

Source: Field work in Kolkata 2010–11

That said, it may be that the way women access information related to work allures towards the constraints they encounter because of their unequal structural positioning within the society vis-à-vis men. Despite the availability of other alternatives such as web-based job portals, their informal interaction in the workplaces continues to be primarily with other women of similar job functions essentially because mingling with the male colleagues may project them as 'available'. Thus, there seems to be a conflict between working in the 'modern' sectors and being a 'good' woman, constricting the operational spaces for these women compared to those working in the traditional one. As put by Radhakrishnan (2009, 208) 'The workplace provides a context in which women assert respectable femininity as a mark of Indian culture, and these assertions inevitably reflect the moral and cultural preoccupations of the new Indian middle class'.

Women's negotiations and resistances

The preceding discussion does not mean to construct women as passive actors incapable of autonomous action amidst social–structural inequities. Undoubtedly, women workers in the new generation sectors are endowed with a more empowering work environment and relatively greater access to information (Kelkar *et al.* 2002). However, as Omvedt and Kelkar (1995) point out,

> It is not simply a question of access to information technology, but of restoring and carrying forward a creative and empowered participation of women in technology development and enhancing women's agency through increased knowledge, skills, and education (cited in Kelkar *et al.* 2002, 112).

In order to appraise if and how the women resist and negotiate their paid work roles in the new generation sectors, one has to understand how they have been able to contravene the social–cultural injunctions, both in their public as well as private lives. While the former pertains to their experiences in the workplace in terms of access to information, scope for professional growth, the latter pertains to their positioning within the household in terms of managing domestic responsibilities, familial attitude towards paid work, participation in household decision making etc. According to Shanker (2008) women working in the IT sector are experiencing emancipatory transitions in the public sphere, but in the private sphere there seems to be little change in the prevailing status quo.

Lack of freedom of mobility is one of the major constraints returned repeatedly by the respondent women. Mobility, as referred to here, not only encompasses ability to freely access the public spaces but also to strive for professional distinction.[15] The present study indicates that while women have succeeded in achieving considerable freedom to move out of their private domains into the public space, their mobility to advance their career continues to be socially controlled and nuanced.

More than half the women respondents working in the new generation sectors had lived alone, outside West Bengal and even abroad, either for education or for job. However, staying away from family after marriage to advance career interests is fraught with familial resistances with only about 30 percent of the married women having been 'allowed' to do so. Further, more than one-tenth of the sampled women reportedly have limited autonomy in matters pertaining to their own mobility. Again about 34 per cent of the respondents feel that their identity as 'women' significantly proscribes free mobility and consequently impede their professional development. Most of these women hail from the new-generation sectors (about 67 per cent), with education post-graduation and above, are married (about 80 per cent) and have children (about 50 percent). Further, more than two-third of the women said that it would not be easily accepted within their families if they were to change their jobs and enter into the ones which would entail greater physical mobility and travelling, the proportion being slightly higher among those working in the traditional academic sector (about 73 per cent) compared to those working in the new generation sectors (about 60 per cent). This may be explicated by the fact that those working in the new generation sectors are much younger with little familial responsibilities compared to those in the traditional sector. Besides, working in these new sectors is perhaps also associated with acceptance of some sort on the part of the family members that the woman may have to travel professionally.

As Kelkar *et al.* (2002, 122) concurs, while single women seem to find a significant change in their mobility enabling them to take up jobs and advance their careers, a large number of married women are still bound by domestic and childcare responsibilities, and are still not as mobile as men. Those who manage to travel do it with favourable family support, often living with joint families and kids.

While the working of women in the new generation sectors does enable the flouting of some of the archetypal social constructs, the performance of women's autonomy and agency is such that there is a 'non-threatening mobilization of women's labour' (Kelkar *et al.* 2002, 126). That is to say, work has to be in sync with respectable femininity and in consonance with the Indian family life. This mode of femininity is viewed as being complementary to a professional and highly competent persona. As Radhakrishnan (2009, 209) observes,

> Professional Indian womanhood of this type is rewarded, while alternative femininities are sanctioned, sometimes gently, sometimes less so. This is not to say that many women do not develop alternative femininities despite such pressures still, such pressures are palpable in the industry, and figure prominently into women's expectations of themselves.

That none of the respondent women wanted to discontinue working, no matter how hard it was to maintain work-life balance, indicated that their work added value to their lives and provided them with much-desired agency. According to them, their work gave them financial independence and a sense of self-esteem as well as welcome break from domestic chores. Hence, they were ready to make little compromises which entailed upholding their adherence to the norms of 'ideal' womanhood and family life but allowed them to work and be self-dependent. Besides, it should also be remembered that Indian women are socialised since childhood such that they consider reproductive roles as their primary responsibility, and hence, their sense of well-being does not merely centre around paid work but also encompasses family and relationships. This was elucidated by the fact that many of the respondents actually gladly agreed to the fact that during mid-career level, family does get primacy over career in the women's lives. Therefore the choices made and decisions taken by these women regarding their careers often do reflect these stereotypes imbibed by themselves.

Conclusion

The new generation sectors have undoubtedly provided women with greater opportunities of work, better working environment, etc. At the same time, however, they seem to have also increased the stress and strains in the lives of women, since their identities continue to be premised around their domestic roles as care-givers and mothers. Besides, the capital driven market forces exploit women's weaker position in the labour market, which in turn is a consequence of their unequal position within the household that restrict them from responding to market changes.

Gender seems to be a constitutive element in the organization of the new economic spaces not in terms of simply being men or women dominated, but also in terms of the functioning, policies and structures of these spaces which survive in invoking engendered stereotypes. That is, the socially legitimized gender roles seem to be casting discernible imprints of gender typing in the workplace by determining and ordaining the departments and occupational hierarchies. It appears that not only do the constructions about the traits of men and women govern the nature of work they are doing; but also the gender role stereotypes which give primacy to women's role as child bearers and caregivers, place them on a career path whereby they are to be largely the followers (Patel and Parmentier 2005).

Finally, it is evident that the proliferation of new economic opportunities in the service sector has widened the scope of women's participation in highly paid skilled jobs in the labour market. Yet, with continuance of women's labour as secondary and invisible, as compared to men's labour, their commitments to career gets overshadowed by their reproductive responsibilities. Prevailing gender constructs also act as barrier to information network which is often kin-based in case of women, but such closed resources may not necessarily work to enhance their employment opportunities or expanded span of work places.

Endnotes

[1]   It must be remembered that it was only with the formation of engineering as a white, male middle-class profession that 'male machines rather than female fabrics' became the markers of technology (Oldenziel 1999). During the late nineteenth century, mechanical and civil engineering increasingly came to define what technology is, diminishing the significance of both artefacts and forms of knowledge associated with women. This was the result of the rise of engineers as an elite with exclusive rights to technical expertise. Crucially, it involved the creation of a male professional identity, based on educational qualifications and the promise of managerial positions, sharply distinguished from shop-floor engineering and

blue-collar workers. It also involved an ideal of manliness, characterised by the cultivation of bodily prowess and individual achievement. At the same time, femininity was being reinterpreted as incompatible with technological pursuits. It was during and through this process that the term 'technology' took on its modern meaning. The legacy is our taken-for-granted association of technology with men (Wajcman 2010).

2   There has been an increased emphasis on everyday technologies that have disrupted the cultural stereotype of women as technically incompetent in technical spheres. A revaluing of cooking, childcare and communication technologies immediately disrupts the cultural stereotype of women as technically incompetent or invisible in technical spheres.

3   The central government of India issued its own India Vision 2020 that conceives of the country evolving into an information society and knowledge economy built on the edifice of information and communication technology. It is therefore evident that the IT and ITES sectors are being posited as the engines of growth in contemporary society. Besides, postmodern cities have also been acclaimed as cities of consumption, rather than production, cities of shopping malls rather than of the factory (Glennie 1998). Indeed in the post-reforms era, these malls have emerged as the temples of post-modern India.

4   Ideally, a detailed list of the employees of the organizations should have been taken as the sampling frame and probability samples could have been drawn. It would have facilitated utilization of the statistical theory of sampling distribution and standard errors in the analysis. However, access to the organizations' employee records could not be secured due to strict company policies of confidentiality. Besides, the conduction of semi-structured interviews took about one hour approximately and this caused disruption to their work schedule. The issue of confidentiality and privacy was also an important concern. Consequently it was extremely challenging to find respondents willing to take the survey and their refusal to be a part of it has to be respected. Eventually, samples have been collected through key individuals in firms and organizations. Respondents have been identified by referral from friends of theirs who are known to me, and then by snowballing from one referral to another. This method does not create a representative sample. Nevertheless, it gives a comprehensive understanding of the dynamics operational in the workplaces as well as in their personal lives.

5   The Likert's scale, although widely used, has certain limitations. This is because the responses measured with the help of this scale are often perceptual hence subjective. Besides, there is some disagreement regarding the process for analyzing the results of a sample of data where the Likert scale is employed. Often comparisons are made assuming that the Likert characteristics under study can be considered as an interval scale (i.e., a variable) or an ordinal scale (i.e., an attribute). Cautions are presented when assuming the interval scale and it has been argued that a more suitable way of analysing the data is to compute percentages of individual ordinal response categories. However, this study uses the Likert's scale in order to collate individual responses into a collective response. This has certain merits. It helps in some sort of standardization because numerical values can be assigned to the individual item responses and these numerical values can also be summed up to an overall score or those items considered as addressing the same underlying construct. Thus it helps in a broad-brush understanding of the response variable under consideration.

6   The significance level of the mean differences is tested using the formula

$(X_1 - X_2) / \sqrt{(SD_1^2 / n_1) + (SD_2^2 / n_2)}$

7   Watts 2009 notes in her study of civil engineers that there is reasonably equal treatment between men and women until women became pregnant, with motherhood being seen as a key differential in a way that fatherhood was not.

8   A study done in the mid 1990s (Webster in Mansell and Wehm 251, cited in Patel and Parmentier 2005) reports that in every country of the world, women are marginalized from the more instrumental and lucrative careers involved with the research and development of IT, and relegated to lower skill and income tiers of IT production.

9   In India, women comprise of 5.8 percent of senior management (Kulkarni 2002, 11) to as low as 3 percent (Chadha 2002, Mehra 2002, Singh 2003) of all administrative positions. They can be seen mainly in HR, IT and servicing activities. Their presence in hard-core production and marketing is much less and still lower at strategic policy influencing levels.

10 Such critiques emphasise that, in addition to gender structures and stereotyping, engrained cultures of masculinity are still ubiquitous within these industries, causing many young women to reject careers and older women to leave the field. This is fundamentally because women are being asked to exchange major aspects of their gender identity for a masculine version, whilst there is no similar 'degendering' process prescribed for men.

11 Most of the employees in the call centers as well as in the retail sector perceive their current work as a stepping stone to a more fulfilling career (Clark and Sekher 2007, 293). However, in the present study, the respondents wished to either shift to back-office jobs during day shift or move to government service, which not only possess greater job security but also would enable them to strike a better work-life balance.

12 Patel and Parmentier (2005) in their study note that 70.5 percent of women agreed that they have to do better than men to get equal professional recognition. This could be linked to the notion of women's work being inherently invisible (see Table 10.1). Therefore, within the paid labour force, a woman would have to achieve more in order to gain equal recognition.

13 It is intriguing to note that the mean number of non-kin contacts for deriving work related information is significantly higher among women working in the traditional sector compared to those in the new generation sectors.

14 Ensel (1979) found that male job seekers were much more likely to reach higher status contacts than were females. Further, women were more likely to use female contacts in job searches whereas males overwhelmingly used male contacts.

15 Guillaume and Pochic (2009) in their study of higher level management officials note that geographical mobility is often presented as the norm to access top executive positions, and refusing the same could be risky. Career progression patterns also involve a strong correlation between age and career ladder steps. Very high potential professionals must be detected before the age of 35 and they need to reach the first levels of senior management positions before they are 40. This rhythm implies continuous involvement at work with no career breaks, and organizational awareness to avoid dead-end positions or organizational hazards that can slow down the career progression. Last but not least, managerial careers are built around the learning of time availability, starting with 'on call' operational constraints and continuing with time consuming responsibilities. This time-consuming pattern reveals the importance of loyalty in corporate careers and the organizations' demands for total devotion. Overall, temporal norms associated either with career progression or working hours are very prejudicial for women. An intense

working involvement is required between the ages of 25 and 35 when they are likely to have children and family constraints. This typical organizational career pattern, linear and progressive, ignores individual life cycles and implicitly assumes that managers are male.

References

Acker, J. 1990. 'Hierarchies, Jobs and Bodies: A Theory of Gendered Organizations'. *Gender and Society*, 4: 139–58.

Banerjee, N. 1999. 'Can Markets Alter Gender Relations'. *Gender Technology and Development*, 3: 103–22.

Basant, Rakesh, and Uma Rani. 2004. 'Labour Market Deepening in India's IT An Exploratory Analysis'. *Economic and Political Weekly*. 39(50): 5317–26.

Britton, D. M. 2000. 'The Epistemology of Gendered Organization'. *Gender and Society*, 14: 418–34.

Clark, A. W., and T. V. Shekher. 2007. 'Can Career-Minded Young Women Reverse Gender Discrimination? A View from Bangalore's High-Tech Sector'. *Gender Technology and Development*, 11: 285– 319.

Cécile, G., and S. Pochic. 2009. 'What Would You Sacrifice? Access to Top Management and the Work–life Balance'. *Gender, Work and Organization*, 16(1): 15–36.

Chadha, R. 2002. Of Mars and Venus, Businessline. Available at http://proquest.umi.com/pqdweb?Did ¼ 0000000270062871&Fmt.

Dewan, Ritu. 1999. 'Gender Implications of the "New" Economic Policy: A Conceptual Overview'. *Women's Studies International Forum*, 22(4): 425–29.

Dilworth, R., and K. Trevenen. 2004. 'When Cities Get Married Constructing Urban Space through Gender, Sexuality and Municipal Consolidation,' *Urban Affairs Review*, 40(2): 183–209.

Ensel, Walter M. 1979. *Sex, Social Ties, and Status Attainment*. Unpublished Manuscript. Albany, NY, State University, New York.

French, J. R., and B. Raven. 1968. The Bases of Social Power. In D. Cartwright and A. Zander (Eds.), *Group Dynamics* (3rd ed.): 259–69. New York: Harper and Row.

Glennie, Paul. 1998. 'Consumption, consumerism and urban form: Historical perspectives', *Urban Studies*, 35(5–6): 927–51.

Gooptu, N. 2009. 'Neoliberal Subjectivity, Enterprise Culture and New Workplaces: Organised Retail and Shopping Malls in India'. *Economic and Political Weekly*, XLIV, (22): 45–54.

Granovetter, Mark. 1974. *Getting a Job. Chicago.* IL: University of Chicago Press.

Granovetter, Mark. 1995. 'Afterword 1994: Reconsiderations and a New Agenda'. *In Getting a Job*, 2d ed., Chicago, IL: University of Chicago Press. pp. 139–82.

Green, E., and Adam, A. (eds.). 1999. *Editorial Comment, Information, Communication and Society*, 2(4): v–vii.

Guillaume, Cécile, and Pochic, Sophie. 2009. 'What would you Sacrifice? Access to Top Management and the Work-life Balance'. *Gender, Work and Organization*, 16(1): 15–36.

Kanter, M. R. 1977. *Men and Women in the Corporation*. New York: Basic Books.

Kelkar, Govind, Girija Shrestha, and N. Veena. 2002. IT Industry and Women's Agency: Explorations in Bangalore and Delhi, India. *Gender Technology and Development*, 6(1): 63–84.

Kemp, S., and J. Squires. (eds.). 1998. *Feminisms: An Oxford Reader*. Oxford: Oxford University Press.

Kirkup, G., Janes, L., Woodward, K., and F. Hovenden. 2000. *The Gendered Cyborg: A Reader*. London: Routledge.

Kulkarni, S. S. 2002. 'Women and Professional Competency – A Survey Report', *Indian Journal of Training and Development*, vol. XXXII(2), April – June: 11–16.

Lin, N. 1999. 'Social Networks and Status Attainment'. *Annual Review of Sociology*, 25: 467–87.

———. 2000. 'Inequality in Social Capital'. *Contemporary Sociology*, 29(6): 785–95.

———. 2001a. 'Building a Network Theory of Social Capital'. In N. Lin, K. S. Cook and R. Burt (eds.) *Social Capital: Theory and Research*, New York: Aldine deGruyter, pp. 3–31.

———. 2001b. *Social Capital: A Theory of Social Structure and Action.* New York: Cambridge University Press.

Mansell, R., and U. Wehn. 1998. *Knowledge Societies: Information Technology for Sustainable Development*. New York: Oxford University Press.

Martin, P. Y. 2006. 'Practising Gender at Work: Further Thoughts on Reflexivity'. *Gender Work and Organization*, 13(3): 254–76.

Massey, Doreen. 1994. *Space, Place and Gender*. Minneapolis, MN: University of Minnesota Press.

McDowell, L., and J. Sharp. 1997. *Space, Gender, Knowledge: Feminist Readings*. Oxford: Oxford University Press.

Mehra, P. 2002. 'Women Managers: To the Top and Beyond'. *Hindu Businessline*, Saturday 27, April.

NASSCOM. 2008. *Gender Inclusivity in India Building Empowered Organizations*, New Delhi: NASSCOM.

Nieva, V. E., and B. A. Gutek. 1981. *Women and Work*. New York: Praeger.

Oldenziel, R. 1999. *Making Technology Masculine: Men, Women and Modern Machines in America*. Amsterdam: Amsterdam University Press.

Omvedt, Gail, and Govind Kelkar. 1995. 'Gender and Technology: Emerging Visions from Asia'. *Gender Studies Monograph* 4, Bangkok: Asian Institute of Technology.

Palmer, A. M. 1996. 'Something to Declare — Women in HM Customs and Excise', in Ledwith, S. and Colgan, F. (eds) Women in Organizations. Challenging Gender Politics, Basingstoke: Macmillan. pp. 125–51.

Patel, Reena, and C. Mary Jane, Parmentier. 2005. 'The Persistence of Traditional Gender Roles in the Information Technology Sector: A Study of Female Engineers in India'. *Information Technologies and International Development*, 2(3): 29–46.

———. 2006. 'The Persistence of Traditional Gender Roles in the Information Technology Sector: A Study of Female Engineers in India'. *Information Technologies and International Development*, 2(3): 29–46.

Radhakrishnan, Smitha. 2008. 'Examining the "Global" Indian Middle Class: Gender and Culture in the Silicon Valley/Bangalore Circuit'. *Journal of International Studies*, 29(1): 7–20.

Raju, S., and I. Baud. 2007. 'Life Aspirations and Embedded Contexts: Gender and Vocational Training in Segmented Labour Markets in Indian Cities', in Annapurna Shaw (ed.) *Indian Cities in Transition*, pp. 412–45, Hyderabad: Orient Longman.

Raju, Saraswati. 2006. 'Gender and Empowerment: Creating "Thus Far and No Further" Supportive Structures. A Case from India', in. Lisa

Nelson and Joni Seager (Eds.) *Companion to Feminist Geography,* pp. 194–208, Malden, MA: Blackwell Publishers.

———. 2009. 'Professional Women, Good Families: Respectable Femininity and the Cultural Politics of a "New" India'. *Qualitative Sociology,* 32(2): 95–212.

———. 2013. 'The Material and the Symbolic Intersectionalities of Home-Based Work In India'. *Economic and Political Weekly,* XLVIII(1): 60–68.

Rosenfeld, R. A., and J. A. Jones. 1987. 'Patterns and Effects of Geographic Mobility for Academic Women and Men', *Journal of Higher Education,* 58(5): 493–515.

Shade, L. R. 1998. 'A Gendered Perspective on Access to the Information Infrastructure'. *Information Society,* 14: 33–44.

Shanker, D. 2008. 'Gender Relations in IT Companies: An Indian Experience'. *Gender, Technology and Development,* 12(2): 185–207.

Singh, K. 2003. Women Managers: Perception vs. Performance Analysis. *Journal of Management Research,* 3(1): 31–42.

Spain, D. 1993. 'Gendered Spaces and Women's Status'. *Sociological Theory.* 11(2): 137–51.

Valk, R., and V. Srinivasan. 2011. 'Work-Family Balance of Indian Women Software Professionals: A Qualitative Study'. *IIMB Management Review,* 23: 39–50.

Wajcman, J. 2010. 'Feminist Theories of Technology.' *Cambridge Journal of Economics,* 34: 143–52.

Watts, Jacqueline, H. 2009. 'Allowed into a Man's World' Meanings of Work–Life Balance: Perspectives of Women Civil Engineers as 'Minority' Workers in Construction'. *Gender, Work and Organization.* 16(1): 37–57.

Witz, A. 1992. *Patriarchy and Professions.* London: Routledge.

11

Gender Equality and Women's Employment in the Banking Sector in India[1]

Supriti Bezbaruah

Introduction

In recent years, the media, both in India and globally, has been replete with stories of women's success in reaching the top-most echelons of the banking sector in India. To name a few, Arundhati Bhattacharya at the State Bank of India, the country's largest bank, Chanda Kochhar at ICICI and Shikha Sharma at Axis Bank, two of India's largest private banks, and Naina Lal Kidwai at the Indian operation of major foreign bank, HSBC. The success of these women in breaking through the glass ceiling is portrayed as indicative of greater gender equality in a country more commonly known for discrimination against women. Beyond media reports, however, women's employment in the banking sector remains under-researched – to what extent have women entered and progressed through the occupational hierarchy? How has the increased presence of women altered traditional gender relations in the workplace? In light of this, this chapter aims to look behind the headlines, and examine women's experiences of work and employment in the banking sector in India.

Based on interviews and a questionnaire survey of bank employees conducted in the National Capital Region (NCR) between 2008–2010, the chapter discusses how gender discrimination manifests itself primarily through gendered organizational practices such as long working hours, the need to network and be geographically mobile. While these are universal constraints for women worldwide, in India, these constraints are linked to traditional norms of femininity emphasizing respectability and the need to prioritize family. When workplace demands conflict with these traditional norms, women invariably adhere to traditional socio-cultural norms at the expense of career advancement.

The chapter is divided as follows – the next two sections set the background by outlining the main trends in women's employment worldwide, and specifically, in the banking sector in India. The following section presents the methodological framework. After this, the gendered patterns of inequalities in the Indian banking sector are examined, followed by an analysis of their underlying causes. The final section concludes.

Gender equality and women's employment

The growth in women's employment is one of the defining features of contemporary labour markets: in 2012, the global female labour force was estimated to be 1.3 billion, of whom almost half were employed in services (ILO 2012, 15, 24). These trends have been attributed to the shift from an industrial economy towards services, linked in turn to advances in Information and Communications Technologies (ICTs) (Coyle 1997; Perrons 2004). The move towards a service-based economy benefits women as requiring less physical labour, services tend to be 'more typically a female-employing sector than was manufacturing' (Perrons *et al.* 2006, 18).

In the Global North, the initial entry of women into service work can be linked to the historical process of industrialization, and the transition away from agriculture in the early twentieth century. The expansion of tertiary services opened up opportunities for women but these were mainly confined to lower-end, lower-wage clerical work (England and Boyer 2009; Game and Pringle 1984; Mazumdar 2007; Prather 1971).

What distinguishes the employment of women in services in the last few decades is the entry of educated women into the previously male domains of high skilled, professional and managerial work (Bradley *et al.* 2000; McDowell 1997). Despite the rise in women's employment in managerial and professional jobs, gender equality remains elusive. Horizontal and vertical segregation persist, and women continue to be under-represented in senior positions (McDowell 1997; Perrons 2009). Women are also disproportionately represented in part-time and informal jobs and concentrated in jobs that offer less pay and status (Burton 1996; Özbilgin and Woodward 2004; Perrons *et al.* 2006).

Women's employment in the banking sector in India

In India, the expansion of white-collar service employment was mainly the result of the expansion of the government, rather than changes brought about by the industrial revolution as in the Global North (Mazumdar 2007). Consequently, the first notable influx of women, mainly middle-class women, into service sector employment occurred only after independence (ibid.). Traditionally, regarded as conduits of social honour (Liddle and Joshi 1986; Standing 1991), upper caste and middle-class women faced severe restrictions on undertaking paid work. After independence, with greater education of women, and changing social attitudes, these restrictions were gradually loosened resulting in increasing numbers of middle-class women entering the workforce. Women, however, were only allowed to work in jobs that fulfilled the criteria of middle-class respectability (Liddle and Joshi 1986; Radhakrishnan 2009). Banking was perceived to be one such respectable occupation, and nationalized banks were instrumental in boosting women's employment in the 1970s and early 1980s (Gothoskar 1995).

Following liberalization, the rapid expansion of the services sector opened up new opportunities for the employment of women, particularly in information technology (IT) services. There is a growing literature analysing these employment opportunities for women in India's new service economy (Basi 2009; Kelkar, Shrestha and Veena 2005; Mitter 2004; Patel 2010; Radhakrishnan 2009, 2011). Withholding the euphoria generated by the increased entry of women into these occupations, some studies have questioned the quality of this employment. For instance, studies show that the jobs involve routine, repetitive work with little upward career mobility (Mitter, Fernandez and Varghese 2004). Some jobs are also showing trends towards increasing informalization in the form of shift work, non-permanent contracts and high attrition rates (Ng and Mitter 2005).

However, the majority of these studies focus on women's employment in the IT sector, with few studies examining women's employment in the banking sector. Women's employment in the banking sector is particularly interesting as it predates economic liberalization (and the associated influence of globalization). Prior to liberalization, the majority of women were employed in clerical positions in nationalized banks (Gothoskar 1995).

Similar to the trends witnessed in developed economies, in recent years, there has been a rise in the proportion of women in managerial positions. Women's share of managerial positions more than doubled from 6.3 per cent in 1996 to 17.3 per cent in 2013 (RBI 1998, Table 1.28; RBI 2014, Table 1.31). This trend was most marked in Indian private banks, where the share of women managers increased from 6.2 per cent in 1996 to 19.2 per cent in 2013 (*ibid.*).

These trends reflect wider changes in the Indian banking sector following economic liberalization in 1991. Prior to liberalization, the majority of banks in India were nationalized (Bhasin 2006; IBA 2013; Shirai 2002). After liberalization, India embarked on two major phases of banking reforms in 1991 and 1999, which focused on among others, privatization, deregulation, increasing competition and reducing entry barriers. These changes resulted in the entry of more foreign banks and the establishment of several new Indian private banks. At present, there are 57 regional rural banks, 27 nationalized banks (including State Bank of India and its associates), 20 private banks and 43 foreign banks (RBI 2013; Ministry of Finance, n.d., cited in Bezbaruah 2015). While nationalized banks continue to dominate the sector, the entry of foreign and Indian private banks has changed the character of Indian banking, resulting in greater competition and customer orientation. Significantly for women, foreign and Indian private banks have been active recruiters of women, particularly in management positions (Bezbaruah 2015).

The Indian banking sector has recently drawn much attention for the success of several women in reaching the senior-most positions. For instance, in 2013, there were eight women at the helm of India's top banks, controlling almost half of the country's banking assets (Chakrabarti 2013; Parmar 2014). While this success has generated claims of gender equality in the Indian workplace, this is counteracted by other studies that indicate that vertical and horizontal segregation, and sexual harassment persist in the workplace (Gupta, Koshal and Koshal 2006; CII 2005).

In seeking explanations for continued gender inequality in the workplace, theorists, primarily from the Global North, increasingly focus on the gendered nature of organizational structures. Whereas organizations present themselves as gender-neutral filled with abstract workers, Acker (1992, 257) contends that 'The abstract worker transformed into a concrete worker turns out to be a man whose work is his life and whose wife takes care of everything else'. The construct of the 'ideal worker' – that is, someone who can work long hours, network, and can relocate and travel as requested (Kelly *et al.* 2010, 283), assumes that employees are not bound by any other domestic commitments.

Thus, the 'ideal worker' becomes equated with the male worker, marginalizing women, particularly those with domestic responsibilities, and contributes to gender inequality in organizations. Supporting this, the most commonly cited factors hindering the career advancement of Indian women included women's domestic responsibilities and gender stereotypes regarding women's roles in the workplace (Budhwar, Saini and Bhatnagar 2005; Gupta, Koshal and Koshal 2006).

Theories of gender and organizations highlight how gendered norms are embedded within organizational structures, and thereby provide a useful lens through which to understand the mechanisms by which women are disadvantaged in the workplace. While these theories shed light on how gender inequality is manifested within organizations, less attention is given to where such inequality takes place. Feminist scholars and geographers have critiqued this neglect of the importance of place. They argue for the need to acknowledge the multiple diversities of women's lived experiences, and the complexities of women's lives, shaped among others, by local, social and cultural factors (Kabeer 2008; Mohanty 1991). For example, studies suggest that cultural practices are among the biggest impediments to the career progression of Indian women (WEF 2009). Following on this, this chapter explores how local social and cultural gendered norms in India influence patterns of gender inequality in the workplace. In particular, I fuse together gender and organization theory with the concept of respectable femininity (Radhakrishnan 2009) to analyse how the increased entry of Indian women into the professional workplace has not resulted in significant changes in traditional gender relations. While the older, pre-independence notion of respectability that emphasized the domesticity of middle-class women has given way to a reshaped notion of respectability that 'includes home and a "safe" job' (Radhakrishnan 2009, 204), the importance of upholding traditional family norms remains paramount. Thus, women are pressured to enact a form of respectable femininity that requires putting family first, 'job second', and to follow a discourse that adheres to strict codes of sexual morality (Radhakrishnan 2009, 202). In a similar vein, Patel (2006, 21) argues that despite the increased entry of women into the workplace, there has been little change in patriarchal relations of power as women's mobility, and thereby, their ability to work is still defined by 'surveillance and "protection" of women's bodies.'

Methodology

The findings of this chapter are based on fieldwork and research conducted in India's NCR during the years 2008–10. The core data are based on a questionnaire survey of 156 women bank employees, and semi-structured interviews with 62 women and 11 men bank employees. Supplementary information was gathered from a questionnaire survey of Human Resource (HR) policies of six banks,[2] and semi-structured interviews with one HR personnel officer in a foreign bank, five government officers and one manager in a business association. The questionnaire survey included questions relating to demographics (age, caste and marital status), terms of work (part-time/full-time) and whether the women had experienced discrimination and harassment. The interviews focused on banking as a career, the main barriers to career advancement, and everyday experiences of discrimination in the workplace.

Research participants were recruited through snowball sampling, initially drawing upon existing contacts within banks and walk-in visits to different banks. The selection of participants was affected by problems of access that are an acknowledged feature of social science research, particularly when doing research with elites such as bank managers (England 2002; Mullings 1999). Within these constraints, every effort was made to obtain as varied a sample as possible. The research participants covered 20 different banks – foreign, Indian private and nationalized. The participants ranged in age from 21–59, and covered a diverse range of household types (nuclear, single, joint family) and seniority levels (from clerical staff to senior managers). All the women had a minimum educational qualification of a Bachelor's degree.

The majority of interviews and surveys were face-to-face, with a few telephone interviews. The interviews lasted from a minimum of half-hour to two hours. Some were recorded on digital recorders, which were later transcribed. Where participants were unwilling to be recorded, interview notes were taken.

Gender segregation in the Indian banking sector

According to nation-wide data, women constituted 19.1 per cent of total employees in the banking sector in 2013 (RBI 2014, Table 1.31). In urban/metropolitan areas, the proportion of women employees increases slightly to 23.5 per cent of total employees. Foreign banks have a marginally higher representation of women employees (31.4 per cent in urban/metropolitan areas in 2013) (ibid.). While this proportion of women falls short of what could be considered equal gender distribution, what is perhaps more notable is that the share of women employees has been steadily increasing, from 13.6 per cent of total employees in 1996 to 19.1 per cent in 2013 (RBI 1998, Table 1.28; RBI 2014, Table 1.31). Women are clearly entering the banking sector in increasing numbers. For example, in 2011, about 40 per cent of the total applicants for nationalized banks were women (Sridhar and Vageesh 2011). More significantly, as mentioned earlier in the chapter, the percentage of women managers has more than doubled during this period.

These trends, along with the visibility of several women in senior positions lend further credence to suggestions that banking in India is increasingly becoming a woman's world. However, such assertions may be premature; the data from this research point to the persistence of vertical and horizontal segregation. First, the data obtained from banks on the gender distribution of employees show that the proportion of women declines markedly from over 20 per cent in junior managerial positions to less than 5 per cent in senior managerial positions[3].

Second, another issue relates to the type of jobs that women occupy. Using a method, albeit subjective, by asking interviewees about their work environment (whether it is mainly men, women or mixed), almost half the women (48.8 per cent) in foreign and Indian private banks[4] observed some form of job profiling (Table 11.1). The research data suggest that sales jobs are heavily male-dominated, while service-related jobs are female-dominated. For example, Lalita, a mid-level manager in a foreign bank observed that 'there are hardly women in (the) sales side' (cited in Bezbaruah 2015). In her team, she was the only woman till one more woman joined recently. At the other extreme, men are rarely seen in front-end customer care or in positions such as executive assistants.

Table 11.1 Job profiling by sex

Type of environment	Sales	Customer service / front-end operations	Other
Mainly women	0	7	1
Mainly men	12	0	1
Mixed	2	1	2

Notes: *a*. The data are only approximate, as it has been extracted from qualitative interviews, and hence, are difficult to quantify. Due to constraints of time, the topic was not always discussed. Some women referred directly to their own teams, others responded based on their observations in their present job or previous bank. The data does not include responses from women in nationalized banks, including those who had previously worked in foreign and Indian private banks, and therefore, had observed similar patterns of job profiling.

b. Customer service/front-end operations also include administrative positions.

Source: Interviews with women in foreign and Indian private banks. n = 43. Number of no responses/did not discuss = 17. Data adapted from Bezbaruah (2015, Table 4.1).

Gender discrimination in the Indian banking sector[5]

The persistence of gender segregation in the Indian banking sector could be an indication that women still face discrimination in recruitment and promotion. The majority of women employees (66 per cent) surveyed for this research, however, discounted this possibility stating that they had never personally experienced overt discrimination and banks treat men and women equally. In general, the majority of women were confident that 'as long as you perform,' work hard and achieve the targets set 'you will get recognition for what you've done' and 'being a woman does not make any difference'.

One reason for this perhaps naive perception could be because employers rarely practice blatant discrimination. Most discrimination is usually covert and consequently, employees often 'erroneously assume that discriminatory conduct is absent from their workplaces' (Gregory 2003, 10). In the Indian banking sector, the interview data indicate that gender does implicitly affect both recruitment and job profiling decisions. For example, Jamini, a 23 year-old assistant in a nationalized bank, said her manager would never openly state it, but always suggested that only men should be hired for sales positions. Vimala, a 24 year-old junior manager in an Indian private bank said the line managers were not 'comfortable' hiring girls for back-end operations in her bank, whereas Abha, a 24 year-old assistant in a foreign bank noted that they 'only prefer girls' for her position.

However, more than direct discrimination, the research data suggests that the main obstacles to women's career advancement were gendered organizational practices, based on the construct of the 'ideal worker' (Acker 1990, 1992; Benschop and Doorewaard 1998). This was most evident when women employees returned from maternity leave. Maternity leave per se was not an issue, with no cases of women being denied their leave. Taking maternity leave, however, particularly for women in foreign and Indian private banks, usually constituted a major setback to their careers, as promotions were linked to performance and achievement of targets, and women's absence from the office during maternity leave was not accounted for. Of the 16 women interviewees from foreign and Indian private banks who were married with children, slightly less than half (43.8 per cent) said that maternity leave has an adverse effect on women's career progression. For example, Bonnie, a 31 year-old, mid-level manager in a foreign bank with a one year-old child, had been working in the same position for three years before she took maternity leave. Even though she was due for promotion, her boss told her she would not get the promotion that year as she had been on maternity leave. Most women, therefore, expect to remain in the same position for a few years if they decide to opt for motherhood.

Women also struggle to combine long working hours with childcare responsibilities. Yet, in order to progress in their careers, women are faced with little option.

> To grow and stay in the organization, you have to work these long hours, there are no shortcuts.
>
> (Brinda, 28 years old, mid-level manager, Indian private bank)

If women are unable to work these long hours, their careers inevitably suffer.

> I find women who are more capable than men but still they are working in lower grade just because of this reason they have to ... give time to their husbands, the children ...
>
> (Gita, 35 years old, mid-level manager, foreign bank)

In some banks, long working hours can be exacerbated by the need for networking. Networking is considered essential for developing client relationships and it can also help facilitate the exchange of ideas between colleagues, and increase one's visibility among senior management (Bezbaruah 2015; McDowell 1997; Ogden, McTavish and McKean 2006). For example, Tara, a 29 year-old, senior manager in a foreign bank, explains that if she is unable to stay late to meet a client because of her childcare responsibilities, her manager would assign these clients to another male employee who could put in those extra hours.

> ... it's quite important because see, end of the day there are targets which are to be executed, so if I have fewer clients, if I have lesser accounts ... then there is a comparison with somebody else who is getting those leads ...

Similarly, the need to be mobile – to travel or to relocate for the job – limits women bound by their domestic commitments. Almost a third of the women interviewed (32.3 per cent) stated that lack of mobility has affected their careers.[6] This is especially the case for senior management positions, which usually entail relocation. Lalita, a 31 year-old, mid-level manager in a foreign bank with a four year-old son recounts

> I've given up a lot because I'm not mobile. My boss, two years back, had told me that I can give you your next band ... you go to Bangalore ... I had a discussion at home, I knew that it won't work out, so I gave it up.

For women in nationalized banks, the mandatory transfer policy in these banks stipulates that managers must get transferred to a different location every three to five years. Crucially, the transfer policy is linked with promotions. Therefore, as Madhavi, a 59 year-old senior manager in a nationalized bank, points out, many women opt out at a very junior level because they do not want to relocate. Since the transfer policy does not apply to clerical staff, of the six clerks interviewed, four of them said they had not applied for promotion to managerial levels for this reason.

Career advancement, respectable femininity and gender relations

Clearly, women's career progression is hindered by organizational expectations of long working hours and geographical mobility. Women, however presented these patterns as the outcome of voluntary choices.

> ... women are voluntarily choosing to opt out of senior positions, it has nothing to do with the structure of the organization.
>
> (Tarini, 30 years old, mid-level manager, nationalized bank)

A closer scrutiny of these 'choices' reveal they are based on traditional norms of femininity, that bear close parallels to Radhakrishnan's (2009) description of respectable femininity enacted by women in the IT sector. Middle-class women can enter paid work, but this work must satisfy the core tenets of middle-class respectability, namely that the work does not conflict with women's family responsibilities, and jeopardize women's sexual integrity (Radhakrishnan 2009, 2011; Liddle and Joshi 1986; Patel 2010).

Therefore, the majority of interviewees (71 per cent) said they chose banking as an occupation because of the respectability associated with it, based on the perception that it is a desk-based job with regular timings that enable women to balance work and family commitments, and does not require travel.[7]

As some of the women interviewed observed, this is no longer the case. Women are increasingly struggling to conform to traditional norms of femininity while working in a modern-day banking environment that demands long working hours, and significant travel and sales to customers at different locations. What is notable from the interview data is that in the final analysis, women consistently chose family over career advancement. About 64.5 per cent of women interviewees had either opted out of promotions and career advancement because of their family commitments or had observed other women doing the same. Single or married women without children either expected or planned for opting out of promotions in the future in order to prioritize family and children (Table 11.2).

Table 11.2 Women employees prioritizing family over career

Responses of women	Number
Personally opted out of promotions due to family commitments	16
Expect to opt out in future when family commitments increase	14
Observed other women opting out due to family commitments	10
Have prioritised family, but hasn't affected career advancement	2
Other (including no responses)	20

Source: Interviews with bank employees, n = 62. Data adapted from Bezbaruah (2015, Fig. 5.2)

This ties in with the concept of respectable femininity under which

> ... the role models are not the women who gave up their families for success, but those who manage to balance the two, most often by sacrificing the climb up the company hierarchy.

(Radhakrishnan 2009, 202)

For example, Oma, who is a 24 year-old and working in sales, has asked to change her profile in anticipation of her commitments after marriage, as she believes that –

> ... after marriage, it's very difficult to manage a sales call...You know, if client is ... free only on weekend, so I have to go there ... but after marriage it's not possible for me to go out ... my responsibilities will be after marriage you know, bacche wacche (children) and all ...

In a similar vein, Tara, mentioned above, admits that after she had her daughter, she was no longer willing to work on weekends or stay after work for drinks with clients, even though she realized it would affect her career prospects.

Work-life balance and the struggle to combine family and work responsibilities are challenges not uncommon among women worldwide. What differentiates the Indian experience is that these responsibilities are heightened by the demands of respectable femininity. A large proportion of respondent women (half the married women surveyed) live in extended family structures. While in many cases, the extended family can provide crucial support, particularly for juggling childcare responsibilities (61.6 per cent relied on parents and in-laws to help with childcare), the expectations made upon women to adhere to traditional roles can sometimes be incompatible with women's career progression. For example, Chitra, a 26 year-old, junior manager in an Indian private bank has been living with her in-laws since she got married. Although her own career aspirations have not changed, she now has to conform to the expectations of her in-laws.

> If you're in a joint family, then the family does not like it (working late)... my expectations of career have not changed but now, I can't stay late, since my in-laws expect it (that I return at an appropriate hour). Earlier, if there was urgent work, I stayed late, but now I can't ... I have to go home and do the cooking.

Chitra's example illustrates the conflicts facing Indian women in the workplace – although women are increasingly entering paid work, they have to still conform to traditional gender roles.

Familial expectations also discourage women from networking, after-work socializing and travel. Such constraints, related to concerns about women's sexual integrity are not just an issue for married women, but also for single women. This is one reason why there are fewer women in sales.

> ... in sales, you have to travel, go out. You also have to sit till late. Sales also mean you have to meet lots of people, and many families don't like it for women.
>
> (Chitra, 26 years old, junior manager, Indian private bank)

Lalita (mentioned earlier) recounts how the husband of one of her colleagues refused to let her change her profile to sales even though this would have improved her career prospects, which had 'come to a plateau' in her current role. One of the main objections of the husband was that 'I don't know what kind of customer you'll be interacting with, people you'll be meeting with.'

Clearly, women's decision-making in the workplace is inextricably linked to family support, which in turn, appears to be shaped by patriarchal relations of power. Consequently, women are not able to do 'that bit extra' that is required for moving up to senior management positions. Most women reach a career plateau at mid-level positions, probably, because as one of the women observes, the family does not 'respect your job that much.'

The emphasis on family also has an impact on women's empowerment as workers. On one hand, women in the banking sector could be considered privileged given that they are well-educated, aware of their rights and working in formal sector jobs that provide a salary and benefits. On the other hand, the constraints of traditional norms of femininity deter women from protesting discrimination in the workplace. Concerned about maintaining respectability and the family's reputation, the women interviewed said that families would not support women in making complaints, as this would entail becoming the 'scene of discussion' (Bezbaruah, 2015). This is especially the case in instances of sexual harassment. Within the cultural norms of sexual respectability, the responsibility for forestalling male attention falls on women themselves (Puri 1999). In such a system, if a woman complains of harassment, the implicit assumption is that they failed to self-monitor their conduct and attire (ibid.) Hence, according to Lalita (mentioned earlier), women prefer to ignore instances of sexual harassment as 'they don't want any kind of social ostracism or social taboo against them and/or their families'.

The research data also does not suggest that women wish to challenge traditional norms of femininity. Instead, there appears to be an unquestioning acceptance that it is women's responsibility to look after the family, as the 'the family is the most important'. Rupa, a 35 year-old, mid-level manager in a foreign bank summarizes this belief, which was a recurring theme in the interviews –

> ... you are the person who's looking after the family, whereas the men aren't. Okay, so you got to take a call over there and take a backseat. Then you've got kids to take care of which happens to be a woman's main responsibility.

The general perception appears to be that it is only the woman who can look after the family's welfare, particularly that of children. For example, Eshal's (a 39 year-old, senior manager in a foreign bank) mother used to work in a nationalized bank. When her father got transferred, her father expected it, and her mother willingly agreed, to forgo promotions so that she could stay with the family. Eshal points out, 'they realized they need a balance, so she compromized.' Eshal felt that this was necessary, as –

> ... it's not that they (families) feel that the wife's job is less important, it's also the factor that a mother is more needed for a child's growth, she can do it better justice, the father is not that competent in handling a child's growth.

Madhavi's (a 59 year-old, senior manager in a nationalized bank) sentiments about her choice encapsulate the feelings of several of the women interviewees that looking after the family's interest gives them a sense of well-being. Several years earlier, Madhavi had opted out of promotions as this entailed moving to Mumbai. At that time, her daughter was about to give her 10th exam (Indian GCSE or O'Level exam), and she did not want to disrupt her studies. So, Madhavi recounts, she decided to forgo her career advancement for her family's well-being. Significantly, she went on to say, '... you may call it a sacrifice ... I don't think it was a sacrifice, it was what I felt was right ... and I have been happy, no regrets.' Kavita, a 53 year-old, senior manager in a nationalized bank also reflects similar thinking. She too, had opted out of promotions to raise her children, but she notes –

> I've enjoyed my children's childhood ... so it's a wonderful thing... I've got seven years left (to retire) and I know they (my family) are the people who are going to be with me, ultimately, you know, it's not about ... I don't want to give myself 24/7 to the bank.

Gender role expectations in the workplace

Apart from family, this research, similar to Radhakrishnan's (2009) study of women in the IT sector, finds that employers, whether consciously or unconsciously also consolidate respectable femininity in the workplace. According to Frieda, a 29 year-old, mid-level manager in a foreign bank, employers assume that women always prioritize family over work.

> ... it's always there, you know, for women ... (the perception that) the family comes first ... And ya, I think at some level, we're always judged or discriminated because of that ... it's very understated, but it is there.

This is most evident when promotions or career progression for women involve relocation or travel. Several women complained that their bosses assumed they would be unable to take up these responsibilities due to their domestic commitments.

> ... the men with me have been made (regional managers)[8] but I have not ... the unsaid reason for not giving it to me is that I would have to travel. Boss would ask me things like, are you geared up for it? How are you going to manage it?
>
> (Chanda, 29 years old, senior manager, Indian private bank)

... [a] lot of men already assume that you will not want to take up those roles ... Like, er, my boss asked me that would you be willing to move to (another city) or any other region, but er, then he even said that ya, most likely I'll not be ... he assumed that it's a no... he'll consider that since my husband is also settled in Delhi... my family is in Delhi, they can't move...

(Tara, 29 years old, senior manager, foreign bank)

Recognizing the pressures on women to conform to the ideals of respectable femininity, banks often try to accommodate women, through practices that give concessions to them. For example, Gita, a 35 year-old, mid-level manager in a foreign bank previously worked in a nationalized bank. Based on traditional concerns about women's safety (which implicitly ties in with concerns about maintaining women's sexual integrity), she recalls that women were often not sent out to travel:

... for loans, people have to go for inspections ... but initially, like, first two-three years, I was never asked to go. Or, if I were to go, I used to accompany someone, so therefore I felt that probably girls are not sent ... just because of consideration ...

Even within the workplace, exceptions were made for women. For instance, Yogita, a 28 year-old, mid-level manager in a foreign bank observes that in some banks, 'if a woman is getting married, she would get one month off. If a man is getting married, he gets one day off.' The problem with getting such concessions, as Yogita notes, is that it can serve to disadvantage women:

... because they want so much personal time off, they're not perceived as serious about work.

Deepanjali, a 44 year-old, senior manager in a nationalized bank suggests that these kinds of concessions by banks may explain why there are few women in senior positions.

Being a woman, you are given concessions, sometimes, of course, not always, like you don't have to travel, go out and meet people. The bank tries to give male counterparts for these jobs ... But the problem is to go higher up, you need wholesome [all-round] experience. If you (are) always taking the softer position, you can't expect to go higher up. It works both ways.

It appears therefore, that by reinforcing traditional gender stereotypes about women's roles through such concessions, banks only serve to 'cloak a glass ceiling' (Radhakrishnan 2009, 209) that hinders women's career advancement.

Conclusion

Women have clearly benefited from the expansion of employment opportunities in the banking sector after liberalization, particularly in managerial positions in Indian private banks and foreign banks. Contrary to media representations, however, women's entry into the workforce has not been accompanied by any significant change in traditional gender relations. Upholding the norms of middle-class respectability was the paramount influence on women's decisions on career progression. Thus, patterns of gender inequality observed in the banking sector, such as the low representation of women in sales, can in part be explained by this focus on respectability. Moreover, the ability of women to advance to senior positions was often hindered by the pressure to conform to traditional gender norms. Linked to this, the family emerges as the main arena in which decisions on what constitutes respectable and appropriate behaviour are made, underlining the importance of the inter-connectedness of the public and domestic sphere in women's working lives.

However, notions of respectability are constantly being reconstituted through modernizing influences. There are emerging signs that perceptions of respectability are slowly changing and breaking away from traditionally prescribed gender roles. For instance, in the banking sector, women are increasingly moving into sales positions.

> ... If you interview a new entrant, you will get a different perspective ... they have no inhibitions about such posts (sales). They are more open to all kinds of postings ... This is also a reflection of society itself ... How society sees it, that also has gradually changed. Before, there was a feeling that women should just go to the office ...
>
> (Deepanjali, 44 years old, senior manager, nationalized bank)

In the domestic sphere, several women interviewed indicated that in-laws are increasingly accepting of the demands placed on women through their work, and are even trying to accommodate this, through taking care of household responsibilities and childcare. Furthermore, more husbands are also more likely to share household responsibilities to support their wives compared to a generation ago. For example, according to Brinda, a 28 year-old, mid-level manager in an Indian private bank with a young child, her husband has been very supportive of her career, and 'takes care of [the] child more than I do'.

These are encouraging indications that there is space for the constant reformulation of notions of respectability in response to global and local influences. This research has shown that the family can play a major role in influencing women's position in the workplace. Ultimately, however, given that the family is shaped by broader societal norms, a fundamental transformation in societal attitudes towards women would be required to achieve gender equality within the workplace.

Endnotes

[1] This chapter is based on the author's book on women's employment in the banking sector in India. See Bezbaruah (2015) for elaboration of some of the findings discussed in this chapter.

[2] However, the response to the survey was quite poor, with only six banks responding, with varied levels of information provided. This is partly due to confidentiality issues and the sensitive nature of some of the information, especially on discrimination and harassment.

[3] Data based on three banks that completed the questionnaire survey. The other banks that responded did not provide sufficient information on gender distribution across the occupational hierarchy.

[4] This pattern of horizontal gender segregation of jobs was less obvious in nationalized banks, as positions were not so clearly distinguished between sales, service and operations.

[5] Quotations from the interviewees in this and the following sections are cited from Bezbaruah (2015).

[6] The majority of these respondents were married women, but 20 per cent of those who said the requirement for travel/relocation affects women's careers were single women. Single women also find it difficult to travel or relocate due to safety concerns.

[7] Women either directly used the work 'respect' to describe banking, or used similar word (regarded, honourable, prestigious), or alluded to the characteristics associated with respectability, such as regular timings, desk-based job, no travelling, preferred by families.

[8] The exact designation has been changed to protect the anonymity of the respondent.

References

Acker, J. 1990. 'Hierarchies, Jobs, Bodies: A Theory of Gendered Organizations.' *Gender and Society*, 4: 139–58.

———. 1992. 'Gendering Organizational Theory.' In *Gendering Organizational Analysis*, edited by Albert J. Mills and Peta Tancred, Newbury Park, London and Delhi: Sage. pp. 248–60.

Basi, J. K. Tina. 2009. *Women, Identity And India's Call Centre Industry*. London and New York: Routledge.

Benschop, Y., and H. Doorewaard. 1998. 'Covered By Equality: The Gender Subtext of Organizations.' *Organization Studies*, 19(5): 787–805.

Bezbaruah, S. 2015. *Banking on Equality: Women, Work and Employment in the Banking Sector In India*. Abingdon and New York: Routledge.

Bhasin, N. 2006. *Banking Developments in India, 1947 to 2007: Growth, Reforms and Outlook*. New Delhi: New Century Publications.

Bradley, H., Erickson, M., Stephenson, C., and S. Williams. 2000. *Myths at Work*. Cambridge: Polity Press.

Budhwar, P. S., Saini, D. S., and J. Bhatnagar. 2005. 'Women in Management in the New Economic Environment: The Case of India'. *Asia Pacific Business Review*, June, 11(2): 179–93.

Burton, D. 1996. 'Gender Relations in the British Banking Industry: Continuity or Change?' *Service Industries Journal*, October, 16(4): 527–43.

Chakrabarti, R. 2013. 'Women Bankers Break Through in India'. *BBC News*. 12 November. Accessed October 2, 2014. http://www.bbc.com/news/business-24867346.

CII (Confederation of Indian Industry). 2005. *Understanding the Levels of Women Empowerment in the Workplace: A Study*. New Delhi: CII (prepared by IMRB International), November.

Coyle, D. 1997. *The Weightless World: Strategies for Managing the Digital Economy*. Oxford: Capstone.

England, K., and K. Boyer. 2009. 'Women's Work: The Feminization and Shifting Meanings of Clerical Work'. *Journal of Social History*, Winter, 43(2): 307–40.

England, K. 2002. 'Interviewing Elites: Cautionary Tales about Researching Women Managers in Canada's Banking Industry', in *Feminist Geography in Practice: Research and Methods*, edited by Pamela Moss, Oxford: Blackwell. pp. 200–13.

Game, A., and R. Pringle. 1984. *Gender at Work*. London: Pluto.

Gothoskar, S. 1995. 'Computerization and Women's Employment in India's Banking Sector', in *Women Encounter Technology: Changing Patterns of Employment in the Third World*, edited by Swasti Mitter and Sheila Rowbotham, pp. 150–76. London and New York: Routledge.

Gregory, R. F. 2003. *Women and Workplace Discrimination: Overcoming Barriers to Gender Equality*. New Brunswick, New Jersey and London: Rutgers University Press.

Gupta, A., Koshal, M., and R. K. Koshal. 2006. 'Women Managers in India: Challenges and Opportunities', in *Management in India: Trends and Transition*, edited by Herbert J. Davis, Samir R. Chatterjee and Mark Heuer, pp. 285–312. New Delhi, Thousand Oaks and London: Response Books (a division of Sage Publications)/Sage.

IBA (Indian Banks' Association). 2013. *Indian Banking Year Book, 2013*. Mumbai: Indian Banks' Association.

ILO. 2010. *Women in Labour Markets: Measuring Progress and Identifying Challenges*. Geneva: International Labour Office.

———. 2012. *Global Employment Trends for Women*. Geneva: International Labour Organization.

Kabeer, N. 2008. 'Paid Work, Women's Empowerment and Gender Justice: Critical Pathways of Social Change'. *Pathways Working Paper* 3. Accessed December 15, 2010. Available at: http://www.pathwaysofempowerment.org/PathwaysWP3-website.pdf.

Kelkar, G., Shrestha, G., and N. Veena. 2005. 'Women's Agency and the IT Industry in India', in *Gender and the Digital Economy: Perspectives from the Developing World*, edited by Cecila Ng and Swasti Mitter, pp. 110–31. New Delhi, Thousand Oaks and London: Sage.

Kelly, E. L., Ammons, S. K., Chermack, K., and P. Moen. 2010. 'Gendered Challenge, Gendered Response: Confronting the Ideal Worker Norm in a White-Collar Organization'. *Gender and Society*, 24(3): 281–303.

Liddle, J., and R. Joshi. 1986. *Daughters of Independence: Gender, Caste and Class in India*. London and New Delhi: Zed Books and Kali for Women.

Mazumdar, I. 2007. *Women Workers and Globalization: Emergent Contradictions in India*. Kolkata: Stree.

McDowell, L. 1997. *Capital Culture: Gender at Work in the City*. Oxford, UK and Malden, USA: Blackwell.

Ministry of Finance (Government of India). n.d. Banking division. Online. Accessed October 2, 2014. Available at: http://financialservices.gov.in/banking_index.asp.

Mitter, S. 2004. 'Globalization, ICTs and Economic Empowerment: A Feminist Critique'. *Gender, Technology and Development*, March, 8(1): 5–29.

Mitter, S., Fernandez, G., and S. Varghese. 2004. 'On the Threshold of Informalization: Women Call Centre Workers in India'. In *Chains of*

Fortune: Linking Women Producers and Workers with Global Markets, edited by Marilyn Carr, pp. 165–84. London: Commonwealth Secretariat.

Mohanty, C. T. 1991. 'Under Western Eyes: Feminist Scholarship and Colonial Discourse', in *Third World Women and the Politics of Feminism*, edited by Chandra Talpade Mohanty, Ann Russo and Lourdes Torres, pp. 51–80. Bloomington: Indiana University Press.

Mullings, B. 1999. 'Insider or Outsider, Both or Neither: Some Dilemmas of Interviewing in a Cross-Cultural Setting', *Geoforum*, 30: 337–50.

Ng, C., and S. Mitter. 2005. 'Valuing Women's Voices: Call Center Workers in Malaysia and India', in *Gender and the Digital Economy: Perspectives from the Developing World*, edited by Cecilia Ng and Swasti Mitter, pp. 132–57. New Delhi, Thousand Oaks and London: Sage.

Ogden, S. M., McTavish, D., and L. McKean. 2006. 'Clearing the Way for Gender Balance in the Management of the UK Financial Services Industry: Enablers and Barriers'. *Women in Management Review*, 21(1): 40–53.

Özbilgin, M. F., and D. Woodward. 2004. 'Belonging' and 'Otherness': Sex Equality in Banking in Turkey and Britain'. *Gender, Work and Organization*, November, 11(6): 668–88.

Parmar, B. 2014. 'Women Fly High at Indian Banks'. *The Hindu Business Line*. 8 March. Accessed October 3, 2014. Available at: http://www.thehindubusinessline.com/news/women-fly-high-at-indian-banks/article5763664.ece.

Patel, R. 2010. *Working the Night Shift: Women in India's Call Center Industry*. Stanford: Stanford University Press.

Patel, R. 2006. Working the Night Shift: Gender and the Global Economy, *ACME: An International E-Journal for Critical Geographies*, 5(1): 9–27.

Perrons, D. 2004. *Globalization and Social Change: People and Places in a Divided World*. London and New York: Routledge.

———. 2009. 'Women and Gender Equity in Employment: Patterns, Progress and Challenges'. *IES Working Paper*, WP 23, February. Accessed June 29, 2013. Available at: http://www.employment-studies.co.uk/pdflibrary/wp23.pdf.

Perrons, D., McDowell, L., Fagan, C., Ray, K., and K. Ward. 2006. 'Social and Spatial Divisions and Work-Life Management in the New Economy', in *Gender Divisions and Working Time in the New Economy: Changing Patterns of Work, Care and Public Policy in Europe and North America*.

Edited by Diane Perrons, Colette Fagan, Linda McDowell, Kath Ray and Kevin Ward, pp. 17–20. Cheltenham and Northampton: Edward Elgar.

Prather, J. E. 1971. 'When The Girls Move in: A Sociological Analysis of the Feminization of the Bank Teller's Job'. *Journal of Marriage and Family*, November, 33(4): 777–82.

Puri, J. 1999. *Woman, Body, Desire in Post-Colonial India: Narratives of Gender and Sexuality*. New York: Routledge.

Radhakrishnan, S. 2009. 'Professional Women, Good Families: Respectable Femininity and the Cultural Politics of a "New" India'. *Qualitative Sociology*, 32: 195–212.

————. 2011. *Appropriately Indian: Gender and Culture in a New Transnational Class*. Durham and London: Duke University Press.

RBI (Reserve Bank of India). 1998. *Basic Statistical Returns of Scheduled Commercial Banks in India*. Mumbai: Reserve Bank of India. Accessed October 20, 2014. Available at: http://www.rbi.org.in/scripts/Annual Publications.aspx?head=Basic+Statistical+Returns.

————. 2013. *A Profile of Banks* 2012–13. Mumbai: Reserve Bank of India. Accessed October 20, 2014. Available at: http://www.rbi.org.in/scripts/ AnnualPublications.aspx?head=A%20Profile%20of%20Banks.

————. 2014. *Basic Statistical Returns of Scheduled Commercial Banks in India* – vol. 42, March 2013. Mumbai: Reserve Bank of India. Accessed October 20, 2014. Available at: http://www.rbi. org.in/scripts/AnnualPublications.asp x?head=Basic+Statistical+Returns.

Shirai, S. 2002. 'Banking Sector Reforms in India and China: Does India's Experience Offer Lessons for China's Future Reform Agenda?' *JBICI Discussion Paper*, No. 2, March. Accessed July 26, 2008. Available at: http:// www.jbic.go.jp/japanese/research/report/discussion/pdf/dp02_e.pdf.

Sridhar, Naga, G., and N. S. Vageesh. 2011. '40% of Job Aspirants in Public Sector Banks are Women'. *Hindu Business Line*. November 11. Accessed November 15, 2012. Available at: http://www.thehindubusinessline.com/ industry-andeconomy/banking/article 2618681.ece.

Standing, H. 1991. *Dependence and Autonomy: Women's Employment and the Family in Calcutta*. London and New York: Routledge.

WEF (World Economic Forum) 2009. *The India Gender Gap Review*. Geneva: World Economic Forum.

12

Women Body Screeners and the Securitization of Space in Indian Cities

Winifred R. Poster*

Introduction

Cities are becoming increasingly securitized. As these spaces become targets of political attack by militant groups, they also become sites of highly organized manoeuvres by the state and private industries.

*   A previous version of this paper was presented in *The City Seminar* at Washington University, St. Louis. I'm grateful to a visiting professorship at the Ontario Institute for Studies in Education, University of Toronto, where I discussed women workers and the state with Kiran Mirchandani, Helen Colley, and Shahrzad Mojab, and surveillance in India with Zaheer Baber. Thanks to Ketan Jain-Poster for assistance in interpreting during the fieldwork. Much appreciation goes to the participants for offering their time and stories for this analysis. All opinions expressed herein are my own.

In India, there have been many such jarring acts of urban violence in urban spaces by militant groups. Especially since 2000, bombings have occurred in most major Indian cities, including Delhi, Bangalore, Hyderabad, and Mumbai. They take place at governmental buildings like the High Court, Parliament buildings, etc., and often in crowded markets, bus stands, commuter trains, cinemas, universities and hotels.

This comes at a time when governing bodies at local, regional, national and global levels have joined in anti-terror campaigns. There has been a growing international rhetoric of 'security' and policies like the 'War on Terror' from the US. Following this trend, Delhi police began waging a campaign called 'Let's Fight Terror Together' in December of 2001, after attacks on the Red Fort and Parliament (Mehmood 2008). Then in 2002, the Indian government passed POTA, the Prevention of Terrorism Act, on the heels of the US Patriot Act in 2001, a sweeping policy that legalized surveillance and other anti-terrorism measures in the US.

As a result, checkpoints have diffused throughout Indian cities, becoming normalized and integrated as features of urban spaces. These checkpoints constitute 'architectures of security', as Jones (2009) argues. Here, the movement of people through the entrances of buildings serves as a geography to regulate terrorism. Curiously, these checkpoints have also become a driving source of women's labour.

In this chapter, I describe how the growth of the security industry is pulling women into new jobs in Indian cities. Occupations in body screening at public and private checkpoints represent more than an emergent employment sector though. They reflect the changing nature of the city itself, which is reorganizing to accommodate militarisation, surveillance, and technology. They also reflect an emergent field of cybersecurity and how it is incorporating women globally. After outlining the details of these jobs, and what it means to be a security screener in India's expanding cities of Hyderabad, Delhi, and Gurgaon, I discuss the opportunities and challenges for women.

Theorizing cybersecurity, labour, and gender

Body scanning reflects a form of labour within the nascent industry of cybersecurity. As I have been charting in a larger analysis (Poster 2012a), cybersecurity involves the use of technology to advance military activities and installations, and the use of the military to protect information and data.

The term sometimes appears in the media to describe the specific act of securing of online data. I use it in a broader manner, however, to describe the variety of ways in which militarism, security, information and technology intersect in the contemporary economy. In this chapter, I explore the labour of cybersecurity in protecting and managing urban spaces.

The work of cybersecurity

Cybersecurity applies to jobs with a range of capacities with technology, levels of authority and skill, and gender compositions. I turn to the literature on information and communication technologies (ICTs) and labour to develop a framework of how these occupations are arranged and inter-related (Table 12.1).

Table 12.1 The information hierarchy of cybersecurity work

Feature of Work	Level of Hierarchy		
	Networker	Networked	Switched Off
Relation to Internet	Sets Connections Designs Virtual Spaces	Online Interactive	Offline Non-interactive
Relation to ICTs (Hardware and Software)	Developer Maintainer	User of Advanced or Specialized ICTs	User of Basic ICTs
Female Composition	Low	Variable	High
Representative Cybersecurity Jobs	Info-Czar Security Engineer	Cyberspy Call Center Worker	Flight Attendant Transit Screener

Note: This framework integrates and elaborates conceptualisations from Castells (2000) and Montagnier and van Welsum (2006). Responsibility for the final form is my own.

Individuals who work and interact through the internet, satellite phones, etc., have different capacities 'to link up with other workers in real time' (Castells 2000, p. 260). Castells describes this as a 'network' relation in the development of ICT work. These individuals are grouped on a scale, from 'the *networkers*, who set up connections on their initiative ... and navigate the routes of the network enterprise; the *networked*, workers who are on-line but without deciding when, how, why, or with whom; the *switched-off* workers, tied to their own specific tasks, defined by non-interactive, one-way instructions'.

From this perspective, the ability of workers to *access the network* is central to the conceptualisation. The most privileged workers are not only able to connect to the internet, but they are responsible for developing the network infrastructure itself. Mid-level workers are the subsequent users – those who navigate it on a daily basis (participating in collective forums, communicating with others, joining virtual worlds, etc.). Marginalized workers are excluded from the network altogether, or else integrated very sparingly. For instance, they may transfer information in a singular direction (e.g., downloading documents), without communicating to others through the network in the process.

Employees also vary in their *tools* for connecting to the network and doing ICT work (Montagnier and van Welsum 2006). High-level workers have a wide spectrum of hardware and software at their disposal as they develop and maintain ICT systems. Mid-level workers often have access to specialized types of software and hardware, especially for their particular industry. Low-level workers have access to, at best, basic software and other simple hardware technologies.

The gendering of cybersecurity

Women have become a conspicuous feature of the labour constellation in this information hierarchy. Cybersecurity has become an occupational niche for women, and alternatively, women have become an integral factor in cybersecurity.

This may seem counterintuitive. After all, both of the fields from which cybersecurity originates – the military and information technology – are egregiously lacking in women. In India, for instance, women's representation in the ICT workforce is at best 35–40 per cent (Poster 2013), and their role in the military is considerably smaller.

The answer lies in seeing these two spheres as dynamically inter-related rather than as separate. First, there is an integration of ICTs into the military. The job of militarism is shifting in the information age. Daily activities are occurring at computers in offices rather than just in the field with guns. The tasks are becoming technical rather than just physical. The bodies needed for these jobs are increasingly mental and gender-neutral, and less linked to brute force strength and masculinity. Furthermore, cybersecurity involves ICT skills in networked communication and interpersonal relations, which women may be socialized towards through early education, and drawn to in their career choices as adults.

The second trend is the reverse – an integration of militarism into the information economy, largely through technology. Increasingly, the work of fighting 'terrorists' is done in everyday life – especially where women are. It is done in transportation, service industries and even people's homes. Thus, while the military and IT sectors may repel women on their own, their recent *merging* has created a formulative mix to make them more inclusive. As illustrated in Table 1, it starts with 'networkers' at the top, i.e., the women info-czars who lead the nation's agencies for military and information security, and engineers who design the military technology systems. In the middle 'networked' level, are the women cyberspies (posing from their homes as militants on the internet) and customer service workers (enforcing state security policies on the phone with the public). At the bottom, are the 'switched off' workers – women flight attendants and transit screeners, who use security information embedded in computers for the surveillance of people's bodies. My larger project considers each of these jobs in detail, and the unique ways that they impact women in cybersecurity (Poster 2012b).

For this chapter, I focus on this lowest level of the hierarchy.[1] As switched-off employees in the information hierarchy, security guards represent women's agency in working with ICTs, as end-users of surveillance technology on the ground. They have less authority than the other categories of info-workers above, in that they are offline. Still, their role is critical in a different way. If networkers are the 'minds' of cybersecurity, this last group of switched-off workers represents the 'eyes' and 'hands' of the cybersecurity infrastructure.

The bodily labour of cybersecurity

What's distinctive about the work of the scanning in the field of cybersecurity is its corporeality. The main task is the surveillance of people's bodies and the objects they carry with them. Women are highly linked to this switched off level of cybersecurity because of the connection of the body to three components of the work – surveillance, information, and services.

To start with, security falls in the category of *service* occupations. 'Interactive' services in particular involve dealing directly with customers and the public. These jobs often require providing physical or emotional care of customers. Employers typically feel these qualities are more suited to female workers. Consequently this sector of the labour force has historically been associated with women (Korczynski and Macdonald 2009; Leidner 1993; MacDonald and Sirianni 1996).

An additional component of security work is *informational* labour. On one level, information drives the practice of surveillance, in that the purpose may be administering watch lists or other databases. As such, security guards are often asked to enforce policies of the state on the bodies of the public. They use specified technology and information embedded in computers (sometimes from the military) in order to monitor everyday citizens and look for potential targets. Alternatively, information is also an outcome of surveillance. Scanners use the body as a source of collecting data. Kirstie Ball notes how: 'the human body and the information it yields, in terms of its make-up and movements, is the starting point for the creation of surveillance practice' (2003, p. 126). In security work then, the informational requirements of the job are intertwined with the corporeal.

Third, and critically for the case of security, is the gendering of surveillance (Ball, Green, Koskela, and Phillips 2009). In many instances, surveillance of women's bodies requires surveillance *by* women's bodies. Social conventions dictate that touching and attention to women's bodies in public places is to be performed only by other women. Accordingly, female workers are needed to do the part-downs and hand-scans of female subjects.

The case of scanning therefore elaborates on the kinds of bodily labour that have been theorized in feminist scholarship. Lan (2001) has illustrated how 'body control' is an integral part of the labour process in the service economy. In this formulation, the body is a primary component of the production process – not just a tool for carrying it out, or a source of labour power. Rather, the body is integral to labour in four ways – the 'exploitative body', offering physical labour and strength for the job; the 'mirroring body', embodying images to display brands and products; the 'disciplined body', performing service identities through gestures and behaviours; and the 'communicative body', imparting emotions and feelings for the job.

The field of cybersecurity offers an additional category for the typology, what one could call the 'surveilling body'. The worker's body, and especially the *female* body, is an integral part of security. It serves a dual purpose – to carry out the physical monitoring of another body (which may require direct touch), and to serve as a gender-appropriate (and therefore 'safe') complement to the body of the surveilled. Thus, when it comes to public security systems, both the body of the worker and the body of the surveillor are key. This contrasts to Foucault's account of the panopticon (1979), where the body of the surveilor is not even necessary for the surveillance process. Here, both are integral to the construction of the job and the carrying out of the monitoring on the public.

Quite in contrast to the middle-tier jobs of the info-hierarchy above (i.e., the networked women who do virtual work), switched-off workers are very closely aligned to the world of the real and the material. Ultimately, the end target of the body is what lowers the status of switched off work in the information network hierarchy.

In the analysis below, I'll show how scanners perform critical functions of surveillance of Indian cities. Through scanning jobs, we see how women's bodily labour is increasingly central to the cybersecurity infrastructure. Yet, the rewards for these jobs do not approximate those of other – higher level – cybersecurity positions.

Women body screeners in Indian cities

The job of security in India: Growth and change

India, like many other countries, has experienced a rapid growth in security occupations. It has an estimated five million security guards, working for 50,000 agencies, as noted by the Central Association of Private Security Industry (Oommen, Undated). Worldwide, the industry generates an estimated $140 billion in revenue annually, and in India, $2 billion (Timmons 2009). While other sectors are laying-off workers, firms in this field continue to hire steadily. Insiders are calling this job 'recession-proof', with a seemingly endless demand. Agencies are reporting boosts in hiring by 10–35 per cent in recent years.

There are several reasons for this boom in the context of India. One is economic. The massive expansion of the economy in the last decade has prompted a parallel geographic trend: outward pressure from Indian metropolitan areas. Demand for residential and business property has ignited urban and suburban sprawl (Ghertner 2011). Land developers have bulldozed farmlands to build shopping malls, office enclaves, and factory parks in the areas surrounding Delhi and other major cities. In turn, there are rising needs for personnel to guard them.

Second, there has been a shift in the kinds of personnel who do security, given the trends of privatisation (Higate 2011). Rather than turning to governmental units, employers are hiring security personnel from private companies. Such private security in India now outnumber police by 2:1, and will soon do so by 3:1 (Oommen, Undated). They make up a labour force that is 1.3 million greater than India's police and armed forces combined (Timmons 2009). Furthermore, private security is likely to take on an even more central role in the future, given that India has a much smaller police force for its population relative to other countries; 'there is one officer for every 1,000 people in India, [which is] less than half the United States average and one-tenth the average in China' (Timmons p. 1).

The Indian state has been sponsoring this trend by passing legislation like the Private Security Agency Act of 2005 and The Private Detectives Agencies Bill, 2007. Under planning is the establishment of the Central Private Detective Agencies Regulatory Board and state regulatory boards, which will standardize the certification and training processes for new employees.

Women securing the city

Guarding the security of Indian cities is increasingly falling in women's hands. In the last few years especially, there has been a sharp upswing in the proportion of women guards. While the percentage of female security guards was roughly 20 percent in 2005, it has since risen by 25 percent in some firms (Subramanian 2009). Moreover, industry experts predict this figure will rise to 50 per cent in the next ten years (Oommen, Undated).

Women have become more and more qualified for these jobs through improved gender access to higher and technical education. In addition though, their role has expanded through targeted recruitment by training companies. Security firms are reaching out to rural areas to attract, train and hire available labour forces, sometimes seeking female candidates in particular (as I discuss more below).

In addition, a key factor in the Indian context is the growth of women as consumers and mobile participants in the city. With the expansion of the middle class, and the relaxing of social rules governing women's mobility in the public sphere, women are now much more active in urban spaces (Poster 2013). Women are working more, entering markets, living alone, travelling at night and generally participating in the social life of the city (Basi 2009; Patel 2010).

As women visit these spaces, their entrance is now monitored and surveilled in the same way as men's. Convention says, however, that women personnel should be the exclusive providers of security for (and surveillance of) women's bodies. This is the narrative that most security companies use to explain the rising trends in women's security employment.

Of course, not all spaces are checked and surveilled. Rather, specific geographies of the city are focal points for this monitoring of women. Firms are hiring women security guards to scan women visitors in high-end hotels, banks, gymkhanas; mid-range retail stores, cinemas, and malls; corporate parks and offices; and some manufacturing sites.

There is also special attention given to transportation sites like airports and the metro. Since 2013, the Delhi Metro Network has hired women as 16 per cent of its 5,000 guards, at 800 women (Fig. 12.1). Plans are to raise this to 25 per cent (Pardaphash Today, 2013). The Metro, which serves a predominantly middle and upper class of passengers, is better protected than the bus system, which is used disproportionately by the working class and poor, and which has recently been the site of brutal abuses against women passengers.

Fig. 12.1 Women security guards for the Delhi metro

Source: Pardaphash Today, 2013

Significantly, however, the demand for women guards runs from the lowest to highest echelons of the socio-political spectrum of city life. For instance, the United Nations Office on Drugs and Crime is training victims of sex trafficking in the security industry (Sangh 2010). These women have been kidnapped from northern India and taken to Delhi and Mumbai to become prostitutes or domestic workers. Upon rescue, the Indian government and UN prepares these women to patrol stadiums and guesthouses, as a means to uplift them in society.

At the elite level, the Indian state has initiated its first female unit of the National Security Guard. These women are charged with protecting female VIPs, as members of the country's top security team (Asia Daily Wire 2012). They will provide security for the women chief ministers and heads-of-state who pass through Delhi, the administrative capital of the nation.

In this way, the global city is marked by circuits of labour mobility at both the top and bottom of the class structure (Sassen 2008). With a widening range of women to be guarded and to do guarding, we see how the field of security in India is increasingly feminized.

What women guards are doing: The skill and work of body scanning

In India, there has been a profound change in what guards do. They used to be primarily 'fetchers of tea at government offices and car washers at wealthy homes', but are quickly 'becoming corporate India's de facto police force' (Timmons 2009). They decide who should enter a designated space. They are pivotal for crisis situations, whether this is in their job description or not. Security guards are often first on the scene for fires and accidents given the slowness of ambulances and fire engines in many parts of India.

Women are now acquiring physical skills for security work though training in fitness and procedures on handling tense situations. They learn how to perform evacuations and how to respond to threats. Some learn mob control, prevention of stranger attack, and weapons use (Secura Security Solutions 2013). Those in certain government sectors learn advanced military procedures and undergo combat training.

Indeed, the military is often a feeder into security professions. My interview with Geeta in Hyderabad revealed that women in airport screening typically work for state military forces, and get six weeks training with these units (Fig. 12.2). In the US as well, 25% transit screeners are ex-military (Transportation Security Administration 2009). In India, women also have a notable history in the police (Pande and Joshi 2000). Many security staff aspired as children to be in either the police or state security units (Subramanian 2009). However, security is becoming more legitimate than police work, in the eyes of parents and family members, as a career for their daughters.

Fig. 12.2 Woman screener at Hyderabad airport from the military

Source: Photo taken by author.

Technology is another key component of security work. The job is becoming highly computerized, and the devices increasingly sophisticated. Many women guards operate small devices like hand-held wands that scan bodies (Fig. 12.3). Other devices are larger, like walk-thru metal detectors. Some are more complex, like video systems which display the contents of baggage (Fig. 12.4).

Fig. 12.3 Woman screener at a Gurgaon mall using a hand scanner

Fig. 12.4 Using video monitors in a hotel in Hyderabad

Source: Photos take by author.

The new wave of surveillance technology is biometric authentication – through iris, retinal, fingerprint and voice scanning. Soon, personnel will be using facial recognition software (Capsi 2013). Some Indian firms already use night-vision goggles and IBM surveillance systems. These technologies are so complex that employers bring in experts from the Israeli military and US marines to train security employees (Timmons, 2009). In the future, personnel in India, like the US and the UK, will be using computerized bio-scanners which look *inside the body*, not just inside the clothes (Domer 2012; McSmith 2013) (Figs 12.5 and 12.6). Inevitably, technology will increase the skill demands on the workers who operate these devices. In this way, the methods for surveilling bodies in India are becoming more complicated and intrusive.

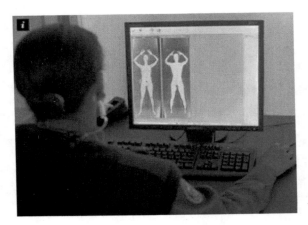

Figs 12.5 and 12.6   The future of security scanning for women – under-clothes body monitoring

Sources: Domer 2012; McSmith 2013.

The job of the security is also becoming more mental and technical than just physical. The core tasks are placing fewer corporeal demands upon workers. Either the devices are smaller and more agile, freeing the user from the need for strength, or the technology is more dependent upon interfacing with software and other visual media than engaging in live combat. These factors increase the social acceptability of women in security.

Discussion

Implications for women workers

Security scanning has provided many opportunities for women in India. For one thing, it offers rural women a chance to earn a living in urban jobs. Many of the recruits, male and female, are from villages where jobs are scarce and many families are impoverished. Rinki, whom I interviewed at a mall in Gurgaon, had migrated from Bihar. Like many other women in security, this is her first paid job (Fig. 12.3).

The industry also appears to be pulling women out of lower paid sectors of the labour market into higher ones. Many women come to this profession from previous jobs in female-dominated services, like beauty industries and retail sales (Subramanian 2009). Men, alternatively, tend to come from higher status jobs in the police and security. Some women are giving up their part-time studies (that they do alongside part-time jobs) to enter these more secure, full-time positions.

In turn, women are earning wages for the first-time, or else greater wages than they had been accustomed to. Plus they sometimes earn more than their male colleagues. Several companies report higher salaries for women than men in the same job. Securitas, for instance, pays women 8,000–10,000 Rupees per month, versus men's 6,500–7,000, for a 12-hour shift. Jupiter Administration and Security Services pays women on average 20 per cent more than men (Hannon 2009). Of course, this trend may be fleeting. The low numbers of women applying to these jobs, in combination with the high demand for female guards, may be momentarily redirecting the 'gender queue' away from men (Reskin and Roos 1990). History shows, however, that the wage differential is likely to swing back towards men after women enter the job in bigger numbers.

Agencies are offering a range of other incentives to entice women into the occupation – refresher courses, bonuses, maternity leave, provident fund (retirement and other social security accounts), etc. (Natu 2005). In some cases, women are able to leverage benefits like jobs close to their homes (Subramanian 2009). These security firms, it seems, are structuring these jobs to ease commuting and help women manage work-family responsibilities.

More indirectly, but still significant, is that Indian women are experiencing empowerment with respect to their familial, social, and economic situations from urban work in security. As one observer notes, this job offers a release from over-restrictive families, "For these women, putting on a uniform was like coming out of their own skin … They saw it as a way of gaining some form of independence" (Bearak 2012, p. 1). Employment in security may help provide unique opportunities for marginalized groups of women, as in the case of UNDOC guards above. Shunned from their home communities due to their histories as trafficked women, they may have few other options and find security work advantageous for more than just the job.

There are drawbacks, however. Despite women's gains, there are vivid signs of gender segregation within the profession. Women tend to be excluded from sectors of the city associated with finance or production, like guarding automatic teller machines (ATMs) and manufacturing plants (Natu 2005). In addition, the job is generally low-paid. Some earn as little as Rs 4000 a month (or $65, at the current exchange rate) (Timmons 2009). This contrasts with other kinds of cybersecurity personnel, like those at the "networker" level of the information hierarchy. An example is software engineering, and those who design and protect internet systems. As one of the higher paying IT professions, a network or system security administrator in the US earns on average $100,000 a year (Lee *et al.* 2009).

With respect to the typology in Table 12.1, this means that women at the 'switched off' level are not benefitting from lucrative, data-intensive sectors of the industry. This is ironic, given their location in the 'Hi-Tech Cities' of India. Cities of Gurgaon, Hyderabad, Bangalore, etc., are known as regions where IT jobs are relatively plentiful. Yet, these women are not accruing similar rewards as their 'Hi-Tech' counterparts. Furthermore, security jobs come with added stresses and personal risks. Workers are placed directly in threat as the 'frontline' staff against criminal, militant, and other kinds of violence.

Lack of labour representation is another problem in these jobs. Rinki and her colleagues in Gurgaon told me that they have no union to negotiate on their behalf. According to a local worker's association, the need for this is critical. Gurgaon Worker's News (2013) reports that employers are forcing security staff to stand for 12-hour shifts, with penalties for taking a rest to sit. Some employers even beat employees when criminal acts occur on their shifts. Especially when there is property damage, employers blame workers for their failure to stop or prevent the incidents.

Another drawback of this emerging labour niche is how it repositions women's relation to the state. While women may gain independence from patriarchal families, they may instead become subordinated to the state. An observer of a female security team for the government reports – "Some of the recruits were simply replacing duty to family with duty for country... They often think it's a massive privilege to serve for the nation with almost the same conviction in the way they would serve a man" (Bearak 2012, 1).

Finally, their work aids in the process of surveillance for the state and private sector. Even if these women are not employed directly for the government, their work facilitates and carries out the technological monitoring of the public by elite institutions. Gender is a critical component of this process. The hiring of women reflects a common state administration technique, in which marginalized segments of the workforce are recruited to enforce government policies against groups of their own kind. An example is how women are hired overwhelmingly as social workers for welfare programs that serve largely female and young populations. In this way, women scanners become agents of the state and private enterprises. They are also enforcers of surveillance against a female public, whether or not they are conscious of or agree to it.

Conclusion

The case of body scanners illuminates a growing convergence of information and militarism in Indian cities, and in turn, a reversal in women's traditional job roles. Women are entering jobs with technological responsibilities and risky tasks of policing which had previously been associated with men. The advantages for Indian women are many. This security industry provides not only new employment avenues for women, but in some cases, higher pay than men in the job. In this sense, it is possible that technology has helped to break some of the gender barriers in ICT-based occupations.

Focusing on the recent field of cybersecurity, I have described how body scanners represent an important labour niche in the contemporary information network hierarchy. As 'switched off' workers, they are the eyes and hands of surveillance on (often female) citizens for the state and private sector. Scanners represent the lowest level of this hierarchy, as their access to data is offline rather than connected through the internet. Yet, their jobs are increasingly technological, with continually upgraded devices for the direct surveillance of the public.

A distinctive feature of the switched-off tier is the way women's jobs are linked to the monitoring of the body. As scholar Pramod Nayar observes, 'the increased use of biometrics ... announces the arrival of India as a technological society' (2012, p. 17), and 'the culmination of a surveillance culture where the body returns as the key figure in any identification' (2011, p. 413).

Accordingly, these security staff in Indian cities perform what I have called here labours of the 'surveilling body'. They provide a dual service to the security infrastructure – performing corporeal monitoring of the public, on one hand, and functioning as gender-appropriate bodies for interaction with female citizens, on the other. Beyond just the labour implications then, this analysis reveals the curious intermediary role of these women in the urban landscape of India. Security personnel are simultaneously protecting and monitoring citizens as they 'guard' the city.

The technologies themselves hold further ironies from a feminist point of view. Indeed, female security personnel are the physical agents of new technologies in the public that some women have found to be exploitative (Redden and Terry 2013). Technologies like metal detectors and full-body scanners are said to constitute a 'virtual strip search' of their bodies. In turn, women have been engaging in covert and overt acts of resistance against these devices, from refusing to walk inside to disrobing completely as a symbolic gesture of protest.

At the same time, other women have found surveillance technology to be liberating. For women trafficked as international brides, these walk-thru metal detectors have also served as a path of women's liberation out of abusive situations. In a recent trend, South Asian women fearful of impending forced marriages have placed metal spoons in their under-garments. The idea is that security guards in the UK would stop them at airport checkpoints, thereby creating an opportunity to escape their captor husbands (McSmith 2013). Body surveillance technology in this case, along with the security employees who attend to it, can help in signalling and rectifying globally coercive experiences for women.

In this light, the work of female security employees may be seen as positive, i.e., in enabling women residents to travel safely in urban spaces. This is especially important in cities like Delhi, which has among the highest rates of gender-based crime in the nation. Consider the case of the Delhi Metro, which as Baber (2010, 480) observes, is helping to improve women's mobility in the region:

> Gender relations, unlike in the larger Indian cities, always under strain in Delhi, are undergoing a subtle but noticeable transformation. 'Eve teasing' or the misleadingly benign euphemism for the rampant sexual harassment of women by so-called roadside Romeos appears to be on the decline. In the past, such harassment of women thrived on the relative spatial as well as the social segregation of the sexes and was a nightmare for single women trapped in overcrowded buses. The Metro brings the sexes together which, while it can create further problems down the road, is, for the moment at least, literally creating new forms of gendered sociality that was unthinkable in Delhi barely a few years ago.

As I have shown, women security guards participate in this new "gendered sociality." While these personnel are certainly protect the transportation system from infrastructural damage, they are also protecting women's bodies from harassment by other passengers. The outcome is creating safer spaces for women's movement in the city.

Cybersecurity, in the process, creates a new and perhaps undefined gender role for these women workers. They are neither hyper-*feminized* as victims of male violence, like the other women in the city who are seen as passive and agentless, nor are they hyper-*masculinized* as male military personnel who are seen as domineering and aggressive. Women guards are intermediaries in the gender continuum. Perhaps the growth of this profession will help mitigate the gender binaries that are so pervasive in mainstream society worldwide (Blackwood and Wieringa, 1999).

Thus, the issue of empowerment for women in the security industry of Indian cities is multi-faceted. As a technology-based field, it has opened new employment paths for women. Indian women are becoming trained in both security technology and self-defence. This job has also become a means of upward mobility for Indian women who were previously unemployed, earning sub-standard wages, and/or facing limited job markets in rural areas. Women are getting training in both security technology and self-defence. In a few cases, employers in this industry are even creating special programs to help women with their work-family balance. All this can provide leverage for women in circumventing patriarchal situations and gaining independence from families. By doing this work, moreover, such workers are also aiding *other women* in metro areas, by facilitating their movements on public transportation and around the city.

Still, there are many costs for women in this profession. They experience segregation into female-typed assignments from employers, and physical risk of violence from the public. And, while body scanning may involve the use of sophisticated equipment, women workers are not necessarily gaining the full rewards of the larger technology infrastructure. Rather, as they enforce cybersecurity on the ground, these women are shielded from many of the benefits (financial or otherwise) of India's 'Hi-Tech Cities' that are afforded to their counterparts up the info-hierarchy, both male and female.

Endnotes

1   This analysis draws from my on-going research on ICT employees in India and the US since the mid-1990s. For this particular study, I conducted interviews with women and men in security industries. I focus on the cities of Delhi, Gurgaon and Hyderabad as regional urban centres for the high tech industry, and sites where surveillance technology is deployed widely. These are also sites of recent militant violence.

Between 2009 and 2012, I talked with security staff of airports, malls, and hotels. (some of their names have been changed for anonymity). Many of the photos in the analysis are taken from these interviews. The interviews were in English or Hindi, with the assistance of an interpreter.

I also examined a variety of materials (websites, newsletters, power points, photos, etc.) from security companies, industry associations, employee representatives, surveillance retailers, research organizations, etc. Finally, I gathered statistical data on women's participation in ICT and military occupations globally from a range of state, inter-governmental, and non-governmental sources.

References

Asia Daily Wire. 2012. *Indian VIPs Wary on Women Guards.* www.asiadailywire.com, October 17. Accessed March 12, 2012.

Baber, Z. 2010. 'Public Transportation in an Era of Neo-Liberal Privatisation – the Delhi Metro'. *Inter-Asia Cultural Studies*, 11(3): 478–80.

Ball, K. 2003. 'The Labours of Surveillance.' *Surveillance & Society*, 1(2): 125–37.

Ball, K., Green, N., Koskela, H., and D. J. Phillips. 2009. 'Surveillance Studies Needs Gender and Sexuality.' *Surveillance & Society*, 6(4): 352–55.

Basi, J. K. T. 2009. *Women, Identity and India's Call Centre Industry.* London, UK: Routledge.

Bearak, B. 2012. On India's Border, A Changing of the Guards. *New York Times*, www.nytimes.com, October 1. Accessed March 12, 2012.

Blackwood, E., and S. E. Wieringa. (Eds.). 1999. *Female Desires.* New York, NY: Columbia University Press.

Castells, M. 2000. *The Rise of the Network Society, Second Edition.* Malden, MA: Blackwell Publishing.

Domer, T. 2012. Cancer Concern Over Newest TSA Airport Body Scanners. *Wisconsin Workers' Compensation Experts*, www.wisworkcompexperts.com. Accessed June 11, 2012.

Foucault, M. 1979. *Discipline and Punish.* New York: Vintage Books.

Gurgaon Workers News. 2013. *GWN Newsletter*, gurgaonworkersnews. worldpress.com, October 18. pp. 1–59.

Ghertner, D. A. 2011. 'Rule by Aesthetics: World-Class City Making in Delhi.' In *Worlding Cities: Asian Experiments and the Art of Being Global*, edited by A. Roy and A. Ong, pp. 279–306. West Sussex, UK: John Wiley and Sons.

Hannon, E. 2009. 'Central and South Asia Demand Up for Female Guards in India.' *PRI's the World*, July 17.

Higate, P. 2011. 'In the Business of (In) Security? Mavericks, Mercenaries and Masculinities in the Private Security Company.' In *Making Gender, Making War: Violence, Military, and Peacekeeping Practices*, edited by A. Kronsell and E. Svedberg, pp. 182–96. London, UK: Routledge.

Jones, R. 2009. 'Checkpoint Security: Gateways, Airports, and the Architecture of Security.' In *Technologies of InSecurity*, edited by

K. F. Aas, H. O. Gundhus and H. M. Lomell, pp. 81–101. New York, NY: Routledge.

Korczynski, M., and C. Macdonald. (Eds.). 2009. *Service Work: Critical Perspectives*. New York, NY: Routledge.

Lan, P. C. 2001. 'The Body as a Contested Terrain for Labor Control: Cosmetics Retailers in Department Stores and Direct Selling.' In *The Critical Study of Work*, edited by R. Baldoz, C. Koeber and P. Kraft, pp. 83–105. Philadelphia, PA: Temple University Press.

Lee, J., Bagchi-Sen, S., Rao, H. R., and S. J. Upadhyaya. 2010. 'Anatomy of the Information Security Workforce.' *IEEE IT Professional*, 12(1): 14–23.

Leidner, R. 1993. *Fast Food, Fast Talk: Service Work and the Routinisation of Every day Life*. Berkeley: University of California Press.

MacDonald, C. L., and C. Sirianni. (Eds.). 1996. *Working in the Service Society*. Philadelphia: Temple University Press.

McSmith, A. 2013. 'Girls Escape Forced Marriage by Concealing Spoons in Clothing to Set off Metal Detectors at the Airport.' *The Independent*, www.theindependent.co.uk, August 15, pp. 13–14.

Mehmood, T. 2008. 'India's New ID Card: Fuzzy Logics, Double Meanings, and Ethnic Ambiguities', in *Playing the Identity Card*, edited by C. J. Bennett and D. Lyon, pp. 112–27. New York, NY: Routledge.

Montagnier, P., and D. van Welsum. 2006. ICTs and Gender: Evidence from OECD and non-OECD Countries. *Organization for Economic Cooperaiton and Development*, www.oecd.org. Accessed July 26, 2010, pp. 1–46.

Natu, N. 2005. 'Malls Seek Female Security Guards'. *Times of India*, www.timesofindia.com, February 2. Accessed February 22, 2013.

Nayar, P. K. 2011. 'Smile! You Are on Camera. The Rise of Participatory Surveillance.' *Rupkatha Journal on Interdisciplinary Studies in Humanities*, 3(3): 410–18.

Nayar, P. K. 2012. 'I Sing the Body Biometric': Surveillance and Biological Citizenship'. *Economic and Political Weekly*, 47(32): 17–22.

Oommen, A. Undated. 'Security Services: A Sunrise Industry.' *Central Association of Private Security Industry (CAPSI)*, www.capsi.in, pp. 57–60. Accessed June 27, 2013.

Pande, R., and S. Joshi. 2000. *Gender Issues in the Police*. Hyderabad, India: S. V. P. National Police Academy.

Pardaphash Today. 2013. 'CSIF Announces 25 Percent More Women Personnel to Guard Delhi Metro'. *Pardaphash Today,* www.pardaphash.com, January 13. Accessed June 14, 2013.

Patel, R. 2010. *Working the Night Shift.* Palo Alto, CA: Stanford University Press.

Poster, W. R. 2012a. 'Info-czars, Airport Screeners, and Online Spies: The Gendering of Cybersecurity'. Presentations in Germany: Paderborn and Humboldt Universities.

———. 2012b. 'The Case of the U.S. Mother/Cyberspy/Undercover Iraqi Militant, or How Global Women Have Been Incorporated in the Technological War on Terror'. In *Globalization, Technology Diffusion, and Gender Disparity: Social Impacts of ICTs,* edited by R. Pande, T. van der Weide and N. Flipsen, pp. 247–60. London, UK: Routledge.

———. 2013. 'Global Circuits of Gender: Women and High-Tech Work in India and the U.S.' *Gender, Sexuality, & Feminism,* 1(1): 37–52.

Redden, S. M., and J. Terry. 2013. 'Feminist Understandings of Resistance to Full-Body Scanning Technology.' *International Feminist Journal of Politics,* 15(2): 234–53.

Reskin, B. F., and P. A. Roos. 1990. *Job Queues, Gender Queues: Explaining Women's Inroads into Male Occupations.* Philadelphia, PA: Temple University Press.

Sangh, B. K. 2010. 'India: Trafficking Survivors Earn their Livelihood as Security Guards.' *United Nations Office on Drugs and Crime,* www.unodoc. org, February, 11–12.

Sassen, S. 2008. 'Two Stops in Today's International Division of Labor: Shaping Novel Labor Supplies and Employment Regimes.' *American Behavioral Scientist,* 25(3): 457–96.

Secura Security Solutions. 2012. 'Women Security Officers and Women Security Guards at Your Service.' www.securasecurity.com, November 1: 1–6. Accessed February 22, 2013.

Subramanian, S. 2009. *Spike in Demand for Female Security Guards.* www. livemint.com, January 23. Accessed December 3, 2012.

Timmons, H. 2009. 'Security Guards Become the Front Lines of India'. *New York Times,* www.nytimes.com, March 3. Accessed February 22, 2013.

Transportation Security Administration. 2009. *TSA Weekly.* www.tsa.gov, May 25–29. Accessed January 26, 2010.

Notes on Contributors

Amit Basole is an Assistant Professor of Economics at the University of Massachusetts, Boston, USA.

Debangana Bose is a PhD Scholar at the Department of Geography, The Ohio State University, Columbus Campus, Ohio, USA.

Karen Coelho is an Assistant Professor at Madras Institute of Development Studies, Chennai, India.

Kiran Mirchandani is a Professor at Adult Education and Community Development Program, Ontario Institute for Studies in Education, University of Toronto, Canada.

Neetha N. is a Senior Fellow at the Centre for Women's Development Studies, New Delhi, India.

Neethi P. is a Senior Lecturer at the School of Development, Azim Premji University, Bangalore, India.

Kaari Mattila works as a Secretary-General at the Finnish League for Human Rights in Helsinki, Finland.

Sanjukta Mukherjee is an Assistant Professor at the Department of Women's and Gender Studies in DePaul University, Chicago, USA.

Santosh Jatrana is Associate Professor and Principal Research Fellow at the Centre for Social Impact Swinburne, Swinburne University of Technology, Melbourne, Australia.

Saraswati Raju is a Professor of Social Geography at the Centre for the Study of Regional Development, Jawaharlal Nehru University, New Delhi, India.

Shruti Tambe is an Associate Professor at the Department of Sociology, Centre for Advanced Studies, Savitribai Phule Pune University, Pune, India.

Supriti Bezbaruah is an independent consultant based in Singapore.

Swati Sachdev is an Assistant Professor at the Department of Geography, Budge Budge College, affiliated to the University of Calcutta, Kolkata, India.

Tanusree Paul is an Assistant Professor at the Centre for Women's Studies, Visva-Bharati, Sriniketan, India.

Winifred R. Poster is Adjunct Faculty at the School of Social Work, Washington University, St. Louis, USA.

Index